✔ KU-483-593

Comparing Media Systems Beyond the Western World offers a broad exploration of the conceptual foundations for the comparative analysis of media and politics globally. It takes as its point of departure the widely used framework of Daniel C. Hallin and Paolo Mancini's *Comparing Media Systems*, exploring how the concepts and methods of their analysis do and do not prove useful when applied beyond the original focus of their "most similar systems" design and the West European and North American cases it encompassed. This book uses a wider range of cases both to interrogate and clarify the conceptual framework of *Comparing Media Systems* and to propose new models, concepts, and approaches that will be useful for dealing with non-Western media systems and with processes of political transition. Among other cases, *Comparing Media Systems Beyond the Western World* covers Brazil, China, Israel, Lebanon, Lithuania, Poland, Russia, Saudi Arabia, South Africa, and Thailand.

Daniel C. Hallin is Professor of Communication at the University of California at San Diego and served as Chair of the Communication Department from 2006 to 2011. He holds a Ph.D. in Political Science from the University of California, Berkeley. His books include *The "Uncensored War": The Media and Vietnam*, *We Keep America on Top of the World: Television News and the Public Sphere*, and, with Paolo Mancini, *Comparing Media Systems: Three Models of Media and Politics*. The last book received the Goldsmith Book Award from the Shorenstein Center on Press and Politics, the Diamond Anniversary Book Award from the National Communication Association, and the Outstanding Book Award from the International Communication Association. Professor Hallin has been awarded the Murray Edelman Distinguished Career Award by the Political Communication Division of the American Political Science Association, a Mercator Professorship of the German National Science Foundation, and fellowships at the Freedom Forum Media Studies Center at Columbia University and the Center for Advanced Study in the Behavioral Sciences at Stanford University. His research covers media and politics, media and war, media and public health, the history of journalistic professionalism, and comparative media systems, particularly in Europe and Latin America.

Paolo Mancini is Professor in the Department of Institutions and Society at the University of Perugia. He chairs the undergraduate program in Communications Sciences and the Ph.D. program in Social and Political Theory and Research at the University of Perugia. Mancini has served as a visiting professor at the University of California, San Diego, and in 1995, he was a Fellow at the Shorenstein Center at Harvard University. In 2001, Mancini was a Fellow at the Erik Brost Institute, University of Dortmund, and, in 2009, at St. Antony's College, University of Oxford. Mancini's major publications include *Videopolitica: Telegiornali in Italia e in USA*; *Come vincere le elezioni*; *Sussurri e grida dalle Camere*; *Politics, Media and Modern Democracy*, with David Swanson; *Manuale di comunicazione politica*; *Il sistema fragile*; *Sociologie della comunicazione*, with Alberto Abruzzese; and *Elogio della lottizzazione*. In 2004, with Daniel C. Hallin, he coauthored *Comparing Media Systems: Three Models of Media and Politics*.

Communication, Society, and Politics

Editors

W. Lance Bennett, *University of Washington*
Robert M. Entman, *The George Washington University*

Politics and relations among individuals in societies across the world are being transformed by new technologies for targeting individuals and sophisticated methods for shaping personalized messages. The new technologies challenge boundaries of many kinds – between news, information, entertainment, and advertising; between media, with the arrival of the World Wide Web; and even between nations. *Communication, Society, and Politics* probes the political and social impacts of these new communication systems in national, comparative, and global perspective.

Other Books in the Series

Continued after the Index

Comparing Media Systems Beyond the Western World

Edited by

DANIEL C. HALLIN
University of California, San Diego

PAOLO MANCINI
University of Perugia

CAMBRIDGE
UNIVERSITY PRESS

CAMBRIDGE UNIVERSITY PRESS
Cambridge, New York, Melbourne, Madrid, Cape Town,
Singapore, São Paulo, Delhi, Mexico City

Cambridge University Press
32 Avenue of the Americas, New York, NY 10013-2473, USA

www.cambridge.org
Information on this title: www.cambridge.org/9781107699540

First published 2012
Reprinted 2012

A catalog record for this publication is available from the British Library.

Library of Congress Cataloging in Publication Data
Comparing media systems beyond the western world / [edited by] Daniel C. Hallin,
Paolo Mancini.
    p. cm. – (Communication, society and politics)
Includes bibliographical references and index.
ISBN 978-1-107-01365-0 (hardback) – ISBN 978-1-107-69954-0 (paperback)
    1. Mass media – Political aspects – Developing countries.   2. Mass media – Political
aspects – Developing countries – Case studies.   3. Mass media – Social aspects –
Developing countries – Case studies.   4. Mass media policy – Developing countries – Case
studies.   I. Hallin, Daniel C. II. Mancini, Paolo.
P95.82.D45C85 2011
302.2309722 – dc23   2011018391

ISBN 978-1-107-01365-0 Hardback
ISBN 978-1-107-69954-0 Paperback

Contents

Contributors

Afonso de Albuquerque, Fluminense Federal University

Auksė Balčytienė, Vytautas Magnus University

Bogusława Dobek-Ostrowska, University of Wrocław

Adrian Hadland, Universtiy of Nottingham, Ningbo

Daniel C. Hallin, University of California, San Diego

Marwan M. Kraidy, University of Pennsylvania

Paolo Mancini, University of Perugia

Duncan McCargo, University of Leeds

Yoram Peri, University of Maryland

Natalia Roudakova, University of California, San Diego

Elena Vartanova, Moscow University

Katrin Voltmer, University of Leeds

Yuezhi Zhao, Simon Fraser University

I

Introduction

Daniel C. Hallin and Paolo Mancini

In writing *Comparing Media Systems*, we deliberately decided to focus on a limited number of similar cases: eighteen nations of Western Europe and North America that by global standards had relatively similar histories as advanced capitalist democracies. As we argued in that book, we wanted to avoid the kind of universalizing approach to comparative analysis in media studies – symbolized by Siebert, Peterson, and Schramm's *Four Theories of the Press* (1956) – that we believed had held back the field for many decades, producing superficial analyses not based in detailed research on particular media systems and often riddled with ethnocentric assumptions. We focused on Western systems not because we thought they were inherently more important than others, nor because we thought they were a natural reference point for comparative analysis, but simply because they were the systems we knew best, and because we knew that there was substantial research available on all of them in languages we could read, enough to make a comparative synthesis possible. Of course, both of these factors reflect the longstanding dominance of the West in global academia. We also believed that because these countries had long been the principal reference points for comparative analysis of media systems – and in general for public discourse about media systems – there would be a great deal of value in subjecting them to more concrete comparative analysis. One of the objectives that we hoped our analysis would accomplish was to demystify the notion of a "Western media model" to some degree, both by showing that there is not in fact a unitary "Western model," because media systems in the Western world have developed according to several distinct patterns, and by treating these systems not as abstract ideals but as concrete social formations that developed under particular historical conditions.

As soon as the book came out, widespread discussion began about how our framework might apply to the rest of the world. Some criticized us for confining our analysis to a narrow range of countries; many asked us, "How does my country fit into your three models?" or "How does your framework apply to the part of the world that I am studying?" These questions were obviously gratifying, but they made us uncomfortable at the same time. We began to worry that instead of putting *Four Theories of the Press* to rest, our book might *become* the new *Four Theories of the Press*, with our three models turning into a kind of universal schema to be applied almost everywhere. We had many conversations with colleagues about these kinds of questions and eventually decided to confront the issues head-on by launching this book project. We began by inviting a group of scholars who studied media systems outside Western Europe and North America to a conference in Perugia in 2007; because the initial conversations seemed fruitful, we then organized another conference in San Diego in 2009, as well as three panels at meetings of the International Communication Association. We tried to enlarge the range of cases as much as we could and to make sure a wide range of world regions – Eastern Europe and the former Soviet Union, the Middle East, Asia, Africa, and Latin America – were represented. However, we did not attempt a systematic selection of cases. Instead, we recruited scholars we had met in a variety of academic settings, many of whom we knew had been reflecting in some way on how to think about the systems or processes they were studying in relation to *Comparing Media Systems*. Obviously the range of cases presented here does not represent an exhaustive or systematic typology of world media systems. For instance, it excludes the case of India, the world's biggest democracy and one of the few news media systems that has been growing in recent years; at the same time it deals mostly with large and relatively rich countries like China, Brazil, Russia, Poland, and South Africa. We emphasize that this volume should not be conceived of as a kind of "Handbook of World Models of Journalism."

In preparing these chapters, we asked participants to address the question of whether and in what ways the three models of our analysis – which we call the Mediterranean or Polarized Pluralist, the North/Central European or Democratic Corporatist, and the North Atlantic or Liberal models – might illuminate the case or cases they studied, while discussing both how those models did and did not fit those cases. We asked them to consider the four dimensions we use to compare the cases in our analysis – the structure of media markets, the degree and form of political parallelism, journalistic professionalism, and the role of the state – and to discuss the ways in which the framework provided by these dimensions did and did not prove useful for the analysis of the media systems they addressed. Finally we asked them to reflect on what other media system models and concepts for comparative analysis might be proposed on the basis of the cases or regions they studied.

The initial focus on the conceptual framework of *Comparing Media Systems* seemed important to giving the book a common structure. At the same time we were well aware that this enterprise involved a kind of contradiction; it ran the risk of producing exactly the kind of universalizing extension of our framework we hoped to avoid. We were calling for an extension of comparative analysis beyond a framework centered on Western cases, and yet we were placing at the center of the analysis a book based precisely on those cases. This issue provoked significant discussion in our meetings. We hope readers will judge the results of the enterprise useful in two ways: first, that the chapters presented here use cases outside the scope of our original analysis to subject the framework of *Comparing Media Systems* to critical scrutiny, and second, that they use the dialogue with our book to produce useful insights that can point toward the formation of new theory. This project is not based on an assumption that *Comparing Media Systems* is a natural starting point for analysis of media systems around the world; on the contrary, we were motivated to undertake this project precisely because we consider the application of our framework to cases outside the regions we studied to be highly problematic in many ways.

The Methodology of Comparing Media Systems and Its Applicability to Other Cases

Comparing Media Systems was based on a "most similar systems" design. The adoption of this approach was motivated by two kinds of concerns. One was practical: We did not feel we could learn enough about a wider range of media systems to be able to analyze them competently, particularly because there was limited systematic research on media systems in many parts of the world and our study was based more on the synthesis of existing research than on primary research. Second, most similar systems designs, as Lijphart (1971) has argued, are useful for "reducing the property space of the analysis," that is, for limiting the number of variables an analyst is forced to deal with. In some studies, this is done to facilitate causal analysis, as the analyst tries to match cases on all but a small number of variables whose effects can be isolated. Our study was oriented toward theory building rather than hypothesis testing; for us, reducing the property space of the analysis was important because we wanted to think through certain concepts and relationships – to unpack the concept of "journalistic professionalism" for example, and to explore how it was related to partisanship and to political culture – and we could only do this coherently if the number of concepts we were dealing with was limited.

One other aspect of the methodology of *Comparing Media Systems* is also important to emphasize here. Our approach to social theory is a historical one. Our analysis was intended as a concrete, historical analysis of a particular group of media systems, not as a set of general categories for understanding media systems regardless of time and place. In particular, our three models were intended as ideal types that would summarize distinct patterns of media system development among particular groups of countries, and they should be thought of as bound to the cases from which they were generalized. To be sure, we did suggest that they could be of some relevance to the analysis of other systems. What we intended was to suggest that the three models might be useful as points of comparison, for noting similarities and differences, and for beginning the process of asking why these similarities and differences existed. We certainly did *not* intend for them to be used as a set of categories *classifying* any and all media systems, nor did we intend that comparative analysis should be carried out by "applying" our three models to other cases, a phrase we often hear.

The chapters in this volume vary in the extent to which they "apply" our categories, critique them, or just use them as a starting point and move on to address other concepts. This reflects the fact that different media systems are more or less proximate to those we study. For example, Bogusława Dobek-Ostrowska ends her chapter on the Polish media system by locating Poland on the triangle diagram we use to represent the relationship of our eighteen cases to the three ideal types. She places it near the middle of the axis that separates our Polarized Pluralist and Liberal models – an interesting finding because many had asked us why the area between those two systems seemed to be unpopulated in our analysis and whether there was some theoretical reason why a mixed model between those two types was impossible. The answer is probably that the absence of cases in that part of our triangle is a historical accident and that in fact many media systems worldwide combine important characteristics – commercialization and politicization – of the Liberal and Polarized Pluralist systems simultaneously. East European scholars were among the first to use *Comparing Media Systems* to analyze their own media systems and tend more than other scholars to fit those cases into our framework, often speaking of the Italianization or Mediterraneanization of East European media systems in the post-Soviet period, even if they do so with important qualifications.[1] This makes a lot of sense. Poland is a part of Europe after all: It was always a part of the European state system, has now been reintegrated into Europe as a member of the EU and is subject to its rules for media policy, and has many media outlets owned by Western media companies. In contrast, Adrian Hadland reports that the South African media system is a "square peg" in the "round holes" of our three models – even if, as a country with strong European institutional and cultural influences and a relatively strong capitalist sector, it probably has many more similarities to our three systems than most developing countries. To try to fit China onto the triangle defined by our three models would simply be silly.

With this in mind, we have organized the first part of this book, which is made up of individual case studies, to move from cases more proximate to those of *Comparing Media Systems*, which can reasonably be analyzed, up to a point, by applying the conceptual framework developed there, toward "most different systems," which clearly represent alternative models and require a very different conceptual apparatus.

If the three models, which form the first component of the conceptual framework of *Comparing Media Systems*, are difficult to transfer outside the original context of our study, this is less true of the media system variables or dimensions of comparison that form its second component. One can ask about any media system, "What is the role of the state?" or "What is the degree and form of journalistic professionalism?" – although it is conceivable that the answers would prove unenlightening in some contexts. In fact, we were struck by the fact that the list of variables we proposed to compare the relationship between mass media and politics in the Western world seemed to hold up reasonably well as we shifted to a "most dissimilar systems" design, at least in the sense that the participants were almost always able to tell a coherent and interesting story about how their cases could be understood in relation to those dimensions. At the same time, it is clear that the particular conceptualizations of these four

---

[1] We offer more extensive reflections on the way we see East European media systems in relation to our framework in Hallin and Mancini (forthcoming b).

dimensions developed in *Comparing Media Systems*, the particular values that the variables connected with them take in our analysis, are tied to the eighteen cases of our original study and often need to be reconceptualized to apply to other cases. In fact, this reconceptualization is where much of the value of this enterprise lies, in the way the authors were forced to rethink our media system variables – to ask, for example, what "political parallelism" might mean outside the context of the European party systems for which the concept was originally conceived – as well as to suggest new variables that might be important within other contexts. In the concluding chapter we focus on some of the most important insights generated by this rethinking.

The core conceptual framework of *Comparing Media Systems* also included one additional component, a set of political system variables, that we proposed were relevant to understanding the different patterns of media system development, the distinction between "moderate" and "polarized" pluralism, for example, or between Liberal and Corporatist models of democratic politics. Many, although not all, of the variables we deal with in this part of our analysis are quite closely tied to the context of West European and North American political history; we suspect they are more difficult than our media system variables to apply outside their original context and so did not ask participants to address them in any standardized way. However, it was one of the most important principles of our approach that media systems had to be understood in the context of social and political institutions more generally, and we sought in *Comparing Media Systems* to build bridges between the fields of media studies and of comparative politics and political sociology. For this reason we did ask participants to think about what literatures on, for example, the nature of the state in their particular political systems might be important for understanding media and politics. Because these literatures are necessarily diverse in a collection of this sort – the literatures on the Chinese communist state or the Arab state are quite different from one another – we do not try to generalize very much about political system variables. However, we address selected points related to these literatures, including, first, the question of party systems and other ways in which political conflict and diversity are structured – crucial for the reconceptualization of the concept of political parallelism – and, second, the relation of rational-legal authority to media systems, which we think is very important to understanding both journalistic professionalism and the role of the state.

Many of the chapters in the book also address the question of convergence or homogenization. In the last chapter of *Comparing Media Systems*, we discuss a historic shift in European media systems that can be understood to some extent as a shift toward the Liberal model of commercialized, politically unaligned, or "catch-all" media. Many of the investigations presented here address the question of whether this process can also be seen in other parts of the world.

The book is divided into two parts. Part I comprises seven case studies: the media systems of Israel, Poland, Lithuania, Brazil, South Africa, Russia, and China. Part II comprises multicase studies and has more of a focus on methodological issues concerning the units of analysis for the comparative study of media and politics. As discussed, *Comparing Media Systems* centers around the concept of a "media system," and the chapters in this part raise a series of issues about this concept as a focal point for comparative analysis: whether media systems should be analyzed as national or transnational; the value of media system "models"; the possibility of focusing on other units such as processes rather than systems; and the question of how to understand structure, agency, and change in comparative analysis. The book closes with a concluding chapter in which we summarize some of the principal conclusions that we believe have emerged from this project and respond to some of the most important issues that the participants have raised about our own analysis and about the future of comparative research on media and politics.

We are very grateful to all the contributors to this volume: We learned a lot from them, and this book is only possible thanks to their involvement in the seminars that paved the way for the book and their willingness to do the often extensive work of developing a chapter that fit the collective enterprise. We would also like to thank a number of scholars who participated in earlier phases of this enterprise and who contributed significantly to the discussions that led to this book, including Mine Gencel Bek, Sahar Khamis, Myung-Jin Park, and Miklós Sükösd. We are grateful to the Regione dell'Umbria, the World Universities Network, and the Institute for International, Comparative and Area Studies of the University of California, San Diego, for funding that made possible our workshops in Perugia and San Diego, as well as other crucial components of this project. Special thanks also to Jackie Tam for patiently and efficiently handling the logistics for the San Diego workshop.

PART I

CASES

2

The Impact of National Security on the Development of Media Systems

The Case of Israel

Yoram Peri

Introduction

"Media systems are shaped by the wider context of political history, structure, and the culture" (Hallin and Mancini, 2004b: 46). Indeed, anyone who wishes to understand the structure of Israel's media institutions today must adopt a broad historical perspective, covering almost ninety years. This journey begins with the formation of a Jewish political entity in Palestine under British Mandatory rule in the aftermath of World War I.

Jewish journalism in *Eretz Yisrael* (as the Jews referred to Palestine), and before that in Central and Eastern Europe where the Zionist movement sprang up at the turn of the nineteenth century, was forged primarily as a wing of this Jewish national liberation movement. A good portion of its leadership – including the Zionist movement's founder Theodore Herzl and other founding fathers like Ze'ev Vladimir Zabotinsky – were themselves journalists or people of letters, who used the press as a vehicle to realize the collective objectives of the movement: revitalizing the Hebrew language and building a national homeland for the Jews.

This state of affairs – a mobilized press – continued even after the establishment of the State of Israel in 1948. The print media, and even more so the radio, continued to be a key vehicle in the hands of political and cultural elites in the process of nation-building and the formation of the new nation-state (Liebes, 2000). The fact that many leaders of the political parties were themselves editors of daily newspapers or editors-turned-politicians strengthened that pattern. Some fifteen years after the establishment of the state, the second stage of media development began with the routinization of the revolutionary project.

Although the state was established in the post–World War II wave of decolonialization and in an underdeveloped region – in what was then labeled the "Third World" – from the beginning the founders adopted a political model based on democratic principles they brought with them from Central and Eastern Europe. Whereas surrounding states had authoritarian regimes, monarchies, or military dictatorships without parliamentary democracy, the new state of Israel was a multiparty parliamentary democracy, founded on consensual rather than majoritarian politics, although with an emphasis on procedural rather than substantive democracy (Axworthy and Johnson, 2008). The media system with its parallelism characteristics was in keeping with this political ecology.

Toward the end of the 1980s and more so in the course of the 1990s, the third stage in the crystallization of Israel's media system developed, and it has continued into the first decade of the twenty-first century. During this period significant changes took place both in the political system and the communication system. These changes were so deep and occurred so quickly that they deserve to be called "revolutionary" (Peri, 2004). Had this trend continued, Israel would have easily integrated into the emerging global media culture, adopted the characteristics of its Liberal model, and manifested this model's "triumph" (Hallin and Mancini, 2004b: 251–9). Yet this did not happen.

The primary reason that this transformation did not occur was that in the sixty years since the establishment of the state, Israelis have been locked in protracted conflict. On an average of once a decade, Israel has engaged in full-scale war – ten wars to date. In between these major clashes, Israelis experienced other forms of violent conflict with neighboring Arab states and with the Palestinian people.

This ongoing conflict has had a definitive impact on Israel's institutional, social, and political arrangements. It has always been at the top of the national public agenda in Israel, demanding the lion's share of national resources and influencing every sphere of life. Protracted conflict has had a major impact on the Israeli psyche as well as on the nature of Israeli political institutions and on the symbolic order (Kimmerling, 2001). The prolonged state of emergency, the intractable conflict, and full-fledged wars in particular have created a "national security culture" and have had a major impact on the form taken by Israel's media system.

The analytic tools used by Hallin and Mancini enable not only a better understanding of the Israeli case but also put this case study in a more theoretical context and enable conclusions to be drawn that are relevant to other cases. Thus, although Israel does not fall into one of the three models proposed by Hallin and Mancini – Polarized Pluralistic, Democratic Corporatist, and Liberal – focusing on the major variables that underlie these models helps deepen an understanding of the Israeli media system.

However, before we analyze the impact of prolonged conflict on the nature of Israeli democracy and the character of its media system, we must first describe in more detail the three stages in the historical development of the media system since the establishment of the state.

The Media's Role in Nation-Building and State Formation

The constitutional structure established with Israel's independence in May 1948 is an expression of the multiparty nature of Israel's parliamentary democracy, which follows the Polarized Pluralist model. The East and Central European political traditions between the two world wars; the nature of the Zionist movement, which was, since its inception in 1897 a voluntaristic and democratic movement; and the democratic orientation of Israel's founding fathers and mothers shaped this constitutional structure.

The political culture embodied consensual rather than majoritarian rule, with an extreme form of proportional representation in the Knesset, the Israeli parliament (it has a very low threshold for entry: only 1 percent or later 2 percent of the vote). Political parties played a central role relative to other organized social groups; such a role is characteristic in Southern European Polarized Pluralist systems. Indeed, Israel at statehood had the features of the organized pluralist model rather than the segmented or individualized pluralist model, with a substantive degree of ideological diversity and conflict, as well as clientelism.

During the first decade after independence, similar to the pre-state period, the Israelis lived within three major cultural and political camps – the Labor, the nationalist, and the religious – with consociational arrangements that kept the camps as a whole together; the party within each camp served not only as a political arm but also as a major provider of social services. Each camp had its own system of education, housing, employment, and health care. Thus political affiliation and close ties to political leaders were useful, in many cases even necessary, for obtaining jobs and services.

In addition to the consociational arrangements, the other reason for the relative stability of such a fractionalized system was that the Labor Party won a plurality, although not a majority, in elections time after time, and it headed every coalition government until 1977. This was a good example of Maurice Duverger's concept of a "dominant party" that reflects the spirit of the times (Arian, 1985).

Since Israel's founding – the fulfillment of the dreams and aspirations of so many generations – the state has played a key role within various social institutions. In other words, there has existed a very high level of "stateness." The state owned and controlled a centralized economy, combining a "statist," or *etatist*, ideology quite common among newly established nations at the time with a Social Democratic outlook that favored a welfare state, as in many Western European countries.

Civic society was weak and controlled by the state. The Constituent Assembly that established the machinery of statehood in 1948 failed to write a constitution, and therefore liberal principles and institutions were late to develop and slow growing. For instance, neither the Constituent Assembly nor the Knesset passed a law that would guarantee freedom of the press, and this principle was only adopted five years after Israel declared its independence – not through legislation but through a Supreme Court ruling.

The Israeli case did not fully fit the Mediterranean model, but could be seen to some extent to embody elements of both the Democratic Corporatist and Polarized Pluralist systems. At the center of society, there was strong support for rational-legal legitimization of the political order, a characteristic of corporatist democracies. Yet a small but influential cultural group, particularly members of the religious community, did not provide this support.

The religious community, at first primarily the ultra-Orthodox groups and later also the national-religious camp, possessed a decisive swing vote in most coalition governments and consequently had far more political clout than indicated by its numerical strength at the polls. These groups opposed the drafting of a constitution and wished to enhance Israel's particularistic nature. They contended that modern Israel should be based on Jewish religious tradition with a leading political role given to the rabbinate, rather than adopting universalistic values and fully integrating into the international community.

Just as the Israeli political system embodied components common in the Polarized Pluralist model of Southern Europe, so did the media system. Within an organized pluralism model, such as Israel's, "where organized pluralism was strongly developed, the media were always integrated to a significant extent into the institutions of group representation" (Hallin and Mancini, 2004b: 54). Yet, since its inception, the Israeli media system has also had some features that are not typical of the Mediterranean model.

One clear manifestation is the media market. Newspaper circulation and news consumption were and still are extremely high, and the consumers have been not only the elite but also the masses. That involvement is a direct outcome of the long Jewish tradition of an extremely high level of literacy and of the crucial role the written word has played in the national movement of a people living under dispersed conditions in the European Diaspora. The uncertainties created by prolonged conflict increased even more the need for information, interpretation of events, and forecasts of future developments.

Yet, in the first era, from statehood until the mid-1960s, Israel did have political parallelism, which is so typical of polarized democracies. In their analysis Blumler and Gurevitch (1995) rely on Seymour-Ure's (1974) notion of press-party parallelism that rests on three criteria: party involvement in mass media ownership and management; the editorial policies of newspapers; and the party affiliation of readers. Furthermore, Israel can be described as having the highest level of parallelism, according to Blumler and Gurevitch's own definition (1995: 64–5), which incorporates several other elements: "The highest degree of partisan involvement exists when the parties are directly associated with running of media enterprises via ownership, provision of financial subsidy or membership on management and editorial boards."

Indeed, during the first era, the media and the political elites were very integrated: Political parties owned the papers, controlled their budgets, and appointed their journalist-editors, and the readers of the various papers consisted of the respective party members.

This pattern actually began in the prestate era during the British Mandate, but it prevailed throughout the first decades following statehood as well. The year that Israel was born, two-thirds of the newspapers in circulation were party papers: Political parties owned, subsidized, and controlled twelve of eighteen dailies published at the time (Peri, 2004: 74). Political instrumentalization – that is, control of the media by outside actors – was high. However, whereas in Italy or Greece for instance, the media were owned by individual capitalists, political parties or other public institutions played this role in Israel.

Indeed, print media were linked extremely closely not only to political parties but also to other political bodies. The Histadrut, the strong trade union federation, owned and published *Davar*, the most important paper of the Israeli left, which supported the ruling Labor Party's party line. The Jewish Agency, the executive arm of the Zionist movement and the state, owned the only English-language daily, the *Jerusalem Post*. The Jewish Agency was also dominated by the Labor Party.

In the early years of the state, the government controlled broadcasting. The *Kol Israel* (Voice of Israel) radio station operated under the aegis of the Prime Minister's Office; its director was a subordinate of the director-general of the Prime Minister's Office. The government's control of the media system was expressed in other ways as well – government subsidies to newspapers in the form of special custom tariffs for imported newsprint, various kinds of tax breaks, and even bulk purchase by the government of "favored" newspapers for distribution to army units or passengers on the national airline El Al. Subsidies were also commonly given to newspapers in the form of advertising space for official announcements by government ministries.

In the first few decades the level of professionalism of the journalists and the press was relatively low. There was no university-level school of journalism, the journalist-politician pattern was common, and the professional organization of journalists was in its embryonic stage. More than anything else, journalists saw their mission as giving a hand to the national and party leadership in their endeavor to achieve the national goals as defined by the political institutions and not by the journalists – which were first and foremost the development and defense of the nation-state.

When David Ben-Gurion, the first prime minister, appeared before the annual convention of the Journalists' Association in Tel Aviv on March 13, 1953, he described how he saw their role: "You must foster in the nation those qualities and attributes that are necessary to improve its ability for productive work for the good of the economy, raise the youths' cultural level and pioneering zeal, and enhance the strength, courage and loyalty to the Israel Defense Forces. If you do that you will fulfill your true mission to Israel and to the entire Jewish people" (Peri, 2004: 76). Even had there been a journalist in the hall who would have subscribed to other professional values, such as the search for truth or placing the administration under public scrutiny, no one had expressed these ideas in public. Several more years had to pass until such values were incorporated into the Israeli journalists' code of ethics.

In the early 1950s, when the level of differentiation between the state and other social systems and the level of professionalism among journalists were low, it is clear why the prevailing journalistic style was advocacy or commentary-oriented journalism rather than neutral and informative or investigative journalism.

The Decline of Political Parallelism

The symbolic significance of Israel's founding father David Ben-Gurion stepping down from power in 1963 and the structural changes that began after Israel's victory in the 1967 Six Day War brought the first buds of liberalization in Israeli culture and politics. This phenomenon also found expression in the media system. During the course of this period, which extended until the end of the 1980s, the dominant party era came to a close, the Labor Party narrative ceased to be the hegemonic one, and a polarized competitive party structure emerged in which two large parties – the Likud and the Labor Party – became catch-all parties. Both established coalition governments during this period and at times formed national unity governments. With the expansion of the economy and changes in social and economic policies, the state also lost some of its power.

The most salient trait in political communication during this period was the collapse of political parallelism. Almost all the party papers ceased to exist, and the commercial papers began to flourish, particularly the two semi-tabloids that controlled the lion's share of circulation and dominated the newspaper market. Although they were not politically neutral like the American tabloids – one supported the Labor government; the other, the right-wing Likud opposition – they were free from party ties, unlike the party papers of the past. Government control of the press, for example, in regard to imposing custom tariffs on imported newsprint, declined as well.

At the same time, a slow process of professionalization of journalism was set in motion, and the first signs of professional autonomy began to appear. The new generation of editors and reporters were influenced by what they saw in the international, and particularly the American, media. Beginning in the mid-1960s and continuing thereafter, most editors were not publicist-type journalists who had risen in the party ranks; rather they were reporters who had climbed the professional ladder of the news departments. This period witnessed the decline of advo-cacy or commentary-oriented journalism and the rise of fact-centered discourse.

Furthermore, journalists and editors, even those of papers that still had ties to political institutions, adopted norms of the adversarial approach. *Davar*, the daily newspaper of the Histadrut, the trade union federation, and the *Jerusalem Post*, which was owned by the Jewish Agency, both still reflected the views of the Labor Party. Yet Erwin Frankel, editor of the *Jerusalem Post*, explained that he resigned from the paper in 1989 because he lacked the freedom an editor should have to express his reading of reality free from the publisher's dictates.

Hallin and Mancini use Frankel's case to illustrate their contention that "in much of northern and Central Europe, a relatively high level of polit-ical parallelism did coexist for most of the twentieth century with a high degree of journalistic professionalism" (Hallin and Mancini, 2004b: 40). In Israel, however, the case of Frankel occurred in the second rather than the first stage, reflecting the weakening of political control, the decline of political parallelism, and the growing awareness of journalists of profes-sional codes.

These changes also occurred in public broadcasting. The 1965 Broad-casting Authority Law established a public council along the lines of the BBC, replacing direct government (i.e., the dominant party in power) ownership of the broadcasting organization. "The most basic feature of politics in consensus systems is power sharing, and the strongest example of power sharing in broadcast governance can be found in systems that tend towards the consensus model" (Hallin and Mancini, 2004b: 51). In Israel this power sharing took the form of the parliamentary model: The make-up of the council that served as a board of governors for broadcast-ing channels reflected the relative power of the various political parties.

The transfer from governmental control to public control reflected not only the decline of the dominant party but also to a certain degree the weakening of the state itself and emerging civil society. Broadcasting was financed by a compulsory annual fee levied on all radio owners (almost the entire public), and a process of professionalization of Broadcast Author-ity personnel began. Although the council continued to have a political nature, the working journalists who operated the stations demonstrated more and more opposition to outside political interference.

Nevertheless, the government continued to wield quite a bit of clout because of its power to appoint not only the chair of the Broadcasting Authority but also its director-general. As we soon see, the government also used the demands of the security situation to tame the nascent independence of the public broadcasting organization.

Toward Adoption of a Liberal Model

If passage from the first stage to the second was gradual, slow and incomplete, entrance into the third stage in development of the media system, which began at the beginning of the 1990s and is still continuing, was accelerated, significant, and dramatic.

As occurred in most European countries, these processes included globalization, contraction of the state, retreat from the principles of the welfare state, and adoption of a neoliberal economy. During this period, as the state weakened and the scope of its roles narrowed, a parallel process – the decline of the political parties – took place. The major parties, compared to the smaller ethnic parties, lost a significant part of the varied functions they had fulfilled in the country that was previously labeled a "party state"; no longer supplying social services, these parties adopted a more strictly political role, primarily nominating political leaders and mobilizing public legitimacy for them. The two major parties, which had always led Israeli coalition governments, were transformed from ideologically identified mass parties rooted in distinct social groups to electoral professional parties oriented not so much to ideology as toward the conquest of the electoral market. Indeed, in 2006 factions split from both parties to join forces to create a new centrist party, Kadima, which won the election that year and stayed in power until the 2008 elections.

At the same time, Israel witnessed the expansion and growth of a civic society that previously has been subject to government's deep penetration. With the weakening of collectivist ideology and the strengthening of individualistic trends in culture, as well as the adoption of postmaterialist values, the operations of interests groups changed. This change was typified by a more individualized pattern of social belonging and a shift from organized pluralism toward individual pluralism.

The primary change in the media system resulted from what has been termed in the literature a "commercial deluge" – the rapid expansion and diversification of the media market and its transformation into a multichannel and market-oriented system. In essence, the media ceased to be an educational and cultural enterprise and became an industry whose primary objective is to make a profit. Radio broadcasting and television's public monopoly was removed, ushering in a "neo-television" era, to use Umberto Eco's term, an era in which television captured the central position in the public sphere that the print media had occupied in the past.

During this time, Israel underwent a visual revolution, transforming what had been "paleo-television," which was introduced in 1968 as a black-and-white "network" with one channel. Franchises were licensed to enable cable and satellite television to offer more than 100 channels from across the globe. The same process was also instituted for radio broadcasts. New media, Internet, cellular phones, and a host of other new digital communication technologies followed television, transforming the way news is consumed in Israel – a society that has a genuine "obsession" for hard news (Gilboa, 2008).

The declining strength of the political machinery of the "party state" and the lessening of the public's trust in politics and politicians took place parallel to the increased status of the media and a move toward professionalization among journalists. The Knesset adopted the Freedom of Information Law in 1999, and political instrumentalism (i.e., dependence on old political organizations) was replaced by an orientation that advocated not only detachment from political parties or the government but even disdain for politicians and politics (although in the beginning of the twenty-first century commercialization began to be a real threat to professionalism).

This disdain for politics was tied to a growing critical disposition among journalists and development of a culture of "critical expertise," a posture that at times has gone overboard, spiraling into cynicism. More and more journalists were acquiring academic degrees in journalism at universities in Israel and developing strong professional ties with colleagues and professional bodies abroad, particularly in the United States: Most of Israel's top writers served for some years as foreign correspondents in Washington, DC.

Impact of Conflict on the Media System

Whether one subscribes to the convergence and homogenization theory of global media systems (as Hallin and Mancini [2004b] have suggested), or disagrees with it (as does McCargo in Chapter 10), it is clear that if the evolution of Israel's media system had continued along the path set in the early 1990s, it would become part of the new global culture of journalism. Had life in Israel not been conducted in the shadow of protracted conflict, it seems most likely that progress toward the Liberal model would have been stronger, with a shift from polarized pluralism to moderate pluralism. In that case, a legal-rational authority would have also spread into cultural groups that adhere to religious and traditional bases of authority, like the Jewish religious parties or the Israeli Arab nationalists.

If not for that protracted conflict, one can assume that the Israeli media system would have converged more fully with the globalization process – developing more in the direction of a global media culture, in which the media are closer to the world of business and farther from the world of politics (Hallin and Mancini, 2004b: 76). Indeed, it is hard to ignore the commercialization of the media and professionalization of journalists that have taken place during the closing years of the twentieth century and the beginning of the twenty-first.

Yet, the protracted conflict put constraints on these processes. The 1967 Six Day War, followed by the occupation of the Palestinian Territories, four decades as an occupying power, and the various uprisings that the Palestinian people in the Territories have launched in an attempt to shake off Israeli rule – as well as the war against Palestinian and Islamic terrorism within Israel proper and the shadow of a nuclearized Middle East – have had a significant impact on the openness of political institutions, political processes, and the media system, obstructing this convergence.

The impact of these wars on politics has been well demonstrated in research on the "national security state." Conventional wisdom holds that conflict and the rise of such a state modify the Liberal model, not only by encouraging a pro-administration bias but also by giving the state a greater role in pushing in the direction of moderate pluralism or even low pluralism by suppressing political differences and emphasizing consensus.

Indeed whenever Israel was involved in actual battle, like the Six Day War, the Yom Kippur War, the Second Lebanon War in the summer of 2006, or the confrontation with Hamas in Gaza in December 2008, the well-known phenomenon of rallying around the flag occurred: People and the media united behind the national leadership and the military. However, the Arab–Israeli confrontation is not about war and peace only. It involves a deep division of opinions in Israel about the country's relations to other states in the Middle East, the future of the Territories, and more than anything else, the definition of Israel's collective identity.

Consequently, a process of de-ideologization and weakening of ideological splits such as the one that occurred in Europe could not take place. There has been no decline in the political and ideological differences that separate parties and different sectors of the public, and the forcefulness of polarized pluralism has not waned. Although at the beginning of the 1960s a liberalization process indeed started, the outcome of the 1967 Six Day War and, all the more so, the 1973 Yom Kippur War led to renewed polarization of public debate over the foundations of Israel's national existence. Nothing could have better illustrated the severity of that deeply divided society than the assassination of Prime Minister Rabin in November 1995. The evolution to moderate pluralism has backtracked to polarized pluralism.

These conditions have had a detrimental impact on the media. On the one hand, the media cannot divorce themselves from the heated political debate, and they continue to reflect the divisions in society. On the other hand they are under constant pressure from both the state apparatus and their audiences to be tamed, because of the external threats and security considerations.

In contrast to World War II and the Cold War, which have brought about the partial integration of the media into the state apparatus, the ongoing Israeli–Arab conflict has undermined the separation of the Israeli media system from political institutions. Under such conditions, one should not be surprised that even in the two newspapers that are basically tabloids, political issues and events in the public sphere have higher newsworthiness value than soft news that originates in the private sphere. On television, politics penetrate into entertainment programs, even more than entertainment values permeate the news shows. News bulletins are transmitted during prime time, current events programs receive very high ratings, and the entire population tunes into 24/7 news radio channels. During the first Gulf War in 1991, television and radio channels merged their broadcasts. In the Second Lebanon War in the summer of 2006 this did not happen, but the public was supportive of such a move.

When the security situation is tense, pressure for consensus and uniformity tends to increase. At such times, the audience is less willing to hear different opinions. Therefore the media cannot completely fulfill its function as the arena where issues are hashed out or hammered out before being brought to the political system for a policy decision. An ongoing state of emergency undermines the readiness for pluralism, tolerance, and liberalism and amplifies public expectations that the media will exhibit more "social responsibility" – be less critical, more committed to collective endeavor, and more supportive of the national leadership. Above all, a state of emergency legitimizes the state's deeper and deeper intrusion into the private sphere and into civic society. It demands that independent and professional considerations of journalists, as well as other professions such as law, accommodate or bend themselves to conform to state logic and *reason d'etat.*

Indeed, although in the 1970s Israeli journalists had already begun to adopt a more adversarial and critical perspective, this did not apply in the security domain. There an attitude of "self-cancellation" of one's worth and autonomy vis-à-vis the powers-that-be, particularly the security establishment, still held. From this standpoint, the 1973 Yom Kippur War played as significant a role for the Israeli media as the Vietnam War did for U.S. media, but the outcomes were not the same. Israeli journalists conceded that their total dependence and trust in the government and uncritical adoration of the top brass were responsible for the media not issuing a warning that war was about to break out.

Yet, despite the lessons that the media learned from their own 1973 blunder, and although the media grew more critical of the political establishment, their attitude toward the security realm changed only slightly. When it comes to national security, there is mounting public pressure to be responsible, to stay in line, to stop being partisan or critical, to bolster public morale, and, above all, to be patriotic.

In the 1990s – during the peace process, which made it appear that the era of warfare was at an end and that Israel was becoming a postwar society – the professional autonomy of the media grew, and journalists adopted a more critical stance. However, the failure of peace talks in the summer of 2000 and the outbreak of the second Intifada with its suicide attacks aimed at the heart of the civilian population led to a serious retreat from these developments. State agencies and the public even more so again exerted pressure for media reorientation, demanding that the media restrain its criticism and circle the wagons.

Thus, in the twenty-first century the media in Israel are enjoying relative strength vis-à-vis the state and other political agents, but are in increasing confrontation with their audience. While gaining more independence from political control, they find themselves under stronger social control. As the state has become weaker and its power to interfere in the media has decreased, the public is exerting much more pressure on journalists to conform their activities to what is seen as appropriate professional conduct.

The consequences are interesting: Pluralism exists, but it is constrained. Criticism of the government is widespread, but is limited in scope, refraining from questioning the basic premises of society. Public debate is conducted within very clearly marked boundaries. Divisions in society and journalists' perception of the need for a free market of ideas do exist, but not within a well-developed internal pluralism, because such pluralism is perceived as weakening the unity of the besieged nation. There is no dialogue between various paradigms, but rather exchanges of positions within the same one; that is the new version of Zionist ideology. Other schools of thought do exist, but only on the margins of society, and they are not represented in public mainstream media. In the field of national security – and in Israel this field covers a wide area – the consensual mode of thinking prevails. Opinions that are considered legitimate are only variations of the central hegemonic paradigm.

In the Second Lebanon War in the summer of 2006, some journalists – for instance, those working for the newest and most aggressive news channel, Channel 10 (in contrast with the other two channels) – tried to report on the war from a somewhat critical perspective; however, their professionalism was "rewarded" with a flood of harsh criticism from the public, which accused Channel 10 of undermining national morale and damaging the Israeli Defense Forces (Weimann, 2007). Indeed, a deeper analysis of the media's criticism has shown that journalist allowed themselves only instrumental criticism, not basic criticism: Although they questioned military conduct and operational efficacy, they refrained from asking deeper questions about Israel's military preferences, strategic decisions, and political worldview (Neiger et al., 2008; Peri, 2007).

Three factors propel the process of *differentiation* of the media according to Jeffrey C. Alexander (1981). On the structural level, differentiation is produced by demands for more universalistic information. Another structural factor is the growth of stronger professional norms and self-regulation within the journalistic profession itself, developments that lead to demands for increased prestige and professional freedom. On the cultural level, the crucial variable is the degree of universalism in national civic cultures, which depends on a range of factors from national religion to the structure of the educational system (Alexander, 1981: 25).

In Israel, ongoing conflict continues to have a negative effect on all three factors. First, instead of an increasing degree of universalism in civic culture, the particularistic-nationalistic foundations of culture have been strengthened, which could be seen more than ever before in the first decade of the twenty-first century. When the peace talks between Israel and the Palestinian Authority, which were based on the premise of territorial separation, broke down in 2000, a post-territorial nationalism developed, and the ethnic cleavage between Jews and Palestinian deepened. If we are bound to live together, not in two distinctive and separate territories, so went the argument, something else should divide "us" from "them," and that is ethnicity.

Second, there is public resistance to adopting professional norms and self-regulation by journalists, with pressure to bend the media system to stay in tune with public opinion. Last, there is an increasing demand for particularistic rather than universalistic information; there is even a negation of the premise that universalistic information does exist. Those who do not see reality the way we see it are by definition supporters of our adversaries, whether knowingly or unknowingly.

Whereas critics of a national security culture tend to look at the pressure exerted by the state or the security establishment as hindering free and critical media, the Israeli case demonstrates a different threat to professionalism: the opposing orientations of the public and media personnel concerning the role of the media in protracted conflicts. This widespread public perception of the media's role is the main obstacle to further adoption of the Liberal model of media system.

One could see this threat to professionalism arising in Israel's latest military confrontations. Wolfsfeld describes the "synergy between journalists, the military, and the government" during the second Intifada (2000–5; Wolfsfeld, 2004). In addition, foreign journalists stationed in Israel who followed the Israeli media during the Second Lebanon War in the summer of 2006 claim that Israeli television did not show viewers at home what the European networks were showing, nor even what the American networks (where support for the Israeli narrative was higher than in Europe) were showing. These journalists charged that Israeli television ignored the suffering of the other side in the conflict and failed to show footage that was liable to raise questions about the government's policies or undermine Israeli viewers' patriotic feelings. Nevertheless the Israeli public still overwhelmingly criticized the media for not being patriotic enough.

Fundamental changes in media systems are product of developments in the political arena, in technology, and in the media profession and culture. Underlying all these changes is the social environment. As long as the media have to operate in a situation of protracted conflict, even if indeed convergence and homogenization are prevailing global forces, the full adoption of the Liberal model of media system is most unlikely.

3

Italianization (or Mediterraneanization) of the Polish Media System?

Reality and Perspective

Bogusława Dobek-Ostrowska

At the beginning of the 1990s S. Splichal (1994) coined the phrase "Italianization of the media" to describe the process of media change in the postcommunist world. Many other scholars in this period also compared Central European media systems to that of Italy, including A. Wyka (2008: 66) and T. Goban-Klas (1997: 40). Quoting Paolo Mancini, Goban-Klas describes the Italian media system as being dominated by the following four features: (1) state control over the media, realized in the direct control over television and indirect control over the press; (2) political party influence on the selection of topics and the structure of the media organizations; (3) a high degree of integration of the media and political elites; and (4) ethical divisions among journalists and media personnel (Mancini, 1991: 139). Goban-Klas argues that "these four characteristics of the Italian system are surprisingly close to the present situation in East-Central Europe" (1997: 40).

A few years later, many scholars expanded their comparative analyses by introducing a new concept: "Mediterraneanization." One such scholar is K. Jakubowicz (2008b: 47), who argues that former communist countries share some features with the countries grouped in the Mediterranean media system: They have undergone recent democratization, they lag in economic development, and they are characterized by a weak rational-legal authority combined with a strong direct influence of state. He adds that their modernization is incomplete or (in some cases) little advanced.

Are these concepts – "Italianization" or "Mediterraneanization" – useful in studies of the Polish media system? Is the Polish media system farther from or closer to the Italian system today? Or is Poland closer to Spain, Portugal, or Greece, the countries that "threw off the last three authoritarian regimes in Western Europe and began successful transitions to liberal democracy" (Hallin and Mancini, 2004b: 89)? Have the media in other countries in Central Europe evolved in a similar or a different way than in Poland? In this chapter I examine whether Hallin and Mancini's models of media and politics are useful for a comparative analysis in Poland and in other postcommunist countries in Central and Eastern Europe.

The Development of Mass Media in Poland

Development of the Press before 1939

Mass press in Poland started to develop relatively late compared to Western European countries. The reasons for this situation are complex. One of the most important was the lack of statehood. Poland had been partitioned, with parts controlled by Russia, Prussia, and Austria. The ruling authorities did not allow or strictly limited publication in the Polish language. A large percentage of the Polish population was illiterate, moreover, and Polish newspapers were read only by aristocrats and intellectuals. Distinguished writers such as Kraszewski, Sienkiewicz, and Prus were the journalistic elite, and as in Southern European countries there was a strong symbiosis between literature and journalism. The journalistic profession started to emerge from the literary groups, politicians writing for newspapers, and social activists. At the turn of the twentieth century there were about 1,000 journalists (Habielski, 1999: 55), many of whom had fled from the Russian-occupied territory to the more liberal Austrian part of former Poland. The vast majority of Polish journalists emigrated in the nineteenth century to Western Europe, mainly France and the United States, where they worked for newspapers addressed to Polish emigrants

The year 1918, when after 128 years of foreign rule Poland gained independence, was a breakthrough in the development of the press. The political system in the interwar years was conducive to the free and independent opinion press. Parliamentary rule, a multiparty political system, and the absence of one dominant political party in the years 1918–26 fostered the development of external pluralism in the press. All the political forces were interested in the unfettered development of the politically engaged press. Most of the newspapers were officially or unofficially connected with political parties, and in this sense we can say that party-press parallelism developed in this period. Circulation remained relatively stagnant, which negatively affected the financial situation of the publishers, who would not have survived without subsidies from the political authorities.

At this time Poland was a very poor country, devastated by World War I and burdened with an anachronistic social structure: Peasants represented 64 percent of the population; workers, 16 percent; intellectuals and office workers, 5 percent; and the lower middle class, about 11 percent (Habielski, 1999: 62). Poor, uneducated rural communities were not part of the public for the press, which was associated with the world of the intelligentsia and well-read city dwellers. The circulation rate went up from 600,000 copies in 1930 to 900,000 in 1939 and it was only 9 copies per 100 inhabitants; the comparable figures were 38 in Great Britain and 27 in France (Habielski, 1999: 75).

The interwar years were dominated by the opinion press, both political and informative, addressed to narrow political and intellectual elites and the aristocracy. The popular press appealing to the less intellectually demanding city dweller first appeared; its articles were short, abridged, and simple, and colloquial usage replaced literary language. However, a profit-oriented tabloid press did not appear.

In the interwar years the professionalization of journalism was clearly visible. However, the profession was still highly political, and the politician-journalist or politician-editor was a common phenomenon. Specialized university programs were created in the late 1920s. The Higher School of Journalism was founded in Warsaw in 1927, followed by similar schools in Cracow and Poznan. In 1939, around 3,500 journalists were employed in all forms of the press.

Hadamik (2005: 214) argues that, in the interwar period, the Polish media underwent a dynamic, rigorous, and far-reaching process of modernization characterized by strong self-organization, differentiation, and journalistic education, while retaining a strong literary, intellectual, and political orientation. She claims that the professionalization of Polish journalism evolved in a direction different from the Anglo-American model. As a Central European country, with a mentality and culture created under the influence of its former occupants (above all Germans and Austrians) for more than one century (1795-1918), Poland adopted tendencies well known in the region, in which the Democratic Corporatist model, rather than the Liberal model, was typical of the democratic media systems.

The Polish press before World War II shared several features found in the press of Southern European countries, such as polarized pluralism, political and literary roots of journalism, and limited access to or lack of commercial and popular newspapers. Church-linked media, typical of the Mediterranean countries, played a significant role in Poland as well. As in Southern Europe, mass-circulation newspapers never developed. However, features characteristic of the Democratic Corporatist model, such as "critical professionalism" of journalists linked with political parties, well-organized formal education in journalism, strong professional associations, and a relatively high level of journalistic autonomy, also developed in the interwar Polish press. Thus the Polish media system in the interwar period was situated between Hallin and Mancini's Polarized Pluralist and Democratic Corporatist models.

World War II ended the development of the pluralist party press system initiated in 1918. Newspapers published in the German- and Soviet-occupied territories were closed down during the war. The only Polish papers published at that time were those published abroad or by the underground resistance movement.

Authoritarian Media System during the Communist Period (1944–89)

The media system in the communist era (1944–89) was created from scratch by the new communist government, as the Soviet press model replaced the external pluralist model in Central and Eastern Europe. As many authors have argued, this model is more complex than its classic portrayal in *Four Theories of the Press* (Siebert, Peterson, and Schramm, 1956). The Soviet press model had as many variations as there were countries dominated by the Soviet regime in Central Europe – from the strongly controlled ones in Romania, Bulgaria, Czechoslovakia, and East Germany to more liberal ones in Poland and Hungary.

The nature of media control and journalistic professionalization in Poland has been analyzed in a very interesting way by J. Curry (1990). Forty-five years of communism destroyed the Polish intellectual elite and the prewar form of journalistic professionalism. It resulted in a complete break with the democratic traditions of the interwar years. The majority of the journalists who had worked in the profession before 1939 were killed in the war, had died, or had emigrated. Only those linked with the communist and socialist press could continue to work. Curry emphasizes that the articulated institutions of direction and control in the communist states were the forces of control inherent in the media production process itself and that journalists were selected and privileged members of their own societies. She adds that the editorial position at all but the most marginal journals was held by a member of the communist party's "nomenklatura" (1982b: 106). In the early postwar years of Stalinism, Polish journalists were recruited from the working class. This generation formed the core of the profession for the next thirty years (Curry, 1990: 25). Another significant group of journalists came on the scene in the 1970s, the generation of Solidarity. Many of them worked for the opposition media inside or outside the country and are still active in the profession today. Their presence marks a significant difference between Poland and other communist countries in this region of Europe.

The Polish media and journalists were atypical (Curry, 1990: 23–4) in the Soviet bloc, because they were more liberal and open than in other communist states. Only Poles, the most independent, disobedient, and troublesome people for Moscow, could travel relatively freely to the West, which allowed them to assimilate democratic ideas faster than other communist societies. It is not by accident that the strongest and most organized opposition to communism developed there.

The press landscape was also much less uniform than in other communist countries in Central Europe. In addition to party propaganda, Polish readers could find excellent reports and essays, as well as entertaining, even sensational news (Curry, 1990: 70; Hadamik, 2005: 215; Pisarek, 1999: 136–7). Criticism of the political regime and ideology was present in many official publications. Another phenomenon was a narrow enclave of publications that did not belong to the state and that are still published today, such as the Catholic weekly *Tygodnik Powszechny*. Poland was a unique communist country in which private ownership existed, amounting to about 10 percent of all the published titles. Cultural magazines often smuggled forbidden contents between the lines (Hadamik, 2005: 216). In the Soviet bloc, Polish radio and television were also the most liberal and "commercialized" at that time. People could listen to Western pop music and watch American movies and soap operas that were forbidden in other parts of the Soviet bloc. Additionally, the wide-ranging underground press and books, which had an impressive circulation even before the 1970s, broke up the monopoly of the official propaganda and state information. Thus a kind of external pluralism existed in a clandestine way, and Poland was perceived by its neighbors as the only window open onto the Western world.

Transformation to Liberal Democracy and the Mass Media Structure in the 2000s

In the early 1990s the Polish media began to undergo a profound structural transformation from a state media controlled by the Communist Party to an independent and free media market. Three groups of publications emerged. Titles owned by the state were transformed into private and self-managing commercial enterprises operating in free-market conditions. Privately owned periodicals and newspapers published before 1989 continued their activity on the competitive market. New publications, such as *Gazeta Wyborcza*, which had appeared on the market before the first semi-democratic elections in 1989, constituted the third group.

In the 2000s the Polish daily press expanded with an increase in the number of free dailies. Axel Springer introduced the tabloid *Fakt* in 2003 and the national quality daily *Dziennik* in 2006. The three main high-quality daily newspapers (*Gazeta Wyborcza, Rzeczpospolita, Dziennik*) together constituted in 2008 about 33 percent of the national newspaper market, the two paid tabloids (*Fakt* and *Super Express*) about 30 percent, and the free tabloids about 13 percent. There are more than ten newspapers representing different political orientations and ideologies. Quality newspapers in Poland addressed to a small elite – mainly urban, well educated, and politically active – seem to be closer to the Polarized Pluralist than to the Democratic Corporatist model. A strong segment of tabloids and free newspapers, together with an important role of cheap magazines and periodicals, is present in Poland and perhaps brings Poland closer to the Liberal model. We know that this segment is absent from the southern region of Europe. However, the overall circulation of newspapers, which declined from about 130 copies sold per thousand in the communist era to about 90–100 per thousand today, is consistent with the Mediterranean pattern. Poland does not have the sports dailies common in Southern Europe; the tabloids perform this function.

The presence of foreign investors in the print media market is a common feature of all the countries in Central Europe. Some publishers took advantage of the economic transformation after the collapse of communism in this part of Europe to enter the young markets in the early 1990s. Rich and experienced in competition, the foreign companies eliminated weak national owners in a short time. A high degree of market concentration has resulted from this process, with pluralistic markets becoming duopolies and owners (Agora, Bauer) controlling more newspapers, more magazines, more television channels, and more radio stations and, as McQuail (2005) claims, with increased power. In Poland and in Central Europe the market is being colonized by external media groups, mainly from Germany, but also from Switzerland. The activity of foreign groups leads to strong commercialization and tabloidization of the media systems; their influence on journalistic professionalization is analyzed later in the chapter.

The commercialization of broadcasting in Europe began in the 1980s. Poland came to commercialization about ten years later than such leaders as Great Britain and Italy, but only two years later than Spain. Polish commercial television was already well developed when the markets in Ireland and Austria opened for private investors. Poland, the Czech Republic, and Slovakia were the leaders in this part of Europe.

With a population of 38 million, Poland was the largest media market among postcommunist countries in Central Europe and thus a very attractive market for many foreign investors. The print media market was soft-regulated, and media groups could enter it without any obstacles in the early 1990s. In contrast, Polish broadcasting regulations contained in the Broadcast Act – passed by Parliament at the end of 1992, one year after private commercial radio stations and television channels started operating – were more rigorous and favored national investors: Only 33 percent of total ownership could belong to foreign companies. Today the majority of the broadcast media owners have national roots, which is an important difference between Poland and other postcommunist countries.

Competition took place within the regulatory framework in compliance with Western European standards, and a dual model with commercial and public service broadcasting was established in 1994. An oligopoly with three main broadcasters – Public Service Broadcasting, RMF FM, and Radio ZET – was created in the radio market in the late 1990s. The biggest share of the radio market is held by the commercial stations (RMF FM and Radio ZET). Oligopoly is characteristic of the television market too. In the case of television, however, the three public television channels are still dominant, and they controlled more than 46 percent of the audience in 2008, although that percentage has since declined. The largest terrestrial commercial TV stations (TVN and Polsat TV) attract about 35 percent of the audience. This structure resembles the Italian system more than that of any other Mediterranean country. At the beginning of the 2000s public channels in Italy attracted about 48 percent of the viewers, in contrast to 35 percent in France, only 25 percent in Spain, and about 15 percent in Greece. The solid economic position of Polish public television is exceptional in Central Europe, where public broadcasting services are weaker, as in the Czech Republic, Slovakia, Estonia, Latvia, and Romania (Jakubowicz, 2007a: 309).

Yet, public television has been commercialized, as reflected in media content and high advertising incomes. More than 70 percent of its revenue comes from a commercial source. In this aspect Poland is more similar to Spain than to Italy or France, where about 45 percent of the revenue comes from advertising. There is one significant difference between public and private broadcasters in Poland: Some private channels try to keep up high standards. Paradoxically, the private TVN network broadcasts more information and news programs than does the public TVP network, and its evening news is more professional than that of private television in Hungary, the Czech Republic, and Slovakia – owned by American or Western European companies – "whose news coverage is characterized by commercialization of the news, human interest perspectives, superficial coverage, tabloidization, sound bites, and a search for scandals" (Sükösd, 2007).

Political Parallelism

Political parties have a different history in Central than in Southern Europe, even in countries in both regions that have undergone recent transformations to democracy. In Spain, for example, the main opposition parties had existed a long time before the collapse of Franco's dictatorship. Later, their émigré leaders came back and continued their activity in the country. These parties are thus well rooted in Spanish society. In Poland and other countries of Central Europe, the process of the formation of political parties started only after 1989 and has been difficult. Many small and weak political organizations sprang up, which had many leaders but lacked sufficient support from the citizens. Politicians and leaders founded parties because the only way for them to enter Parliament and pursue a serious political career in the state administration was to lead a party. Herbut (2002: 110) calls this process the colonization of the public administration by political parties. Party system consolidation and elimination of small organizations took more than fifteen years in Poland. In the early 2000s two parties became dominant: the right-wing PiS and the centrist PO. The left is marginalized in Parliament despite a significant group of left-oriented voters.

Throughout Poland's twenty years of democracy, political leaders, presidents, and governments have aimed to secure media control. Success came easy with public media but less so with private media. Blumler and Gurevitch (1995: 64–5) describe five degrees of mass media partisanship. Three of them can be seen in various segments of the Polish media system. Polish parties do not own media enterprises, the highest degree of partisanship, although some do have a relationship with public broadcast media controlled by politically affiliated broadcasting bodies and with the quality newspaper *Rzeczpospolita* (since August/September 2006). The second degree, described as voluntarily fixed partisanship, is typical of many parts of the Polish media system. The parties may count on the unconditional and unswerving loyalty of particular media; for example, *Trybuna* and *Przegląd* support the left, and the quality newspaper *Dziennik*, which belonged (2006–9) to the German Springer publishing conglomerate, has a strong center-right orientation. The latter paper is an exception among the newspapers published in Poland by foreign companies, which generally prefer to avoid any political identity. At the third level degree of partisanship, the media may back a favored party, but this support is conditional. The majority of private Polish print and broadcasting media, such as *Gazeta Wyborcza*, TVN, and Polsat TV, operate at this level. The fourth level, ad hoc support given in an unpredictable way, can be found above all in tabloids such as *Fakt* and cheap entertainment media. The fifth level represents nonpartisanship and political neutrality: Blumler and Gurevitch (1995: 65) claim that it may be exemplified by broadcasting organizations that are obligated by law or charter to refrain from political support. No media in Poland correspond to this level.

The Polish public broadcasting system can be described as a "politics over broadcasting system," in which appointments to the governing body entrench political control, and the news agenda is not governed primarily by journalistic judgments of "newsworthiness" but by political policy (Hallin and Mancini, 2004b: 108). The process of public media politicization was visible during the presidencies of Wałęsa and Kwaśniewski, but has intensified with the presidency of Lech Kaczyński, which began in December 2005, and the government of Jarosław Kaczyński from July to September 2006. The adherents of Kaczyński's PiS party were appointed to the National Broadcasting Council (Figure 3.1), replacing adherents of the left parties connected with Kwaśniewski. The government of Kaczyński monopolized public media and the national newspaper *Rzeczpospolita*, which is 50 percent owned by the state but had a reputation of being an independent quality daily. Jakubowicz (2008a) calls this process the "etatization of democracy," and many scholars consider the period of Kaczyński's government as the deconsolidation of democracy.

Content analysis of the evening news of the public broadcasting stations (Łódzki, 2010; Nieroda, 2008) has shown that with rare exceptions public radio stations and TV channels have been partisan and have favored the ruling party in a visible way from the beginning of the transformation in 1989. A low level of commitment to civic values in elite

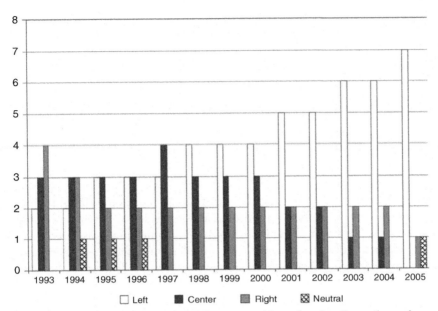

FIGURE 3.1. Political preferences of the National Broadcasting Council members during the presidency of Lech Wałęsa (1993–5) and Aleksander Kwaśniewski (1995–2005; Głowacki, 2008: 84).

political culture, passivity of society (very low voter turnout in elections), and, in general, an unprofessional media have contributed to this pattern. As explained later, journalists themselves played a central role in purging fellow journalists in public media after each change of government. Let me add that control exercised over the media is not automatically reflected in electoral results. Since the first presidential election in 1990, the political parties have been in control of public radio and television. However, even though they had easy access to publicity, they lost almost all elections. The parties and candidates whose attitude toward this media was unfavorable or even hostile won those elections (Dobek-Ostrowska, 2001: 63).

Commercial media, which belong to both national and foreign investors, have shown more resistance to political pressure. Because they are owned by Polish holdings and media groups like Agora, Polsat, ITI, and Eurozet, those groups themselves decide on their content. Unfortunately, independence does not always lead to objectivity and impartiality. In contrast to public radio and television, the process of political control over commercial media content is hidden from public view. The integration of political elites and media personnel is not observed: Politicians are not directly involved in media industries, nor are media owners or journalists involved in politics. Undoubtedly, this is a positive factor that, in the future, may stop the media politicization process and consolidate professional journalistic ethics. However, some private media owners do not bother to conceal their political preferences, and privately owned media do manifest sympathies and antipathies toward a given publisher's political line.[1]

Content analysis of the Polish quality newspapers and the evening news shows that these media are dominated by an "advocacy" style of journalism similar to that of Southern Europe. Interpretation and political commentaries dominate reporting, and in this sense, patterns of Polish journalism are closer to the French or Italian commentary-oriented political reporting than to the news and information-based Anglo-American model, although Polish journalists are not as strongly opinionated and politically engaged as, for example, Greek journalists. In contrast to the quality newspaper sector, local newspapers enjoying a monopoly of their markets and some national quality newspapers belonging to foreign investors do not engage in the political sphere and ideological divisions because any kind of political involvement could reduce their income. Thirty percent of Polish readers choose tabloids, which are not found in the Polarized Pluralist model, and in this sense Poland resembles more closely the Liberal model. As in Britain, party identification does affect the readership of tabloids – *Fakt* is somewhat conservative, whereas *Super Express* avoids political connections.

Although Polish media are in many cases opinionated and politically partial, they do not have stable alliances with political parties. In contrast to Spain or Italy, the degree of party politicization has declined considerably in Poland. Media support is unpredictable for political parties and politicians, and in the last twenty years the media have changed their political preferences many times. The large number of political parties and the instability of the party systems have fostered this behavior.

One clear difference between Central and Western Europe is the high degree of foreign press ownership in Central Europe. Content analysis

---

[1] The main Polish opinion newspaper *Gazeta Wyborcza* has a left-center orientation; the media belonging to the controversial foundation of Father Rydzyk (Radio Maryja radio station, TV Trwam, and the small national newspaper *Nasz Dziennik*) support uncritically the Kaczyńskis and their conservative party PiS; and TVN, one of the dominant TV stations, belongs to ITI and is in a permanent conflict with the Kaczyńskis and PiS.

of the Polish media (Dobek-Ostrowska and Łódzki, 2008: 233) lets us clarify how foreign ownership affects political parallelism and journalistic professionalism. The main aim of the Western companies has been making a profit, and this aim has affected media coverage and the quality of journalism. Acquiring tabloids (Springer in Poland; Ringier in Czech Republic, Slovakia, Hungary, and Romania) and entertainment media (Bauer, Burda, Edipress, etc.) was the best way for those companies to achieve economic dominance. However, Western publishers did not implant the profit-making strategies that they had used in their mother companies to their new daughter companies in postcommunist countries. The empirical data collected by Woźna (2008: 160) show that the German group Verlagsgruppe Passau did not decide to copy its conservative daily *Passauer Neue Presse* but introduced a neutral one. This was because the group was afraid that Polish readers might not accept a strongly politicized regional newspaper. Now the company publishes a national daily that marginalizes political content. Political neutrality or rather depoliticization of newspapers owned by foreign investors, not only in Poland but also in the whole region, is a strategy that might help them in unfavorable political and economic situations.

The content analysis carried out by M. Röger (2010) concludes that newspapers belonging to a foreign owner often have very different political preferences from those that the same company publishes in its home market. It may be surprising that the tabloid *Fakt*, which belongs to the German Springer conglomerate, is anti-German. Röger concludes that *Fakt* is more "geared to the market and profit than to the ideological basis of its parent company" (2010:280). The commercial logic followed by Axel Springer leads this publisher to drown ideology in the icy waters of cold calculation. In 2008 the German Journalists Association in Landau-Hessen passed a resolution that it was unacceptable for the editor to insult Germans in his newspapers in Poland and to insult Poles in his tabloid *Bild* in Germany. As a consequence of the resolution Axel Springer was awarded the title "Hyena of the Year" by the Polish Journalists Association because his newspapers published in Poland fuel anti-German attitudes.

There is no single answer to the question about the level of political parallelism in Poland. The media are politicized, the result of both political culture and tradition. Publicly owned media have been dominated directly by political actors since the beginning of the 1989 transformation, being controlled by the political group in power at any time. In the case of public media, then, we can clearly talk about a high level of political parallelism. Private opinion media owned by Polish owners do not have any formal connection with political parties. They create their content in an independent way, but they have more or less obvious political sympathies and antipathies. The third group, the media belonging to foreign companies, above all the tabloids, tries to be neutral because it is better for business. Poland is thus a mixed system in terms of the degree of political parallelism, resembling in some ways the high levels of the Polarized Pluralist model and in other ways the depoliticization of the Liberal model. An evolution toward the Liberal model has been hastened in a visible way by foreign ownership that dominates the print media in Poland.

Journalistic Professionalism

As in the Mediterranean countries, journalism in Poland has deep political and literary roots, and the profession was already well developed before 1939. The professional organization and journalists' unions were relatively strong, which is more typical of the Democratic Corporatist model. As noted earlier, the first school of journalism was created in 1927. During the communist period, formal education in journalism was much better than in other countries of the Soviet bloc. Jane Leftwich Curry's research on journalists in Communist Poland is part of Hallin and Mancini's (2004b: 39) discussion on the nature of journalistic professionalism. They claim that many aspects of professionalism existed, even though there was no separation between political and media institutions, and thus it may be misleading to include that component of separation in the definition of professionalism. She argues that despite the official ideology and censorship that regarded the media as instruments of the party, Polish journalists developed a strong professional culture (1990: 23–4): They were both highly politicized *and* highly professionalized (1990: 177). Media personnel were more flexible and better prepared for full freedom than in other communist countries. Polish journalists had a strong sense of identity and their distinct role in society (Curry, 1990: 30; Hallin and Mancini, 2004b: 39). Alongside those journalists who were totally subordinate to the regime, there was a large group of insubordinate and disobedient journalists from whom the Solidarity, underground, and opposition press developed. However, journalists in the official and censored newspapers and magazines also managed to develop some independence. Weekly opinion magazines, such as *Polityka*, *Kultura*, *Przekrój*, and the magazine for the Catholic intelligentsia *Tygodnik Powszechny*, are good examples of papers that provided a space for the development of independent Polish journalism. The best Polish journalists – Janina Parad-owska, Jacek Żakowski, and Jerzy Baczyński – worked for the fifty-year-old magazine *Polityka* during the communist period and still work for this magazine today. After 1989 a new group of journalists started work-ing for the free and politically independent opinion newspapers, although there was no radical change in media personnel in Poland, as occurred in the Czech Republic, Slovakia, and the Baltic countries. Except for those most discredited and dedicated to the communist regime, journalists were allowed to continue doing their jobs.

Hallin and Mancini indicate three dimensions of professionalization – autonomy of the profession, consensus on professional norms, and public service orientation. What do journalistic professionalism and profession-alization of journalism mean in Poland twenty years after the collapse of communism? What kinds of professional skills do journalists have? Is journalistic professionalism well developed, as in the Democratic Corpo-ratist and the Liberal models, or is the level of professionalization lower, as in the Polarized Pluralist model? Does it take an information-oriented form, as in the Liberal model, or a more commentary-oriented or "publi-cist" form as in the Polarized Pluralist or Democratic Corporatist models?

About 70 percent of all the materials published in the Polish press can be classified as providing information; the remaining 30 percent is dedicated to solving problems and to genres that involve "publicist" writing (Bortnowski, 1999: 53). It should be emphasized that "publicist" writing has a long tradition in Poland:

> Polish journalists are still inclined . . . to take a position and to present their own view. In this way advocacy journalism and political engagement are not deemed to be unprofessional. . . . The ability not only to gather and package information but also to analyse reality and to express this to the public, preferably in an outstanding individual way, is still regarded as a very important professional skill. (Hadamik, 2005: 218–19; see also Bajka, 2000; Gross, 1999)

In this sense Poland again combines characteristics of journalism in the Liberal model with other characteristics more typical of the Polarized Pluralist or Democratic Corporatist models.

As in many countries, journalists in Poland vary widely in their level of prestige, skill, and autonomy. At the top of the profession are two groups. The first is made up of the most popular and visible journal-ists and anchors working for the TV evening news and opinion pro-grams. They are famous not only for their brilliant analyses on TV but also as the authors of analytical and critical articles or columns in opinion newspapers and magazines. Well-known reporters and "publicists" in the print press make up the second group. Many of these reporters belong to an older generation that entered journalism before the transition to democracy. In contrast to other postcommunist countries in Central Europe, in Poland the old journalists' generation is free from negative connotations.

What about other Polish journalists who are not so brilliant and talented? The rapid growth of Polish media over the last twenty years has resulted in a decline in the quality of journalism. Young journalists and newcomers to the media often have no professional skills or basic knowledge. Additionally, to cut costs, publishers of tabloids and "light" media often prefer to employ paid amateurs rather than experienced professionals. Lower standards go together with a widespread demand for sensational, entertainment-style journalism.

In fact, there are two kinds of journalism in Poland. There are only a few but very important media outlets that try to keep up a high level of journalism. These are the main quality dailies like *Gazeta Wyborcza* and *Rzeczpospolita* (until 2006); financial and economic dailies like *Gazeta Prawna, Gazeta Podatkowa, Puls Biznes*, and *Gazeta Giełdy Parkiet*; and some opinion magazines like *Polityka, Newsweek*, and *Tygodnik Powszechny*. Journalists linked with this kind of media are in the minority. The majority of the media and their personnel belong to the other group. Weak consensus on journalistic standards and limited development of professional self-regulation, similar to the Mediterranean pattern (Hallin and Mancini, 2004b: 113), reflect the fact that journalism in Poland, to a large extent, is not an autonomous institution but acts under pressure from the political and business world.

Many surveys confirm that Poles perceive the journalistic profession as a service to the public. The majority of society (more than 60 percent) trust the media. This percentage is higher than in other European countries. For example, 20 percent of respondents in Great Britain and 30 percent in Sweden declare that they believe what journalists write (Waniek, 2007: 163). The reality of media performance, however, suggests that public service is not the dominant pattern. Hallin and Mancini coined the term "instrumentalization," which is very useful in studies of the media in Central Europe. All democratic societies in this region have had to struggle with a strong tradition of political instrumentalization of the media, which is rooted in communism. After 1989 the new political elites adopted this pattern. Politicians and leaders of political parties do not see anything improper in their relations with the media. Each winner of the elections tries to control the media. In the sector of public media, as noted earlier there are no obstacles that can stop politicians: Public media are the tool of political communication and propaganda of the ruling parties.

In contrast, private media have achieved sufficient independence from politicians during twenty years of democracy. Media conglomerates based in other industries (for example, the travel, construction, telecommunications, and oil industries) are absent in Poland, and media owners, both national and foreign, have not formed any political alliances, although some do have political biases. Even if political instrumentalization may be absent in commercial media, however, it has been replaced with commercial instrumentalization. Hallin and Mancini describe some forms of commercial instrumentalization, such as product placement or advertisers' demands for influence on media content. Those demands are clearly visible in Poland. Foreign and national owners of tabloids and entertainment media are not interested in political content because it could reduce their audience. In this sector, however, the media model of the public sphere has been replaced by the market model (Croteau and Hoynes, 2006: 39). In Poland as in all postcommunist countries in Central Europe, private companies sell their products to consumers, but do not serve the citizens and the public interest; profits are more important than the promotion of active citizenship. The chase for profits leads the media to commercialization and the deepening of tabloidization, and we can find only a few media – some opinion and Catholic newspapers and a few radio stations – that try to maintain "the ethic of public service." This kind of instrumentalization also affects public media, particularly television, which operates under strong economic pressure and competes with commercial channels. Both kinds of instrumentalization limit journalistic autonomy and threaten journalistic professionalization (Blumler and Gurevitch, 1995: 66; Hallin and Mancini, 2004b: 37).

There is no press ombudsman system in Poland, but there have been some moves toward systems of self-regulation. The major media organizations, including the public television and *Gazeta Wyborcza*, have their own codes of conduct, whereas some smaller media outlets have at least a general system of ethical guidelines. In addition, journalists' organizations have developed their own internal codes of ethics and a system of journalists' courts. After lengthy consultations and discussions, journalists' organizations agreed to adopt in 1995 a very brief, seven-point document titled "Media Charter of Ethics." It declares that journalists should perform their jobs in accordance with the following principles: honesty, objectivity, separation of information from commentary, truthfulness, respect and tolerance, putting the interest of the audience first, media freedom and responsibility. All existing journalists' organizations and major media organizations signed the charter. The signatories established the Council of Media Ethics in 1996 – a body consisting of well-respected media professionals who are charged with guarding the principles of the Charter and providing interpretations and reports on cases of the violation of ethical standards. Like most press councils, it has no authority to impose formal sanctions, but its opinions and judgments are perceived as important by the media, journalists, other political institutions, and society more generally. No press council exists at the national level in any of the Mediterranean countries discussed by Hallin and Mancini, so this is one more instance in which the Polish case departs from the Polarized Pluralist model and incorporates an element normally found in the Democratic Corporatist model.

There are two large associations for professional journalists and a smaller one; these are defined in large part by politics and religion, in a manner similar to the Mediterranean pattern. The Polish Journalists Association (SPD) was created in 1951. It supported Solidarity in 1980 and as a consequence was dissolved a few years later by the communist regime. The association was reanimated in 1989. It now has about 3,000 members who mainly profess a conservative ideology and support right-wing parties. The second large organization is the Association of Journalists of the Republic of Poland (SDPR), with more than 7,000 members. It was founded by the communists in 1982 to replace a pro-Solidarity SPD whose activity was illegal at that time. Its members are linked with the left. Both organizations are relatively strong and have central and regional offices in the major cities. Yet they differ in their assessment of history, ideological preferences, and sympathies for political parties, and these differences are reflected in frequent conflicts between their members and in media content. The conflict is visible above all in the public media after elections when a change in government takes place. Then, the ruling party appoints a new management board of public radio and television. The adherents of the winning party take up posts that the adversaries are obligated to leave. Very often this "clean-up action" is carried out by journalists linked with or supporting the new government, not by politicians. The Catholic Journalists Association that was founded in 1991 is the third association. It is a small organization and in principle is outside the mainstream of conflict, but Catholic media outlets, both those owned by private groups and those owned by the church, play a significant role in Polish society.

Poland seems to be close to the Democratic Corporatist or Liberal model in terms of journalistic professionalism, but this appearance is deceptive. As Jakubowicz notes (2002: 210), in addition to economic reform, democratization, de-monopolization, and decentralization, professionalization is also crucial to ensuring a free media. He argues that, although some elements of professionalization are apparent, the tradition of politicized journalism is still deeply rooted in Poland. The majority of journalists were and still are today far from being objective; they represent partisan political viewpoints and are convinced that their civic responsibility requires them to promote what they personally consider to be the best political course for the country (2002: 210). It is not clear what kind of journalistic professionalism is typical of Polish journalists. I agree with Hadamik (2005: 222) who claims that it is a mixture of the old and the new. She argues that, although many traditional values of journalistic culture have survived up to now, this culture is evolving and being modernized under pressure from global developments and trends.

What level of journalism professionalism does exist in Poland? Is it more similar to the Polarized Pluralist or to the Liberal model? This is an important question that cannot be answered unequivocally at the moment. We observe a process that is operative globally, in all of Hallin and Mancini's models, through which journalistic work and organizations are being changed under pressure of technical and economic but also political factors. We agree with Witschge and Nygren (2009) that these factors disrupt the established professional status, roles, and practices of journalists and, most importantly, journalists have become a "semi-professional" group (2009: 54). The changes in the journalistic profession in Poland are typical of trends observed in the world today, in the Liberal, as well as in the Polarized Pluralist and Democratic Corporatist models.

The Role of the State

Blumler and Gurevitch (1995: 63–4) describe three areas of state control of media: control over (1) appointment of supervisory and governing bodies of public service media, (2) over media finances, and (3) political control over media content. How are the media controlled in Poland? Are these areas of state control visible there? Does the state control the public and private media in the same way?

Each democratic state in Europe (except for Luxemburg) plays an important role as the owner of public service broadcasting, and this is also the case in Poland. All the facilities and holdings of public television and public radio belong to the State Treasury. The state also holds 49 percent of the shares of the opinion daily *Rzeczpospolita*; the remaining 51 percent belongs to the British media group Mecom. In addition, local governments own many local weeklies and magazines. In many cases these periodicals are the only medium that exists in these local communities, which means that government-owned local press is the main channel of political communication at this level.

Relations between the state and the public media differ significantly from relations between the state and the private media. The print media, which are totally in the hands of private owners (apart from *Rzeczpospolita* and local publications), are considered less important by politicians. Politicians focus their attention on television, which they believe is the most influential channel of political communication.

The first and most important means of control indicated by Blumler and Gurevitch (1995: 63) is making personnel appointments in the media that belong to the state. This form of control is a powerful instrument of subordination. As Blumler and Gurevitch suggest, it mixes two elements: the right to make political appointments and a belief that political criteria are relevant to the selection of media personnel (1995: 63). Since 1989, the system of appointment in the publicly owned broadcasting media has been based on candidates' political credentials, and no ruling party or governing coalition has deviated from this form of public media control since then. This pattern of political intervention reflects a majoritarian democracy marked by deep conflicts among the main political parties and a lack of political consensus, and it situates Poland closer to the Polarized Pluralist system than to countries classified as the Democratic Corporatist or Liberal Models.

Hallin and Mancini (2004b), drawing on work by Humphreys, Kelly, and others, distinguish four models of public media governance in Europe – the professional, civic, parliamentary, and government models. They note that in majoritarian systems, parliamentary and governmental control are often essentially indistinguishable. A high level of state intervention in public service broadcasting prevails in Poland, as in many of the Mediterranean countries. The main regulatory body for the broadcasting media in Poland is the National Broadcasting Council, whose members are appointed by the Seym, the Senate, and the President. The Council elects members of the public radio and public television supervisory boards. Only one member of the National Broadcasting Council is nominated by the Minister of the State Treasury. These boards appoint the managers and staff of public media. This system of governance has allowed the ruling party together with its coalition partners to control the media effectively. Opposition parties were not represented in the National Broadcasting Council from 1993[2] to 2007.

In 2006 all members of public institutions and media bodies, mainly linked with the outgoing leftist president and government, were replaced by new members connected with the coalition of Jaroslaw Kaczyński's PiS and two small populist parties. Kaczyński's party has significantly advanced the instrumentalization of the publicly owned media. This party has controlled not only the broadcast media but also the daily *Rzeczpospolita*, which was at one time regarded as among the most professional and independent media outlets in Poland, since 2006. In that year the government took advantage of the moment when the British media group Mecom bought shares in *Rzeczpospolita* from the Norwegian company Orkla and appointed an editor connected with the PiS. The editor's political orientation was soon noticed, and many journalists decided to leave the editorial board. Similarly, politically affiliated boards have elected politically affiliated executive directors of public radio and television. In fact, from 1989 to 2008, twelve directors of public television have been appointed because of their political affiliation, sometimes after long and fierce fights between political parties (see Figure 3.2). A good example of control over appointments and the loyalty system was the nomination of an ordinary politician, who was strongly connected with the ruling PiS party, as the director of public television in March 2007.

In 2007 the PiS lost the legislative elections, but thanks to a regulation the party had introduced two years before, it retained control over the public media through 2012, setting up an unusual situation in which public media would remain in the hands of the opposition party. If a government cannot control public media by appointment, as with the case of the PO government that succeeded Kaczyński, it looks for other instruments. One of them is control over media finances. The ruling PO party tried to amend the media law passed in 2005 by the previous Parliament

---

[2] The Council was established in 1993 by the Radio Television Act passed by Parliament in December 1992.

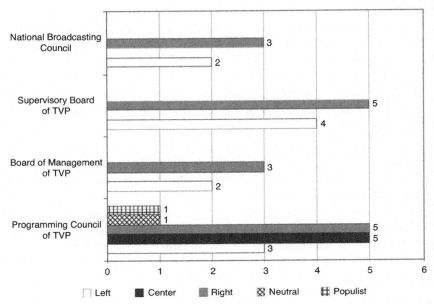

FIGURE 3.2. Political preferences of members of the National Broadcasting Council and supervising bodies of public television TVP, 2005–8 (Głowacki, 2008: 89).

and signed by President Lech Kaczyński. When this turned out to be impossible, the government of Tusk decided to limit its financial support for public radio and television companies. Limiting public funding would have a serious impact on public radio, which is financed from public sources, though less so on public television, for which commercial revenues provide 70 percent of its budget. This control instrument is not very effective in the case of the private media, which receive no subsidies from the state.

In terms of the role of the state, then, Poland is clearly a mixed case. There is strong state intervention in many parts of the media sector, and that intervention tends to be party-politicized, consistent with the pattern of the Polarized Pluralist model. Public television is relatively strong, although lacking independence from both commercial and political pressures. State intervention in private media is limited, and Poland does not have the systems of press subsidies associated with the welfare state tradition in the Democratic Corporatist countries of Northern Europe or in France or Italy; in this respect, like Spain, Greece, and Portugal, it could be said to shade to the Liberal side of the Polarized Pluralist model.

Rational-Legal Authority and Clientelism

Hallin and Mancini (2004b: 55) stress the role of a rational-legal authority in the formation of media systems. They indicate the importance of clientelism and the relatively slow development of a rational-legal authority in Southern Europe. We can observe the same processes in the postcommunist countries of Central Europe.

The most important characteristic of Weber's rational-legal authority is bureaucracy as an autonomous administrative apparatus based on professional civil servants who should be free from pressures from political parties and organizations, individuals, and social groups. Before 1989 the Polish bureaucratic apparatus and the juridical system were dependent on the Communist Party, which had a monopolistic position in the Soviet regime. Since 1989, the bureaucracy and the judiciary are in theory independent but in a fact come under the pressure of political elites. As Gwiazda (2008: 19) argues, the civil service was particularly vulnerable to political pressure. Each new government started with a "purge" in the public administration. The turnover in personnel and the appointment of loyal people often without the needed experience weakened the status of the civil service corps. The ruling party controls and penetrates not only the public administration but also the judiciary and all the enterprises owned by the state, including the media owned by the State Treasury.

In general, a weaker rational-legal authority translates into a prevalence of clientelism. Jakubowicz (2007a: 311) emphasizes the importance of clientelism in Central and Eastern Europe, and it is defined as a central problem for Polish political parties by Gwiazda (2008: 6):

Poland as a communist state has a long tradition of a political culture based on clientelism and personalized relations. In communist Poland, public administration operated under the Communist Party's nomenklatura system, according to which all appointments to the administration were made on the Communist Party's recommendation.

Paradoxically, the collapse of the Soviet regime in 1989 neither eliminated nor weakened the nomenklatura system. Instead, the nomenklatura of a single Communist Party was replaced by a multiparty nomenklatura. From 1989 onward each party that won an election in Poland dismissed people at the top of the civil service corps connected with the previous government and appointed their own people. Herbut (2002: 110) calls this process the "colonization of public administration." Clientelism and patronage characterized both postcommunist and post-Solidarity parties (Kochanowicz, Kozarzewski, and Woodward, 2005). For the last twenty years public administration has reflected the governing parties. An empirical study by Gwiazda of the SLD in 2001–5 (the Social Democratic Party with postcommunist roots) and of the PiS in 2005–6 (the conservative party with post-Solidarity roots) shows that party patronage was present in both administrations. The process was advanced by Kaczyński's party, which prepared a special list of candidates for posts in public administration. The party also established more ministries and enlarged the civil service corps.

Clientelism is also evident in local communities. The empirical data presented by Rutkowski (2008: 65–6) show that clientelism is deeply rooted in those societies and is called *kolesiostwo*. As mentioned, many local newspapers and periodicals are in the hands of local governments, and they are dependent on local leaders and ruling groups. As a result local media are involved in local election campaigns, supporting their candidate. If their candidate wins the election, the media receive rewards – the best posts in local power and the protection of friendly businesspeople. This award system is an important way to consolidate networks. This analysis shows how a patron who is a local leader absorbs the media and business into a clientelistic relationship.

The degree of clientelism locates Poland close to Southern European countries, but clientelism in Poland is weaker than in Spain or Greece. For example, in Spain the PSOE was the ruling party for fourteen years. Over such a long period of time the members of the party built stable networks and strong linkages that facilitated the development of corrupt and clientelistic relationships. This phenomenon, called the "caciquismo" or "amiguismo del PSOE," was well known in the last years of Gonzalez's government and continued in subsequent governments. In the case of Greece Samaras (2000: 14) claims that a long-term "bureaucratic clientelism" has given the powerful PASOK party a substantial and loyal clientele of some 40 percent of the electorate. Frequent changes of governments in Poland and short times in power do not allow clientelistic networks at the national level to deepen and consolidate. Many Polish scholars agree that there are no clientelistic relationships between the ruling parties and the private media, which would also distinguish the Polish case from those of Spain, Italy, or Greece. The owners of private television channels and radio stations do not get involved in politics, although that does not mean that they are not partisan. They do not keep company with leaders and political parties and they do not offer them news space or book contracts, in contrast to such media moguls as Murdoch or Berlusconi (Street, 2001: 124).

Conclusion

The Polish media system can be understood as a hybrid of the Polarized Pluralist and Liberal models, with a few elements of the Democratic Corporatist model and the country's postcommunist legacy. Certainly it has many characteristics of the Polarized Pluralist model. The system is characterized by a small circulation of daily newspapers and the central position of the electronic media. The media, above all the press, strongly focus on political life, and external pluralism and the tradition of commentary-oriented journalism are important. Instrumentalization of the public broadcasting media by the government and political parties is evident. Journalistic professionalism is at a lower level than in the Democratic Corporatist or the Liberal model. Relationships between the media and political elites are characterized mainly by conflicts over the autonomy of journalism. The state plays a significant role as the owner of public radio and television.

About twenty years after the collapse of communism, the Polish pattern is closer to the Mediterranean model, and it is rooted to a large extent in the high degree of ideological diversity and conflicts. The Polish media system in the first decade after 1989 had many features typical of the Italian and Spanish systems. We can agree with Školkay (2008: 38), however, who says that if we use Hallin and Mancini's categorization, then we realize that in the 1990s it was the Polarized Pluralist model that was dominant in Central and Eastern Europe as well as in Poland, whereas in the 2000s a strong process of privatization, competition, commercialization, and tabloidization in the late 1990s (Dobek-Ostrowska and Głowacki, 2008: 16) pushed the Polish media system toward the Liberal model. Today, the Liberal model is increasingly mixed with the Polarized Pluralist model in this region of Europe. We can also agree with Jakubowicz (2007a: 311–12) who says that the media systems in Poland and other countries in Eastern and Central Europe are affected by the same processes of change as their Western European counterparts, including strong neoliberal tendencies. Yet his opinion that "[g]iven all the political and cultural experience and heritage, a vision of the Liberal system is unrealistic, the Democratic Corporatist model is more realistic, but in a distant future" (2007a: 312) is rather questionable. Similar processes of change are also visible in the Democratic Corporatist countries,

Bogusława Dobek-Ostrowska

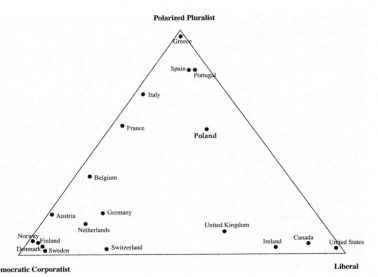

FIGURE 3.3. Position of the Polish media system on the three-models triangle of Hallin and Mancini (2004b).

especially in Scandinavia (Nord, 2008: 108; Roppen, 2008: 85–9). Nord concludes that the Nordic media systems have developed as a hybrid of the Democratic Corporatist and Liberal Models (2008: 108). The relation of the contemporary Polish media system to Hallin and Mancini's three models is represented in Figure 3.3.

4

Culture as a Guide in Theoretical Explorations of Baltic Media

Auksė Balčytienė

Introduction

Limited scholarship, particularly in other than national languages, has contributed to a situation in which the three Baltic countries are still "terra incognita" for many scholars outside the geographic and cultural region of northeastern Europe. Because of their peripheral location and cultural marginality, it is not surprising that even today in international contexts these countries are often represented in a rather mystified, mysterious, sometimes romantic way.[1]

From the Western point of view, the Baltic countries have often represented the East, whereas for the East these countries seemed to be part of the West. This duality in interpretations, combined with the geopolitical, cultural, and linguistic marginality of the Baltic states, has contributed to the development of a certain rhetoric of intellectual preservation and self-realization (Hoyer et al., 1993; Lieven, 1994).

At the end of the twentieth century the three Baltic countries recovered their independence and for the second time in the century reappeared on the world map. On both occasions – in 1918 and in 1990 – the three countries came back into existence through the revival of their histories, languages, and their cultural heritage, rather than through the exercise of power. It was the "Singing Revolutions" of the three Baltic nations

---

[1] Examples can be provided from Prosper Merimee and his short horror story "Lokis" (written in 1869) – its action is set in nineteenth-century Lithuania and is full of vampire-like activities – as well as much more recent and contemporary novels such as *The Corrections* by Jonathan Franzen and the suspense novel and thriller, *Hannibal Rising*, by Thomas Harris.

that in 1990 destroyed the entire Soviet Union, and the three nations have emerged from political nonexistence to become political entities and historical actors.

There have been many attempts by researchers to address Lithuania, Latvia, and Estonia collectively as a Baltic region. The countries on the northeastern side of the Baltic Sea – particularly, Lithuania, Latvia, Estonia, and also Finland[2] – have remained on the periphery for a long time. Throughout the centuries, the small Baltic nations have repeatedly faded in and out of the European history. The ideas of Christianity and modernization also gained ground in the northeastern region of the Baltic Sea much later than anywhere else in Europe. Lithuania converted to Christianity only in the fourteenth century, in 1387. Precisely for this reason the uniqueness, cultural diversity, and multilayered codes of cultural meanings of these nations have survived and are recognizable in modern politics and culture, while the countries themselves remain in the margins of global ideas and experiences, as well as in a kind of ideational isolation. Although attempts to analyze the three Baltic states as a geographic region may overall be justified, especially when taking into consideration the historical events of the twentieth century (the establishment of independent states in 1918 and then fifty years of Soviet occupation), the three Baltic countries manifest a number of significant differences in their histories and cultures as well as in languages and ethnic composition.

It is misleading to assume that the three nations have taken identical paths and have played identical roles in their own histories, as well as in the histories of their neighbors. Lithuania, for example, boasts a very ancient culture and a very rich history of being a strong political power in medieval and Renaissance Europe. In 1569 the Kingdom of Poland and the Grand Duchy of Lithuania formed the Polish-Lithuanian Commonwealth.[3] The new union created the biggest country in the region, stretching from the Baltic Sea almost to the Black Sea. It included not only modern Poland and Lithuania but also Belarus and Ukraine. It

---

[2] For quite some time Finland was also envisioned as a Baltic nation, and only after 1944 did the country opt for Nordic membership. Indeed, Finland has been affected by the major European conflicts to the same degree as the small Baltic countries south of the Finnish Gulf. However, Finland, as well as the rest of the Nordic countries, had a more advantageous geographic location. Finns have learned their history lessons and made wise political choices in the twentieth century, so they kept successfully out of Cold War conflicts.

[3] The union was a unique political entity and possessed unique features. Its political system was characterized by strict checks on monarchical power.

existed until 1795 when, after the Third Partition of the country, its different parts were incorporated into tsarist Russia. In contrast, Latvia and Estonia lost their statehood in the thirteenth century and became part of the political and cultural sphere of the Baltic Germans. Throughout the centuries, Latvia was strongly influenced by German and Swedish powers, while the history of Estonia is inseparable from Danish and Swedish influences. However, in the nineteenth century, despite those many differences in their historical memories and cultures, all three Baltic nations were subjected to tsarist Russia's rule. The three Baltic countries emerged on the international scene as modern states and independent political actors only in the twentieth century.

Except for certain differences in their histories of development, the Baltic nations nonetheless share important similarities, which arise from their smallness and their linguistic marginality, as well as from ideals of cultural preservation. In the small Baltic countries, the recognition and protection of national languages, national identities, and cultural traditions have played an instrumental part in their national awakenings. The struggle for their languages and cultural acknowledgment has led those countries to their modernization. Culture has always played an instrumental part in the histories of the three countries – in Lithuania, Latvia, and Estonia politics emerged on the basis of culture. Moreover, issues of nationalism and cultural autonomy were more important in the histories of party development and political mobilization in those countries than the class conflicts that shaped party systems in Western Europe. As is demonstrated in this chapter, cultural protection, national resistance, consolidation, and survival have been the primary aims of the Baltic nations for many centuries. Even in modern times, their political and economic developments have been mostly regarded as tools to achieve those aims. The centrality of cultural concerns in politics, media history, and media policy distinguishes Lithuania and the Baltic states generally in important ways from the West European cases analyzed in *Comparing Media Systems*.

Media and Politics in the Baltic States

Historical and Cultural Roots of Baltic Journalism
In Lithuania, the development of culture and print tradition was closely related to the history and the social role of language in its intellectual life. Moreover, we must recognize the multifaceted tradition of the state's political and cultural development. For many centuries Lithuania

was envisioned as a multiethnic, multireligious, and multicultural political entity. In early modern times (sixteenth to seventeenth centuries),
Lithuanian culture was strongly influenced by German culture from East
Prussia.[4] Despite tolerance and openness to outside influences, the longing
for authentic culture and its practice have been reflected in various layers
of culture including some relics of paganism and a distinct kind of Romanticism. After the formation of the Polish-Lithuanian Commonwealth in
the sixteenth century and later when both countries were incorporated
into the Russian Empire (from 1795 until 1918), Polish gradually became
the language of culture. The Lithuanian nobility also spoke Polish.

In the nineteenth century, not only Lithuania but also other Baltic
countries (Latvia, Estonia, and Finland) and to some extent Poland
(all these nations were provinces of the Russian Empire at that time)
went through strident Russification; this process was especially severe in
Lithuania where press prohibition was installed after the national uprisings against tsarist rule in 1861 and 1863.

Until 1864, all works of Lithuanian literature were written and printed
exclusively in the Latin alphabet. However, in the second half of the
nineteenth and early twentieth centuries – from 1864 until 1904 – print
culture in Lithuania was severely affected by a ban placed by the Russian
tsar on publications in the Lithuanian language and Latin letters.

However, in spite of various prohibitions on the use of Lithuanian language in schools and religious services, cultural life continued. Children
were secretly taught Lithuanian in unofficial schools from books that
were printed and distributed clandestinely. The books were published in
East Prussia (which is also often called Lithuania Minor), and book smugglers brought thousands of books into the country, becoming legendary
political rebels and heroes of the national revival.[5] Thanks to the efforts
of these devoted people, the tradition and the language persevered, while
the cultural press and literature they brought became the object of the
pursuit of national self-expression. By the end of the nineteenth century

---

[4] In the East Prussia region a large number of books, such as translations of the Bible,
psalm books, grammars, dictionaries, and primers, were published. The first periodical
publication in the national language, *Nusidavimai Dievo karalystėje*, was printed in
Lithuania Minor in 1823. The first newspapers in Lithuanian were published significantly
later than in many other European languages. They appeared later than the Estonian
Luhhike Oppetus (1766), the Latvian *Latviesu Arste* (1768), the Polish *Merkuriusz Polski*
(1661), and the first Finnish newspaper founded in 1771 by the Aurora Society in Turku.
[5] More than 100 periodicals in the Lithuanian language were published outside the country.
In total, book smugglers secretly brought into Lithuania more than five million books.

the nation came together in protests against the press ban. Over the four decades of the press ban, various Russian government institutions of the time received the total of more than 100 appeals to lift the Lithuanian press ban and allow Lithuanian publications to be printed in Lithuania. The resistance had religious as well as moral motives: People claimed that their children could not be properly educated and that public morals suffered as the Lithuanian language was banned in churches (Tyla, 2004).

All these actions deeply influenced the national consciousness. According to historians, when the Russians imposed the press ban in the mid-nineteenth century, the authorities did not consider the Lithuanians to be a distinctive nationality. However, by lifting the ban, the tsarist government essentially recognized the existence of the Lithuanians as a nationality (Senn, 2004). The resistance had begun from religious motives, but it deeply influenced the national consciousness, and the Russians were forced to recognize this.

Certain similarities to the events just described can be found in the development of protest movements in the second half of the twentieth century, during the Soviet occupation. With the secret protocols of the Molotov-Ribbentrop pact in 1939, Nazi Germany and the Soviet Union divided the countries of Central and Eastern Europe between themselves, and the three Baltic states were incorporated into the Soviet Union. The Baltic states underwent a radical social and political transformation. Everything that belonged to the cultural sphere, including the press, theater performances, art exhibitions and film, were strictly supervised and regulated by the Communist Party and its apparatus.

Despite the system of total control, many underground publications[6] were published, and a kind of "semi participatory" channel was born in the cultural sphere within the subdued Baltic countries. The state apparatus strictly controlled official media, and the only medium in which parallel spaces and alternative discourses could be developed was within the sphere of the arts. According to Aleksandras Štromas,[7] when free communication is suppressed or otherwise impossible, and the political public sphere is nonexistent, the cultural sphere acquires a certain consolidative function. Indeed, in Soviet times the Baltic national consciousness

---

[6] Among the samizdat publications *Katalikų Bažnyčios kronika* (The Chronicle of the Catholic Church) was the biggest (self-published) publication in the Soviet Union, continuously published from 1972–89. Other samizdat publications were the publications (from 1946–53) of partisan poems, songs, and diaries (many of these authors remained unknown).

[7] A Lithuanian émigré political scientist.

was maintained through cultural functions such as preservation of cultural traditions, folk songs, and distinctive poetry. A common heritage allowed all ethnic community members to communicate on a free and understandable basis, which also required a specific literacy to comprehend hidden meanings in Aesopian language. By developing and maintaining hidden discourses, the subdued Baltic nations were desperately trying to restore the past, including their culture.

Within the cultural sphere and the arts, all Baltic countries paid lip service to the official ideology, while maintaining a tradition of participation in the national opposition to the regime. Creativity in all its forms – theater, literary press, and song and dance festivals – became a substitute for other functions such as political participation, which under democratic conditions may be performed without any help from the arts. Topics like the preservation of the cultural heritage, the protection of language from Russification, problems with education, and the pollution of the environment saw daylight despite careful ideological control.

Even in the times of the First Republic of Lithuania (1918–40), because of restrictions such as a distinctive practice of press supervision, the literary genre was among the most developed in printed media. At that time, the Lithuanian press acted as a public catalyst: National dailies published translations, opinions, and reviews. The press as a publishing outlet also motivated young writers to produce and publish their works, thereby intellectually enlightening the public.[8] Through such activities the press enabled Lithuanians to identify themselves as Lithuanian. "Lietuvos sulietuvinimas" (making Lithuania Lithuanian) was a key phrase of that time. In their search for a national identity, Lithuanians rejected elements of culture that did not seem appropriate to them. At the same time, they sought appropriate approaches to the development of a national culture, particularly in Scandinavia and France.

Over the years, the literary perspective has gradually changed into a political one – from erudite and literary journalism to journalism that incorporated the mythmaking power of fiction and political advocacy. In the first half of the twentieth century, the writing dealt with the actuality of observed life, but because of its literary character the press was opinionated: It attempted to convey impressions and fuel emotions, rather than to provide facts. The close linkage between journalism and literature was also apparent in how professional organizations of journalists

---

[8] A significant feature of Lithuanian literature of that time was its romanticism.

and publishers, as well as journalism training and education, evolved.[9] The journalism of that time did not require much more than the skills necessary for any writer; journalists and writers founded joint professional associations, while specific education in journalism did not become institutionalized in universities for a long time.

In sum, the modern histories of the Baltic countries have been very fragmented, their statehood traditions very weak, and democratic regimes very short. What becomes clear from looking at the Baltic states' historical memory and tradition is that culture is inseparable from national identity, and when that identity is threatened, cultural life grows more intense and becomes more important. Thus Lithuanian, Latvian, and Estonian journalism evolved from a literary tradition and were cultivated as a part of the cultural sphere. In different periods (especially during Soviet times) it was the cultural sphere (literary and cultural press, theatrical performances, national song and folk dance festivals, etc.) that accommodated the most diverse functions – of education, development of national consciousness, and, later, in times of Gorbachev's perestroika, of political mobilization. With the political thaw of the 1980s, which stimulated the emergence of diverse interests and sociopolitical pluralism in Lithuania, Latvia, and Estonia, new issues and new topics emerged in the press. The media immediately discarded all taboos of the past, yet it soon found itself in a moral and normative vacuum. Confusion arose as to how to behave in the changing public sphere where the old patterns did not work and the new ones were yet to be introduced or adapted. There was no consensus on how to use the newly achieved freedom or what guidelines to follow.

Political Parallelism

With the political thaw and Gorbachev's perestroika in the late 1980s, national reform movements were born in each of the Baltic countries. Consequently, the dominant ideologies in each country split into at least

---

[9] The Union of Lithuanian Writers and Journalists held its first meeting in Kaunas in 1922, with twenty-two founding members on board. The organization was reorganized in 1929 as the Lithuanian Journalists' Union (LJU) with about seventy members. At that time, the most popular form of journalism training included courses organized by the Lithuanian News Agency ELTA (founded in 1920), newspapers (e.g., *Trimitas*, 1926), as well as extramural studies called Journalism Courses at Home (1933) for which more than 500 participants registered. The academic institutionalization of the profession began with the establishment of the Department of Sociology and Journalism at Vytautas Magnus University in Kaunas in 1941 (Balčytienė et al., 2009).

two identifiable ideological streams – the old official (Communist) and the new reformist (nationalist).

Indeed, in all three Baltic countries, political parallelism was especially strong during the political breakthrough years. With the diversification of political society, the press in Lithuania, Latvia, and Estonia rapidly diversified along ideological lines in the same way as in the other Central and Eastern European countries. However, by the mid-1990s, the last party newspaper had vanished in Lithuania, and signs of party affiliation disappeared from all dailies. Newspapers announced themselves as "free and independent." Today, political parallelism, at least in the West European sense of stable alignments of media with parties or political/ideological tendencies, is mostly absent from the Baltic states.

One very concrete factor in the rapid collapse of the political parallelism that characterized the immediate postcommunist period was the provision in the media law introduced in Lithuania in 1996, restricting party ownership of media. This provision was a strategic attempt to use policy to limit the dominance of certain ideologies and potential foreign (Russian) interests. In the long run, however, this restriction has weakened the party system in Lithuania. With no channels to mobilize their voters, the political parties have gradually and significantly diminished their ideological "left–right" leanings.

Clearly, however, deeper historical forces are also important to the understanding of the absence in of political parallelism (in the West European sense of word) in the Baltic countries. Part of the story has to do with suppression of the development of multiparty politics by totalitarianism and part with the pattern of Lithuanian politics before communism.

In contrast to countries with long democratic traditions, the idea of mass parties is not deeply rooted in the political systems of the three Baltic states. In Lithuania, political life is confusing and blurred. The ideological markers that are relatively stable in Western democracies (social democratic, conservative, liberal, agrarian, green) fluctuate widely in all three Baltic countries, depending on the context and the personal agenda of whoever invokes them.[10] The history and democratic tradition of the multiparty political life and of press freedom in Lithuania are rather short – democracy lasted only a few decades in the first half of the twentieth century (between 1918 and 1940, with a mild authoritarian regime from 1926) and was reestablished with the political breakthrough of 1990.

---

[10] The situation in Latvia is a bit different from Estonia and especially from Lithuania. Latvia is the only new EU member state whose principal political cleavage among political parties is not socioeconomic, but ethnic.

Although the ban on publications in the Lithuanian language was lifted in 1904, censorship endured and freedom of the press was achieved only when independent states were established on the eastern side of the Baltic Sea in 1918. Even then, a different kind of censorship endured. In Lithuania military censorship was proclaimed after independence because the young state thought it was obliged to control information in its territory because of its unstable social and political conditions.

There was a short period when Lithuania was called a multiparty republic and its media was not censored. The period from 1920 to 1926 – approximately eight years if counting from the establishment of independence in 1918 – is considered to be a classical democratic period in Lithuania with two dominant parties and a number of marginal parties on the political scene. The military coup d'état that brought the Nationalist Union to power in December 1926 reinstated censorship. The state imposed a ban on ideologically and politically varied publications, especially those produced by the Christian Democrats and the Peasants' Party. The ruling Nationalist Union presented information through political lenses, and propaganda was almost equated with journalism.

The new law on media in 1936 imposed even more severe restrictions on the party press. All parties were banned except the Nationalists. The dominant ideology was reflected also in the character of publications. At the same time, because of subsidies provided for news publishing and distribution, some of the periodicals were indeed strengthened.

In the Soviet period, the partisanship of the press meant that it accommodated ideological views but only the ones that incorporated certain parts of Marxist ideology. As Štromas (2001) explains, totalitarianism has its peculiar characteristics. Its distinctiveness from other dictatorship systems lies in its requirement of a total and active captivity. In contrast, authoritarian dictatorships leave the public sphere relatively uncontrolled and isolated from politics; thus, they "imprison" only partially. Totalitarianism requires active participation of people in all the spheres of society, but only on such terms as are accepted by those in power, as, for example, through feigned participation in the activities of ideological youth and professional organizations. According to Štromas (2001), such kind of "imitated freedom" creates a peculiar existential situation. The individual has to be active and participating, but he or she can participate only in a way that is tolerated by those in power – the Communist Party.[11]

---

[11] The Soviet Union was a state that did not allow any kind of ideologically unprotected association outside the Communist Party. For instance, churchgoing, a historically tested activity that sustains societal integration, was tolerated, but there were permanent

In this situation, as explained earlier, a substitute for the political public sphere gradually emerged in the subdued nations in the sphere of culture. The literary press, cultural and educational publications, plays, poetry, and folk performances were rich in allegorical expressions and metaphors. These productions provided an understanding adequate for the public to comprehend hidden meanings about what the nation had lost and what it had to preserve to survive. To some extent this cultural sphere emerged and was maintained as a national survival project. One reason why such an alternative public sphere could have been possible was the distinctiveness of the Lithuanian, Latvian, and Estonian national languages. Although all official communication was primarily done in the Russian language, each Baltic country used its national language in schools, the mass media, and public life. This division between official and alternative spheres could be interpreted as a form of political parallelism.

However, this history also meant that, in the Baltic states, issues of nationalism and cultural autonomy were more important in party development than the kinds of class conflicts and conflicts between tradition and modernity that shaped party systems in Western Europe. In Lithuania, for example, party structures grew up in the framework of national resistance movements that took place at the end of the nineteenth and the beginning of the twentieth centuries. The newly born parties supported different cultural ideas and gradually differentiated into political ideologies supporting nationalism, liberalism, Christian democratic, and social democratic ideals. Yet these political parties were very weak, and institutionalized structures were absent. Their ideological identities were also very weak because the opportunities (for example, through the press or through elections) to mobilize public support were practically nonexistent.

In modern Lithuania, the absence of partisanship traditions has contributed to the situation in which clear political leanings on the scale of right–left divisions were not able to develop, and consequently, a partisan press in which these leanings could be discussed, explained, and defended was absent. Clearly, in none of the Baltic countries does the

attempts to weaken its functioning and place it under the control of national representatives of the Communist Party – the nomenklatura (Antanaitis, 1998). Although one may claim that there existed nongovernmental social organizations such as trade unions, professional organizations, creative unions, and groups formed under "artificially voluntary participation" that were not subject to specialized control from the Communist Party, in fact public participation was based on a demonstrative rather than a natural interest.

distinction between political right and political left mirror the pattern of twentieth-century Western Europe. Ideological cleavages designated as centrist, conservative, and liberal are found in public discourse; however, these are words and concepts that fit well in party programs and political rhetoric, but do not mean much beyond that. Lithuania's political party system is quite volatile both in terms of the frequent formation of new parties and changes in existing parties. Nearly every parliamentary term a major political party either splits into several smaller parties or these merge into a completely new unit. Every four years several new political parties take part in the elections, although not all manage to meet the electoral threshold. Moreover, political life in Lithuania revolves around personalized politics. Parties are built around personalities and temporary, transient (most often populist) issues, rather than well-defined economic and social goals. In this political context commercialism rules, and media discourse is filled with sensationalism that gives a very fragmented view of society; in this sense it could be said that the three Baltic countries have jumped into the period of secularization, bypassing the period of media dependence on political leanings.

In referring to an absence of direct party-press parallelism or, more broadly speaking, of political parallelism, I do not want to indicate that the press has no ideological leanings or that the media do not play the role of a political actor. In Western Europe, the strength of advocacy traditions in journalism is linked to the development of institutional ties between the media and the system of parties and organized social groups. In Lithuania, opinionated journalism is associated with country-specific constraints such as its historical path of development, absence of partisan traditions, strong literary roots, and reliance on the role of language in the process of national identity formation, rather than with the development of a politically diverse society. Moreover, the absence of stable ideological alignments does not imply that the media have no connections with political and economic interests.

In contrast, today's politics in Lithuania is shaped by power fights between different interest groups in which clientelistic (or particularistic) interests guide choices, rather than ideological conceptions of the public interest. The competition is structured around power games, rather than the rules of fair play. Both businesspeople and politicians find it easier to buy media (in a direct or an indirect sense – through hidden advertising and other means of exerting pressure) than to feel responsible for the fate of the free market and liberal democracy. The media, too, becomes an active player in public power games by putting pressure on other actors (business companies and political parties) and demanding financial support. A significant number of studies disclose connections between positive or neutral reporting and advertising in the dailies purchased by business companies or political parties in an election period. For example, in 2007, the Lithuanian chapter of Transparency International announced the results of its research about the level of corruption in Lithuanian media. According to its data, 13 percent of businesspeople who participated in the survey and who had dealings with Lithuanian media in 2005–6 said they paid the media through advertising or commercials to publish positive material or suppress negative information. Most often respondents claimed they bribed the press; national TV channels were described as less corrupt than local ones.

Indeed, political and economic forces, while remaining anonymous, interfere with editorial independence and autonomy by setting the agenda for the media. Consequently, an absence of internal press freedom or editorial autonomy is a manifestation of a media system that has not yet been fully separated from the existing political system – in a society where values and norms are structured around immediate political or economic goals (and power games, which change depending on the situation), the idea of the public interest turns out to be very loose. As a result, the true public sphere is squeezed and marginalized, or it emerges and is maintained as a substitute public space via new technological and communicative forms such as the Internet media and online social and public networks, or cultural and niche channels.

The new media and social networks in the Baltic states are of exceptional importance: In comparison to Internet media developments in the West, all Central and Eastern European (CEE) countries clearly stand out in terms of new media use. Internet penetration in CEE is clearly higher than the European average (between 60 and 70% of individuals in the Baltic states are Internet users), and these countries have the largest numbers of households connected to the Internet via fiber-to-the-home networks. Moreover, the most popular online media in those countries are those online-only news portals that do not have any connections to mainstream media such as dailies or broadcast stations. Exciting links among journalism, civil society, and democracy are emerging in new media/alternative, media/blogosphere developments in CEE countries.

On the Boundary of Two Missions: The Role of the State

In the Baltic countries, the state's relationship to the media has a dual character. In many ways, the state's role toward the media is rather passive. Media regulation is very liberal, and liberal market ideals dominate in the government's policies. None of the Baltic countries has any laws against media concentration, for example, nor is there any regulation of foreign ownership in the mass media or, for the most part, of advertising content. In contrast, there are important ways in which the state plays a fairly active role in imposing certain restrictions and media regulations.

As Hallin and Mancini propose, the role of the state can be assessed according to its functions as media owner, regulator, and funds provider (Hallin and Mancini, 2004b). In Lithuania, according to the law, the only media that the state has ownership rights to is the Lithuanian National Radio and Television (LRT), the public service broadcaster. The state does not own other kinds of media nor, according to media law, can any political party act as a public information provider or own or be associated with media. Although there are some exceptions, the state in the Baltic countries does not play a significant role as a provider of funds. It mainly funds minority and cultural publications. Although these funds provide significant subsidies for some small, regional, and local media and for cultural and minority publications as well, they are mainly described as attempts to correct "market failures." The funding is significant in enabling media outlets to diversify their output, yet its long-term impact on the media system is limited because it is given only for short-term projects.

This "laissez-faire" policy structure reflects the political context of the postcommunist period. In the early 1990s, as the three Baltic countries went through a process of media nationalization, memories of state censorship, blacklisting, and bias during the communist era were still foremost in people's minds, and any proposals for the participation of the state in media matters raised very sensitive issues. The process of drafting statutory regulation was shaped by the lobbying of business interests of large media groups and by conscious decision making intended to gradually destroy the power of the state over the media and to grant the media the freedom to regulate themselves.

At the same time, the role of the state in Lithuania is affected by a tradition in its political culture that regards the state as a protector of national identity, cultural heritage, and the like. The development of culturally sensitive policies – to protect the language, the country's cultural heritage, its folklore, and national traditions – is perceived as a fundamental role of the state, alongside the role to act in the public interest. Elements of Lithuanian culture are manifested in more active forms of state involvement in media and culture, many of which are absent in the other Baltic countries.

One manifestation of the role of the state as cultural protector has to do with language. Lithuania is perhaps the only country in the world that imposes fines for improper use of the national language in the mass media. Lithuanian has the status of the state language, and media are required by law to show audiovisual programs and motion pictures with translations into the Lithuanian language or with subtitles. The law has provisions on how the language should be used in state and governmental institutions as well as in education, and it requires that foreign names must be written in the state language. The exceptional importance of the Lithuanian language is evidenced in other cases as well – for example, in publicly funded research projects a special status is assigned to projects that deal with Lithuanian philology and history of the language.

Another particular institution through which the representation of the public interest comes into play is the press ombudsman; the official title is the Inspector of Journalists' Ethics. The Inspector and the office on ethics represent the public interest and report on media performance in terms of how it adheres to media law; basic editorial standards are defined in the Law of Provision of Information to the Public and are legally binding on all media. Lithuania also has a Law of Protection of the Juveniles from the Detrimental Effects of Public Information, which regulates more than a dozen types of information.

The role of the state in Lithuania is thus marked by duality and ambiguity. In some ways it resembles the role the state plays in the Liberal model countries in which media regulation is limited and a laissez-faire mindset is dominant. At the same time, it has some similarities with state performance in the Democratic Corporatist countries through the representation of public interest, provision of subsidies, and the like. It could be said that in the Baltic countries the media and the state compete with each other to satisfy the public's expectations. Both the media and the state seek to offer "what the public wants" – when the public wants a stronger hand (a protector), this is manifested in a stronger role of the state; when the public wants to learn about political wrongdoings, the media have the freedom to uncover them. Indeed, each of those actors – the media and the state – wants to control the other (through imposing certain restrictions, for example, on the amount of political advertising in the media; through revealing political wrongdoings) and at the same time each tries to avoid being controlled by the other.

Journalistic Professionalism

Journalism performs different roles and functions in different systems, and its performance is therefore strongly shaped by contextual features. In this respect, a historical retrospective of how this profession evolved in Lithuania, Latvia, and Estonia, and which contextual conditions have influenced and shaped it becomes of critical importance. As previously discussed, in the small Baltic nations, the print culture grew within the framework of the preservation of cultural traditions and national consciousness building, as well as public movements associated with those aims. In the period of their First Republics (1918–40), the journalistic professions in Lithuania, Latvia, and Estonia were fully institutionalized. Previously scattered activities of writing, editing, and publishing gained some characteristics of a profession with the establishment of professional organizations of writers and journalists and the development of professional codes of ethics. These initiatives were developed by people involved in book publishing as well as general education. Quite a few early press workers had received journalism training in other countries (the United States, Germany, and France). However, most professionals were unable to study abroad and could only develop their competencies and skills through self-education, by exchanging printed lectures and other learning materials published in periodicals.

The role of the Catholic intelligentsia in promoting journalism in Lithuania can be seen in different ways. On the one hand, university lectures in journalism were introduced at the Faculty of Theology and Philosophy of Vytautas Magnus University in Kaunas in 1925–6 and in 1939–40. On the other hand, while promoting the circulation of some conservative publications, the clergy hampered the periodicals of a more neutral nature. Getting rid of foreign influences was considered to be the most important condition of creative work. Attempts to secure and defend the purity of the national culture promoted ethnoculturalism and pushed the society toward cultural self-isolation.

It took quite some time before university programs to educate journalists and press workers were in place. It was not until 1941, when the Department of Sociology and Journalism at Vytautas Magnus University in Kaunas[12] was established, that the journalistic profession acquired an institutional status. This was the only university in the three Baltic states that included journalism in its academic curriculum. The lifespan

---

[12] In the period from 1920 to 1940 Kaunas was a provisional capital of Lithuania. At that time Vilnius and its region were incorporated into Poland.

of journalism training at the university level, however, was very short. In 1943 Nazi Germany shut down the whole university.

In the Soviet period, journalism was taught in the universities of Vilnius (Lithuania), Riga (Latvia), and Tartu (Estonia). Mass communications was a large Soviet industry and an instructive tool, used to promote the government line. This attitude affected the function of the press. The role of journalists was to educate, motivate, and mobilize society. Required skills were truthfulness, objectivity, and thoroughness, but only within narrow ideological borders.

In the period of political breakthrough the media acquired a role of mobilization, integration, and service. With its explosive outburst of national pride and determination, the "Singing Revolution" brought the euphoria of freedom, including the freedom of the written word. This was a "golden age" of Baltic journalism. The collapse of the Soviet regime fractured old concepts of professionalism. The press in general discarded most taboos of the past. It disclosed Stalinist crimes in detail; the sufferings of the deportees of 1941 and 1944–52 were described and published in memoirs. Soviet crimes and accident reports were published with regularity and discussions followed. Special sections of newspapers were dedicated to the analysis and interpretation of the nation's history.[13]

In fact, the newly born media and journalists found themselves in a situation completely different from the ideologically defined context of the past – in a kind of "normative vacuum" in which old values became extinct and new values were absent (Lauk, 2008). The new times required a new logic of professionalism, but the knowledge and understanding of how to create it were absent. Examples were sought from abroad, but very often these did not work or did not match practices that press workers were used to.

A natural choice made by the media at that time was to reinstitute what the nation had lost with communism – to abolish censorship and to restore the old names of the newspapers of the First Republic. These changes were combined with a search for outside institutional models for inspiration and attempts to import those models and adapt them to national contexts. The processes of restoration and adaptation were quite complicated and not without certain problems; for example, the institutions imported from

---

[13] During the national awakening, details that were almost unknown to young people came into focus in public discourse: the declaration of independence of 1918, the annexation of Lithuania in 1940, and the guerilla movement until 1953. After all the official lies of the communist press, this seemed to be the only way to regain a sense of national, cultural, and personal integrity.

other countries (the ideals of professional journalism from the Liberal model countries or systems of media self-regulation from the Nordic neighbors) had different meanings and implications when transplanted into a different cultural context.

As mentioned, by comparative standards, Lithuania has a relatively strong system of institutionalized self-regulation that comprises two institutions: the Ethics Commission of Journalists and Publishers (Ethics Commission) and the Inspector of Journalists' Ethics (the ombudsman). In 1996, the experience of the Scandinavian states was used to guide the self-regulation system in Lithuania. Several years later, the system developed further, becoming more nationally specific, and the new Ethics Code was accepted in 2005.

Despite these formal institutions and despite the establishment of press freedom and media pluralism, serious problems in media performance are evident. The marketization of journalism, weakness of public service media, and nonprofessionalism of journalists are widely reported in the countries of this geographic region.

Although on the structural level, press freedom and media pluralism seem to be institutionally established, media performance analysis reveals a different story. Traditions of democratic newsroom management are missing in Baltic newsrooms, as most media are hierarchically organized structures where major decisions are taken by editors in chief or those having middle management positions. Journalists have little or no voice in mainstream media. Media also do not have established routines for coping with external pressures. According to journalists themselves, there is no censorship in the media, yet a certain degree of self-censorship exists, but of a different character: Whereas in Soviet times self-censorship meant resigning oneself not to discuss specific issues in public (except when written in Aesopian language), today it means altering content to fit a particular situation that is comfortable financially. In addition, working conditions in the newsrooms pose a serious threat to the professionalization of journalism. The fear of losing their job pushes journalists to follow instructions they receive from their managing editors. As mentioned in the section on political parallelism, instrumentalization of journalism by outside interests is common in Lithuania today, undermining professional autonomy. Some years ago a report by Transparency International mentioned a case in which a list of major advertisers was hanging on the notice board in the newsroom of one national TV channels, meaning that no negative material should be announced about them. An analysis of publications in three Lithuanian dailies from 2004–6 noted the tendency not to publish negative articles about major advertisers; the same study also found that some newspapers even started publishing negative articles about some companies, in an effort to force them to take out ads.

It also needs to be mentioned that there are cases in which journalists have protested against internal pressures in media newsrooms. For instance, when the Respublika media group bought the Lithuanian news agency ELTA, the majority of ELTA journalists left their jobs because they claimed that the new owners tried to influence the news content. Almost an identical case was registered in Latvia when journalists and editors of the national daily *Diena* left their jobs when the Scandinavian owner of the paper, Bonnier, sold the business to unidentified investors with supposed links to Russia.

To conclude, the culture of Baltic journalism in some ways adheres to the Liberal model, for example, in the application of laissez-faire principles. However, weaker journalistic traditions, the lack of public knowledge and debates on media, the lack of organized self-criticism, and weaker self-regulation have caused significant deviations from the Nordic examples in particular. Therefore secularization, competition, and consumerism are keywords describing professional journalistic culture in the Baltic countries today; in many cases, media instrumentalization as well as business parallelism is another appropriate descriptor.

Mixed Model Countries: Small Nations with Active Media and Passive Publics

As if following the invitations by Daniel C. Hallin and Paolo Mancini, many scholars have identified the development of media institutions in Central and Eastern Europe with conditions these authors identify as the Polarized Pluralist (the Mediterranean) model.[14] However, the earlier discussion shows that what is popularly called the Mediterranean model of postcommunist countries' media does not directly apply to the media of the Baltic states. Despite similarities among these countries, the process of Mediterraneanization (or Italianization as some scholars called these developments[15]) of the media has limited applicability, and

---

[14] This idea (media Mediterraneanization) is mainly developed by the Polish scholars (Jakubowicz, 2008b; Wyka, 2008) who indicate that the Polarized Pluralist model best describes the media situation in their country. In Poland, political parallelism is strong, and other indicators of the model are applicable.

[15] Splichal (1994: 145) draws a parallel between media development characteristics in the countries of East and Central Europe and Italy. His argument is that several

certainly, not all postcommunist countries can be artificially situated around the Mediterranean Sea as proposed in some studies.[16]

A brief examination of the Baltic media shows they have many significant elements from each of Hallin and Mancini's models. For example, in the Baltic states, as in the Polarized Pluralist model, newspaper reach and newspaper circulation numbers are comparatively low[17] (in this context Estonia is a little different, having higher press readership than Lithuania or Latvia); journalism developed later as a profession than in other countries in Europe; and elements of clientelism and instrumentalization are quite significant. In addition, the role of the state is mixed because it combines a very interventionist role with a pattern of weak regulation.

As in Democratic Corporatist countries, elements of corporatist arrangements are found in the Baltic countries. For example, the Baltic states have institutionalized systems of media self-regulation (with the exception of Latvia). In Lithuania the Broadcast Council that governs public service broadcasting includes elements of the civic model often found in Democratic Corporatist systems – both political and ideologically independent (professional and institutional) representation.[18] Finally, as in Liberal model countries, laissez-faire media policy prevails in many respects, and "media logic" tends to dominate the communication process. As research studies have found, in the Baltic states, media organizations are driven by profit-oriented motives of attaining the highest audience reach and highest advertising revenues (Balčytienė and Harro-Loit, 2007; Balčytienė and Lauk, 2005). Tabloid and commercial media play a very strong role, public service media are weak, market-oriented

characteristics of the Italian system and of other Southern European countries, such as partisanship of the media, strong integration between media and political elites, and weak professional consolidation of journalists, are also significant for East and Central Europe. The author claims that one principle for the organization of the public sphere in those countries is the integration of media with politics and business.

[16] Although southeast European countries (Romania, Bulgaria) would fit into this geographic region, media developments there do not directly follow such a path (Gross, 2008).

[17] Newspaper reach (WAN, 2006): Estonia (68.5%), Latvia (64.7%), Lithuania (56%); total number of newspapers and number of dailies: Estonia (143 and 16), Latvia (130 and 22), Lithuania (328 and 22).

[18] The structure of the LRT Council is designed to accommodate interests of different groups: Four people are nominated by the president, four by parliament (representing different political fractions), and four by associations: the science council, education council, bishops conference, and the union of creative artists. At present, each of the twelve members in the council has professional linkages to media (they are media scholars, editors, journalists, screenwriters, poets, and writers); two of the council members are party members.

discourse has penetrated into all media sectors (print, broadcast, and online), generic diversity in media has decreased, and topics are covered with personalized and human touch aspects. Such performance contrasts with media systems that are either dominated by the party press or are characterized by structures of political parallelism.

This kind of comparison with the three groups of countries discussed in Hallin and Mancini's analysis is informative and descriptive, but in the end it is not sufficient to answer the question they pose at the beginning of their text: "Why are media in the Baltic states as they are?" A fundamental goal in the studies of postcommunist media must be to find new analytical variables to analyze the diversity of national media systems.

Therefore, I propose that there is a need to explore how culture influences the social structure and symbolic organization of a given society. As mentioned, throughout the centuries, it was the cultural sphere that carried out the numerous functions of national consolidation, linguistic preservation, and survival of Baltic nations. As Baltic histories reveal, empires have collapsed because of nationalism. One hundred years ago, it was the disintegration of the Russian Empire that enabled Poland, Finland, and the Baltic states to become independent; in more recent times – in 1990 – the Baltic nations were the first countries to break away from the Soviet Union. Culture has been and continues to be instrumental in (re)shaping modern consciousness and social reality in the Baltic countries. Although we may imagine that the role of culture is negated in contemporary world by commercial media practices, culture can still be a serious analytical dimension that can guide the theoretical exploration of media systems in Central and Eastern Europe.

The very active role of contemporary Baltic media is among the main findings of this chapter. This role has emerged and been shaped by specific historical conditions. Culture in general and the media as a transmitter of cultural ideals had a dual (official and unofficial) function in Soviet times; media and literary culture also played a fundamental and missionary role of cultural (linguistic) preservation and national consolidation in the second half of the nineteenth century. It can be assumed that the dominating role the media play in today's environment is a peculiar derivative of its earlier missions. The only difference is that contemporary media does not rise to the ideals of moral authority and spiritual representativeness once assigned to the cultural sphere.

The tradition of centrality of culture in history as well as intellectual life interacts with important and distinctive characteristics of the Baltic states in the postcommunist period that reinforce the tendency for media to dominate public life. The trend toward media centrality and its increasing commercialization is reported in many countries around the world. Yet, in the Baltic states this process has its country-specific character. Briefly, the Baltic societies are shapeless, blurred, or somehow unsolid. They are characterized by low and decreasing public trust in political parties, commercialization of the press, lack of ideological diversity, lack of transparency in editorial leanings, and high public aspirations with popular politics. Such an unclear situation contributes to a growing value crisis in the country. When values are unclear or mixed, the ground is laid for populism and commercialism to emerge and dominate in the public sphere. As de Albuquerque describes in his chapter, in a context where political cleavages are blurred, other parameters of analysis (for example, the role the media play as being politically weak or active) need to be taken into account.

As mentioned, the party system in Lithuania is still a blurred reality. The lack of public political participation in the Baltic states is associated with the weakness of political parties, the absence of value divisions on the left–right scale in the party system, as well as other features. Usually people are motivated to vote when they identify with parties and when they are able to defend this identification. The parties' weakness, vague ideological background, unarticulated values, and their convergence provoke the media to play a very active role; the function of publicizing the activities of parties and interest groups is transferred to the media. Consequently, having such an artificial but dominating mission the media are no longer a channel for spreading political ideas or just a mediator between politicians and society. On the contrary, the media become the "creator" of politics. In this context, the culture of political communications is based on the practice of public relations as well as media logic.

5

On Models and Margins

Comparative Media Models Viewed from a Brazilian Perspective

Afonso de Albuquerque

The publication of Hallin and Mancini's book *Comparing Media Systems* was a turning point for comparative media studies. Given the tremendous impact of the book, the question soon arose whether it would be possible to apply the categories proposed by Hallin and Mancini in a broader, worldwide comparative effort. The authors themselves discuss this possibility in their book. On the one hand, they recognize that the consistency of the models they proposed is indebted in part to the fact they have studied a relatively limited and homogeneous group of countries (2004a: 6). On the other hand, they show some optimism in this regard, given that they believe that the models that exist in Western Europe and North America tend to prevail also in the rest of the world. In this chapter, I critically examine the categories proposed by the authors, and this proposition in particular, with a focus on the Brazilian media system.

In the first part of the chapter, I discuss the three-model system both from a theoretical and a methodological point of view. Two main problems are of concern. The first refers to the very concept of "model" as used by the authors. I argue that when they suggest that the Western models "tend to be dominant globally" they are in fact using two very different concepts of a model. When they apply the term to the Western countries, they use it in the sense of "*models from . . .*" – that is, methodological entities that *exist only as research tools*. When they apply the term "model" to non-Western countries, however, its status changes and becomes a "*model to . . .*" – that is, normative parameters that *are used in the real world*. The second problem refers to the way Hallin and Mancini define the Polarized Pluralist model and, in particular, their suggestion that it would explain some traits of media systems in Eastern Europe and the former Soviet Union, Latin America, Middle East, Africa, and most Asian countries (Hallin and Mancini, 2004b: 36). Here, I suggest that such a broad use of the concept risks converting it into a catch-all concept that includes everything that does not fit into the other two models.

In the second part of the chapter, I use the four sets of variables proposed by Hallin and Mancini to explore some characteristics of the Brazilian media system. Some authors (Azevedo, 2006; Hallin and Papathanassopoulos, 2002) have pointed out that the Brazilian media system has many traits in common with the Polarized Pluralist model. However, the data collected indicate not only some similarities between them – mainly in the structure of media markets – but also some noteworthy differences: Brazilian broadcasting media have been almost entirely privately owned since their inception; political parallelism does not apply easily to the Brazilian media, both because political parties do not play a central role in presidential countries such as Brazil and because the leading media organizations have adopted a catch-all attitude regarding their public; and Brazilian journalists have defined their professional identity with reference to the American model, although they have reinterpreted it a very particular way.

The categories created by Hallin and Mancini shed light on many important aspects of the Brazilian media systems, but leave others in the shadow. Thus, in the third part of this chapter I examine some problems not discussed in depth in *Comparing Media Systems* and propose some new categories to deal with them. The first problem relates to the difference between *central* and *peripheral* media systems. A media system is peripheral to the extent that it defines itself with reference to foreign models, and it is central to the extent that it can be used as a reference for other systems. I believe this distinction is very important in a worldwide comparative analysis. The second problem refers to the system of government – presidential or parliamentary – as an important variable for explaining some traits of the relationship between the media and the political agents. Finally, I discuss the limitations of the concept of political parallelism for analyzing the Brazilian political/media system and propose to replace it with a schema that articulates two variables: the strength of political parties and the degree of engagement of the media in political activity.

Models from... and Models to...

When applied to the original scope of analysis of *Comparing Media Systems*, the use of the term "model" does not look problematic. The models elaborated by Hallin and Mancini are ideal types, that is, conceptual devices designed to describe the relationship between media and politics in a group of eighteen countries of Western Europe and North America. In the book, they present three models of media systems. The *Democratic Corporatist* model is described as having an early and solid development of a mass press, strong professional associations and a well-established professional culture in journalism, a tradition of state intervention in defense of the ideological plurality of the media, and a public service model of broadcasting. The *Polarized Pluralist* model has a low-circulation press that is directed mainly to a small elite, a weak professional culture in journalism, a high degree of political parallelism between the political system and the media system, and patterns of instrumentalization of the media by political and economical interests. *Liberal* model media systems have a high-circulation mass press, although not as high as the Democratic Corporatist ones; information-oriented journalism with internal pluralism; strong professionalism, although without institutionalized self-regulation; and a market-dominated media.

The Liberal model is dominant in the Anglophone countries on both sides of the Atlantic (United Kingdom, Ireland, United States, and Canada); the Democratic Corporatist model is found in North and Central Europe (Germany, Austria, Switzerland, Netherlands, Belgium, Sweden, Norway, Denmark, and Finland); and the Polarized Pluralist model is dominant in Southern Europe (France, Italy, Spain, Portugal, and Greece). However, the authors say that those countries must not to be taken as pure examples of the three models. For example, the United Kingdom mixes features from the Liberal and the Democratic Corporatist models, and France combines some characteristics from both the Polarized Pluralist and Democratic Corporatist models. Yet the media systems of individual countries are not homogeneous: For example, media systems in Catalonia and Quebec are different in many ways from the media in the rest of Spain or Canada, respectively. Thus, the media system models proposed by Hallin and Mancini must to be understood as simplifications made from empirical data, which are useful mainly for analytical purposes. That is the central reason why I propose to refer to them as "models from...."

However, when Hallin and Mancini write that "the models that prevail in Western Europe and North America tend to be dominant globally" (2004a: 6), they make a subtly different use of the term "model." In that context the term "model" has a normative meaning, rather than a descriptive or analytical one. In this sense, models are standards by which social agents usually guide their behavior in concrete circumstances. They exist and have an effect in the real world, notwithstanding their abstract character. I call this type "models to...." The three models proposed by Hallin and Mancini are "models from..." when applied to the countries represented in the original scope of their study; however, for the rest of the countries of the world they are not equally "models to...."

Since the 1980s Liberal model values (such as the association between press freedom and market freedom) and practices (such as the commercialization of the media) have spread around the world, as a consequence of the process of economic globalization and in connection with the commercialization of the media in many countries. This process has been often described as an Americanization of the media of such countries (see, among others, Hallin and Mancini, 2004b; Negrine and Papathanassopoulos, 1996; Swanson and Mancini, 1996). In contrast, the emphasis that the Democratic Corporatist model puts on the conception of a "common good" and the equilibrium between media autonomy and state intervention has nourished a discourse of resistance against the hegemony of the Liberal model. The same does not apply to the Polarized Pluralist model. Notwithstanding the influence that the media and political culture of some Southern European countries (mainly France, but also Spain and Portugal) have exerted abroad (especially in the Latin American countries), it would not be appropriate to discuss the Polarized Pluralist model per se as the source of such influence. After all, according to the authors, one of the chief traits of the Polarized Pluralist model is the absence of consensual values among media and political actors (see also Chalaby, 1996). Thus, how could the absence of unifying values exert some kind of normative role?

In a way, the Polarized Pluralist model is defined in a negative manner relative to the Liberal and the Democratic Corporatist models. The prevalence of such a model would be a result of the absence of the circumstances that rendered possible the development of the other two (e.g., a solid mass press, significant autonomy of media from the state and political parties, and a tradition of professionalism among the journalists). At the same time, Hallin and Mancini suggest that the Polarized Pluralist model may have an almost universal use in the analysis of non-Western countries. What does this suggestion mean? Should the Polarized Pluralist model be taken as merely a negative version of the other two models, a kind of less developed countries' model? Or, alternatively, would it be possible to identify traits in common between the media systems of the Mediterranean countries they analyzed and the non-Western countries?

In an article published before *Comparing Media Systems*, Hallin and Papathanassopoulos (2002) made a comparative analysis between the four Southern European countries analyzed in the later book and the media systems of three Latin American countries: Brazil, Colombia, and Mexico. The authors focused their analysis on five characteristics: (1) low levels of newspaper circulation, (2) tradition of advocacy reporting, (3) instrumentalization of privately owned media, (4) politicization of public broadcasting and broadcast regulation, and (5) limited development of journalism as an autonomous profession. They conclude that the same characteristics that distinguished media in the Southern European countries from those in the rest of the European Union were present "usually in more extreme forms" in the three Latin American countries' media systems (2002: 175). The authors maintain that the concept of clientelism can be very useful in explaining the traits shared by the seven countries they analyzed. From the five specific characteristics analyzed, only one – tradition of advocacy reporting – is not defined in a negative manner. The others are defined as the absence of some qualities that can be found in the rest of the European Union countries: a high newspaper circulation, a considerable independence from the media vis-à-vis private interests and political ends, a strong public service tradition, and significant autonomy of journalism as a profession. In a similar way, clientelism, the chief analytical category used by the authors, is also defined in a negative way, in contrast to rational-legal authority. The authors provide convincing evidence that both the Southern European and the Latin American media systems are very different from the other Western European and North American countries, but they are not so persuasive when they suggest that they have other significant characteristics in common.

It seems only fair to ask if the label "Polarized Pluralist model" is adequate for a broader use than the one originally intended in *Comparing Media Systems*. The authors borrow the concept from Sartori's 1976 book *Parties and Party Systems* and use it in opposition to another Sartorian concept, "moderate pluralism." However, the two categories are far from adequate for illustrating the entire framework presented by Sartori. In fact, the main contrast that he proposes is between *competitive* and *noncompetitive* party systems. Sartori identifies three types of noncompetitive party systems – no-party, single party, and hegemonic party systems – and four types of competitive party systems: the Polarized Pluralist system quoted by Hallin and Mancini, the Moderate Pluralist, the two-party, and the atomized party systems. The emphasis on the opposition between polarized and moderate pluralism is partially justi-fied by the restricted focus of their study – all the Western European and North American countries have competitive party systems. Yet this emphasis is not entirely justified given that some of them, like the United States or the United Kingdom, have two-party, rather than pluralistic party systems.[1] In addition, Sartori (1976: 131–73) applies the category "polarized pluralism" to a very limited set of countries, in specific histor-ical circumstances. This contrasts with Hallin and Mancini's suggestion that the Polarized Pluralist model could have an almost universal utility as an analytical tool. It remains an open question whether the framework proposed by Sartori provides a good basis for a global-scale comparative study about the relationship between the media and political systems. As with most comparative studies of political parties (Wolinetz, 2002), its premises are too much grounded on the Western European experience. For example, they describe better the role that political parties play in the parliamentary system, which prevails in Western Europe, than their role in the presidential system. I return to this issue later.

The Four Dimensions for Comparative Analysis and the Brazilian Media System

In this part, I analyze the Brazilian media system in light of the four dimen-sions presented in *Comparing Media Systems*: (1) structure of media mar-kets, (2) political parallelism, (3) professionalism, and (4) the role of the state. My aim is to identify traits in common or significant differences between the Brazilian media system and the three models proposed by Hallin and Mancini.

The Structure of Media Markets
In their analysis of the structure of the media markets of the countries of North America and Western Europe, Hallin and Mancini focus on four variables: (1) the rates of newspaper circulation, (2) the audience of the

---

[1] Maybe it would be useful to consider the Democratic Corporatist model and the Liberal model as roughly corresponding to Sartori's moderate pluralistic and two-party systems, respectively.

TABLE 5.1. *Newspapers with the Highest Circulation, Brazil 2005*

Newspapers	Daily Circulation
Folha de S. Paulo	309,383
O Globo	276,385
Extra	267,225
O Estado de São Paulo	231,165
Zero Hora	174,617

Source: IVC.[2]

newspapers and the role they play as mediators in the political communication process, (3) the relative importance of newspapers and television as sources of news, and (4) the historical roots of the newspapers. How does the Brazilian media system perform regarding them?

First, Brazilian newspapers have a very low rate of circulation. According to data from the Institute for Verification of Circulation, in 2000 the rate of newspaper sales per 1,000 adult population was 60.6.[3] In the same year, the corresponding rates for the four Mediterranean countries examined by Hallin and Mancini were 129.4 for Spain, 121.4 for Italy, 82.7 for Portugal, and 77.5 for Greece. These rates were the lowest among the countries discussed in *Comparing Media Systems*. Comparatively, the rate of newspaper circulation was 719.7 for Norway, 408.5 for the United Kingdom, and 263.6 for the United States. In 2005 the Brazilian rate had dropped to 45.3 newspapers sold per 1,000 adult population.

Second, Brazilian newspapers are addressed to a small urban elite, just like Southern European ones. From the five newspapers with the highest circulation (see Table 5.1), four are elite-oriented – *Folha de S. Paulo, O Globo, O Estado de São Paulo*, and *Zero Hora* – and only one, *Extra*, targets a popular readership. According to Azevedo (2006: 95), Brazilian newspapers adopt a restrained writing style, give priority to economic and political themes, and balance their low penetration among the popular classes with a great capacity to set the agenda, frame questions, and influence perceptions and behaviors at the elite level.

Third, the Brazilian media system has often been described as being significantly television-centered. In contrast with the low newspaper readership, 90 percent of Brazilian homes have at least one television set

---

[2] See http://www.anj.org.br/?q=node/177.
[3] See the Web site of the Associação Brasileira de Jornais (National Newspapers Association). http://www.anj.org.br/?q=node/183.

(Azevedo, 2006). In contrast to newspapers and, until recently, radio stations, television is structured around national networks that play a very important role in building a homogeneous national culture (Ortiz, 1988). Television receives 58.7 percent of the advertising media budget, and Globo Network, the main television network in Brazil, gets more than three-quarters of this amount. Currently Globo Network has 55 percent of the audience share (Lima, 2004).

Fourth, Brazilian press had a late development. During the colonial period, Portugal made consistent efforts to reduce the economic, political, and intellectual autonomy of Brazil. In contrast to Spain, which created universities in its colonial territories, Portugal limited the education of the Brazilians and forbade them to have printing facilities until 1808, when the Portuguese Court moved to Rio de Janeiro, escaping from the invasion of their country by Napoleonic troops. The independence of Brazil in 1822 stimulated a rapid expansion of the press. During the rest of the nineteenth century, most publications were leaflets, pamphlets, and short-lived newspapers, dedicated chiefly to political polemics (Lustosa, 2000). Only at the turn of the twentieth century did a more consolidated, institutionalized press come to exist in Brazil, mainly in Rio de Janeiro, then the capital. The replacement of a monarchy by a republican government in 1889 and changes in the urban environment – mainly in Rio de Janeiro, whose population almost tripled, from 275,000 inhabitants in 1872 to 811,000 in 1906 – served as a powerful stimulus for intellectual life (Chalhoub, 1986, 1996). Under the influence of the *Belle Époque* spirit, Brazilian intellectuals dreamed about taking part in a *République des Lettres* and making a living from literature. They were largely frustrated, however, given that the publishing business was not strong enough to allow it (Sevcenko, 1983). Newspapers were the only exception to this state of affairs. Thus being a journalist was a sine qua non condition for living the literary life (Miceli, 2001).

The influence of the American model was decisive in changing Brazilian media. This influence can be traced to the 1930s, when a commercial model of radio, inspired by the American trusteeship model, developed in Brazil (Almeida, 1993). This influence became stronger during World War II, and in the 1950s, a new type of journalism – more information oriented and inspired by the American model – began to develop (Albuquerque, 2005). Television also began to operate in 1950. The TV stations stayed essentially local until the 1970s, when improvement in the technologies of communications and a huge investment from the Brazilian state allowed the creation of nationwide television networks.

As described earlier, Globo Network was the main beneficiary of this structure. Not only did it occupy a hegemonic position in the Brazilian television scene but it also became an important player in the global market, as an exporter of programming, mainly *telenovelas* (Mattelart and Mattelart, 1989; Porto, 2006).

Political Parallelism

The concept of political parallelism refers to Seymour-Ure's notion of party-press parallelism, used to evaluate the degree of connection between the media system and the party system. Hallin and Mancini use this concept in a broader sense than did Seymour-Ure; they are interested in evaluating the strength of the liaisons between the media organizations and general political tendencies (and not only political parties). They present five criteria to evaluate that strength: (1) media content, (2) organizational connections, (3) the tendency for media personnel to take part in political life, (4) the partisanship of media audiences, and (5) journalists' role orientation and practices (advocacy journalism versus neutral information or entertainment).

Until the 1950s journalism was thought of mainly in terms of a "publicist" role, and most journalists came from the lower ranks of the oligarchy. Political commentary, notes in honor of powerful people, and above all editorials were valued journalistic genres. Doing well in these activities would allow journalists to initiate political careers or at least to get an easy job in the public bureaucracy (Miceli, 2001). After the 1950s Brazilian newspapers progressively shifted to a more *fact-centered model of journalism* (Chalaby, 1996). This does not mean that journalism in Brazil changed entirely from one moment to the next, however. During the brief democratic period that endured from 1946 to 1964, most Brazilian newspapers still showed some of the traits that define political parallelism. *Media content* was strongly tied to political interests: Newspapers often acted as the public voices of political groups. For example, the paper *Última Hora* was created to support the election campaign and the government (1951–4) of the former dictator Getúlio Vargas, and it defended his legacy after Vargas killed himself; other papers, such as *Notícias Populares*, were founded to oppose him (Goldenstein, 1987). These *connections* with political actors were essential for the survival of the newspapers as organizations. Their low circulation and the absence of significant private advertising investment did not allow for the development of a market-based press. Rather, the economic health of the newspapers depended on the government investments, advertising by state-owned organizations, loans "to be paid on doomsday," and also on bribes (Ribeiro, 2001, 2006; Waisbord, 2000).

Some newspapers had partisan audiences, too. When Carlos Lacerda, a maverick politician from the conservative party União Democrática Nacional, was fired from the traditional newspaper *O Correio da Manhã*, in which he worked as a columnist, his supporters backed a campaign to name "a newspaper for Carlos." The campaign was successful, and as many as 34,000 people donated money to help Lacerda build the newspaper *Tribuna da Imprensa*. The number of contributors was close to the newspaper's circulation in the 1950s, which oscillated from 25,000 to 45,000 (Ribeiro, 2006). Obviously, the coming of a new style of journalism did not displace in the short run either the role orientation of *journalism as advocacy* or the tendency of *journalists to take part in politics*.

The military regime (1964–85) had a devastating impact on political parallelism, however. It dissolved all political parties and replaced them with a noncompetitive two-party system, in which the opposition party Movimento Democrático Brasileiro was supposed to perform a very moderate opposition role, taking part in the elections and being defeated by the governing party ARENA (Aliança Renovadora Nacional; Kinzo, 1988). During this period most media organizations were either subservient to the government or were under censorship (Smith, 1997). Only small, independent journalistic organizations known as *imprensa alternativa* (alternative press) tried to resist this state of affairs (Kucinski, 1991). From a financial point of view, however, the military regime era was an auspicious time for the leading media organizations. They profited from the significant growth of the market economy and from massive investments by the military government (Ortiz, 1988). As a consequence, by the end of the military regime they were able to play a more active political role in the transition to and consolidation of the new democracy (Guimarães and Amaral, 1988; Lima, 2004).

As democracy became more consolidated in Brazil, most of the leading news media organizations adopted a market-driven, catch-all attitude. They made an effort to distance themselves from particular political groups and took measures to increase internal pluralism in their political coverage (Matos, 2008; Porto, 2002). However, this does not mean that they adopted a more passive attitude toward politics. For example, *Folha de S. Paulo* has maintained that when their readers buy an copy, they provide the newspaper with a representative mandate. Based on this stance, *Folha de S. Paulo* has claimed the responsibility for "intervening in public debate, and supported by facts and objective data, changing beliefs and habits, influencing the behaviour of institutions, either public or private-owned" (Folha de S. Paulo, 1984: 42; see also Albuquerque and Holzbach, 2008).

Professionalism

Hallin and Mancini discuss three dimensions of journalistic professionalism: autonomy, distinct professional norms, and public service orientation. How do these apply to Brazilian journalism? Let us begin by discussing *professional norms*. Since the 1950s the American journalism model has exerted a significant influence in Brazil, which is far earlier than in most other countries. The use of a fact-centered text style and methods of gathering and processing information on a large scale became a matter of professional pride for Brazilian journalists, allowing them to think about themselves as mastering a specialized craft. Even today, the adoption of the lead at the beginning of the news text as opposed to the ancient literary style is described as one of the main traits that distinguish true (professional) journalists from amateurs (Jobim, 1954; Ribeiro, 2003).

However, this does not necessarily imply that Brazilian media has become "Americanized." The circumstances that allowed the development of American journalism were not present in Brazil: There was no solid market economy, individualistic culture, or political culture that valued the freedom of the press. As a consequence, the Brazilian news media and their journalists redefined the rhetoric (such as the concepts of objectivity and journalism as a Fourth Branch) and the practices (such as the interview) they borrowed from American journalism, sometimes in very peculiar manners (Albuquerque, 2005). To better understand how this transformation occurred, it is necessary to take a closer look at the process of adaptation of American journalism. Understanding the particular way in which Brazilian journalists and news media adapted the American model is as important as recognizing the changes that resulted from it.

The development of journalistic professionalism in Brazil was facilitated by economic and political circumstances that allowed the owners of conservative papers and communist journalists working for them to establish an unspoken alliance (Albuquerque and Roxo da Silva, 2009). This alliance allowed a large number of leftist journalists – most of them affiliated with the Brazilian Communist Party (Partido Comunista Brasileiro

[PCB])[4] – to be hired, and some came to hold key positions in the conservative newspapers.[5] The newspaper publishers had commercial reasons and the communist journalists had political reasons for working together. The publishers had to modernize their newspapers to survive in an increasingly competitive market (Ribeiro, 2006), and that included adopting a more fact-centered style of journalism. To do so, they needed a new kind of journalist, and for many reasons, the communists were in a good position to be that kind of journalist. Meanwhile, infiltration in the newspapers provided the communists with organizational resources (providing jobs and political protection for their militants) that they could use for the benefit of their party. However, these journalists knew there was a price to pay for their infiltration: They could not look threatening to the publishers, or the schema would break down (Abramo, 1988; Kucinski, 1998). Thus, in practice, the PCB converted party discipline into journalistic discipline. By providing some stability to the newsrooms, communist journalists helped ensure that the conditions for the transformation of Brazilian journalism were met. The language of professionalism was convenient for both owners and journalists. It allowed them to communicate, notwithstanding their different beliefs and objectives. From the point of view of the owners, professionalism helped assure some discipline to their newsrooms; for the journalists, it helped assure some *autonomy* in the exercise of their work (Soloski, 1989).

Yet the military that ruled Brazil from 1964 to 1985 could not easily accept the massive presence of communists working in the newspapers. To restrict the hiring of new communist journalists, in 1969 they imposed a law (decree-law 972) that required a university degree to work as a journalist, believing that this criterion would guarantee professionals with a more technical than a political background. The strategy was only partially successful. On the one hand, the influence of the traditional

---

4 It is not possible to estimate precisely the percentage of journalists who were communists, because the PCB was outlawed, and thus communist activism was a clandestine activity. However, from a group of fifty-five journalists active in the 1960s–70s who were interviewed by Alzira Abreu (2003), 43% reported having taken part in leftist movements or parties and among them 61% reported having taken part in the PCB. This corresponds roughly to one-fourth of the journalists interviewed.

5 Augusto Nunes, Elio Gaspari, and Roberto Müller Filho are some examples of journalists who were editors-in-chief of leading newspapers and newsweeklies and who were affiliated with the PCB. Claudio Abramo, who was editor-in-chief of the two most important newspapers from São Paulo – *O Estado de São Paulo* and *Folha de S. Paulo* – used to define himself as being a Marxist, but not a communist.

communist networks declined sharply during the 1970s. On the other hand, the new journalists had far from the technical profile intended by the military. In fact, many were more radical than the older communist journalists. The new radical journalists saw themselves as exploited proletarians, whose interests were identical to those of the working class and thus clashed with the publishers' interests (Abramo, 1997). These journalists began to build their professional identity in the universities, far from the newsrooms. Given that the universities became the fulcrum of the leftist resistance to the regime (Almeida and Weis, 1998), the journalists were taught to believe that the media were the ideological apparatus of the state, at the service of the interests of the bourgeoisie and the military dictatorship. In addition, the new journalists were more ready to believe that their jobs depended mainly on their *individual* talents (that is, the competency attested by a university), rather than on political and personal favors; thus they were less inclined to have feelings of personal gratitude regarding their employers or colleagues.

In these circumstances, the unspoken agreement between the owners of newspapers and the journalists who worked for them could not prosper. In 1979 the journalists of the São Paulo State went on strike. They fought for better salaries, but they demanded something else too: recognition by their bosses of the Consultative Council of Newsroom Representatives (Conselho Consultivo dos Representantes de Redação [CCRR]), which would work toward reinforcing the authority of the Union of Journalists within the newsrooms.[6] The publishers were not ready to provide this recognition and reacted severely to the strike, firing many journalists and greatly reducing the autonomy of the newsrooms. Because the publishers concluded that the old communist journalists were not able to maintain discipline in the newsrooms, they were removed from their editorial posts and replaced by new journalists, more submissive to management interests.[7]

---

[6] The Consultative Council of Newsroom Representatives was created by the Union of Journalists of São Paulo in 1977–8. Perseu Abramo, one of the most distinguished defenders of the CCRR, says that its main purpose was to provide the journalists with democratic representation inside the newsrooms. He defines the CCRR as a journalists' instrument of pressure "against the publishers, and, as a consequence, against the establishment" (1997: 289).

[7] The newspaper *Folha de S. Paulo* provides the best illustration for this. Its "Folha Project" aimed to reorganize entirely the process of news production, with the aim of giving management total control over it. In a three-year period, hundreds of journalists were fired, or they resigned because of their inability to conform to the requirements of the

The legal requirement of having a university degree in journalism had a significant impact on the development of the cultural identity of Brazilian journalists. Notwithstanding the authoritarian character of decree-law 972, the National Federation of Journalists (Federação Nacional dos Jornalistas [FENAJ]) endorsed it, motivated by corporatist interests (reserving posts for the people who had a university degree in journalism). As a consequence the normative focus of Brazilian journalists shifted from the questions "what is journalism?" and "how must it be exercised?" to "who can legally work as a journalist?" As Adghirni put it, in Brazil a person with a university degree in journalism will always be a journalist, even if she or he works in another profession" (2004: 142). All in all, the development of a solid public service orientation did not find fertile ground in Brazil. Despite the widespread use of a public service rhetoric by the Brazilian journalists, this very same rhetoric has often served as a cover-up for other purposes: to allow conservative newspapers to employ communist journalists or to justify job privileges for people with a university degree in journalism.

The Role of the State
In *Comparing Media Systems*, Hallin and Mancini suggest that the state plays four main roles regarding the media: (1) exerting censorship or other types of political pressure, (2) endowing the media with economic subsidies, (3) owning media organizations, and (4) providing regulations for the media in the name of the public interest. To what extent are they useful for explaining the Brazilian case?

During its history as a republic, Brazil has alternated between authoritarian and democratic periods of government. During the first government of President Getúlio Vargas (1930–45) – particularly during the period of the *Estado Novo* (New State), which lasted from 1937 to 1945 and had Nazi-fascist inspirations – and during the military regime (1964–85), the media were systematically censored. However, the logic of *censorship* was different in these two periods. During the *Estado Novo* censorship was fully institutionalized. In 1939 the regime created the Press and Propaganda Department (*Departamento de Imprensa e Propaganda*). Its responsibilities included both censoring the media and disseminating the regime's values and perspectives (Velloso, 1982). In contrast to the *Estado Novo*, the military regime tried hard to veil its authoritarian character. It

project. Even Octavio Frias Filho, who was mainly responsible for the project, described it as "draconian" (2003).

also systematically censored the press, but it attempted to hide it from the public. There was no formal entity responsible for censoring the press: The orders always came "from above." To be effective, this kind of censorship relied on a "culture of fear" installed among journalists (Smith, 1997). Both the *Estado Novo* and the military regime also occasionally resorted to physical violence to intimidate journalists. After the end of the military regime, political censorship almost ended in Brazil. However, intimidation and violence against journalists remain significant in the country, particularly in small towns.

The limited number of readers and the insufficient investment from private advertisers rendered impossible the full development of a market-based press in Brazil (Silva, 1991; Waisbord, 2000b). As a consequence, *state subsidies* have played a very important role in the economic life of media organizations. State-owned banks have provided generous loans for media organizations, and state-owned companies are responsible for a large part of their advertising budgets. During the military regime, the state made a huge investment to build first a microwave and then a satellite-based communications infrastructure necessary to allow television broadcasting across the entire Brazilian territory, in the name of national integration. Thanks to this, TV Globo jumped from a local TV station based in Rio de Janeiro to become a major network, one of the biggest in the world (Mattelart and Mattelart, 1989).

The state has never played an important role as an *owner of media organizations* in Brazil. Similar to what happened in the United States, broadcasting media in Brazil have been almost entirely privately owned since their inception. Thus, in contrast to what happened in Europe and in many countries around the world, the Brazilian broadcasting media structure was not deeply challenged in the 1980s and 1990s. There was no place for a "commercial deluge" simply because Brazilian media already had a commercial character. In fact, Brazilian broadcast television had developed a very particular communicative style, which has remained remarkably stable for decades – for example, the prime-time schedule has continued to be based on a mixture of *telenovelas* and newscasts – and was not significantly affected by the process of globalization. Thus, the association between commercialization and Americanization makes much less sense in Brazil than in the European countries.

Finally, there are some central questions regarding the regulation of the media. In a sense, the Brazilian media are even less regulated than American media. In contrast to the United States, an independent regulatory agency was never established in Brazil. Historically, the power to allot radio and television licenses has been monopolized by the executive branch (Porto, 2006: 130). There is an important exception to that rule, however. Political broadcasts have been regulated since 1962. Law 4115 provided parties with free time on radio and television in order to broadcast political ads, and in 1974 Law 9601 forbade candidates and parties from purchasing time for paid advertising. Both rules remain valid today (Albuquerque, 1999; Duarte, 1980). Most free airtime is allotted to the political parties in proportion to the number of seats they have in the lower house of the National Congress. In local elections, the number of seats in the local and city chambers are also taken into account. As a rule, there are not many content restrictions on political broadcasts (Albuquerque, 1999).

New Variables and Categories

In this part of the chapter, I discuss several traits that distinguish Brazil from the three-model framework presented by Hallin and Mancini and, based on this discussion, propose new categories and schemas for a worldwide comparative analysis. First, I emphasize the importance of distinguishing *central* from *peripheral* media systems. Second, I present the system of government as a significant variable for understanding the relationship between the political and media systems in a given country. Finally, I criticize the concept of political parallelism as being inadequate to account for the different kinds of relationships between the media and the political systems that go beyond the original scope of *Comparing Media Systems*, and I propose a schema that crosses two variables – the relative strength of political parties and the level of engagement of the media in politics.

Central and Peripheral Media Systems

The distinction between peripheral and central media systems is a classic one that can be identified in different forms in theoretical perspectives as diverse as development theory, cultural imperialism theory, and cultural studies. This distinction takes its raison d'être from colonialism, which, from the sixteenth century on, has put the Western countries in the center of the world system. It is possible to suggest that this distinction is implicitly recognized by Hallin and Mancini themselves, when they write that the models they analyzed "tend to be dominant globally." Here, I propose classifying as *peripheral* those media systems that have been primarily structured in reference to foreign models (understood in the sense of "models to . . .") and as *central* those media systems that serve as models for the others.

We must use the terms "central" and "peripheral" with some caution, however. To begin with, they must be understood as *relative* concepts. Media systems occupy a more or less central (or peripheral) role relative to the others; there are no "pure" central or peripheral media systems. When used in a broad sense, we can apply these terms even to the eighteen countries analyzed in *Comparing Media Systems*. The dictate "either the state or the United States" (Hallin and Mancini, 1984: 232) neatly indicates the relatively peripheral position of Canada vis-à-vis its powerful neighbor. The same can be said about the position of Ireland in relation to the British media system.

The concept of periphery proves to be particularly useful when applied to countries that are former colonies and that have defined their national identities in reference to (and against) their European colonizers (see, for example, Daniels and Kennedy, 2002). Latin America offers a very interesting case in point. In a similar way to what happened in the United States, the Latin American countries shared language and culture with their former colonizing metropolises (Anderson, 1983). However, the colonization of Latin America and the United States followed very different logics. Settlers in the United States were strongly influenced by the ideal of building a new world, *alternative* to the one they left in Europe. They also enjoyed a significant degree of autonomy in the administration of their local affairs (Bellah, 1967; Tocqueville, 1969). In contrast, Latin American colonies were considered to be *extensions* of the colonizing powers, and their colonization was strongly determined by the state. Even though the independence process of the Latin American countries has been strongly influenced by that of the United States, in practice the pathways to independence were very different. In a way, the Latin American countries have experienced a double sentiment of displacement. They perceive themselves as *others* in relation both to their formal metropolises (other Spanish or Portuguese people) and to the United States, the prototypical model for "America" and the "New World" (Feres Junior, 2004).

The analysis of peripheral media systems must focus on the relationship they maintain with foreign media models. It is not sufficient to say that these media systems are influenced by foreign models and that they adopt their principles and practices. The identification of the peripheral countries as merely passive recipients of media contents and formats in contrast to the central countries is too simplistic. Similarly, the differences between the original model and the form that it takes in the peripheral systems cannot be adequately explained as the result of its failed implementation, even if the agents involved in the process say so – as when Brazilian journalists refer to Brazilian journalism as a caricature of the American system (Herscovitz, 2000; Silva, 1991). These differences result from an *active* effort of *adaptation* of the foreign models to the specific social and cultural characteristics of the different peripheral media systems.

The adaptation of the Anglo-American Fourth Power rhetoric in Brazil provides a good example. Two different Fourth Power discourses served as references for Brazilian journalists: the *Fourth Estate* discourse and the *Fourth Branch* discourse.[8] The Fourth Estate discourse describes the role of the press in terms of a counterpower, whose main purpose is acting as a watchdog at the service of the citizens to prevent governmental abuses. It is a strongly normative discourse, associated with a Liberal view of the media.[9] The Fourth Branch discourse refers to the checks and balances system of American government and describes the press as playing a mediating role between the branches of government and between the government and the citizens of the country (Cater, 1965; Cook, 1998). In Brazil, both discourses were reinterpreted in reference to a native model of Fourth Power, which originally had nothing to do with the role of the press: The *Poder Moderador* (Moderating Power) was created by the first Brazilian constitution, in 1824, under the argument that a fourth force would be necessary to arbitrate the conflicts between the executive, the legislative, and the judicial branches, enabling them to work together. The legal existence of the Poder Moderador ended in 1889, when the Brazilian government shifted from a monarchy to a republic. However, the belief that three constitutional branches needed a fourth force to arbitrate their disputes remained an important trait of Brazilian political culture. Between 1946 and 1964 the military was supposed to play that role, as the supreme guardian of the constitution.

---

[8] In this chapter I use the term "Fourth Power" as a general concept that includes other, more specific conceptions about the role of the press vis-à-vis the political institutions. Sparks (1995) proposes a different classification based on three concepts: Fourth Power, Fourth Estate, and watchdog.

[9] Two examples of such normative use of the concept of the Fourth Estate are Lawson's analysis on the role of the press in the Mexican democratization process (2002) and McNair's discussion on the failure of Russian press in acting as a "genuine 'fourth estate' debt to a succession of pro-censorship bills made by the conservative-controlled parliament" (2002: 84–5).

In 1964, it took control of the government in a coup d'etat and ruled the country until 1985. After the end of the military regime, the leading media organizations claimed the responsibility for playing such role, by creating a Fourth Power discourse that combined references to the Fourth Estate and Fourth Branch discourses with the Brazilian tradition of Poder Moderador (Albuquerque, 2005).

The peripheral (or central) condition is not unchangeable. The relationship between central and peripheral media systems is dynamic and historically situated: A given media system can move from a more peripheral to a more central place, and vice versa. The growing influence of American-born concepts and practices in the Western European media systems (Hallin and Mancini, 2004a) indicates the shifting of the American model to a even more central position, at the same time as the status of those media systems status becomes more peripheral in comparison to it. In contrast, some media systems – for example, some East Asian ones (Keane, 2006) – that usually have been considered as peripheral seem to be moving to a more central position. Not all aspects of a given media system move equally, however. The *telenovelas* produced by some Latin American countries, such as Brazil, Mexico, Venezuela, Colombia, and Argentina, have come to occupy a considerably more central position in the world media system (Mato, 2005; Mattelart and Mattelart, 1989), but the journalism that these countries produce has mostly peripheral traits.

System of Government

For a long time, presidentialism has been almost ignored by comparative political research. When it finally got some attention at the end of the 1980s to the early 1990s, it was mainly negative. The presidential system was described as being essentially a source of political instability: The temporal rigidity of presidential and congressional mandates facilitates institutional deadlock, either when there is a very unpopular president or stiff opposition between the president and the congress (Linz 1994); the presidential system promotes an extreme form of majoritarianism, which marginalizes minority views in a "winner-take-all" logic according to Linz (1990); and it promotes personalism and, as a consequence, weak political parties (Mainwaring, 1995). All in all, the presidential system was described as a peril for democracy and as being strongly associated with authoritarian regimes. More recently some authors have challenged this view. Cheibub, for example, argues that "[f]rom a strictly institutional point of view, presidentialism can be as stable as parliamentarism" (2007: 3). Shugart and Carey (1997) observe that, during the twentieth century, the parliamentary systems were more likely experience the breakdown of the democratic regime than presidential systems, if we consider only Third World cases.

In *Comparing Media Systems*, Hallin and Mancini did not consider the system of government – parliamentary or presidential – to be a significant variable for explaining the relationship between the political and the media systems. In an earlier comparison of media and politics in the United States and Italy (Hallin and Mancini, 1984), however, they paid a lot of attention to it. Why did this variable disappear from *Comparing Media Systems*? Probably it has to do with the sample of the research. In the earlier study, one presidential country was measured against one parliamentary one. In *Comparing Media Systems* the United States is the *only* country with a purely presidential system, in a sample of eighteen countries. Yet, the distinction between presidential and parliamentary government can prove very useful in a global comparison. Presidentialism is essentially a Third World phenomenon – the United States being the lonely exception to this rule (Shugart and Carey, 1997) – and a particularly important trait of Latin American countries.

How does the presidential system of government affect the relationship between media and politics? Here, I maintain that the separation of powers affects both the manner in which the media organizations represent politics and the role that they intend to play in it. Media representation of politics is affected in two main ways. First, media tends to focus on the president as an individual person – presidents literally give government *a body* – to the detriment of collective agents such as political parties. Second, in a presidential system media tend to reinforce the emphasis on the administrative aspects of government, rather than on party politics. Schudson (1982, 2002) has emphasized the influence of the Progressive Movement in the development of an administrative view of politics among American journalists. No similar movement existed in Brazil, but the administrative view of government also prevails over the political one and has become even more dominant in recent years (Porto, 2002). Both the emphasis on political individuals (rather than on collective forces) and the focus on administrative aspects of the government (rather than on party politics) contributed to promoting a generalist, catch-all attitude in the media. Separation of powers also affects the way the media deal with the government. As discussed earlier, in presidentialist countries, the media play a very important intermediary role by allowing the three branches to communicate with each other and with the public. However, the news media do not play this role in the same way everywhere. In the United States the news media perform this role by denying they do so. It is precisely because the news media claim to provide only objective information to the public that they are perceived as a central institution for democracy (Cook, 1998). On the contrary, in Brazil they claim to play a far more active role, arbitrating the disputes between the branches and taking sides "in the name of the national interest" (Albuquerque, 2005).

Beyond Political Parallelism

Political parallelism is the least clearly defined category among the four variables that comprise the theoretical framework of *Comparing Media Systems*. It refers to the concept of party-press parallelism, proposed by Seymour-Ure (1974: 159): "The same social forces that find expression in a party or parties of a political system tend to find expression also through the press." To measure the level of parallelism, Seymour-Ure proposes four criteria, which relate to some of the characteristics of political parties: (1) *organization*, meaning "the ownership and management of a paper by a party" (1974: 160); (2) the loyalty of a paper to the party *goals*; (3) the correspondence between the *supporters* of a party and the readers of a paper; and (4) the ratio between parties and papers. Thirty years later, Hallin and Mancini note that examples of a one-to-one connection between media organizations and political parties have become harder to find. For this reason, they propose a broader definition of political parallelism that refers to the association between the media and general political tendencies, which are not necessarily related to particular parties. Their diagnosis seems to be correct, but the solution proposed may be questioned: Can the term "parallelism" still be useful when applied to situations in which the political cleavages are not as obvious as they used to be?

I propose that political parallelism not be considered as a single variable, but as the result of the combination of two variables. First, a single variable assumes the existence of a political system in which the party lines are clear enough to allow the observer to perceive them (as their "reflections" in the media). Second, it assumes the existence of a politically active media, in the sense of taking explicit political positions. Hence political parallelism describes a situation in which media organizations systematically embrace specific party lines. Defined this way, *political parallelism* reflects only one of four possible types of relationships between media and politics. However, there are three other possibilities. In the second one, the party lines are also clearly defined, but the media refrain

TABLE 5.2. *Types of Media–Politics Relationships*

	Politically Active Media	
Party Lines	**Strong**	**Weak**
Clear	Political parallelism (Polarized Pluralist model)	Public service media (Democratic Corporatist model)
Unclear	Media as a political agent (Moderating role)	"Objective" media (Liberal model)

from taking an explicit position in the name of a *public service* ethics. In the third possibility a nonpolitically active media associate with a political system in which the party lines are unclear. In the fourth one the media play a very active political role, despite the fact that party lines are unclear (see Table 5.2).

Among these types, three can be easily related to the models proposed in *Comparing Media Systems*: Political parallelism corresponds to the Polarized Pluralist model, public service media to the Democratic Corporatist model, and "objective" media to the Liberal model. The fourth type, the media as a political agent, has no corresponding model in the book. In this situation, the media explicitly take part in political debate, but do not do so as representatives of the view of the political parties. Exploiting their catch-all character, they claim directly to represent national interests in a more legitimate way than the political parties and even the formal political institutions. I cannot identify at the present a model – in the sense of the three models proposed by Hallin and Mancini – that would be equivalent to this situation, but I believe that the moderating role that the Brazilian media claim to play regarding the political forces and institutions furnishes a good example (Albuquerque, 2005).

Conclusion

The Brazilian media system is believed to have many traits in common with the media systems in Southern European countries (Hallin and Papathanassopoulos, 2002). Azevedo (2006) goes further and classifies it as an example of the Polarized Pluralist model. However, the examination of the Brazilian media system according to the four dimensions of analysis proposed by Hallin and Mancini – the structure of media markets, political parallelism, professionalism, and the role of the state – shows a more complex picture.

The data concerning the *structure of the Brazilian media market* seem to support Hallin and Papathanassopoulos's claim that Brazil, like other Latin American countries, presents, even more strikingly, characteristics of the Mediterranean media systems: low circulation of newspapers, orientation toward the elites, late development of the press, and the huge influence of television as a source of news. However, it must be noted that the first three characteristics are defined *in contrast* to the full development of a mass press; hence in a negative way. To put it another way, this means that both Southern European and Latin American media systems are different from the ones in the countries classified as having the Democratic Corporatist and the Liberal models, but they are not necessarily similar to one another.

The examination of the three other dimensions of analysis reveals more differences than similarities between the Brazilian media system and the Polarized Pluralist model. First, *media/politics parallelism* does not appear to be particularly strong in Brazil. I have stressed that parallelism is more difficult to measure in countries with a presidential system than in those with a parliamentarian one, because political parties play a less active role in the government. In addition, most leading news organizations seem to adopt a catch-all, market-driven attitude. This does not mean that they avoid taking explicit political positions. They do take such positions, but their agenda and positions are not reducible to the agendas of the political parties; the opposite is more likely to happen.

Things seem even fuzzier regarding *professionalism*. Brazilian journalists have been influenced by the norms of the American (Liberal) model of journalism since the 1950s, thus far earlier than their colleagues in most other countries, and they have built their identity and professional pride around them. However, this does not mean that Brazilian journalism is similar to American journalism: Brazilian journalists have radically adapted the American model to their country's cultural and social characteristics. The American independent model is usually thought of as opposed to political militancy. In Brazil, however, communist and other leftist journalists played a major role in the adaptation of this model. The influence of the communists shrank during the 1970s, under the influence of decree-law 972, which established the university degree in journalism as a prerequisite to the professional practice of journalism. This changes resulted in a new kind of professional identity among Brazilian journalists, a strongly corporatist one based on the defense of job privileges for those with a university degree in journalism.

Finally, let me present some observations about the role of the state. Similar to what happened in some of the Southern European countries studied by Hallin and Mancini, Brazil has a remarkable history of censorship and of repression of journalists. The state and state-owned organizations have also played a very important role in providing economic subsidies for the media. However, in contrast to other countries, the Brazilian media have been almost totally privately owned since their inception.

Summing it up, the categories coined by Hallin and Mancini prove to be very useful for a comparative discussion about many features of the Brazilian media system, but they cannot deal with every significant aspect. To take them into account, I suggest adding two variables to the authors' schema: the opposition between "central" and "peripheral" media systems, and the system of government (presidential or parliamentary). In addition, I suggest that the concept of political parallelism be reviewed. Instead of considering it as a variable, it would be more productive to think about it as a specific type of media–politics relationship, which results from the combination of two variables: (1) the clarity of party lines and (2) the degree of political activity of the media. The Polarized Pluralist model, as defined by Hallin and Mancini, combines a political system with clear party lines with politically active media. I have identified three other possible combinations: (1) the "objective" media, corresponding to the Liberal model (non-politically active media/unclear party lines); (2) the "public service" media, which corresponds to the Democratic Corporatist model (non-politically active media/clear party lines); and (3) the media as a political agent, which has no corresponding model in the authors' schema, but has important traits in common with the Brazilian media system (politically active media, unclear party lines).

6

Africanizing Three Models of Media and Politics

The South African Experience

Adrian Hadland

Much has already been said and written about the lack of new or developing democratic countries in the sample used to populate Hallin and Mancini's three-model paradigm (2004b). This has indeed been the subject of considerable criticism (Couldry, 2005; Hampton, 2005; Nisbet and Moehler, 2005). Yet the objective of extending Hallin and Mancini's framework to the dozens of democracies that sprung up during the Third Wave of the 1990s is a daunting and ambitious task. Most of the world's democracies are relatively new and are systemically diverse (Diamond, 1996). Even within sub-Saharan Africa, a number of typologies have been proposed over the past three decades aiming to capture the features of political regimes, many of which are undergoing processes of substantial social and political change (Nisbet and Moehler, 2005).

The often fraught process of democratic consolidation has thrown the contested interests and roles of the state and the media into stark relief. It is my contention that the experiences of new democracies offer a critique of the three-model paradigm that is highly relevant and that demands expansion and revision of the original framework. Certainly, Hallin and Mancini noticed the bias toward mature democracies, acknowledging it in their text and indeed calling in it, as well as in subsequent interactions with the scholarly world,[1] for a broader consideration and application of their theory and for the inevitable proposal of alternate or additional variables and models. This indeed is the very purpose of the

---

[1] Such as at the "West Meets East: Comparing Media Systems" conference, University of Wrocklaw, Poland, 2007, and at the International Communication Association conference in Chicago, 2009.

current collection of essays and is eloquent proof of the authors' stated intention.

In this chapter I attempt two tasks. In keeping with the work of other authors in this volume, my first task is to evaluate South Africa's political and media systems against the Hallin-Mancini paradigm. The fit is not a comfortable one, with South Africa exhibiting features of all three of the Hallin-Mancini models, in particular the Polarized Pluralist model but also elements of the Democratic Corporatist and Liberal ones. This positioning coincides with that of most other authors representing emerging or new democracies in the developing world and underlines calls for a new model or models to represent this group. My second task is to build the foundation for the development of a new model or models of media and politics, based on the African experience.

Locating South Africa within the Three-Model Paradigm: Four Dimensions

In this part of the chapter, I analyze the South African media system in reference to the four dimensions of Hallin and Mancini's analysis: structure of the media markets, political parallelism, professionalism, and the role of the state.

The Structure of Media Markets

Race, language, and ethnicity were immensely powerful predictors of media consumption in the South African marketplace during the apartheid era and continue to be so since the advent of democracy in 1994 (Futurefact, 2004). Pre-1994, media audiences were very clearly demarcated by race and by language, and print and broadcast media products were unambiguous about their targeting. This separatism was founded on the political ideology of the day, which espoused (and enforced) the separation of the population according to race. Yet although apartheid has gone, the segmentation of media audiences according to race, ethnicity, and language continues. With some notable exceptions, white and black South Africans (and black South Africans from different ethnic groups) generally watch different television stations, read different newspapers, and listen to different radio shows.

The import of race, language, and ethnicity muddies the water not only with regard to the characterization of the media market but also as far as political parallelism is concerned (see the later discussion). They have a profound impact on the structure of the market, just as they do on the relationship of the media to the state and society in South Africa. This impact is not highlighted in the Hallin-Mancini paradigm, which deals with largely homogeneous democratic societies. And although the currency of race has an impact on South Africa's history that may be unique, many other emerging democracies (and some mature ones too) contend with similarly powerful social cleavages, including race, class, immigration, poverty, culture, and language.

Allow me briefly to sketch the development of South Africa's media. South Africa's newspaper industry has a long, complex history going back to the nineteenth century. Typically, scholars have clustered the print media into three ethno-linguistic categories: the English-language press, the Afrikaans press, and the black press (Hachten and Giffard, 1984; Potter, 1975; Switzer and Switzer, 1979; Tomaselli, Tomaselli, and Muller, 1987). From the early nineteenth century until the 1940s, the English-language press dominated print media in South Africa. Owned overwhelmingly by mining interests and populated by immigrant British editors, journalists, and printers, English-language newspapers sprang up in all the major metropolitan centers. They had all the hallmarks of classic, quality English commercial broadsheets: larger-than-life editors, intrepid (if underpaid) reporters, organized print unions, a highly commercial mode of operation, and an overarching commitment to liberal notions of freedom of the press. If this press had represented the South African press in its entirety, the country would certainly have fallen fair and square into Hallin and Mancini's Liberal model of media and politics.

Yet the Afrikaans-language press established in the 1920s had grown into a powerful force by the time the Afrikaner-based National Party won political office in the late 1940s. This was a press with very different rules. It was unashamedly partisan and party political. The first daily newspaper in Afrikaans, *De Burger* (later *Die Burger*), was edited by Dr. D. F. Malan, who went on to become both the leader of the National Party in the Cape as well as prime minister. Politicians, journalists, and readers alike assumed that newspapers in this sector played a small but important part in the strategic mission to wrest and retain control of the South African polity and to consolidate and propagate Afrikaans language and culture. Until the mid-1980s it was unheard of for an Afrikaans newspaper to be critical of senior National Party politicians, of apartheid policies, or of South Africa's foreign policy.

Then things did change, slowly at first with the birth of the first radical anti-apartheid newspaper, *Die Vrye Weekblad*, in the mid-1980s, then with the formal ditching of support for apartheid, and finally with the gradual embracing of more classic, liberal press values. The duopoly operating in the Afrikaans-language press soon graduated into monopoly as Nasionale Pers came not only to dominate the Afrikaans-language sector but also became the largest media company in the country on the back of its major investment in Internet, satellite, and new technologies from the early 1990s. Nasionale Pers now operates in fifty countries in Africa, Asia, and Europe and is far and away the country's biggest media business in any language or languages. It no longer publishes only Afrikaans-language newspapers. One could not easily fit the Afrikaans press as a whole into the Liberal model, certainly not before the 1990s, although many of its media products now meet most of the criteria.

The "black press," as it has been conceptualized by scholars, is quite a different phenomenon from either the English-language press or the Afrikaans press. A missionary press was born during the colonial era and printed and distributed small-volume periodicals with an educational or religious content. In the 1930s, entrepreneur Bertrand Paver established the Bantu Press and started selling newspapers on a much larger scale to black South Africans. However, the newsprint shortages of the war years, followed by the polarization and repression of apartheid, led to these papers (and some magazines) being closed down, sold, or de-politicized.

Although a radical black press emerged in the 1940s and '50s, it was soon declared illegal and, as a result, remained very small. Black readers read both English and Afrikaans newspapers, and it was not until the 1990s that a black-owned press aimed specifically at black readers was allowed to develop. In 2004, the hugely successful launch of the first tabloid – and many others subsequently – propelled the black press into a mass phenomenon for the first time in South Africa's history. Even so, this press is owned by the already dominant corporate players (Nasionale Pers, Independent Newspapers). This category, therefore, is a mix with both a strong advocacy-oriented history and periods of strong, liberal press inclination.

I have argued elsewhere that the ethno-linguistic categorization of the South African print media is conceptually unhelpful (Hadland, 2007). None of the categories – English-language, Afrikaans, or black – are mutually exclusive, and collectively they blur a much more important distinction that cuts across all the categories. South African newspapers and magazines historically either were advocacy oriented or fell more into the classic Liberal model. They either campaigned with specific political objectives in mind, whether the support of apartheid or its demise, or they adopted a more neutral, "objective" stance. Historically, the South

African print media therefore has strong elements both of the Liberal model and of the more partisan inclinations and the associated clientelism of the Polarized Pluralist model. I call these the two traditions of South African journalism.

This historical dualism reflects a heated contemporary debate concerning the role of the media. On the one hand, there are those who call for a media that is more developmentally oriented, that supports the democratically elected government rather than instinctively criticizes it, and that embraces the "national interest" objectives of racial reconciliation and economic development. This is the manifestation of the advocacy-oriented perspective and has been called developmental journalism, development support communications, and even sunshine journalism by scholars over the years (Ogan, 1980; Wasserman and De Beer, 2005). On the other hand, some scholars and practitioners argue that serving the "public interest" is the media's main responsibility, in line with traditional Fourth Estate values of autonomy and impartiality. This is, of course, the liberal perspective.

The clash of these two historically derived perspectives in a contemporary context has had substantial implications for media–state relations in democratic South Africa. Arguably, it underpins the deterioration in the relationship between media and state (Wasserman and De Beer, 2005), ensures the continuing partisanship of the public broadcaster, and has fed the interventionist inclinations of what I call an "acquisitive" if democratic state. I deal with developmental journalism in more detail later.

Even though South Africa's newspaper industry has shifted from being primarily focused on an urban elite to a more mass-based appeal and its influence on policy arguably outweighs its size, print remains the poor cousin of broadcast in terms of audience. South Africa's broadcasting sector was deregulated shortly before democracy in the early 1990s, a free-to-air television channel was introduced, paid-for-view by satellite arrived, and more than 100 community radio stations were launched. Recent figures indicate that 78 percent of adults in South Africa claim to have watched television in the past week, and 92 percent of South Africans listen regularly to the radio (Milne and Taylor, 2006). This far exceeds newspaper readership. Clearly, any assessment of South Africa's location in the Hallin-Mancini paradigm needs to reflect not just the print media but the important broadcast sector as well.

The key characteristics of the Polarized Pluralist model, say Hallin and Mancini, are to be found in the closeness of political actors to the media, in the dominant focus of the media on political life, and in the relatively elitist nature of journalism. In all of these ways, South Africa exhibits the symptoms of polarized pluralism. Since the unbanning of the ANC in 1990, South Africa has a history of close relations between political actors and the media. This is true whether one speaks of media ownership (key ANC officials such as Cyril Ramaphosa and Marcel Golding currently own significant portions of major newspaper and television companies), of the media acting as the conduit between elites (especially evident during the negotiations period of the early 1990s), or of former editors or journalists moving on to become senior government officials or representatives.

Hallin and Mancini's emphasis on political coverage as a common dimension of the Polarized Pluralist model also applies clearly to the South African case. An overly dominant focus on political life indeed threatened to undermine the print media itself, as circulations plummeted in the months after the country staggered over the democratic finish line and put Nelson Mandela into the presidency (Hadland, 2007). Even with the arrival of the tabloids, the South African print media remain heavily focused on educated (literate) readers residing mainly in the urban areas. Local newspapers are predominantly free in the urban areas, whereas in the countryside (inhabited by 50 percent of the population), circulations are smaller, choices very restricted, and newspapers are generally sold. Given that South Africa has eleven official languages, few can claim that even the country's broadcast media adequately meet the needs of South Africa's diverse population, most particularly in the rural areas where choices are limited at best.

In common with the Democratic Corporatist model, the South African media market has a degree of political parallelism, a strong interventionist state with traditional limits on state power, and a sophisticated pattern of civic life. However, this corporatism does not find its way into the media in any systematic way, and neither does a wide variation in political tendencies. Horwitz (2001) has lauded the deeply democratic and accountable process fueled by civil society activism by which South Africa framed its communications policy in the post-1994 period. Although this process has been influential with regard to broadcasting and, to some extent, in the community print media field, it has not made a deep impression on the mainstream print media.

South Africa's multiplicity of forums and stakeholder involvement in policy processes might also have indicated its leaning toward the Democratic Corporatist cluster. Yet although some of these forums remain important (such as the National Economic Development and Labor

Council), there is also evidence that the impact of these civil society structures is diminishing (Calland, 2006). The South African media market also exhibits clientelism, significant shortfalls in mass literacy, and inadequacies in access to the media, together with an emphasis on a regional and national press, which prevent it from being an authentic member of the Democratic Corporatist cluster.

Similarly, the mature commercial element of the South African media market and the sharp separation of quality from sensational press would signal that it may form part of the Liberal media cluster. However, it also lacks the predominance of local titles, the limited state role, and the informal regulation that are the hallmarks of the liberal press. Overall, South Africa provides a poor example of any of the Hallin-Mancini models, even given the ideal-type flexibility inherent in their design. South Africa has elements of the Liberal, Democratic Corporatist, and Polarized Pluralist models, just as it has characteristics (such as the influence of race, ethnicity, and language) that have not been emphasized in any of the three.

Political Parallelism

When considering the Hallin-Mancini dimensions of both political parallelism and state intervention, how one characterizes the South African state becomes crucial. If the state is considered to preside over an illiberal or even pseudo-democratic system (Diamond, 1996) that deteriorates in quality with each overwhelming electoral majority by the ruling party, then this constitutes a different set of forces with which the media must contend compared to a liberal democracy in which one party has legitimately built powerful, broad, and sustainable support among the electorate.

Contrary to some scholars (Giliomee and Simkins, 1999), I understand the latter to be the case, but with the important caveat that the ruling party's dominant position in South Africa has indeed spawned a range of weaknesses over the past fifteen years that, unchecked, will diminish the quality of the country's democracy over time. These weaknesses include a lack of accountability within the architecture of the political system (the Slabbert Commission outlined this in detail in 2002) together with the complacency and acquisitiveness that power seems naturally to generate among its proponents and that are fueled by patronage, corruption, and secrecy.

The ruling party, the African National Congress, in removing its own incumbent president and in setting out a new set of policy guidelines at its party congress in Polokwane in late 2007, made clear its own discomfort with the direction the party had taken in its first fifteen years of office. In particular, it identified the centralization of power, the remote location of high officeholders from the electorate, and the lack of a sufficiently pro-poor economic framework. However, the new ANC with Jacob Zuma as its figurehead has not only signaled that it has bought into its predecessor's at times illiberal views on the role of the media but also plans a much more intense intervention in the media, including through the establishment of a statutory media tribunal. Zuma himself is currently involved in a libel suit against South Africa's best known political cartoonist, Zapiro. It is in this light of these recent developments that the relationship between media and state in South Africa needs to be considered.

The overwhelming success of the ANC in all four postapartheid democratic general elections since 1994 has generated heated debate among scholars. For Giliomee and Simkins (1999), the ANC has used the ballot box to vault itself into a position of electoral dominance that has negative implications for the quality of South Africa's democracy. Their work drew on a literature concerning dominant one-party democratic systems that has grown voluminous over the past two decades, fueled by ongoing successes of powerful political parties in Mexico, Taiwan, Japan, Italy, Israel, and in several African states such as Botswana and South Africa (Bratton and Van der Walle, 1997; Diamond, 1996; Lindberg, 2006; Pempel, 1990).

Other scholars have downplayed the potential longevity or significance of the ANC's electoral strength, pointing to an array of checks and balances, including formal corporatist structures, that militate against prolonged domination (Friedman, 2006). Indeed, some have argued that given South Africa's substantial developmental challenges, together with its fundamental racial and ethnic cleavages, a dominant majority party is exactly what is required to assure stability, growth, and the consolidation of democracy (Reddy, 2006). The ANC itself has attacked the suggestion that its strength potentially undermines the quality of democracy, arguing that this opinion is grounded in racist assumptions surrounding the capacity of black citizens to govern effectively (Suttner, 2004). These allegations and counterallegations have polarized the field, leading one scholar, Roger Southall , to propose a "soft" version of one-party dominance (2005: 64).

The extent of political parallelism within South Africa's media and political matrix is therefore somewhat difficult to determine. There is no party political press as such, unlike in France or Greece, but this lack may be understandable in a political environment that is dominated by one party with a powerful president at its head (see Albuquerque's Chapter 5 in this volume). Certainly, the ruling party dominates media coverage. A survey of sixteen newspapers and five television channels conducted in the four-month lead-up to the 2004 national election found an overwhelming dominance of ruling party coverage (Schreiner, 2004). It does seem apparent that the exhaustive coverage of the ANC at election time within the South African media reflects the dominance of the party within the polity more generally. This suggests a close political parallelism, but it does not reflect the parallelism that exists within any of the other Hallin-Mancini models. Instead, it is suggestive of a different model, one that matches a high degree of political parallelism with the tendency of the mass media to act as an instrument of clientelist networks and neopatrimonial politics (see Nisbet and Moehler, 2005).

Hallin and Mancini do cite other constituents of political parallelism, including an emphasis on commentary rather than neutral news, the activist role of newspapers in mobilizing readers to support political causes, a party-politicized public broadcaster, and strong ties or alliances between politicians and journalists. South Africa does not have a commentary bias in its journalism, in the French style, nor do newspapers, radio stations, or television channels conduct campaigns around party political issues. However, there would be grounds to argue that the public broadcaster is indeed party politicized and that its work is heavily influenced by the prevailing elite of the ruling party (Glenn and Duncan, 2008). There is also a strong link between the media and political personnel, but even then it would be difficult to argue that young journalists are entering the profession with an eye to a future in a political party or even in government.

There is clearly a degree of political parallelism in the South African media–state model, although it is far from uncontestable. The poor fit is demonstrative of two elements of a Hallin-Mancini critique: the failure of the model to consider the class of emerging democracies in which one political party has hegemony and South Africa's political history in which race, ethnicity, and language are key determinants of media consumption. Evidently, the term "Polarized Pluralist" falls far short of capturing the South African model, but it is also true that the Liberal or Democratic Corporatist models also fail for similar reasons.

Professionalism
There are three dimensions, or indicators, of journalistic professionalism, according to *Comparing Media Systems*: autonomy, the development of

distinct professional norms, and a public service orientation. The notion of a public service orientation has two meanings in the South African context. It could describe a state-funded initiative to provide information or content, as is performed by the state broadcasting body in the classic Liberal model sense. Or, it could refer to the notion of a developmental media aimed at generating responsible coverage of emerging democratic states. In this chapter, I mean the latter. Together these indicators of journalistic professionalism outline an important dimension of a media system that has key consequences for the functioning and development of that system.

South Africa has little in common with the Democratic Corporatist model when it comes to journalistic professionalism. The Democratic Corporatist countries of Northern Continental Europe have high levels of journalistic professionalism including a common consensus on standards and a high level of autonomy. They have strong, formalized systems of self-regulation, including influential press councils, as well as established journalistic qualifications and accreditation. Journalism is considered a public trust in the Democratic Corporatist models, and the state intervenes strongly with subsidies to ensure diversity. Journalists are frequently involved in decision making as well as in the ownership and management of media titles. Media content is frequently partisan and opinionated.

Few of these elements apply to contemporary South Africa. There are pockets of journalistic professionalism and a history of its nurturing, but also clear evidence of its deterioration (Steyn and De Beer, 2002). A formalized system of self-regulation is in place through the workings of the Press Ombudsman of South Africa for the print sector and through various regulatory structures for the broadcast sector (such as the Broadcast Complaints Commission of South Africa). For print, in particular, the system is weak, lacks teeth, and, in some cases, has been ignored altogether by industry players (*Die Son v. Family of Brett Goldin*, 2005). The state intervenes, but not to inject substantial subsidies or to materially affect diversity, particularly in the mainstream media. Journalist involvement in ownership or even in strategic decision making is rare. Media content is usually portrayed in the "informational style" (neutral, objective, liberal) rather in the opinionated style of more overtly partisan titles.

South Africa has much in common with the Liberal model, although it also has some clear deviations. Commercial papers have developed with relatively little interference (commercially at least) from the state since the nineteenth century. However, South African journalism has an equally strong heritage of advocacy journalism, most especially in what has been described as the Afrikaans and black media. Political neutrality has been as heavily emphasized as partisan advocacy in the development of South Africa's media.

The journalistic professionalism that has been the hallmark of the liberal press is also in decline. Editors are diminishing in stature and, with them arguably, the extent of independent journalism. The principal journalists' union, the South African Union of Journalists, closed down in the mid-2000s and has not been replaced. Various studies have diagnosed serious skill shortages in the sector (Steyn and De Beer, 2002). Journalists still do follow their own news selection and presentation criteria and do occupy a "distinct occupational community" in most news organizations. However, self-regulation (in the print media) is currently much more formal in South Africa than in most Liberal model systems. The industry-established Press Ombudsman, as ineffective as it can sometimes be, is still the only body to receive and hear complaints and continues to operate free of state influence or control. Overall, however, there are strong similarities between South Africa and the Liberal cluster, including the perceived, gradual diminishment of journalistic professionalism.

Finally, South Africa does have a number of commonalities with the journalistic professionalism that is evident in the Polarized Pluralist model. The media in this model are frequently used as a tool to intervene in the political world. Polarized Pluralist systems have weak consensus on journalistic standards and limited development of professional self-regulation. In South Africa, there is consensus on journalistic standards, but it has markedly deteriorated (Hadland et al., 2007). In general, the level of journalistic autonomy is lower in the countries populating the Polarized Pluralist cluster.

South Africa's experience is certainly that instrumentalism is on the rise and journalistic autonomy is under threat. Instrumentalism has been in strong evidence since 1994, most evidently and consistently in the manipulation of news coverage and commentary at the national broadcaster. The bias toward the ruling party during election periods, cited earlier, is another clear example of rising instrumentalism. The threat to journalistic autonomy is twofold: First, the extraordinary commercialization of the media since 1994 has placed strain on journalistic ethics and independence (Hadland et al., 2007). Second, heavy pressure has been placed on journalists and their organizations to buy in to the notion of developmental journalism, which restrains criticism of the state and its policies, most particularly those regarding race, redress, transformation, and affirmative action.

The notion of developmental journalism was first coined in Asia in the late 1960s (Ogan, 1980). Initially proposed as a new method of (investigative) journalism that focused on state-led development programs and policies, the concept soon became associated with "government say-so journalism" (1980: 3). This brought it into direct conflict with the principles and purveyors of traditional liberal journalism and heralded a debate that remains confused and largely unresolved.

In South Africa, the debate has gravitated into a contest over the role of the media in postapartheid society. On the one hand, the government argues that the media should be acting in the "national interest" rather than in the traditional, libertarian (and market-oriented) notion of the "public interest." The national interest conveys a more developmental approach (McQuail, 2005) in which the media are expected to support the democratic and developmental project of postapartheid South Africa. In turn the national interest is informed by Black Nationalist thought that implies striving toward equality and a redress of previous imbalances (Wasserman and De Beer, 2005). The rise of a developmentalist agenda calls to mind features of the Democratic Corporatist model in which the media, for instance, in the Scandinavian countries, have actively promoted consensus around social democratic modernization and solidarity.

In South Africa, the dispute between the public interest and the national interest was most infamously encapsulated by heated exchanges between the South African National Editors Forum and then President Thabo Mbeki (Wasserman and De Beer, 2005); it has underpinned numerous incidences of antagonism between the state and the mainstream media in South Africa since 1994 (Johnston, 2005). It also informs the government's growing irritation over criticism of its foreign and domestic policies. Finally, it places pressure on journalists of all races to embrace the government's developmental agenda and soften criticism of an authentically elected state with a democratic mandate to govern. This pressure is reinforced with a racial, cultural, and nationalistic call-to-arms. These dynamics, which are not unique to South Africa, have no weight in the Hallin-Mancini typologies.

Overall, measuring South Africa's experience against Hallin and Mancini's indicators of autonomy, it would seem evident that South Africa falls closest to the Liberal model in terms of its journalistic professionalism. However, there are clear signs of a deterioration of many of these qualities, a growing affinity with elements of the Polarized Pluralist model, and demonstrable similarities with the Democratic Corporatist model.

The Role of the State

Since 1994 a significant realignment in the relationship between the media and the state has taken place in South Africa. This was inevitable with the regime change from apartheid to democracy, but it is clear in retrospect that both media and state have struggled to come to terms with their new roles and responsibilities. The consequence has been heightened tension between the majority party in government, the African National Congress (ANC), and the media: "At best, the ANC's relationship with the political press has been distant and neurotically suspicious; at worst, pathologically hostile" (Johnston, 2005: 13). What is the basis of this hostility?

It is my contention that even though South Africa has enshrined freedom of the press into its 1996 constitution, the degree and breadth of state intervention are unequivocally on the rise. This might seem paradoxical, particularly if one is sympathetic to modernization theory. Yet the trend itself is delineated by an inherent dichotomy unique to postcolonial state formation: on the one hand, the imperative to embrace the principles and political processes of democracy, and on the other hand, the strength of values such as loyalty to or respect of tribal elders that are inimical to a prying, critical media together with a national development agenda that demands the media's co-option by an acquisitive state. At root is an understanding by the state that the media possess great social and political power. As Joel Netshitenzhe, CEO of the Government Communication and Information System, said in 2002, "Media as an institution is not a victim waiting to be abused. It is a repository of immense ideological, economic, social and political power" (cited in Wasserman and De Beer, 2005: 199–200). In the state's bid to harness all forms of power for its urgent project of social and political transformation ("the national democratic revolution" as it is termed in South Africa), the media are an obvious and indeed essential partner.

A range of interventions in the media have been attempted, embarked on, or are planned by the postapartheid South African state. Space constraints prevent a full description, but let me briefly mention several interventions. In the legislative domain, the state continues to make use of apartheid-era legislation to try to curtail media freedom (Tomaselli, 1997: 8), despite repeated requests by the media industry to have these laws repealed (Barratt, 2006). New legislation has also introduced measures that limit the media, such as the Films and Publications Amendment Bill introduced in 2008 that proposed the vetting of all newspaper and magazine content. A number of current and former senior government ministers have also launched lawsuits against media personnel and companies for invasion of privacy and defamation, among other charges. These include the former minister of health, Manto Tshabala-Msimang (suing the *Sunday Times* for breach of privacy) and President Jacob Zuma (suing Zapiro and the *Mail & Guardian* for defamation).

The state has sought to limit the media's access to official statistics and information. The repression of information concerning South Africa's controversial arms acquisition program (Feinstein, 2007), the reluctance to furnish adequate statistics on HIV/AIDS prevalence (Steinberg, 2008), and enduring efforts by the police to conceal damaging crime statistics (Mtyala, 2009) remain stand-out examples. State departments have also routinely refused journalists access to information, in spite of a specific law, the Promotion of Access to Information Act, that provides for this access within thirty days. In August 2009, South Africa's Constitutional Court ruled in favor of a journalist, Stefaans Brummer, who had been consistently denied information on a tender by the Department of Social Development – but the court process took two years (Mabuza, 2009). This denial of rights in spite of existing constitutional and legal provisions is a common tool in state relations with the media across Africa (Tettey, 2001).

The state has also attempted to compete with the media in South Africa, initially with plans to publish a daily newspaper under the auspices of the ruling party, and then, when that was prevented by party factionalism, through the launch in 2005 of the country's largest free magazine, *Vuk'uzenzele* (circulation of up to two million copies). The state has used its advertising muscle (in 2004 it was the sixth biggest advertiser in the print media [Hadland, 2007]) both to circulate its propaganda (by paying for coverage) and to guarantee its access to, for instance, the community media (Hadland and Thorne, 2004). In 2002, the state created the Media Development and Diversity Agency (MDDA), ostensibly to promote diversity in the community media sector but in reality to take a more strategic role. In 2009, the MDDA used government funds to carry out an investigation into media ownership and control in South Africa (MDDA, 2009).

State media policy since 1994 has been unashamedly interventionist, successfully as in the regulation of the broadcast sector (Teer-Tomaselli, 2004) and less so with regard to the print sector (MDDA, 2009). To correct this latter failure, the ruling party resolved at its national congress in Polokwane in late 2008 to implement a statutory media regulatory body to be known as the media tribunal. This was intended to at best augment, but in likelihood replace, the print sector's self-regulatory mechanism, the press ombudsman. The state has interfered in the generation of media content, for instance through its manipulation of the public broadcaster (Oppelt, 2008); has mobilized race and charges of racism in an attempt to shape the news agenda (the South African Human Rights Commission held controversial hearings into racism in the media in 1999), and has called on the media to embrace a developmental stance that would constrain media criticism. Finally, the state has poached senior staff from media organizations to become spokespeople for the government and has encouraged political officeholders to take up ownership and board-level positions in media companies (for instance, Parliament nominates the board of the South African Broadcasting Corporation, and it is approved by the president).

Although Hallin and Mancini's indicators focus on the likelihood of state intervention per se, *Comparing Media Systems* does not devote much time to analyzing different forms of such intervention, particularly of the coercive type in young democracies. This lack of attention is not surprising perhaps, because governments in Denmark or Great Britain are unlikely to send paramilitary police into newsrooms to sort out the editor. Sadly, this is a more common phenomenon in newer democracies, most particularly in Africa. Tettey (2001) lists a number of different forms of coercive intervention, often in blatant contravention of an African country's own legal or constitutional provisions. These at times unorthodox modes of intervention include "various acts of silent or overt reciprocity" among African governments aimed at stifling the media, corporal punishment, the use of state-owned media to discredit media critics, the passage of laws making insulting the president or members of parliament punishable offenses, and a number of "very indirect ways of hurting the media, by using the citizenry or their supporters as agents of intimidation and violence" (Tettey, 2001: 17).

We find in South Africa too a disconnect between constitutional rights and actual state practice. Within the deeply sympathetic framework of constitutional rights, many loopholes exist and countertendencies have emerged, as alluded to earlier. Although the political system has seen the establishment of a constitutional and legal framework that includes fundamental protection for a free press, it is apparent that a powerful democratic state is also more than capable of stalling, if not reversing, the process of differentiation between media and state to ensure that its own narrative is the one that predominates in the mass media.

There are elements of this analysis that may – at this stage – be uniquely South African. Yet there is also plenty of reasons to suspect that the experiences and the challenges they pose to the Hallin-Mancini paradigm may well be applicable not only to emerging democracies in Africa but also elsewhere in the world. Naturally, further comparative research involving other new democracies, particularly those emerging with authoritarian pasts and fragile presents, would be instructive.

Hallin and Mancini contend that the greater the degree of intervention by the state, the further away the media system is from the Liberal model. In the Democratic Corporatist model, high levels of intervention are common, although they do not necessarily affect autonomy because of the presence of strong rational-legal authority. In the Polarized Pluralist model, interventions can have a much stronger influence on autonomy, because they commonly signal a partisan public administration and judicial system, a patron-based distribution system for social resources, and a highly divided and contested political terrain served by an equally divided and partisan media.

South Africa would appear to be a mix of all three models. It has a significant and increasing degree of state intervention, but relatively strong rational-legal authority, and does not have the partisan public administration or judicial system of the Polarized Pluralist model. Emerging democracies, as diverse as they can be, appear to present a different category of democracy in which inherent or traditional values militate against the kind of drift toward the Liberal model described in *Comparing Media Systems*. In South Africa's case, this resistance toward greater liberalism is strengthened by a lack of accountability within the political architecture. The consequence has been an increasing concentration of power in the executive arm of government (Gumede, 2005) that is by no means typical of the differentiated media and political systems populating the Liberal model. This lends credence, furthermore, to critics' concerns (as well as to Hallin and Mancini's own anxiety) that the dynamics of power is an underrepresented concept within the three-model paradigm.

On Africanizing a Model of Media–State Relations

The application of the South African case study to the Hallin-Mancini paradigm has generated a number of challenges. Most notably, South Africa is a poor fit for any of the three models, a square peg faced by three round holes. Are these characteristics unique to South Africa, or can we begin to sketch a model of media–state relations that is regional or even African?

South Africa, as firmly as it is physically rooted to the geographical landmass that is Africa, has long pondered its connections, identity, and role on the continent as a whole. As much as racism and subjugation were features of Africa's colonial relations, only South Africa developed colonialism into the fully fledged and formal notion of apartheid. Only South Africa has formally indigenized its erstwhile colonial oppressors into a new national identity. This alone seems to confer uniqueness to a country that has also long enjoyed an infrastructural and economic advantage over its neighbors and indeed over most of the continent. I would argue that South Africa, just like every other country on the continent, has features and dimensions that are unique to its own history. This diversity does not diminish the clear and overarching commonalities that all African countries share. In fact these commonalities have fueled decades of pan-African theorizing, a notion that is once again gathering prominence and currency. I therefore can neither condone South Africa's extraction from the continent nor the design of a model of media–state interrelationships that is exclusively or uniquely South African. Instead, I claim that, collectively speaking, Africa has a contribution to make to the Hallin-Mancini hypothesis and that fertile ground exists for the design of an alternate model or models populated by the experiences and dynamics of postcolonial African democracies.

Some work has already begun in this area, with Bratton and Van der Walle (1997), Diamond (2002), and Nisbet and Moehler (2005) proposing typologies of African political regimes. Furthermore, Nisbet and Moehler (2005) have proposed five models of political communication systems applicable in sub-Saharan Africa: open democratic, liberalized democratic, liberalized autocratic, closed autocratic, and repressive autocratic. They base these models on the type of political regime, together with the degree of press freedom and of control exerted on media organizations within legal, political, and economic domains (2005: 14).

The typologies are a useful starting point even though, as Nisbet and Moehler concede, they are powerfully path dependent and seek to find linkages among media infrastructure, socioeconomic development, and type of regime that cannot be proven. Nonetheless the Nisbet-Moehler typologies are a reminder that, even within sub-Saharan Africa, the diversity of political regimes and of media systems makes the construction of ideal types an ambitious objective. This challenge is made more evident when confronted by the lack of empirical data, which makes comparative studies difficult either within the subcontinent or beyond. If we were to rely solely on quantitative data to make progress with theorizing on media–state typologies in Africa, we would have to wait a long time before any compelling conclusions could be drawn. Even South Africa, arguably the most developed country on the continent, last carried out a census almost ten years ago.

Although geographic proximity is not uniform across the models, Hallin and Mancini do argue that this variable is often a relevant factor in assembling media system clusters. Africa clearly has a collective geographic coherence. Given the diverse set of political systems and media sectors that Africa evidently contains, we may have to rely on thematic commonalities to sketch a model that would seem to capture the most important features of the continent's media–state relationship.

Just as in the original three-model paradigm, an African-based model of media–state relations would necessarily be an ideal type. It would therefore not be reflective of every trend and nuance, and contradictions would not perforce rule the model inoperative. Just as Germany is classified under the Democratic Corporatist model in spite of a host of features that would suggest otherwise, so Ghana, South Africa, and Egypt can be clustered even if individual elements of each of these systems might militate against a collective model.

Let us consider whether an African-based model of media and state might be a useful addition to the analysis. Is there anything different, even unique, about Africa that might not be applicable, for instance, to other nations of the global South? Can any form of homogeneity be conferred on a continent as diverse, complex, and interconnected as Africa? Are there similarities in the evolution of democracy in an African context that differ substantially and critically from those in other parts of the world, not least in the more mature systems of the global North?

A number of studies point both to the uniqueness and to the coherence of the experiences, values, and architecture of politics on the African continent (Bratton and Van der Walle, 1997; Lindberg, 2006; Piombo, 2005). In a study of 101 elections in thirty-six African countries, Shaheen Mozaffar (2006) argues that the structure of the party system in African countries is unique: "The data shows that African party systems area typically concentrated around a small number of parties, and often around a single dominant party surrounded by many small parties. The data also shows that concentrated party systems persist in the face of high levels of electoral and legislative volatility."[2] This is puzzling because

---

[2] Mozaffar defines electoral and legislative volatility as follows: "Electoral volatility refers to the net change in the distribution of votes, and legislative volatility refers to the net change in the distribution of seats, between political parties from one election to the next" (2006: 1).

in most regions of the world, high levels of volatility typically coincide with fragmented party systems." She offers a number of explanations for this apparent "anomaly," including Africa's ethno-political demography, its historical legacies, a range of institutional variables, and the political skills and strategies of its politicians (Mozaffar, 2006: 7–8).

In his brilliant and seminal work *Citizen and Subject* (1996), Mahmood Mamdani also argues the case for Africa's unique and coherent character. "I seek to establish the historical legitimacy of Africa as a unit of analysis," he claims in the work. Mamdani argues that Africa was the last part of the world to be colonized. The lessons learned in the process of older colonial conquests, such as in India and Indochina, were applied to Africa but with a key difference. Where initially colonization took place in part for trade and to "civilize," in the last period – the so-called scramble for Africa – the purpose became the consolidation and preservation of political and economic power (1996: 286). This resulted in a unique process of colonization and in "a specifically African form of the state" (1996: 286):

> To grasp the specificity of colonial domination of Africa, one needs to place it within the context of Europe's larger colonizing experience. The trajectory of the wider experience, particularly as it tried to come to grips with the fact of resistance, explains its midstream shift in perspective from the zeal of a civilizing mission to a calculated preoccupation with holding power, from rejuvenating to conserving society, from being the torchbearers of individual freedom to being custodians protecting the customary integrity of dominated tribes. This shift took place in older colonies, mainly India and Indochina, but its lessons were fully implemented in Africa, Europe's last colonial possession. (Mamdani, 1996: 287)

The principal characteristic of this unique African state was its bifurcated nature. On the one hand, the state exerted power over urban areas using the language and principles of civil society and civil rights; on the other hand it imposed authority over rural areas using customary law and culture.

Although African countries were reformed in a diverse number of ways in the postindependence period, according to Mamdani, the result was more or less the same: "No nationalist government was content to reproduce the colonial legacy uncritically. Each sought to reform the bifurcated state that institutionally crystallized a state-enforced separation of the rural from the urban and of one ethnicity from another. But in so doing each reproduced a part of that legacy, thereby creating its own variety of despotism" (1996: 8).

The features of this postcolonial African model include the preponderance of a dominant single party, a state-sponsored initiative to deracialize civil society and to redistribute its benefits, the exacerbation of interethnic tensions, attempts to detribalize local government, economic development within a context of unequal international relations, the rise of clientelism, a growing gulf between the urban and the rural, and serious obstacles to democratization. Indeed, Mamdani characterizes "deracialisation without democratization" as "a uniquely African outcome" (1996: 32). All of these factors are important when contemplating media–state relations within what Mamdani argues is a unique and coherent African context.

For instance, ethnicity is by no means an African issue, but it does hold great pertinence, as Mamdani suggests, in so many realms of public life on the African continent – from public administration and formal party politics to the distribution of scarce resources – that its presence has to be both acknowledged and assessed. A recent study of the Kenyan press (Ismail and Deane, 2008) identified the local media's exacerbation of ethnic tensions as one of the primary triggers of postelection violence after that country's most recent national elections. Ethnicity matters in Africa and reaches deep into the media and into the state, often shaping the relationship between the two (Cruise O'Brien, 1999).

Furthermore Mamdani argues that South Africa is far from an exceptional case and indeed clearly illustrates the fracturing of ruled peoples that lies at the heart of the postcolonial African bifurcated state: "Apartheid, usually considered the exceptional feature in the South African experience, is actually its one aspect that is uniquely African" (1996: 27). He suggests that postcolonial African states seesaw between centralizing power in a bid to detribalize local government (centralized despotism) and decentralizing power in an effort to deemphasize the urban–rural fracture (decentralized despotism). The label of despotism clearly argues that democratization is far from operational within the model.

Mamdani presents one view, but it is clear that, at this historical juncture, scholars are revisiting the nature of the state in Africa and elsewhere. Santos argues that the "suicide of neo-liberalism" heralded by the global economic meltdown of 2008 has prompted a profound reevaluation of the role and function of the state (Santos, 2008). The market, he argues, has shown itself incapable of regulating a democratic and humane polity effectively, and state intervention has become necessary in even the most liberal of economies.

The African state, dismissed by scholars for decades by a range of negative adjectives ranging from predatory to corrupt, has ironically come to offer within its modus operandi an alternate and stable instrument for development (Olukoshi, 2008). The developmental state is gaining ground just as the laissez-faire Washington consensus is losing it. Although the limitations and weaknesses of the African state in its current format are evident, profoundly affected as they are by colonial legacies, powerful elites, global corporate power, and racial and ethnic cleavages, the interventionist nature and inclination of the African development state are clear.

Similarly the values and culture that underpin African states, which were, more often than not, established as Santos argues by top-down constitutional formation processes (as opposed to the bottom-up process of Latin American states), exert a profound influence within emerging democratic polities. Where, for instance, is the place of ancestors in the three-model paradigm? Where is religion? Where are different languages and how do they collude and collide? Where is ethnicity? Where are the pluri-nationalisms; migrant, transitory populations; and pan-Africanism that loom so large in the discourse and in the realities of contemporary African life?

Like the Habermasian public, the Hallin-Mancini framework is predicated on bourgeois rationality and on assumptions and values that are not dominant within what might be an African model. New technologies and developments within the media, such as the explosion of local community radio and of cell phone usage, offer a range of new potentialities around social cohesion, mobilization, and resistance. They also offer destructive possibilities that may exacerbate ethnic, racial, and national cleavages, which could do much to reverse or even undermine democratic consolidation altogether. How does the Hallin-Mancini model cope with a country that can at best be only loosely described as democratic or alternatively with a country that once was democratic but that has now fallen, perhaps temporarily, into a state of autocracy, crisis, or war? If a model (or set of models) based on African media–state experience were to be created, what would be its features in the conceptual framework of *Comparing Media Systems*?

The African media landscape has strong features of political parallelism, with media products, ownership, and audiences frequently reflecting ethnic, linguistic, racial, or clientelist features. There is often a direct link between journalists and politicians or businesspeople with strong political affiliations. Professionalism is generally low and is affected by a lack of resources for training, poor educational systems, and weak journalistic organization. In many African countries there is a strong sense of the importance of the media's Fourth Estate functions, which is reflected in numerous instances of great bravery and resilience. Media regulation and control, through press councils, tribunals, or government structures, are usually tight, with journalists subject to a broad range of legislative, regulatory, political, and sociocultural restraints. Journalists are often imprisoned or otherwise victimized. State intervention is pervasive and diverse. This invasiveness is based on the growing demands of an acquisitive, if democratic, state commonly dominated by one political party or movement. This dominant party overwhelms media agendas, media narratives, and the extent and topics of debate within the public domain. It considers the media not just an important, but an essential and even natural tool, in the consolidation and extension of its hegemonic power. This is in spite of the party's public and often historic commitment to democracy and the constitutional and legislative enshrinement of the freedom of the press.

Conclusion

In this chapter I attempted to locate South Africa's media–state system in the existing three-model paradigm and found it sits comfortably in none of the models. Perhaps its closest match is the Polarized Pluralist model, in keeping with other developing or emerging democracies cited in this volume, but the fit is inexact at best. I have found features that do not match this model and that are more closely tied to the Democratic Corporatist or Liberal models. I began in this chapter to examine the basis for an alternate, possibly African, model, and although this new model is far from fully formed, I hope these introductory observations do not preclude the possibility. Certainly scholars have begun to toy around with typologies that might allow comparative work among regimes and media systems in the subcontinent, even given the paucity of quantitative data.

At first glance, there does seem to be sufficient evidence for enough homogeneity among African states, enough shared historical experience, a sufficiently communal pool of values and culture, and also a range of obstacles, risks, and challenges held in common to justify the conceptualization of an African-based model or models. There will inevitably be overlaps with the three current models and a dialectic perhaps with new models being developed that speak to the experience of countries in Eastern Europe and in Asia. In the end, such a model will assist not only in locating Africa within the Hallin-Mancini paradigm but will also allow the countries within the African model to evaluate their own trajectories of development relative to the countries of the North and to each other.

7

The Russian Media Model in the Context of Post-Soviet Dynamics

Elena Vartanova

Studies of Russian society have traditionally highlighted the particularity of the country's historical path and the irregular, irrational nature of Russian culture (Kangaspuro, 1999). Scholars have described Russia as characterized by numerous contradictory features. Not surprisingly, the nature and structure of the modern Russian media system reflect political, economic, and sociocultural developments deeply rooted in the country's history.

During the two last centuries Russia has experienced a permanent transition:

- from an agrarian society and imperial monarchy in the early nineteenth century
- to a rapid, though uneven growth of capitalism and rise of a diverse party system under the rule of an authoritarian ruler (tsar) in the second half of the nineteenth century (interrupted by World War I early in the twentieth century)
- to a short-lived bourgeois multiparty democracy in February–October 1917
- to the socialist revolution (early twentieth century), resulting in the emergence of the Communist Party monopoly and state-controlled planned economy and eventually to years of "mature socialist democracy" characterized by economic recession and degradation of political communication to propaganda
- to a "perestroika" (reconstruction), as a policy of top-down Communist Party reforms that resulted in the collapse of the USSR

- to the establishment of Russia as an independent state accompanied by
  a liberalization process and the introduction of a market economy and
  political systems inspired by "Western" models of liberal democracies

The cultural context and the character of Russian social institutions
and their interrelationships have had serious effects on the media and
journalism model, producing different outcomes as compared to Hallin
and Mancini's three models of media and politics (2004b). This chapter
describes the particular features of the Russian media model using the
major determinants of *Comparing Media Systems*, compares it with the
models proposed in that book, and explores the concept of homogenization as applied to the Russian media system.

Formal Laws versus Informal Norms

Along with Hallin and Mancini other authors have analyzed the interplay between the major driving forces of media systems and their roles
and functions in the society. Nordenstreng and Paasilinna (2002: 194)
refer to the state, the market, and civil society as agents shaping a media
model. McQuail (2005: 220) argues that media always are at the center of three overlapping kinds of pressures – economics, politics, and
technology – that shape media structure, conduct, and performance. To
these pressures Curran and Seaton add "culture" by stressing the role of
national traditions, public opinion, and society (Curran and Seaton, 1997:
326).

The last point seems important for understanding media systems in
their respective national contexts, and the emphasis on culture and traditions and their impact on interrelations between a society and its institutions, including the media system, is crucial to explaining the wide diversity of media models produced by the same set of variables. Hallin and
Mancini's analysis has proven that even among "most similar systems,"
characterized by "relatively comparable levels of economic development
and much common culture and political history" (Hallin and Mancini,
2004b: 6), it is possible to observe the formation of at least three different models characterized by distinct national circumstances and distinct
historical, cultural, and intellectual traditions.

The reasonable way to construct media and journalism models in diver-
gent or the most different economic and sociocultural contexts would
be not to mechanically apply Hallin and Mancini's three models globally, but instead to look at outcomes and peculiarities produced by the

evolutionary logic of the media systems and the interplay of the major variables identified by Hallin and Mancini. A valuable point here comes from North's approach to institutional economics:

> It is the admixture of formal rules, informal norms, and enforcement characteristics that shapes economic performance. While the rules may be changed overnight, the informal norms usually change only gradually. Since it is the norms that provide "legitimacy" to a set of rules, revolutionary change is never as revolutionary as its supporters desire. . . . The implication is that transferring the formal political and economic rules of successful Western market economies to Third World and Eastern European economies is not a sufficient condition for good economic performance. Privatization is not a panacea for solving poor economic performance. (North, 1994:366)

This approach highlights the fact that in transitional economies legal statutes and formal rules often have been disturbed by influential informal practices such as norms of behavior and self-imposed codes of practice. Interactions between the formalized structures and nonformalized norms might produce conflicting, contradictory, and inefficient outcomes in different societies.

In the early 1990s the Russian media system was transformed in the context of the construction of new political and economic institutions – open competitive elections, the end of the Communist Party monopoly, a formal decrease in state influence over the national economy and sociocultural institutions, and the introduction of a market economy. It appeared as though the Russian media had at the same true borrowed many features from an ideal "Western" model, including abolition of censorship, freedom of press concepts and related legislation, privatization of media, a shift to more objective reporting, and increasing control by journalists and editorial boards over news production. However, the deliberate rhetorical orientation of political and media elites toward Western media simply masked a poor understanding of the complexity and dissimilarities of the post-Soviet society, which did not permit the media system to duplicate or efficiently reconstruct the Western experience. Political and cultural circumstances in Russia – for example, the set of informal rules and enforcement practices – significantly differed from European and North American realities. Therefore the transformation of post-Soviet media systems could not be explained as a linear and universal movement toward an imaginary and uncritically understood ideal Western media model. Splichal has defined revolutions in Eastern European media systems as imitations (Splichal, 2001). Gross has used the notion of resemblance, which implied superficial (or misleading) similarity (Gross, 2004: 112, 119).

The most evident political pressures on Western media systems are found in Southern Europe where media are "closely aligned to politics" and their activity is determined by political considerations (Papatheodorou and Machin, 2003: 39). A similar point is also made by media research in Central and Eastern European countries: "Like their Southern European counterparts, they also display features of 'state paternalism,' or indeed 'political clientelism'..., i.e. the situation when politics pervades and influences many social systems" (Jakubowicz, 2007b: 304). However, even compared with "most similar cases" of "state paternalism" or "political clientelism" in postsocialist systems, there exist considerable differences that should be explained by the diversity of informal constraints in national environments. The role of the state in the Russian media system as formulated by Ivanitsky (2009: 114) substantially differs from its role in Southern or Central Europe:

For centuries journalism as a social institution in Russia has been developed free from economic considerations while the role of the economic regulator has been carried out by the state which in turn secured the paternalistic foundations in the journalism. According to this hypothesis, it was the state which defined the particular journalism modes such as Court journalism, Imperial journalism, Communist Party journalism.... However, the state while liberating the economic activity in the media was not ready to relax the control over the content. This has produced practically unsolvable tension for the media themselves trying to function both as commercial enterprises and as institutions of the society.

The main focus of media system analysis in Russia should be on interrelations between "the state" taken as a theoretical and cultural concept, as the quintessence of power in Russia, and other institutions, both old and new, such as the market economy, political parties, certain state agencies and agents, and the journalistic profession.

Attempts to Conceptualize the Russian Media Model

As Russia has passed through its postsocialist transformations, its national media system has been influenced by the multifaceted dynamics of the transitional period. This transition has involved complicated processes of establishing a new political culture, economic institutions, and commercialization driven by a profit-making economic logic of the market economy. Yet because new political institutions and economic structures were not accompanied by systematic change in everyday cultural practices, the struggle for the redistribution of power and economic wealth among new elites made transformations in media in Russia as well as in many post-Soviet states more a "democratic civic masquerade" (Gross, 2004: 113) than real (r)evolution. Institutional change – for example, the adoption of new media and advertising laws, public declarations by decision makers in support for press freedom – has been accompanied by old rituals in relations among politicians, new media owners, journalists, and audiences (McCormack, 1999).

Media and Market: Press Developments in Post-Soviet Russia
Changes in the media started with the adoption of the Law on Mass Media (1991) that reaffirmed the inadmissibility of censorship (article 3) and guaranteed unlimited (except by existing legislation) freedom to seek, obtain, produce, and disseminate information; to found media outlets; and to own, use, and manage them (article 1). The crucial provision was that which allowed the establishment and operation of nonstate-owned (private) media.

The erosion of the old system began with the process of privatization in the media industry in 1992. Media dependence on advertising has resulted in the emergence of new business models, which have promoted more media products and commercialization of the content market (McNair, 2000). In the late 1990s–2000s the annual growth of the advertising market provided media with resources to support nonpolitical general-interest tabloids, the development of FM radio, and the rapid evolution of private entertainment TV channels. The progress of the media market has been directly linked to improvement of the economic situation and an increase in living standards of Russians in the early 2000s. In turn this has stimulated national advertising; ads for new domestically produced items like cosmetics, food, and beverages began to dominate in TV, radio, and print media.

Russia has become one of the four most rapidly growing advertising markets in the world and comprises part of the economically economically attractive group of BRIC countries: Brazil, Russia, India, and China. The annual growth of the Russian advertising market in recent decades was about 30 percent, which is quite atypically high for more mature media markets. The financial crisis of 2008–9 has demonstrated the increased dependence of Russian media on advertising, as the recession in the advertising market has resulted in the decline of print media circulation, job cuts in newsrooms, and closure of media outlets.

TABLE 7.1. *Changes in Newspapers' Circulation in Russian Federation from the 1980s–2000s*

	Circulation		
Newspapers	Mid-2000s	Mid-1990s	Mid-1980s
Argumenti i Fakti (weekly)	2,900,000	2,802,584	33,500,000
Komsomolskaya Pravda (daily)	1,925,000	683,391	17,000,000
Sovetsky Sport (daily)	508,800	No data	5,000,000
Trud (daily)	374,700	No data	18,000,000
Izvestiya (daily)	371,400	464,930	8,000,000
Sovetskaya Rossiya (daily)	300,000	199,216	4,500,000
Pravda (daily)	100,300	96,103	11,000,000
Selskaya zhizn (daily)	92,000	1,000,000	10,000,000

Source: Ovsepyan (1999).

The structure of the Russian media system has dramatically changed since the early 1990s and the country's transition period. The hierarchical national newspaper system began to be transformed into a horizontally organized regional/local press market dominated by nonpolitical local publications. The major trend in the newspaper market was the repositioning of former communist or Komsomol (Communist Youth League) dailies as popular newspapers targeted at the largest possible audience. As a result, the most successful papers, such as the national *Komsomolskaya Pravda* or the Moscow-based *MK/Moskovskyi Komsomoletz*, managed to reestablish themselves as circulation leaders at the national and regional (Moscow) level with obvious characteristics as politically scandalous tabloids.

In 2008, the overall circulation of the Russian press was 7.8 billion copies (see Table 7.1). Of these, 2.7 billion copies represented the national dailies, 2.6 billion the regional press, and 2.5 billion the local press. The overall number of titles has increased significantly from 4,863 (1991) to 5,758 (2000), yet total newspaper circulation has radically dropped from 160.2 to 108.8 million (a 67.9 percent decrease), with the share of nationally distributed newspapers falling to 36 percent. Among the key reasons for this dramatic decrease was the ruination of the postal distribution system. The Russian press market is divided between quality dailies, which are mostly business oriented, and popular newspapers tending to tabloidization. In 2008, the overall audience for Russian national dailies was about 11.3 percent of the urban population, whereas the overall audience for national and business weeklies was about 24.2 percent of the urban population (Rossiiskyi rynok periodicheskoi pechati, 2009: 17).

With the dramatic decline in newspaper circulation has come the replacement of the print media by television at the top of the media hierarchy. Since the mid-1990s, TV has become the leading mass medium. About 94 percent of Russians watch TV every day, and 99 percent of Russian households have at least one TV set: About two-thirds have color sets, but 45 percent still possess black-and-white sets. In 2006, the authorities issued 14,290 broadcast licenses, but the core of the national TV market is made up of nine channels available to more than 50 percent of the population. Russian TV is a mixture of two models, one being state controlled and the other purely commercial, with the state both formally and informally remaining the major actor in the TV sector. Regardless of ownership structure, Russian TV is financed primarily by advertising and sponsorship (De Smaele and Vartanova, 2007). Radio is another rapidly growing segment of the Russian commercial media system; the number of stations has increased both because of advances in commercial music radio broadcasting and fragmentation of the audience.

The growth of media markets has introduced greater competition and new challenges to the instrumental use of media by politicians. As audiences came to enjoy a growing variety of media channels, targeted to diverse, fragmented audiences, the potential for manipulation and abuse of public opinion began to decrease. Although for years the Russian political elite remained a major player in shaping frameworks of political communication, Russian media gradually began to experience new pressures from audiences. It responded with well-known strategies of tabloidization, infotainment, and the expansion of popular entertainment formats addressed to a mass audience (Fomicheva, 2005). The new values of commercializing Russian media have gone hand in hand both with the global advertising industry's attempts to stimulate consumption and with the wishes of the Russian political elite to safeguard political stability and secure the loyalty of the electorate. Searching for viable economic models, the Russian media have come a long way from the Soviet past, although not in the direction expected in the early years of glasnost (Sparks, 1998).

This process of change has not followed the same path as the rise of the mass-circulation press in Northern Europe or North America, which made available a vertical process of communication to mediate between political elites and ordinary citizens (Hallin and Mancini, 2004b: 22). This different trajectory can be explained by differences in historical and social developments between Russia and the West. The birth of the mass press in the West was the result of rapid economic development brought about by industrial capitalism, urbanization, progress in mass literacy, and an increase in political participation in the context of still immature media systems. Although the Russian political system tried to copy media models of the Western European democratic societies, at least superficially, the entire sociopolitical context and culture of political communication in Russia were different. The transition of the Russian economy from a planned, state-controlled, and highly ideologized system to a market system was followed by economic depression, the loss of societal unity, disappointment in politics and economic reforms, and a moral crisis in society. The high educational level of the population achieved in the previous Soviet period could not guarantee rapid economic growth based on consumption, and reformation of the political system could not be translated into an increase in living standards. Consequently, the high political activity of Russians in the mid- to the late 1980s turned to social apathy in the mid-1990s, and values of individual success and hedonistic lifestyles became popular among Russians, making their life values similar to those of Western Europeans (Goryainov, 2009: 114).

To a great degree the state of Russian mass-circulation newspapers reflects these social dynamics. The repositioning of Russian newspapers in the 1990s did not result in the establishment of new segments of political newspapers or the imposition of new political agendas on existing dailies that would have produced new modes of political communication. On the contrary, the newspapers were characterized by severe crises that led either to increased political sponsorship and manipulative use of newspapers or to growing sensationalism. The construction of Russian free-market capitalism on the wreckage of Soviet-type socialism involved the reestablishment of the state bureaucracy as a major agent of economic life and the subsequent integration of the emerging market and the state. Indeed, as McNair correctly describes Russian transformations in the 1990s, "the result was the creation of a hybrid (hyper) capitalism" (McNair, 2000: 82) having a clear statist color.

Privatization of former state (and Communist Party) property was controlled by state officials, many of whom were the same people in office before the political transformation. During the 1990s – the decade of intensive integration of the Russian state and business – new elites mixed the old rituals of the power elite with aggressive strategies of new business leaders in attempts to privatize the most lucrative pieces of state property. Thus, an important outcome of the development of Russian post-Soviet capitalism became the rise of the "media-industrial complex" comprised of several influential clans and driven by new integrated political and business elites backed by the state. A particular area of business interest of these clans was media whose ownership allowed "the complex" (e.g., the Russian power elite) to exert an enormous degree of influence on the media system and media policy (Khlebnikov, 2001; Puppae, 2000). For many large media companies, profit-making motives, although important in the context of the emerging media industry, became clearly subordinated to the political interests of their owners or political "controllers," who instrumentally used them during election campaigns until the end of the 1990s.

The new vision of the state as a core of national identity emerged after the election of Vladimir Putin as the Russian president in 2000, which became a landmark in the development of the media market as well. The presidential administration reinforced control over political programs on national (federal) TV channels, and mass-circulation newspapers lost to national television not only as advertising venues but also as actors in the political process. The defeat of media oligarchs seen as to disloyal the political elite, such as Beresovsky and Gousinsky, made the Russian media industry more competitive and transparent, but content remained commercially attractive and politically risk-free. In the conditions of a market-driven economy affected by the rise of an integrated political-economic elite and low political activity of voters, the development of the mass-circulation press in Russia could not follow the same lines as described in Hallin and Mancini's analysis: It could not form a system that would integrate a mass public into a process of democratic political competition. After the collapse of the daily Soviet newspaper system, Russia's new regional/local press was either highly commercialized and sensationalized or instrumentalized by informal state–business alliances.

Media and Political Parties: Parallelism in the Russian Way

The modern Russian media system has deep roots in Russia's national history. Its origins were laid down by the birth of the first Russian newspaper, *Vedomosti* (1703), when the Russian political elite realized the potentials of print periodicals as an essential means of social management. *Vedomosti*, set up by Tsar Peter the Great after his European trip, was intended to become a tool for elite communication. For centuries thereafter, the Russian political system was managed in a top-down way by the ruling bureaucracy, and Russian power structures did not include political parties. Some researchers claim that, until the end of the nineteenth century the societal need for political parties was weak, and only the development of the working-class Social Democratic movement at that time pushed forward the formation of its bourgeois alternatives (Zassoursky and Esin, 2003).

The role of the newspaper in constructing a political party system was formulated for the first time by the Bolshevik leader Vladimir Lenin. He emphasized the political newspaper as the core of the infrastructure of a mass political party: "[T]he first step towards creating desired organization... should be the founding of an All-Russian political newspaper.... Without a political organ, a political movement deserving this name is inconceivable in the Europe of today" (Lenin, 1901). Lenin attached three basic functions to the political media: propaganda, agitation, and organization. However, he relied on the Russian paternalistic tradition that subordinated journalism to the political elite, and laid down the foundations of "one-party democracy," which was subsequently supported by the media system. Pivovarov (2002) argues that Lenin, as a "demiurge of a new order," enormously influenced Russian political culture of the following century, which later led to some common features between the Soviet authoritarian and the functionalist (McQuail, 2005: 98–9) media concepts: Both described mobilization (organization) and integration and cooperation (agitation) as key media functions.

A short period characterized by the rise of a multiparty press system in February–October 1917 was unable to provide a basis for a tradition of political debates and the party press, especially because that press system was soon ended by the October Communist revolution. However, until the late 1920s the concept of Bolshevik/communist press freedom did permit internal debates in the Communist Party, which could be assessed as a forum of political communication of different political views within the framework of one ideology. This political communication represented more than merely intra-party disputes, but rather debates of different political movements that existed under the umbrella of the non-united Communist Party. Only after the new economic policy (NEP) ended in 1928–9 and the overall monopoly of Communist Party ideology was established did the short-lived, weak tradition of public political debates vanish for decades. The ideological monopoly of the Communist Party during the years of rapid economic growth made the idea of a multiparty press completely impossible.

Soviet modernization, which was accomplished during the twentieth century in several waves – in the NEP years, in the 1930s–'50s, and in the 1960s–'80s – encompassed features of the Western modernization process in the field of economics, but not in politics. Vishnevsky (2010: 36) argues that the Soviet conservative modernization "permitted the USSR to accept and even implement many instrumental achievements of the Western societies (modern technologies, some forms of life styles, science, education, etc.) but could not create adequate social mechanisms of their self-development (such as market economy, modern social structure, civil society institutions, political democracy, etc.)." The introduction of a free press model as glasnost media policy in the mid-1980s might be seen as the first attempt to bring about some form of autonomously developing modernity.

Beginning in the early 1990s the Russian media system enthusiastically welcomed social change as an alternative to the existing ideological monopoly of the state and Communist Party elites, in the expectation of more freedom and independence in media performance. The 1990s were characterized by the emergence of new political parties, which laid the foundations for new conditions for political pluralism:

The collapse of the Soviet Union and the creation of the Russian federation forced both Russian political parties and the media to forge a new relationship in a post-Soviet society.... Rather than encouraging the growth and the development of a range of political parties, media outlets in Russia have worked at supporting relatively narrow groups of elites. While the growth of political parties has stalled, at the same time the presidential administration and other powerful bureaucracies have improved their ability to create, market and win elections for a chosen few political parties and presidential candidates. (Oates, 2006: 66)

In these new political conditions both old political and emerging business elites became key players in the media scene, creating a particularly Russian form of political parallelism. In this form of political clientelism a young, integrated state–business elite has supported the use of political media in new circumstances as traditional instruments of political elite management. Russian "media–political clientelism" was characterized by the sale of media advocacy skills to competing political-economic groups who "sorely wanted them for reputation management and electoral campaign success" (Roudakova, 2008: 43). This relationship's lack of durability and its instability testified to the less political and ideological than commercial motivations of journalists and media organizations, especially at regional and local levels (Roudakova, 2008: 44).

Some media scholars have argued that in the 1990s the role that used to be played in democratic election processes by political parties in Russia was taken over by television. Since 1993 the major national TV channels – ORT and NTV in particular – have mobilized the electorate to a much higher degree than any other political organization. The Russian journalist Rykovtseva has proposed the term "airwaves (or broadcast) party" for the role of television, "pointing out that parties that do not exist outside of a stream of flickering electronic images are . . . merely a reflection of the popularity of television rather than a real political phenomenon" (cited in Oates, 2006: 80).

During the first years of transition most Russians remained passive in constructing new political parties. On the one hand, the longstanding tradition of a political party monopoly stimulated attempts of elites to construct a similar dominant mass political party from above – Russia's Choice (1993), Our Home is Russia (1995), Unity (1999), and United Russia (2003). Most of the attempts failed, because many Russians were disillusioned with pressures coming from elites in shaping Russian politics. The growing individualization of Russians left people alienated from real politics beginning in the mid-1990s. Manipulation of public opinion during presidential and parliamentary election campaigns in 1996, 1999–2000, and 2004 – known as the "information wars" of the late 1990s – made Russians critical of the media's role in the political process and of the interrelations between media and "broadcast" political parties in organizing elections. As Oates argues,

[T]he Russian media, particularly television, have been used to subvert development of a pluralistic party system, with appealing broadcast campaigns outpacing the growth of responsible parties that are accountable to the electorate. As a result, these ephemeral "broadcast" parties and candidates increasingly are able to win votes at the cost of more accountable parties and candidates. (Oates, 2006: 66)

One important dimension of media models and political parallelism is the connection between public broadcasting and the political system. Hallin and Mancini (2004b: 30) describe several models of this relationship, including the government model characterized by direct government control or control by the political majority. This is certainly the closest model to the Russian case, although the philosophy and values of public service broadcasting (PSB) had never been legally or even publicly declared in Russia. Several attempts have been made to introduce the concept of public service into the practices of Russian broadcasting. The privatization of the national broadcaster *Ostankino* and its conversion into a national shareholding company Obshestvennoye Rossiskoye Televideniye (Public Russian Television [ORT]) were "only used to roughly mask mixed state–corporate exploitation of ORT with the dual goal of promoting the influence of the political elite by establishing tough controls over public opinion and garnering commercial profits through uncontrolled transmission of advertising" (Vartanova and Zassoursky, 2003: 98).

Thus, the role of media in the construction of Russian political parties has been limited, although still instrumental. Media were used to promote the interests of emerging elites, some of whom tried to legitimize themselves as political parties. Even conflicts and "information wars" in the Russian media in early 2000s served more as "a means of intra-elite, rather than mass communication" (Roudakova, 2008: 44). New independent political parties failed because the crucial force in the Russian political power game has remained the state.

Media and the State

The relationship between the state and media in Russia has always defined the nature, main features, and conditions of the media system (Akhmadullin, 2000: 26). Trachtenberg points to the fact that "relations with the state and society and a broad cultural context within which the Russian media had been developing had nothing in common with the 1st Amendment to the USA Constitution. Moreover, these relations have nothing in common with the whole Anglo-American tradition that sees proper functioning of the mass media as a fundamental element of civil society and of the system of representative democracy" (Trachtenberg, 2007: 122).

In Russian public communications, relations between the state and a citizen have involved a clear subordination of the individual to a social power that has always been associated in the Russian context with the state. As Count Uvarov, the minister of education of Nicolas I, said, a Russian citizen had no right to address the public freely. It was a privilege given by the state and taken by the state (cited in Trachtenberg, 2007: 123). The Western European/American idea of a social contract that implied the mutual responsibility of state power and mass media for society had taken in the Russian context a nationally specific form in which the state did not need an intermediary between itself and society and the society did not consider itself as something autonomous and independent from the state. Moreover, by tradition Russians have viewed the state through the dichotomy "we–they" and believed it to be something alien to the nature of ordinary people. At the same time they viewed it as a sacral force, a guarantor of the unity and the very existence of the Russian nation and society. Scholars have emphasized that paternalistic relations between citizens and power elites, and between people and their leader, are deeply embedded in the Russian character and define the nature of Russian political and media culture (Batalov, 2002).

This orientation conflicts with a notion of rational-legal authority proposed by Weber and developed by Hallin and Mancini as an institution "to be relatively autonomous from control by government, parties, and particular politicians, and to be governed by clear rules and procedures" (Hallin and Mancini, 2004b: 56). They argue that the degree of instrumentalization in media systems diminishes in societies with stronger rational-legal authority. In the Russian case many concepts that make sense in the West European cultural context have been inapplicable. Neither the state nor the public have supported clear and transparent rules for the media, as they have for other political and social institutions. Russians perceive media as an essential part of the power structure and traditionally "see themselves as media subjects, without the rights of either media citizens or media consumers" (Oates, 2006: 192). This is a consequence of the tradition of people's subordination to the state and their simultaneous alienation from it, the contradiction that governs the relationships of ordinary Russians and the state. Post-Soviet changes in the media system were aimed to liberate the media from top-down, official (Communist Party and the state) control, introduce political diversity, privatize media ownership, and promote new professional values (Jakubowicz, 1995: 127; Paasilinna, 1995). Of all aims the most difficult to realize has been the state's withdrawal from the media. It was difficult partly because during the last two decades the Russian state has changed several times its attitudes to the media, as well as its goals and media policy.

The first period of change in state–media relations – the early 1990s – was characterized by a decrease in the state's visibility in the media system. Media organizations were privatized, and numerous private media companies were set up in all segments of the media system – press, TV and radio, news agencies, and audiovisual production. The strong market-driven direction of Russian media companies originated not only from profit-driven motivations or deficiencies of an immature civil society but also from the strong belief that only commercial motives might be "regarded as mainly limiting state penetration without having any unfavorable consequences" (Splichal, 1994: 135). This was linked to the belief in "decentralized market competition as a vital antidote to political despotism" (Keane 1991: 45). However, already in the mid-1990s it was becoming clear that the emerging integrated elite comprised of state officials and new capitalists had combined efforts to control the Russian media system even if their initial objectives might have been different.

The second period of post-Soviet state–media relations – in the mid-1990s – was marked by the state's attempts to restructure its relationship with the media. This took place in the context of Yeltsin's presidency and his politically "polycentric" regime based on the balance of different power centers such as oligarchic clans, industrial-financial groups, and regional state administrations. Although the Russian state tried to put the media and journalists under its control, it failed because of the disintegration of power centers and multiple tensions inside the state as a complex institution. However, the media were used instrumentally by various agents of power representing both state officials and businesspeople. As Resnyanskaya put it, "[B]usiness elites bartered the loyalty and information support of their owned media for financial and economic preferences from the state" (Resnyanskaya, 2007: 55).

In exchange for using media that were backed by new business elites to orchestrate favorable public opinion, the state provided the new media owners with enormous economic and image/reputation advantages. As Boris Berezovsky, the well-known entrepreneur and media owner of 1990s, said, "I have never got financial profits from ORT operations. . . . Political profits have been infinite, economic – none" (cited in Resnyanskaya, 2007: 56). This statement is in line with Koltsova's point about the most typical connections between the business and political elite in 1990s: "[B]oth see media first of all as weapons to gain political capital – a vital resource that later can be converted into all other forms of capital outside the media domain" (Koltsova, 2005: 224). In the 1990s the symbolic capital provided by media ownership was crucial for the new media-industrial complex, and the struggle for media property among the new oligarchs actually reflected the struggle for a better relationship with top state officials: Those officials used informal connections to business to gain media support, especially during election campaigns, providing in exchange favorable conditions for those particular media outlets. Muratov argued that NTV, the first independent TV channel and considered to be the most objective and important channel in 1994–6, "has joined the Presidential /Boris Yeltsin – E.V./ re-election campaign on the side of the President. . . . In appreciation of this help NTV has gained from the President the license to use the whole channel (before it started broadcasting only from 18:00 hours) and about one million dollars for further development, the sum subsidized by the state company Gazprom" (Muratov, 2008: 26).

The third period in Russian state-media relations – in the 2000s – inspired by the emergence of Putin's "monocentric" political regime, was aimed at the improvement of political management and a decrease in internal conflicts, such as struggles of ethnic groups for more independence, terrorism attacks, clashes of capital and regional economic agents, and so on. It was also intended to subordinate other centers of political power, including the Parliament (State Duma), to the president. In this context political parties were established, but their independence from the state was illusory. Some researchers define this process as re-etatization of the Russian media landscape (Dubin, 2005), confirmed by the fact that in the early 2000s various state agencies reestablished financial or managerial control over 70 percent of electronic media organizations, 80 percent of the regional press, and 20 percent of the national press (Fossato, 2003).

As a result, Russian media, especially nationally distributed TV channels, have been increasingly used by the state as tools to support the vertical power system, create a unified national identity, and minimize politically incorrect debates. The key new element of this period was the attempt of the Russian state to accelerate the process of nation-building and formation of common values that could cut across ethnic and regional divides (Kosto, 2000). Federal TV channels remained the only nationally diffused instrument through which the state could make its massive attempts to construct a new "national idea" and media policy (Becker, 2004).

At the same time the media played a tacit role in the power system of Russia: While the state was exercising its policies to make TV less politically engaged, the advertising and media business easily filled "empty" niches of political programming with entertainment content. The growing commercialism of advertising-based TV naturally supported the state strategy to depoliticize Russian journalism. Paradoxically, the aims of the state converged with those of the advertising industry, and commercially determined content became both a means of increasing depolitization and instrumentalization of political communication and of stimulating consumption.

At present the duality of authoritarian attitudes to mass media and journalism – an "etatist" media policy deeply rooted in the framework of state influence on media combined with the growing market-driven economy – has become the most crucial characteristic of the Russian media system (Nordenstreng, Vartanova, and Zassoursky, 2002). Koltsova also correctly points to the fact that often state actors use their institutional influence on the media to solve private problems. This happens because power groups emerge informally, exceeding the boundaries of the state as an institution. Consequently, "the 'state' cannot be seen as a unified actor. 'State' actors tend to form temporary alliances among themselves and with external agents and pursue their short-term group interests rather than the interests of the state" (Koltsova, 2005: 227).

Therefore the Russian state has mostly exerted informal pressure on the media. For instance, private media companies appoint top managers who meet the approval of state authorities. State pressures include both negative and positive measures:

- A selective use of legal sanctions (tax or customs legislation, fire safety and sanitary regulation) such as the NTV case in the early 2000s (whereas many violate the rules, only media failing to show loyalty are punished)
- The denial of access to information (a ban on attending press conferences held by state agencies is quite typical)
- The strategy of bringing lawsuits against media organizations, often on defamation grounds
- Acquiring ownership of local and regional newspapers that are consequently financed and operated as offices of local agencies and local authorities
- Barter and other kinds of exchange such as providing personal privileges or access to closed sources of information and communication channels

Although the Russian state is increasingly trying to establish a more up-to-date framework of media policy using legislative mechanisms, initiatives of the evolving media business, and even actions of media activists, especially concerning Internet regulation and performance, state–media relations remain very traditional. Passing legislation on politically sensitive issues (access to official information, coverage of terrorism) is still quite difficult, and the state exerts informal pressures on agenda setting and control over selection of key media managers for national TV. Attempts by the state to instrumentalize media have not ceased. The next crucial question that we have to address is the role of journalists and their professional behavior in the context of this system.

Journalistic Professionalism

Russian journalism as a profession had a rather late start. Although the first newspaper in Russia was set up three centuries ago, its uninterrupted evolution as a profession only began in the decade 1825–34. Despite severe censorship pressures, Russian journalists, who were identified mostly as writers, laid down foundations for public debates, particularly on general cultural questions (Mirsky, 1999: 124). Literary journals were the major form of print journalism, and literary criticism was the leading genre until nearly the end of the nineteenth century. The Russian vision of literature presupposed a much broader social and cultural role for it than in other countries, thus often merging it with journalistic activity. In the history of Russian journalism one could easily trace many journalistic projects realized by famous writers – Alexander Pushkin, Nikolai Nekrasov, Fyodor Dostoyevsky, Leo Tolstoy, and Anton Chekhov (Martinsen, 1998).

Another crucial feature of prerevolutionary Russian journalism history was the existence of censorship. Since the introduction of pre-publication censorship in 1804, journalism in Imperial Russia never experienced – even formally – freedom of speech. In the reign of liberally minded Tsar Alexander II (1855–81) a transition was made from legislation on prior censorship to a punitive system based on legal responsibility. Censorship laws were not abolished legally until the 1905 Revolution, and the first Law on Freedom of Information was accepted only by the Temporary Government in April 1917. Yet this freedom was short-lived, as the decree was in force only until October 1917. In Soviet Russia (1918–end of 1980s) the ideologically determined censorship system operated under the central censorship office, Glavlit. From 1922 on, it subjected the performing arts and all mass media to preventive censorship, suppressing political dissidence by shutting down "hostile" newspapers. This government censorship also led to a self-censorship tradition that still has an strong impact on professional practices.

Soviet media theory defined journalism as "a social activity of collection, transmission and periodical dissemination of information through mass communication channels aimed at propaganda and agitation" (Ovsepyan, 1979:7). Soviet journalism had a clear normative character; professional norms included the priority of accuracy over topicality and timeliness, the supremacy of feature and polemic genres involving personal judgments and opinions, and the role of "publicistics" (political or moral essays with moral reasoning) linking journalism to ideology.

The move to new professional values and practices in Russian journalism began after the break-up of the Soviet Union in 1991 (McNair, 1991). The Russian Law on the Mass Media (adopted on December 27, 1991) emphasized the inadmissibility of censorship and highlighted the values of the freedom of the press; later the Russian constitution included the main thrusts of this law (De Smaele and Vartanova, 2007).

The well-known formulation of journalists' roles as propagandists, agitators, and organizers "lost its inevitability whereas a new answer was bound to emerge demanding [a] new approach to the profession itself" (Pasti, 2007: 11). Respect, bordering on admiration, for the philosophy of freedom of speech among journalists was almost limitless, and thus new practices began to be adopted enthusiastically, although uncritically.

Changes in the media system brought about a new understanding of the profession in which standards of investigative journalism held the central place. Famous investigations of the late 1990s were primarily focused on the Stalinist or early Soviet past rather than on contemporary problems of an ineffective economy or political stagnation and passivity. Russian journalists interpreted professional autonomy mostly as liberation from any kind of interference with their journalistic practices: The very idea of professional autonomy became equivalent to the abolition of any kind of censorship and responsibility to anybody except journalists themselves. Journalism became more autonomous than independent, characterized by "an anomaly with an almost impossible degree of media autonomy" and, consequently, more free than responsible (Nordenstreng and Paasilinna, 2002: 195).

However, this value change coincided with the difficulties of privatization of the former state and Communist Party media property. In the early 1990s Russian media organizations formally passed into the hands of their employees – their editorial and technical staff – but new business models to support editorial independence were not set up. Conflicts arose because the formal liberation from censorship had not been safeguarded by new financial solutions. As part of the developing media-industrial complex neither state agencies nor new media owners continued to support the financial operations of newspapers and TV and radio stations. Formally declared freedom and autonomy of media professionals came into conflict with the efforts of the new owners to use these new professional values to further their own interests. Convinced that formal interference into newsroom operations was at an end, journalists could not quickly understand and respond to managerial efforts to introduce self-censorship. Proclaiming formally the ideals of press freedom and serving informally the interests of their new proprietors or sponsors, Russian journalism in the 1990s lost the moral legitimacy gained in the first years of perestroika, becoming one of the most publicly criticized professions. The decline in journalism's moral standing occurred under conditions of economic crisis, new social stratification, and impoverishment of the majority of Russians in the late 1990s, a time in which, as Gross correctly puts it, nonpartisan "universalist" media perhaps would have contributed more directly to the process of resocialization than the politicized media – an "extreme manifestation" of Western party-press parallelism – that in fact prevailed during that period of "media wars" (Gross, 2004:116).

In the 1990s–2000s, Russian journalism faced several professional and moral conflicts. The first major conflict derived from the double-sided nature of Soviet journalism that socially and culturally belonged to creative literature, but was also a politically and ideologically deter-mined profession. The national system of journalism education was car-ried out both by universities where it originated in philological faculties and by high communist party schools. For decades, the mixture of the two fields – philology and ideological work – defined journalism as a pro-fession. Soviet journalism incorporated a robust literary tradition, and political or moral essays incorporating moral and ideological reasoning became part of the core of Soviet journalistic professionalism. Journal-ists' personal opinions were expressed in most articles, responding to a normative demand of communist ideology for a journalist to be an active citizen and propagandist of the Communist Party line (Ovsepyan, 1979). Naturally, this demand directly linked the idea of professionalism to the idea of instrumentalization and explains why shifts from instrumental-ization of journalism to its professionalization since the mid-1990s were painful and problematic (Pasti, 2007).

As Russian society shifted to the demands of the market, journalism was affected by new trends. Processes of standardization and commodi-tization have changed the environment in the newsrooms and have led to the establishment of new professional values – sensationalism, pro-moting the creation of large audiences, an appeal to mass tastes, and entertainment values. The decline in journalism as a creative profession was paralleled by the birth of new creative but openly commoditized pro-fessions in advertising and public relations that outsourced talents from journalism. Professional standards of advertising and public relations eroded journalistic values, and concealed advertising, image making, and information wars became widespread phenomena in Russian journalism of the late 1990s to early 2000s (Zassoursky, 2008: 19–39).

Professionalization in Russian journalism has been an uneven pro-cess across different segments of the media system. The growth of business media is one example of Russian journalism's transformation. Koikkalainen argues that "business publications are among the first media enterprises when introducing international models, styles of practices. They have the role of lighthouse, promoting market economy, and this role includes also adopting and testing imported journalistic practices" (Koikkalainen, 2007: 188). Thus a special segment of the media system that serves the needs of the economy might be considered an important vehicle to promote new media structures and professional practices.

In recent decades several surveys have been conducted to find out the professional standards and ideals of Russian journalists. Sosnovskaja (2000) interviewed St. Petersburg journalists in 1997–9 and found that journalists' identity ten years after perestroika looked less stable than during the Soviet era, although it differed greatly from one age group to another. Young journalists were more market oriented and more often expressed their desire to work in PR and commercial journalism, characterized by blurred borders with advertising. They had frequent and close contacts with foreign education and journalistic values and saw themselves as apolitical. At the same time, the interviews showed that it was difficult for Russian journalists to assimilate into the professional environment of Western countries. Their professional identity differed too much, for example in literary style and attitude to facts and opinions (Sosnovskaja, 2000: 156–95).

Reflecting on developments in Russian journalism in the 2000s, one of the most well-known Russian media critics, A. Pankin, emphasizes the paradoxical coexistence of media independence and a low level of freedom of speech. By independence he means the growing decentralization of the media system and the increasing formal autonomy of newsrooms from state agencies and political parties; this autonomy was based on advertising business models. In contrast, growing political centralization, restructuring of public sphere under the new "national idea," and "sovereign/managed democracy" promote consent to instrumentalization of journalism, its use as a tool of political campaigns, and self-censorship in editorial offices (Pietilainen, 2002: 135).

Russian Media: A Statist Commercialized Model

The results of post-Soviet transformations in Russian political, business, and managerial culture and also for the nature and character of the Russian state remain very contradictory. Research on social transitions has pointed to the fact that an essential problem remains the gap between structural changes and changes in cultures, organizational practices, daily routines, and people's behaviors (Shkaratan and Iljin, 2006: 130).

Recent post-Soviet media trends parallel those in Western media systems. Commercialization of content strategies, deregulation of electronic media, broadening of the scope for commercial enterprise, and private ownership that ignited conflict between public and private forces are easily identifiable in Russian media (McQuail, 2005). Many of these trends are similar to the process that Hallin and Mancini have called convergence or homogenization driven by the "commercial deluge" of the 1980s–'90s (Hallin and Mancini, 2004b: 252–3). The shift to the market-driven logic in the post-Soviet media has brought about expanding commercialization, the increasing role of technology, and secularization (Hallin and Mancini, 2004b: 261–7).

Foreign scholars have often argued that the Russian media model substantially differs from Western European ones (Becker, 2004; De Smaele, 1999). The reason for this difference may lie in the unique character of Russian society and culture as rooted in its geopolitical position, the complexity of its historical heritage, and the multiethnic, multicultural, and multilinguistic nature of Russia. Political and cultural pressures of the authoritarian traditions of Imperial Russia and the Soviet Union definitely also play a role. The contemporary Russian media model should be viewed as a synergy of different features that might be found in various national contexts. The synergy of Western and Asian elements found in the Russian media system is sometimes regarded as a distinct Eurasian hybrid system.

The geographical character sometimes observed in media system models – the fact of regional similarity – is rooted not simply in proximity but also in geopolitical and cultural commonalities. Hallin and Mancini's three models reflect media system development in geographic regions that are characterized either by similarities in economic and cultural life (Protestantism and industrialization in the North) or by patterns of influence between different countries (United Kingdom to Ireland or Canada, the United States or France to Italy and the Iberian peninsula). The idea of cultural commonalities seems to be vital also for understanding media systems in post-Soviet countries, because the similar histories and common patterns in the economy and lifestyles of the largest Eurasian Imperia have very deep historical roots. Although there remain many unanswered questions about how the geopolitical dimension and its social consequences affect media systems, their structures, and performance, it is obvious that countries of the post-imperial and post-Soviet space provide the closest media models for the Russian one.

Many post-Soviet media systems have a number of features of a non-Western/non-European nature, including the existence of a state–market complex and its significant influence on media, formal and informal links between political or integrated political/economic elites and journalists, a specific culture of media audiences and elite–journalist relationships, tolerance on the part of audiences to an instrumental use of media by the state and political clans, and a paternalistic culture of media management. These are also typical of transitional or authoritarian neoliberal countries of Southeast Asia (Kit-wai Ma, 2000: 27, 32; Lee, 2000: 125, 133–4; Park, Kim, and Sohn, 2000: 121). Many of these features are present in Hallin and Mancini's analysis of the Polarized Pluralist/Mediterranean media model, but they are not as visible and influential as in many media contexts outside Europe. On the basis of Hallin and Mancini's categorization "the Russian media system has been classified as closer to the Mediterranean media system that to other Western-type systems, although no systematic analysis of the Russian media systems has yet been conducted" (Nieminen, 2009, 108–9).

The current analysis has proven that, although it is close to the Polarized model, Russian media differ from it in one crucial dimension, and this is the state–media relationship, including the role played by the state and state agencies in shaping media structures, policy, and journalism practices. Yet what really distinguishes a Russian media model from the three described in *Comparing Media Systems*? In the most crucial respect, it involves a different division of roles and pressures compared to Liberal, Corporatist, and Polarized models. H. de Smaele argues that in Russia Western influences seemed to be restricted primarily to the market area, responding to a newly emerging "market demand," whereas a "social demand" understood in Western media through concepts of the public sphere, the pluralist and independent Fourth Estate, and the conversion of journalists into an autonomous professional group is largely absent. Emphasizing the Eastern dimension of Russian societal and cultural practices, de Smaele proposes a "Eurasian" media model (De Smaele, 1999: 173–89).

The key difference between Hallin and Mancini's models and the Russian system is a strong relationship between media, journalists, and the state, legitimized by a shared belief – consciously or unconsciously – in the regulatory/decisive role of the state (or state agencies). This belief is the basis for the statist mentality embedded as the core characteristic of the authoritarian media model (Becker, 2004: 139–63). As far as making media policy is concerned, it is impossible to overestimate the importance of the role of the integrated political–business elite. By embracing political and business elites the Russian state has become the main driving force in media policy whatever goals it pursues, whereas audiences (or the public) have been mostly shunted aside. The role of civil society in the general community and in the journalistic community in particular remains contradictory. Leading journalists and media managers have been integrated into the state and therefore have been included in the process of social management. The traditional paternal character of the media–state relationship in which the media still play the role of an innocent and obedient child (Vartanova, 2002: 66) remains central to the Russian system.

Nevertheless, bearing in mind the statist nature of the Russian media model, it might be incomplete to describe it only through one of its characteristics, although crucial, such as paternalism or neo-authoritarianism. In the past two decades the statist character of the Russian media has been challenged by the growing commercialism of the media industry. The profit-based logic of media organizations using the matrix of the Liberal model has put Russian media far beyond traditional practices. A contemporary Russian media model has emerged in the transitional postmodern fragmented society characterized by a struggle of conflicting multiethnic, multiconfessional, and multicultural interests in which values of modernization and knowledge confront the paternalistic mentality of Russian audiences and journalists. The level of unevenness in terms of economic wealth and access to ICTs (information and communication technologies) has become another factor that produces specific external pressures on the Russian media system. In addition, the discrepancy between media rhetoric and everyday practices of audiences produces growing distrust and disappointment of citizens in mainstream political media. Finally, marginalized forces opposing state influence in the media – investigative and opposition journalists, Internet activists, and active audiences – have been active in promoting a free press, a free Internet, and ethical norms in new media. With the widening support of new media in Russia, this last trend seems to be very typical of the Western European media landscape.

Russia's media model in its complexity differs from the three models of media systems described by Hallin and Mancini, although it certainly has many of the features of the Polarized Pluralist model and some of the Liberal model. Taking into account national history, pressures of the authoritarian traditions of Imperial and Soviet Russia, cultural practices, features inherited from Soviet journalism, the emergence of the market in the media industry, and trends in journalism, we might describe the Russian media model as statist commercialized.

8

Understanding China's Media System in a World Historical Context

Yuezhi Zhao

If Hallin and Mancini's comparison of media systems in the developed capitalist democracies of Western Europe and North America is based on a "most similar systems" design (2004b: 6), to bring in the Chinese media system into a worldwide comparative project is to bring one of the "most dissimilar systems" into the messy picture of non-Western empirical reality. Moreover, although I share Hallin and Mancini's desire to give a long overdue "decent burial" to *Four Theories of the Press*, which they characterized as a "horror-movie zombie" that "has stalked the landscape of media studies ... for decades beyond its nature lifetime" (2004b: 10), to give today's Chinese media system a decent depiction compels me to exhume at least parts of the skeleton of *Four Theories* as starting points. I do so even though I immediately realize the unpleasant and discomforting nature of such an exercise and even though I agree with the now well-established critiques of *Four Theories* as a case of Cold War–tainted theoretical modeling (see also Nerone, 1995). Yet, more than two decades after the pronounced end of the Cold War, a major mutation of the Soviet communist model as described in *Four Theories* is still alive and kicking in a rising China that is not only continental in geographical size but also more populous than all the eighteen countries that Hallin and Mancini's *Comparing Media Systems* covers put together. Furthermore, contrary to Hallin and Mancini's observation about the growing influence of the Liberal model throughout the world, China's CCP-led one-party rule has proven to be highly resilient and adaptive (Heilmann and Perry, 2011; Jacques, 2009; Nathan, 2003; Perry, 2007). Based on her study of the post-1989 Chinese media and propaganda system, a core component of the CCP's ruling apparatuses, Brady has even gone so far as to conclude, "The CCP-led political system, the one Party-State, is now as entrenched as the political systems in Western countries" (Brady, 2008: 202). If so, what does an analysis of the Chinese media system have to offer for comparative media studies?

To prepare the groundwork for analyzing the Chinese media system, I first discuss in this chapter some of the theoretical challenges in analyzing media systems beyond Western Europe and North America in relation to Hallin and Mancini's three-model (Liberal, Democratic Corporatist, and Polarized Pluralist) comparative framework and the legacy of the Soviet model in China. Then, I describe the Chinese media system in terms of Hallin and Mancini's four comparative dimensions: the development of media markets with an emphasis on the mass-circulation press, political parallelism, and the degree and nature of journalistic professionalism and of state intervention (2004b: 21). However, whereas an implicit narrative about the rise, consolidation, and expansion of capitalism in Western Europe and beyond may have led Hallin and Mancini to discuss the market first and the state last, a counternarrative centering on anticapitalist and anti-imperialist social revolutions in the periphery of global capitalism and an acknowledgment of the overwhelming role of one of the resultant postrevolutionary states – the CCP-led Chinese state – compel me to start my discussion with the state. Substantive and structural considerations also necessitate a discussion of party-press parallelism and professionalism in one section and political parallelism in another.

Provincializing Europe and the Legacy of the Soviet Model in China

Following those who have long advocated internationalizing media theory (Downing, 1996) and de-Westernizing media studies (Curran and Park, 2000), Hallin and Mancini explicitly distance themselves from Western-centrism in their analysis, cautioning specifically against a "tendency to borrow the literature of other countries – usually the Anglo-American or the French literature as thought it could be applied unproblematically anywhere" (2004b: 2). The book's explicit Western empirical focus also opens the way for provincializing Western media systems by treating them as concrete historical formations rather than abstract ideals. Nevertheless, extending a Western-generated comparative framework to the rest of the world may still engender a Western-centric mode of analysis; that is, at the end of it, the rest of the world's media systems are likely to be found inadequate to any of the Western models and the kind of Western modernity of which these models are integral parts.

In this context, Chakrabarty's project of "provincializing Europe" offers a helpful entry point for scholars of non-Western media to engage with Western-based theoretical categories without reproducing the subalternity of non-Western media studies. As Chakrabarty (2000: 42–3) argues, such a project does not call for a "simplistic, out-of-hand rejection of modernity, liberal values, universals, science, reason, grand narratives, totalizing explanations, and so on." Rather, it foregrounds historical struggles:

These struggles include coercion (both on behalf of and against modernity) – physical, institutional, and symbolic violence, often dispensed with dreamy-eyed idealism – and this violence plays a decisive role in the establishment of meaning, in the creation of truth regimes, in deciding, as it were, whose and which "universal" wins.... The project of provincializing Europe therefore cannot be a project of cultural relativism. It cannot originate from the stance that the reason/science/universals that help define Europe as the modern are simply "cultural-specific" and therefore only belong to European cultures.... The project of provincializing Europe has to include certain additional moves: first, the recognition that Europe's acquisition of the adjective "modern" for itself is an integral part of the story of European imperialism within global history; and second, the understanding that this equating of a certain version of Europe with "modernity" is not the work of Europeans alone; third-world nationalisms, as modernizing ideologies par excellence, have been equal partners in the process.

Consequently, although Duncan McCargo's assertion in Chapter 10 that North America and Western Europe are not the norm but the exceptions to how the media work in much of the world may be empirically true, such a simple inversion ignores the question of asymmetric power relations and overlooks the history of unequal encounters between North America and Western Europe on the one hand and the rest of the world on the other.

Following Chakrabarty's argument and along with de Albuquerque's insistence in Chapter 5 on the importance of distinguishing between central and peripheral media systems, I believe it is necessary to analyze the world's media systems in their structural relationships – not simply in comparative terms, which tend to flatten asymmetric power relations between the systems under comparison. In particular, it is important to acknowledge that the Western systems' acquisition of their distinctive features vis-à-vis those of the rest of the world is an integral part of the story of European imperialism and American hegemony within the history of global media development. Comparative analysis is "useful in sorting out relationships between media systems and their social and political settings" (Hallin and Mancini, 2004: 4), and *Comparing Media Systems* did discuss the impact of the "world powers" status of countries such as the United Kingdom and the United States on their media systems, especially on state and media relationships. However, its focus on media systems in the West, which "happen" to constitute the systems of former and contemporary imperial powers, has afforded it the privilege to focus more on the relationships between a media system and the social and political settings of a given country within the containment of the modern (Western) nation-state. For example, when the authors describe the U.S. system of broadcasting and analyze the minimal role of the U.S. state in this sector, the massive foreign broadcasting operations of the U.S. state as a global hegemonic power do not register as a part of the American media system. Yet, in many non-Western countries, including China, the modern media system was often a Western imposition to begin with – colonial and missionary agents set up the first modern newspapers in colonized or semi-colonized port cities, often in foreign languages. During the Cold War, China and other communist countries devoted vast resources to jam Western-state–sponsored broadcasting signals. Even today, the penetration and influence of Western media and the imperative to build a strong domestic resistance against them – motivated at least in part and in rhetoric by Chakrabarty's earlier mentioned spirit of Third World nationalisms – continue to figure as a dominant issue in the development of non-Western media systems.

Furthermore, as Chakrabarty points out and as underscored by the turbulent history of media system development during what Wang (2006: 29) has called China's whole "revolutionary century" – from the Republic Revolution in 1911 to the death of Mao in 1976 – and during the no less dramatic post-Mao period, there have been and continue to be historical struggles over different "universals" and "truth regimes" in the world's media systems. It is necessary to acknowledge these struggles as we compare the world's different media systems. Written within the context of the Cold War and with an unapologetic anticommunist stand, *Four Theories* foregrounds an unfolding struggle between two universals and their respective regimes of truth and freedom – the universal of liberalism versus the universal of communism, and the liberal notions of freedom and truth versus the Soviet notions of freedom and truth. As Chakrabarty has argued, academics are not neutral to the struggles between the different universals (2000: 43). The influential role in global journalism gained by works such as *Four Theories*, which was relentlessly promoted in journalism studies both within and outside the United States, often with U.S. state support, was part and parcel of the story of the West's winning of the Cold War. Subsequently, a fundamentalist mutation of liberalism known as neoliberalism triumphed as a global ideology to drastically reshape the world's media systems. It was within this post–Cold War world historical and ideological context that *Comparing Media Systems* gave *Four Theories* a "decent burial." Although *Comparing Media Systems* does not make any direct reference either to Fukuyama's "end of history" thesis or Huntington's "third wave" democratization argument, the book's geographical focus on Western Europe and North America – the triumphant side of the Cold War – along with its explicit effort to move beyond *Four Theories'* preoccupation with "philosophies" or "ideologies" to focus on empirical analysis, does give it an "end of ideology" feeling. To be sure, as Wang (2006) has observed, there has been a tendency toward the rise of a "depoliticized politics, from East to West" in the post-1960s era. This process underpins what Hallin and Mancini described as the decline of party politics in the West. In China, one witnessed the degeneration of Cultural Revolution politics into depoliticized factional struggles and the subsequent rise of Deng's pragmatism in post-Mao CCP politics.

However, this does not mean the "end of ideology," let along the "end of history." On the one hand, we have witnessed "the clash of fundamentalisms" (Ali, 2002), that is, the return of History in a horrific form in the "war against terror" – a protracted conflict between religious fundamentalism and Western, especially American, imperialism. On the other hand, the collapse of the Berlin Wall and the triumphant of neoliberalism as a global ideology have not buried the communist and socialist critique of Western modernity once and for all. In Asia, instead of collapsing, the communist states in China, Vietnam, and Laos have managed to sustain their one-party rule by continuing to claim allegiance to socialism – no matter how hollow such rhetoric might be. In North Korea, a more rigid form of communism remains in place. In India, the world's largest democracy, radical Maoist guerrillas have mounted a sustained and widespread rebellion in the hinterlands, threatening to destabilize the country. In a more counterintuitive development in 2008, Maoists in Nepal, after waging many years of armed struggles, won 38 percent of the seats in the Nepalese Constitutional Assembly. In Latin America, the communists are still in power in Cuba, while Venezuela claims to build "socialism for the 21st century." Despite the horrors of Stalinism, the Cultural Revolution, and the Khmer Rogue, and notwithstanding the postmodernist intellectual challenge to all forms of universalism, various versions of communist and socialist universalism continue to invoke fears and hopes in different corners of the world. Most ironically, as I discuss in the last section of this chapter in relation to media and ideological debates in post-reform

China, Maoist socialist universalism has reemerged as a powerful critique against Dengist pragmatism precisely because of the reform-era CCP's de facto shedding of its socialist colors.

In addition to its methodological and conceptual problems, *Four Theories* only traced the "Soviet model" "from its roots in Marx through its mutations in the gardens of Lenin and Stalin" in the USSR (Siebert, Peterson, and Schramm, 1963: 106) and paid no attention to its mutations in the gardens of Mao in China. More importantly for the purposes of this chapter, Leninist and Maoist legacies continue to cast a long shadow in China's post-Mao media system. It is beyond the scope of this chapter to compare both the significant differences between the Soviet and Chinese communist media systems and the different paths of reforming them in the USSR and China, leading to the collapse of the former and the resilience of the latter. However, suffice it to say that uneven capitalistic development within the world system and, more significantly, uneven development within peripheral capitalism that created a large urban–rural divide and engendered peasant-based revolutions in Asia are partly responsible for the resilience of one-party communist rule in this region. Moreover, and without having to endorse cultural essentialism, historically and culturally embedded notions and practices of statecraft and state–society relations are also important considerations. For example, there are powerful continuities between Confucian and communist modes of rule in China, both of which are based on an implicit contract between the people and the state (Jacques, 2009). As Roudakova's Chapter 12 underscores, it will indeed be very productive to pursue a processual and practice-oriented approach in studying media and political relations worldwide.

In China, a CCP-led and peasant-based social revolution in the first half of the twentieth century engendered a Maoist media system that sinified the Leninist press theory and the Soviet model (Stranahan, 1990; Zhao, 2011). In 1949, a counterhegemonic media system that had grew out of the communist movement since the founding of the Chinese Communist Party (CCP) in 1921 became the hegemonic media system with the establishment of the People's Republic of China (PRC). To be sure, liberal intellectuals did not like the system and they challenged the party's monopoly of the press and crusaded for its liberalization when Mao initiated the "one hundred flowers campaign" in 1957. However, these voices were soon suppressed during the ensuing "Anti-rightist Campaign." During the early years of the Cultural Revolution (1966–1976), more radical, decentralized, and even extra-state communication outlets and practices – namely, Red Guard tabloids and information networks – temporarily destabilized this system amidst heightened ideological and factional struggles (Zhao, 2008a: 197–9). Nevertheless the official media system of the early postrevolutionary era quickly restabilized itself after the initial chaos and sustained its monopolistic status during the rest of the Mao era. The system regained part of its legitimacy in the immediate post-Mao era and served as a powerful communication platform for the post-Mao CCP leadership to forge an ideological consensus around "reform and open up" in 1978 (Zhao, 1998).

However, by 1989, students and urban intellectuals – whose predecessors had embraced communist universalism with "dreamy-eyed idealism" and had been the main protagonists in the creation of the official media system – had once again become disillusioned, and they started to reembrace Western liberal capitalist democratic media values and practices. The reform of the official media system inspired by liberal notions of press freedom and professional autonomy was a key dimension of the political struggles leading to the 1989 pro-democracy movement (Zhao, 1998). In fact, when the movement started in spring 1989 and Chinese journalists marched with students to demand the Chinese media to "tell truth, not lies," Chinese students, urban intellectuals, and journalists were leading the pack in the worldwide struggles against the ossified system of state socialism. However, in China, liberal reformers and their urban middle-class constituencies lost their battle for liberal universalism and Western-style democracy. Whereas Mao and his generation of communist revolutionaries mobilized China's lower social classes to win the 1949 communist revolution, students and urban intellectuals of the 1980s were unable and even unwilling to establish communication networks that connected them with China's industrial workers, let alone its vast rural population (Zhao and Schiller, 2001). State violence, deployed in the name of defending socialism against "bourgeoisie liberalization," secured the continuing domination – at least in official ideology – of communist universalism over liberal universalism and of the Leninist and Maoist media organizational principles over capitalist liberal democratic media organizational principles. In 1999, in yet another ironic turn of history and in a development that defies any linear narratives of modernization and secularization, the Chinese media system was caught in an intensive battle with yet another regime of truth – that of the quasi-religious, nativist, and postmaterialist Falun Gong movement (Yu, 2009; Zhao, 2003). In particular, this movement's militant media activism, including its high-tech campaign to disrupt Chinese state satellite broadcast transmissions and its success in hacking into state-run cable television systems, contributed to the Chinese state's fortification of its regime of control (Zhao, 2008a).

In short, to bring the Chinese media system into a worldwide comparative project necessitates a recognition of its Leninist and Maoist legacies in relation to the worldwide struggles against capitalism and Western imperialism and an understanding of ongoing struggles between different universalisms and different regimes of truth – politically, religiously, or culturally inspired – and how these struggles have shaped the transformation of media and politics.

Beyond "Intervention": The Dominant Role of the Chinese State

Hallin and Mancini discuss the role of the state last in their four comparative dimensions. Moreover, they frame this discussion in terms of "intervention," which presumes a natural state of affairs before and beyond intervention. In doing so, they have excluded a potential role of the state in the initial formation of the European and North American media systems. In addition, in their work, the state's structural role in shaping the media is discussed in terms of ownership, funding, and regulation, whereas its ideological role is analyzed in terms of it as a source of information and "primary definer" of news. Understanding the role of the state in the Chinese media system, however, entails us to move beyond an "intervention" framework. Above all, it requires us to resist the Western-media–framed temptation to not only start with the Chinese state's highly authoritarian regime of control but also to understand it as antithetical to capitalistic developments. In fact, this regime of control has been both a precondition and a consequence of China's accelerated development in the post-1989 era. Among other things, it has suppressed autonomous communication of Chinese workers and farmers and has engendered "cheap labor" as one of China's key "comparative advantages" in the post–Cold War neoliberal global political economy (Zhao, 2008a). At the same time, for the Chinese as well as for many other peoples outside the core of Western capitalism, the struggle for the establishment of a modern nation-state is a historical accomplishment. Precisely because of this particular history of state formation, the state, despite all its authoritarian and patrimonial dimensions, is invested with the normative expectations of promoting positive freedoms, defending territorial sovereignty, promoting national integration, as well as engendering social economic developments. It is this dimension of the Chinese state's role in the media system that must also be highlighted in this analysis. In Asia, whether in a communist state or a developmental state of the democratic or authoritarian type, the media were assigned a major role in the task of national development – even under the tutelage of mainstream Western communication scholars such as Wilbur Schramm (1964). It is precisely in this context that "development journalism" or "development media theory" was proposed. As McQuail (1994: 131) elaborates, within this model, "[t]he responsibilities of the media are emphasized above their rights and freedoms."

Despite its highly caricaturized nature, Schramm's comparison of the Soviet system with the traditional authoritarian system in *Four Theories* captured something that remains paramount in understanding the role of the state in today's Chinese media. That is, whereas the older authoritarian system limited what the media could do negatively, "[t]he Soviet system has defined the function of mass communications positively . . . the emphasis is rather on requiring the press to do certain things . . . for example . . . to increase the 'political awareness' of the masses, to rally the population in support of the leaders and their program, and to raise the level of efficiency of the workers, etc" (Siebert et al., 1956: 140–1). As they pointed out, "[T]he Soviet system was built as a part of change, and to help accomplish change" (1956: 141). In the aftermath of the collapse of the USSR that gave birth to new nations, an argument has been made that the USSR, rather than being communist in any meaningful sense, might have been regarded more accurately as a powerful form of developmentalism. Thus, "20th century communism was as much, if not more, about the logic of uneven development of world capitalism as it was about the logic of class and capitalist exploitation" (Desai, 2008: 418). In China, communism, nationalism, and developmentalism were closely intertwined historically in the mobilizing ideologies of the CCP (Lin, 2006), which came to power by relying not only on the gun (i.e., armed struggles against the Nationalist and Japanese armies) but also the pen (i.e., the winning of cultural leadership and the forging of a revolutionary hegemony through a communication system organized along the Leninist concept of the press as the party's collective organizer, agitator, and propagandist). Moreover, consistent with my earlier point about the importance of cultural tradition and complementary to Roudakava's objective of "bringing culture back into the state" in Chapter 12, that this Leninist concept of the state's role in media "sticks" in China can be partly explained by the fact that it meshes well with the Confucian notion of the state's responsibility to "inculcate in the population a sense of shared values and culture based on Confucian principles" (Jacques,

2009: 84). As Jacques has argued, contrary to Europe, where such matters were not considered to be the responsibility of the state and, until the late nineteenth century, were left to the church, "[t]he Chinese state saw moral instruction, amongst both the common people and the elites, as both desirable in itself and also as a means of exercising social control" (2009: 84).

To be sure, the CCP's programs and its ideological and moral doctrines have changed dramatically in the post-Mao period. As the party increasingly shed its communist colors, nationalism and developmentalism have dominated CCP politics, and Confucian morality has overshadowed communist morality. Nevertheless, the CCP continues to articulate different versions of Marxism and socialism, claiming to "build socialism with Chinese characteristics," and it continues to integrate the Chinese media system with its programs of providing moral guidance to the population and engineering economic development and social change. Whether it is to use the media to promote state-sanctioned "socialist core values" and ethical norms (Zhao, 2011) or to mobilize the media for earthquake relief (Sun and Zhao, 2009), the CCP, in what Hallin and Mancini would describe as a most quintessential form of party-press parallelism, is actively using the media to shape the contours of Chinese modernity through its control of the media.

Furthermore, based on lessons learned from the outbreak of the pro-democracy movement in 1989 in China and the collapse of Eastern European communist governments and the USSR, in which the ideological and structural liberalization of the media was believed to be a major contributing factor, the CCP set out to strengthen its leading role in media and ideology: This effort has been a defining feature of post-1989 party leaderships under both Jiang Zemin and Hu Jintao. The following excerpt from a speech by Hu Jintao (Hu, 2004) is particularly significant:

The ideological field has always been an important battle ground in the fierce struggles between us and enemy forces (*didui shili*). A problem in this front will lead to social chaos, even the loss of regime power...a very important reason from the disintegration of the Soviet Union and the collapse the Communist party there is Gorbachev's advocacy of "ideological pluralism" and the so-called "glasnost," along with the repudiation of Marxism as a guiding ideology, which resulted in the riotous flow of non-Marxist and anti-Marxist trends.

Another area in which the Soviet model and the revolutionary legacies of Chinese state formation continue to cast a long shadow is media ownership. One of the key components of China's post-Mao economic reforms has been the phenomenal expansion of the private sector and the massive privatization of state-owned enterprises in the overall Chinese economy. A concurrent development has been a gradual entrenchment of private property rights in the Chinese constitution, which was amended in early 2004 to protect private property. In March 2007, China's National People's Congress approved a highly controversial property rights law to consolidate private property relationships. However, the Chinese state's legacies in promoting public ownership and its professed commitment to socialism have posed an ideological limit on privatization. In the media sector, although the Chinese state has not only drastically curtailed its role in subsidizing media operations but has also targeted the media and cultural sector as new sites of profit-making and capitalistic development (Zhao, 1998, 2008), the state continues to restrict private capital, let alone the privatizing of existing media outlets. Here, Lenin's theory about the difference between bourgeois "formal" press freedom and that of Soviet or proletarian "substantive" press freedom based on the expropriation of press ownership by the big capitalists casts a long shadow. The CCP not only historically defined public ownership – which it then equated with state ownership and direct control – as the foundation for "socialist press freedom" but also has waged a protracted battle against the emergence of privately owned newspapers as a hallmark of "bourgeois liberalization" both during the Maoist and the reform era. As the state has cultivated the media's entertainment function and accommodated private capital's profit-making rather than speech-making imperative during the reform era, it has developed a complex and differentiated policy regime regarding private capital participation in the media and cultural industries. Because the production and distribution of news and informational content is deemed "sacred," ownership of news media outlets, including newspapers and broadcast stations, continues to be monopolized by the state. Meanwhile, full or partial ownership of the peripheral areas of the media and culture industries, including the production of film, television entertainment, and advertising, as well as audiovisual distribution, has been opened up to domestic private and foreign capital. In this way, the state retains strategic control over the media system and its ideological orientation, but no longer monopolizes production and distribution, especially in entertainment, lifestyle, and business areas (Zhao, 2008b, 2011).

Although the post-Mao Chinese state recognizes the media as incorporating both propaganda organs and profit-making enterprises, it remains wary of private capital because there is no guarantee that private news outlets will not turn their back against it and support oppositional forces, especially during times of political crisis. Given that even CCP-controlled news outlets ended up advocating "bourgeois liberalization" in 1989, such a consideration is perhaps not groundless. Furthermore, just as the CCP continues to be compelled to sustain the idea of socialism as a more just and equitable social order vis-à-vis capitalism, there continues to be an ideological barrier to sanctioning private media ownership despite the intellectual influence of liberal press theory, which equates a free press with a privately owned press. Media ownership by private capital undermines the conceptual and institutional foundations of the Chinese socialist state: It means the acceptance of a news outlet as first and foremost a private profit-making business, contrary to the CCP's Lenin-inspired definition of press freedom as being first and foremost freedom from capitalistic control. "He who opens up the press to the bourgeoisie, he who does not understand that we are marching toward socialism in great strides" – Lenin cursed in 1917 (Chen, 2002:143). With the USSR's collapse as hindsight, there is probably a real fear that the acceptance of private news media ownership may indeed mean one more step toward "capitalist restoration" both in theory and in practice. As I have argued elsewhere (Zhao 2008a, 2008b, 2011), this is not a step any CCP leader, still claiming to be the heir of the Communist Revolution and building socialism, can take easily.

Along with the CCP's role in reemphasizing the ideological field, the state's role in media regulation has expanded dramatically. The commercialization and rapid expansion of the media system, particularly the involvement of nonparty entities in media production and distribution, have led the state to strengthen the structural management of the media through specialized government agencies. China's global reintegration centering on its accession to the World Trade Organization (WTO) in 2001, especially the pressure of transnational capital entering the Chinese market, has made government regulation of media industries a further necessity. The versatile and dispersed nature of the Internet has created another regulatory frenzy on the part of the Chinese state. However, contrary to regulatory agencies in the Liberal model, which typically operate at arm's length from the government, China's media regulators are government departments subject to CCP propaganda department directives. Moreover, instead of passing laws about the media, which would inevitably invoke debates at the National People's Congress (NPC) over the meaning of the constitutional guarantee of press freedom, the state has opted to authorize relevant government departments to legitimate its preferred media structure by administrative "regulations" (*tiaoli*), which only require approval by the State Council, China's cabinet. Finally, because major media outlets are still organizationally affiliated with the CCP and government institutions, the state retains its power to appoint media officials. As I discuss later, the Chinese state has also established a comprehensive system of managing journalistic credentials.

History, Technology, and Media Market Formation in China's Compressed Hypermodernity

Hallin and Mancini's analysis of the Western media markets focuses on the print press and distinguishes the North European and North American mass press's engagement in "vertical" communication by mediating between political elites and ordinary citizens from the Southern European elite press's involvement in a "horizontal" process of debate and negotiation among elite factions (2004b: 22). Although China has become the largest global newspaper market both in terms of the number of newspaper titles and the number of newspaper copies published (98.6 million copies of 955 titles, accounting for 14.5 percent of the world total of 6,580 titles; Wang, 2005), a deep rural–urban divide and the relatively small number of newspaper sales per 1,000 adults immediately give the impression that the Chinese media market is more akin to the Southern European model. In 2004, newspaper sales per 1,000 adults were 75.86 nationally, below the world average. However, Beijing and Shanghai stood at 274.2 and 268.1, respectively (Wang, 2005), surpassing not only the Southern European countries but also the liberal countries of Canada and the United States.

Apart from a pattern of uneven urban–rural development that perhaps surpasses anything that existed and still exists in the West, history – China's revolutionary history and a hyper-modernist post-Mao development era that condense hundreds years of development in the West – and technology (that China first experienced a television revolution and then a digital revolution in two decades) are key factors in the unique formation of China's media markets. In particular, the Chinese media market formation has resulted in the existence of two distinct and yet institutionally intertwined press sectors or subsystems ("markets" is not the appropriate word here): the party organ sector, which traces its roots to the revolutionary period and does not operate in accordance with market calculations, and the market-based post-Mao mass press sector. Furthermore, the role of the media in the Maoist model of political communication means that the distinction of "vertical" versus "horizontal" communication is more blurred in the Chinese context.

As I discussed previously, China's media system is rooted in CCP revolutionary theories and practices. The most formative moment of this history was Mao's sinification of the Leninist press model in Yan'an in the early 1940s, which resulted in a tradition of the party press that serves as a channel of communication not only between the party leadership and local party officials but also between the party and the broad public. The party press as the party's mouthpiece became a quintessential instrument in Mao's "mass line" model of political communication in which the party as the revolutionary vanguard articulates the inspirations of the masses and turns them into systematic party programs and policies, which are in turn propagated, implemented, and modified through the praxis of the masses (Stranahan, 1990; Zhao, 1998, 2011). In theory, this model contains both vertical and horizontal dimensions and combines both elitist and popular participatory tendencies. Furthermore, the fact that the press is only an integral part of a much larger propaganda and ideological mobilization system has meant that party organs were rarely consumed individually, as is the case in the Western context. Instead, newspapers, mostly publicly subscribed to by government offices and work units and local village committees, were read by a large number of individuals. During the Maoist era, newspaper reading sessions at work units were part of the weekly workday routine; newspaper reading windows were mounted in urban public spaces. Although penetration of the print press was low in the rural area, the radio broadcasting system featured a prominent and nationally accessible "news and press digest" program that carried the most important newspaper editorials and press headlines throughout the country.

Central and provincial party organs, many of them with huge circulation numbers, were the dominant newspaper form during the Maoist era. Today, party organs published by party committees at and above county levels – a total of 438 titles in 2005 and most of them dailies – remain the dominant newspaper type in China (Wang, 2005). Although some of the party organs in metropolitan cities have transformed themselves into market-driven mass-appeal newspapers based primarily on private subscription and street sales, the majority, led by the *People's Daily* and *Guangming Daily* at the central level and provincial party organs at the regional levels, continue to depend on publicly subsidized subscriptions. With the retreat of party propaganda work at the workplaces – for example, there are no longer mandatory newspaper reading sessions – as well as the growth of market-oriented papers as more attractive reading alternatives for the general public, party organs have become more "official" in their readership make-up; that is, they have become newspapers aimed primarily at officials, especially upper-level party leadership, enabling them to publicize their programs and work priorities among the party's rank-and-file members. Consequently, post-Mao era party organs have acquired a status that is more akin to the elite press in the West.

Yet the party press tradition matured in Yan'an is not the only one that has shaped today's Chinese media. China's semi-colonial metropolitan cities were the birthplace of the "first commercial revolution" in the history of modern Chinese media in the first half of the twentieth century. Along with official propagandist newspapers published by the Nationalist government, mass-appeal commercial papers molded after the Western liberal tradition – both serious news-oriented broadsheets and entertainment and soft-news–oriented afternoon tabloids or "evening papers" as they are called in China – as well as elite intellectual papers flourished in Shanghai, Tianjin, and a few other metropolitan centers before 1949. When the CCP established the party press system throughout the country in 1949, it was fully aware of the cultural gaps between a journalistic tradition growing out of armed struggles and a peasant-based social revolution in the hinterlands and that growing out of urban commercial journalism in the coastal areas. Recognizing the popular press as a means to establish its revolutionary hegemony over an urban population immersed in "bourgeois" culture, the CCP not only allowed some of the commercial afternoon tabloids from the pre-1949 era to continue their operations but also created nearly a dozen other afternoon tabloids. Although these afternoon tabloids did not deviate from the party line, their content was more diversified and their subject matters closer to everyday urban life. Thus, even from the very beginning of the PRC, there was an entertainment- and lifestyle-oriented tabloid sector within the party press structure. Although these papers were eventually eliminated during the Cultural Revolution, a mass-appeal commercial sector has returned with a vengeance after the post-Mao period, with the beginning of the "second commercial revolution" in the history of modern Chinese media development in the post-Mao era.

If the commercial revolution in the British press was the result of "calculated liberalization" aiming at containing a radical working-class press (Curran, 1978), and if the American "penny revolution" ushered in the decline of the partisan press (Schudson, 1978), China's post-Mao commercial revolution in the press, compelled by a government fiscal crisis that made a state-subsidized press no longer viable, was neither politically calculated, nor has it led to the decline of the party organs. Rather than liberalizing entry by private media firms from the outset, party-state organs themselves spearheaded the process of commercialization, adopting and containing the market mechanisms within the existing structure (Zhao, 2000a, 2008a). In the press sector, the licensing system and the sponsor unit system ensured the state's control over the fundamental industrial structure during the processes of commercialization and market-driven expansion. Party committees and party organs have been "structured in dominance" with a policy-ensured advantage in "conquering" the mass market. In fact, China's mass-appeal newspapers – the "evening papers" and the "metro papers" – are directly affiliated with party committees or existing party organs. The "evening papers" were revived or newly published in the 1980s and early 1990s by major provincial and municipal party committees as second papers intended for the urban family, or by provincial and municipal party organs as their urban subsidiaries.

The second category of urban mass-appeal papers, the "metro papers" or the urban omnibus morning dailies, which emerged in the mid-1990s, are subsidiaries of provincial and national party organs. These papers, accounting for the second largest category of daily newspapers, are vehicles for provincial and central party organs, which are mandated to serve both urban and rural areas and are thus unattractive to advertisers, to reach the commercially lucrative mass-appeal market in core Chinese urban centers. At the same time, because these papers are affiliated with central or provincial party organs and are thus above the political jurisdiction of municipal party authorities, they are able to write critical reports on municipal affairs. These papers, which operate as semi-autonomous business units of the traditional central and provincial party organs serve as the perfect media for the party to reach the rising affluent urban consumer strata and reconstitute them as the new power base. At the same time, these papers function as "cash cows" that cross-subsidize the traditional party organs. Thus, if the revolutionary and Maoist-era CCP had only the traditional organs to reach both its rank-and-file officials and the masses, party-controlled media commercialization has now enabled the CCP to divide the task among two primary press segments: the traditional party organs, which serve as means of intra-party communication between its leadership and its grassroots units, and the mass-appeal papers, which serve as a means by which the CCP renegotiates and rearticulates the terms of its hegemony with the rising urban middle class.

To be sure, just as the traditional party organ structure includes not only a small number of "targeted papers" for various social groups (i.e., workers, women, and youth) but also a small number of newspapers targeted at the intellectual elite, notably the *Guangming Daily* and the *Wenhui Daily*, commercialization has contributed to the rise of two powerful elite niche markets. One is the intellectual-oriented press, most notably the now defunct *Shanghai Economic Herald* in the 1980s, and the *Nanfang Weekend*, a nationally circulated subsidiary of the Guangdong provincial party organ *Nangfang Daily* known for its liberal orientation. The second niche market comprises a handful of influential business papers catering to China's rising business class and fashioning themselves after the *Wall Street Journal* and the *Financial Times*. They appeal to a different kind of "elite" – intellectual and business elites with liberal and technocratic orientations – from the readership of the traditional party organs, which tends to be party officials.

The press remains central to the Chinese media system, and the Chinese state set a target of reaching 90 newspapers per 1,000 people by 2010 (Zeng, 2008). However, as is the case in the rest of the developing world, an analysis of media market with a focus on the press is utterly inadequate, if not a case of misplaced emphasis. Instead, it is television that has the widest population reach in China, and the CCP had sanctioned the centrality of television in its propaganda system as early as 1982 when it established China Central Television's (CCTV) prime-time national news program, *Xinwen Lianbo* (Joint Newscast), as the primary news outlet for the announcement of the day's most important political news. Although the press played an important role in the political and social ferment that led to the 1989 urban-based pro-democracy movement, it was *Heshang* (River Elegy), a highly controversial six-episode televisual commentary – a genre that is unique to 1980s Chinese television – broadcast twice by CCTV in 1988, that served as the most powerful text of both intra-elite and popular communication in the pre-1989 era (Zhao and Guo, 2005: 525–6). In the 1990s, when the post-1989 CCP tried to reestablish its hegemony over Chinese society by curbing official corruption and addressing urgent social issues, it authorized CCTV to launch its high-profile investigative show *Jiaodian Fantan* (Focus Interviews). In turn, this national program pioneered a genre of journalism that is influential not only in local television but also in the press. Although the press is the hallmark of print capitalism, Western modernity, and bourgeois rationality, constituting the historical "public sphere" in advanced Western capitalist democracies, until the rise of the Internet, television – state controlled, monopolistically operated, and highly commercialized – had been the most influential medium shaping China's rapidly transforming market society. Furthermore, continuing the Maoist traditions of newspaper reading in the public and integrated propaganda, Chinese television news is still highly print based and verbal oriented, rather than image driven, and it displays a high level of synergy with the press in terms of content. Instead of delivering "sound bite news" (Hallin, 1992), *Xinwen Lianbo* regularly delivers screens after screens of verbal texts from official documents and speeches, with voiceovers. *Xinwen Liaobo* and other major CCTV news programs also frequently announce the editorial titles and news headlines of major newspapers, as well as of Xinhua News Agency major articles. CCTV2 has a program entitled *Ma Bing Reading Newspapers*, in which host Ma Bing presents selected news stories from the press.

Finally, perhaps more than any other society – partly because of the conventional press and broadcast media's highly controlled nature and partly because of the very success of the Chinese state in promoting information technologies – the Internet and the mobile phone have experienced explosive growth in China, becoming influential "fourth" and "fifth" media, respectively – after newspapers, radio, and television. By 2009, China had more than 300 million Internet users and 500 million mobile phone subscribers. One the one hand, Internet users are predominantly urban, young, and male and are concentrated in the coastal regions, which has intensified the urban bias of the Chinese communication system. On the other hand, the participatory and interactive properties of the Internet, its less easily controlled nature, the explosive growth of a rural migrant population in Chinese cities, along with the state's deliberate strategy of allowing more leeway in online communication, have enabled the Internet public to significantly broaden the terms of political discourse in China. Since the early 2000s, the Internet has in many instances played a leading role in setting the news and public debate agenda of the entire Chinese media system, facilitating bottom-up communication (Qiu, 2009; Tan, 2006; Yang, 2009; Zhao, 2008a). At the same time, beyond the Western-media–constructed image of the Chinese state as the world's most notorious Internet controller, the CCP has been proactively incorporating the Internet into its system of communication, thus carrying the Maoist tradition of "mass line" communication into the digital age (Zhao, 2011). On the one hand, the state has strategically established and subsidized the Web sites of major central propaganda organs – most notably the People's Daily's Web forum – even though it had systematically withdrawn media subsidies in general. On the other hand, "government officials [are] browsing the Internet to exchange opinions with netizens" – as *China Today*, an English-language Chinese newsmagazine proclaimed (Li, 2009: 13). For example, Hu Jintao chatted with netizens to mark *People's Daily*'s sixtieth anniversary in June 2008, projecting an image of a central leadership listening to the voices and concerns of Internet users. In March 2009, when China's National People's Congress was in session, Xinhuanet.com opened a space entitled "Premier, Please Listen to Me" for netizens to send their concerns to the top leadership (Li, 2009: 13). In a sense, it can indeed be argued that the Internet has concurrently empowered the state and society (Zheng, 2008), facilitating both vertical and horizontal communication. Similarly, the mobile phone, through short message services (SMS), has not only played an important role in undermining state control of news in events such as the outbreak of SARS but also in mobilizing social protests, including widespread nationalistic protests in urban China (Qiu, 2009; Zhao, 2008a). Although the nature of mobile-phone–facilitated political mobilizations in China and other places remains a matter of scholarly debates (e.g., Castells et al., 2006; Rafael, 2003), clearly it is no longer adequate to analyze conventional news media as the most relevant forums of mediated political communication. If the Habermasian concept of the "public sphere" is historically linked to the rise of the printing press in Western Europe, scholars of Chinese media and communication are only beginning to grasp the role of information and communications technologies (ICTs) in reconstituting China's social class relations and redefining the nature of China's postrevolutionary and post-reform "public sphere" in the twentieth century (Hong, 2011; Qui, 2009; Yang, 2009; Zhao, 2008a). Not surprising, the potential role of social media in China's ongoing transformation emerged as a hot topic in spring 2011, in the aftermath of the so-called "twitter revolutions" in the Arab world. However, it is very important to avoid any technological deterministic and media-centric analysis of social change.

Instrumentalization and Professionalization: Complexities, Tensions, and Accommodations

The official "mouthpiece" definition means that, overall, the Chinese media system has the highest level of political instrumentalization, displaying all the features of a quintessential party-press parallelism (Hallin and Mancini, 2004b). The dominant media institutions are organizationally affiliated with party and state institutions. Media content advocates the official ideology of the CCP and its political programs. The revolving door system between media and party officials is not only formalized but also constantly honed with innovative personnel management practices (Zhao, 2008a). Not only it is routine for party propaganda officials to be appointed as media managers or vice versa, but also selected media executives are assigned temporary party leadership positions to strengthen their party loyalty and gain the perspective of a party official – for example, a middle-level deputy CCTV news director may become a deputy party secretary in a county for a year before either returning to his or her job or being promoted to a higher media management position. The journalists' official role definition is ostensibly to be party propagandists.

Furthermore, because commercialization has been more or less contained with the existing media structure, it has not undermined political instrumentalization in any substantial way. As scholars of Chinese media have noted since the early 1990s, Chinese media development is one of "commercialization without independence" (Chan, 1993), and the Chinese journalistic field remains one of "professionalization without guarantees" (Yu, 1994). More counterintuitively, the emergence of blunt forms of commercial instrumentalization and the abuse of the party's journalistic power – including journalists receiving cash payments for writing promotional pieces ("paid journalism") or extorting businesses by threatening to write negative pieces, as well as news organizations issuing press cards to nonjournalistic personnel who then use the journalistic privilege for profitable gains – have motivated the state to strengthen its normative and occupational control over journalists. Starting from 1991, party and state authorities, in conjunction with the official journalistic association, the All China Journalists Association, have launched sustained campaigns to combat journalistic corruption, including promulgating journalistic professional ethics and codes of conduct (Zhao, 1998: 81–2). State-led codification of professional ethics became "an occasion for the regime to transform its political authority into a moral authority over the journalistic community" (Pan and Lu, 2003: 225). In a more extraordinary development aimed at controlling the journalistic corps and, in official rhetoric, to protect the interests of journalists, the Chinese state centralized the management of press cards by subjecting journalists to a national system of professional certification and licensing. In 2003, as part of the Hu Jintao leadership's attempt to strengthen official ideology and fortify the media's "mouthpiece" role, authorities launched a nationwide compulsory training program for journalists. With the exception of journalists who already had a high professional rank (in China, journalists, like university professors, are on a professional ranking system), all journalists, regardless of whether they had a journalism degree, were required to take a training program in official ideology, media policies and regulations, journalism ethics, Marxist press theory, and related topics. Journalists who completed the program were issued a nationally registered license in January 2004 (Zhao, 2008a: 29). On March 1, 2005, the State Administration for Press and Publications centralized the authority of licensing journalists by implementing its "Management Measures on Journalists' Licenses." Under this new system, a journalist's license, renewable for a five-year term, is also subjected to an annual review.

If one defines professionalization according to North American ideals of political neutrality, "objectivity," and autonomy from political parties and governments, then Chinese journalism utterly lacks professionalization. However, as Hallin and Mancini argue in the case of Northern and Central Europe, "a relatively high level of political parallelism did coexist for most of the twentieth century with a high degree of journalistic professionalism, and indeed to some extent these continue to coexist" (2004b: 41). In China, party-press parallelism coexists with various aspects and degrees of professionalization, partly because of and partly despite of the party's political instrumentalization. Furthermore, if one understands political parallelism broadly to mean the extent to which a media system reflects political divisions, it is clear that the Chinese system contains considerable "external pluralism" – articulating, sometimes dramatically and more often in opaque ways, intra-party and intra-elite divisions, ideological confrontations, and conflicting social interests. I discuss professionalization in this section and take up the question of media and political division and ideological confrontations in the next section.

Professionalization is not simply proclaimed; it is practiced. Moreover, just as there are different dimensions of professionalization in the West, including "autonomy," "distinct professional norms," and "public service orientations" (Hallin and Mancini, 2004b: 35–6), Chinese journalists appropriate diverse and often conflicting ideas of journalism to construct and "localize" professionalism through "their improvised and situated practices" in a rapidly transforming media system (Pan and Lu, 2003: 215). Thus, professionalism as an ideology is "truncated and fragmented in Chinese journalism" (Pan and Lu, 2003: 230). Like journalism in many parts of the non-Western world, Chinese journalism has a strong advocacy and social reform tradition. Underpinning this tradition is an enduring notion of "speaking for the people" wherein the "people" could either have a class character (as in the Maoist definition of "the people" vis-à-vis "class enemies") or a populist character (as opposed to the "elites"). Just as the American penny paper *New York Sun* of the 1830s made the universalist claim that "it shines for all," CCP press theory proclaims that the party's mouthpiece is also the mouthpiece of the "people" (after all, the central CCP party organ is titled *Peoples' Daily*) and that the party serves the people. As the CCP turns journalists into its publicists, it is not completely inconceivable that journalists as social reformers find in party journalism a means to achieve their "public service" objective. Within the framework of traditional Chinese culture, there is the notion of the Confucian intellectual as "the conscience of society and voice of the people," with a mission "to enlighten the public to recognize their and the nation's interests" (Pan and Lu, 2003: 219). Although it is possible to view this journalistic role definition as distinct from that of the party (Pan and Lu, 2003: 219), an argument can be made that the CCP, in sinifying the Leninist vanguard model into its paternalist mass line, has effectively fused its notion of the party's mouthpiece as the people's mouthpiece with that of the Confucian role of the scholar official as the conscience of society and as a social strata whose role is precisely to "enlighten the public to recognize their and the nation's interests": The difference is, whereas the CCP historically spoke the class language, the Confucian tradition speaks the paternalist populist language. As the post-Mao CCP suppresses the class discourse and redefines itself as a party of all people, China's nominally communist state is increasingly transformed into a paternalist and welfarist Confucian state (Bell, 2008).

To be sure, there have been longstanding internal conflicts within the CCP over the press's role, most notably between a popular participatory model and a more bureaucratic and elitist model. This conflict was carried to its extreme during the Cultural Revolution, with the established and highly bureaucratized party organs on the one hand, and the big character posters and Red Guard tabloids on the other. Journalists and media scholars have also at times tried to redefine the mouthpiece role in favor of the "people" both in theory and in practice (Zhao, 1998). Thus, when journalists set out to expose official wrongdoings and speak on behalf of "the people," it is possible for them to conceive of themselves as "truly" fulfilling the role of the party journalist. In short, "serving the people" in the Chinese context has served as a basis for a Chinese notion of professionalism in the same way the "public service" ethos does in the Western context.

At the same time, contemporary Chinese journalists continue to be influenced by Anglo-American notions of autonomy and even impartiality, and they have found inspiration not only directly from Anglo-American journalism but also indirectly from indigenized Anglo-American models in pre-communist China. Along with Leninist party journalism, indigenized by the CCP, commercial journalism, influenced by the Anglo-American liberal tradition, flourished in metropolitan China under the Nationalist regime. One of the most influential Chinese commercial dailies of the pre-1949 era was titled *L'Impartial*, with its chief editor Zhang Jiluan espousing the famous credo of "not to be partisan, not to be bought, not to pursue self-interests, not to be led blindly." As Pan and Lu (2003: 221–2) relate, contemporary Chinese journalism educators and journalists often recite Zhang's motto favorably, and the ideas imputed to precommunist journalistic icons such as Zhang – journalistic autonomy and editorial independence – bear partial similarity to Western-style journalistic professionalism. Today, many Chinese journalists and journalism educators continue to find inspiration in the Anglo-American liberal model, and market-oriented media outlets proclaim objectivity and impartiality in their news reporting without rejecting their CCP-mandated role of maintaining the "correct orientation to public opinion" (*zhengqu yulun daoxiang*). Citing a *Nanfang Weekend* editorial, Pan and Lu (2003: 231) explain that objectivity in this context "means reporting fact from the vantage point of journalists being not only witness but also catalysts of the social changes led by the Communist Party." Even the official Web site of the State Administration for Press and Publications espouses the values of "truthfulness, objectivity, impartiality, orientation, conscience, ethics" all at the same time. Moreover, Chinese journalists, like their American counterparts who tend to apply the norms of objectivity relatively (Hallin, 1986), invoke and deploy different professional norms and different, even contradictory, facets of what Hackett and I have described as the "regime of objectivity" in accordance with their own ideological framework (Hackett and Zhao, 1998). Thus, in one case, professionalism is understood as passionately crusading for a given cause and dramatizing the social meaning of a news event, whereas in another case, professionalism is defined in terms of suppressing passion and presenting the "bare facts" (Zhao, 2008a: chap. 5).

Finally, there are areas of ambiguity and overlap between the CCP press tradition and Western-style professionalism centering on journalistic relative autonomy. Theories and practices of critical reporting encompass one such area. One interesting point that Schramm mentioned as a distinctive feature of the Soviet press system is that the system has "moved beyond forbidding the press to criticize the regime, to the point actually that they are fairly free in inviting criticism of the minor functioning and functionaries of the regime" (Seibert et al., 1963: 140). Carrying out "criticism and self-criticism" in the media is a manifestation of one of the CCP's "three great superior traditions" (the other two are "seeking truth from facts" and "the mass line"). As a reportorial genre, "criticism and self-criticism" – the publication of contained and constructive criticisms of the party's work in a specific area – originated in the CCP's early revolutionary period. It became more regularized in the early 1940s and was formally promoted by the CCP Central Committee's April 19, 1950, "Decision on Carrying out Criticism and Self-Criticism in the Press" (Zhao, 2011). This tradition of specific criticism of concrete work was completely overshadowed by the "Create Criticisms and Great Debates" of the Cultural Revolution as ideological differences and factional struggles intensified. However, it was quickly resuscitated in the early reform period after Deng restored the CCP's Leninist discipline and forged a reform consensus. By the mid-1980s, the party state's anti-corruption imperative had necessitated media exposure of corrupt officials. However, by then, the liberal discourse of the press as a "watchdog" of the government had gained influence and the more Western-sounding notion of "public opinion supervision" gradually replaced the Maoist notion of "criticism and self-criticism." By the time CCTV's *Focus Interviews* established itself as the exemplary "public opinion supervision" reporting genre in the mid-1990s in response to the CCP's intensified campaign against official corruption (Zhao and Sun, 2007), the notion of "criticism and self-criticism" had disappeared in Chinese political and journalistic discourses. Instead, media scholars began to rearticulate the party's call for media surveillance against corruption in terms of the Western notion of professionalism (Pan and Lu, 2003: 227), while journalistic practitioners at CCTV's *Focus Interviews* explicitly modeled their investigative shows after CBS's *60 Minutes*, espousing the motto of "speaking with facts" (Zhao, 1998, 2000b).

Media and Political Divisions within and beyond the CCP

A discussion of media and political divisions in China's one-party state formation requires a number of theoretical moves. First, one must understand political practices as a praxis informed by theory and imagine political divisions beyond a notion of political pluralism as reflected in the formal institutional framework of multiparty democracies. Second, one needs to move beyond Cold War–inspired images of the CCP as a totalitarian monolith on the one hand and as a political apparatus afflicted with factional struggles on the other. Rather than merely "reflecting" political divisions embodied in institutionalized multiparty politics and formal electoral processes, the Chinese media under CCP control have been highly constitutive of political struggles, which were spoken of as "line struggles within the party" in the pre-reform era, and of fundamental theoretical and policy debates over the direction of Chinese society.

Wang has observed that an outstanding characteristic of twentieth-century China's revolutionary transformations "had been the continuous and intimate connection between theoretical debate and political practice" (2006: 32). Throughout the CCP's history, "every great political battle was inextricably linked to serious theoretical considerations and policy debates," ranging from "conflicting analysis of the question of revolutionary defeat following the catastrophe of 1927, through the theoretical disputes of the early 1930s on the social character of the Chinese revolution . . . to the debates on contradiction during the Cultural Revolution" (Wang, 2006: 33). Although the absence of institutionalized mechanisms for inner party democracy meant that these debates and differences often found their "resolution" through faction fights, in Wang's view, "it is precisely these theoretical battles that maintain a party's internal vitality and ensure that it does not become a depoliticized political organization. Subjecting theory and practice to the 'line struggle' also functions as a corrective mechanism, enabling the party to recognize and repair its errors" (2006: 33). As Wang (2006: 33) goes on to note,

During the Sixties China had developed a wide-ranging theoretical agenda, revolving around such questions as the dynamics of history, the market economy, the means of production, class struggle, bourgeois right, the nature of Chinese society and the status of world revolution. There were heated exchanges between different political blocs on all these questions.

The Chinese media system was deeply implicated in these debates, and the Cultural Revolution, which aimed to revitalize CCP politics after its stagnation and bureaucratization in the post-1949 era but ended up transforming political debates into polarized factional struggles and symbolic violence of the most destructive kind, generated some of the most heated political debates over China's developmental path in the history of Chinese politics. Furthermore, as a precursor to the Cultural Revolution, and in an extraordinary moment in the history of twentieth-century party politics in the world, the Chinese media system spearheaded an international debate on the "Soviet revisionist line" between the CCP and Communist Party of the Soviet Union (CPSU). The *People's Daily*'s notorious "Nine Commentaries," published between June 9, 1963, and July 14, 1964, in the form of a series of "open letters" to the CPSU, epitomized probably the highest point of partisan politics and the sharpest political division in the media in a world historical context – if one understands international media history to also include that of communist countries. As Wang (2006: 33) argues,

After the Cultural Revolution, many of those who had suffered in the process came first to detest and then repudiate the "line struggle" concept. On regaining power in the late Seventies they sought to suppress this type of argument in the name of party unity, rather than to analyse the conditions whereby "line struggle" had degenerated into mere power play. This not only resulted in a thoroughgoing suppression of the political life of the party, but also destroyed the possibility of exploring the relationship between the party and democracy. Rather, it laid the foundation for the statification – i.e. depoliticization – of the party.

Consequently, the Chinese political system was transformed from a party-state system into a "state-party" system, in the same way and as part of the same world historical process in which Western political parties transformed themselves into "state parties." That is, rather than political parties having a specific representative character and political values, their character and political values become increasingly indeterminate within a broad macroeconomic consensus. Instead of functioning as a stimulant for political ideas and practices, political parties become depoliticized structural functional machines for capturing state power, resulting in the hollowing of democratic politics in the West. Because the Chinese case is a symptom of this worldwide dynamic toward the neoliberal politics of depoliticization, Wang's point is well taken when he argues that those analyses that avoided "recognition of the generalized crisis in party politics and attempt[ed] to prescribe the best means of reforming the Chinese system – including setting Western-style multi-party representative democracy as the goal of Chinese political reform – are themselves only extensions of this depoliticization" (Wang, 2006: 35).

Ironically, the politics of depoliticization in the post-Cultural Revolution era was consolidated by one more highly politicized "Great Debate" – the debate on "truth criteria" in the Chinese media in 1978. Although such a seemingly abstract and philosophical debate appears irrelevant and even absurd to the dominant Western notions of politics

and political communication, it assumed fundamental political importance because of the intimate connection between theoretical debate and
political practice that had historically characterized CCP politics and
given it its vitality. It was precisely this debate – which rejected Mao's
teachings as the ultimate truth and established the pragmatism in the
doctrine of the "practice criterion" of truth – that enabled the Dengist
faction, known as the "reformers" in the West, to dethrone the theoretical, ideological, and political authorities of what was left of the "Cultural
Revolution" Maoist left, known as the "conservatives" in the West; this
allowed the former to legitimate and consolidate their power to pursue the
policy of "reform and open up." Furthermore, as Wang (2006: 34) notes,
although Deng severed the organic relationship between theory and political practice with the pragmatic notion of "crossing the river by feeling
for the stones," debates about socialism, humanism, alienation, the market economy, and ownership both within the CCP and Chinese society
as a whole continued to shape Chinese media discourses in the early and
mid-1980s.

Although the repression of 1989 temporarily ended political debates,
by 1991 and 1992, tensions between the CCP's socialist claims and its
capitalistic-oriented economic reform policies had intensified, and the
Chinese media were once again caught in an intra-elite debate. Facing a
Beijing media scene dominated by national party organs under the tight
control of a CCP central propaganda department that espoused a more
"conservative" position, Deng, who had no official party position by
then, found it necessary to travel to southern China and mobilize the
more liberal-oriented Shanghai and Guangdong media to advocate his
line. In what must have been seen as the most effective imposition of
depoliticization, Deng consolidated the post-1989 Chinese political and
ideological order for accelerated market-oriented development by proclaiming his own "truth" in his "southern tour" talks – that is, "development is the hard truth" – and by imposing his famous "no debate" degree;
that is, there should be no open debates in the media about whether the
reform policies were capitalist or socialist. This decree, which was quickly
adopted as an official CCP position under the leadership of Jiang Zemin,
effectively sealed off any media space for debates over the fundamental
direction of China's social transformation. It consolidated the ground for
a process of party-controlled commercialization that further integrated
the media with the interests of the country's political, economic, and
intellectual/cultural elite, accelerating both political instrumentalization
and commercial instrumentalization at once.

It is within this political economic and ideological context that Chinese journalistic professionalism and *Focus Interviews* of the investigative reporting type I described as "watchdogs on party leashes" emerged to neutralize social tensions and smooth the rough edges of a market-authoritarian society (Zhao, 2000b, 2004; Zhao and Sun, 2007). For an entire decade (1992–2002), it appeared in the Chinese media that the Chinese "end of ideology" moment had arrived. That is, a "market reform" consensus had been secured, fundamental political debates over China's reform path had ended, and all that was needed was to solve practical administrative problems – including the problem of official corruption – through the investigative reporting of journalists as part of a rising urban middle class with state-sanctioned professional credentials and market-guaranteed financial means. Within this general ideological framework of the depoliticization of both state and market, "divisions over questions of development become technical disputes about market-adjustment mechanisms. Political divisions between labour and capital, left and right, are made to disappear" (Wang, 2006: 39).

However, as I already alluded to earlier, by 1999, the Chinese media system had found itself caught in an intensive ideological battle with the grassroots-based Falun Gong movement over fundamental categories such as truth, rationality, science, and ethics (Zhao, 2003). By 2005, intra-party divisions between what Li (2009) described as the more "elitist" and more "populist" factions within the CCP leadership had intersected in complicated ways with elite intellectual politics and grassroots popular class politics – including a revived Maoist discourse – to generate heated political and ideological debates. While liberal and neoliberal intellectuals crusaded for accelerated market-oriented reforms and even political liberalization along Western-style multiparty democracy and (Western) "universalist values" (*pushi jiazhi*), old revolutionaries, left-leaning intellectuals, and grassroots online critics of market-oriented reforms mounted successive waves of criticism against the further privatization of China's state-owned economic sector, the entrenchment of private property rights in the Chinese legal system, the dominance of Western-style market economics and neoliberal ideology, and the economic exploitation of laborers. Different sectors of the print and broadcast media took different positions and articulated different social interests in a multifaceted Chinese "public sphere," with the Internet, which reflects more popular and grassroots tendencies in Chinese society, playing an instrumental role in spearheading these debates (Zhao, 2008a). By March 2006, even China's National People's Congress – the "public sphere" within the Chinese state that is not known for being a place of open political debates – was "consumed with an ideological debate over socialism and capitalism that many assumed had been buried by China's long steak of fast economic growth" (Khan, 2006). That this observation was made by the *New York Times* was perhaps even more significant.

To be sure, these debates were limited in many ways. Moreover, the party's censorship regime eventually curtailed them, and the Hu Jintao leadership in any case did not intend to break Deng's "no debate" curse in any substantive way. Nevertheless, it remains the case that one of the world's most tightly controlled media systems generated some of the most lively and spontaneous challenges to the politics of neoliberal development and depoliticization several years ahead of the spectacular implosion of neoliberalism as the global ideology par excellence in 2008. In doing so, China's Internet users, led by a small anti-neoliberal counter-elite within intellectual and media circles, mounted a challenge to the domination of an "iron triangle" of political, business, and academic/media elites in public discourses on policy issues. These debates not only reinjected an important social dimension into China's emerging market economy but also raised fundamental questions about the future of Chinese socialism. It remains to be seen whether these debates are symptomatic of the beginning of "repoliticization" in the aftermath of the bankruptcy of neoliberalism and the 2008–9 global economic-financial crisis. Certainly, Internet-based debates and political struggles in China have contributed to a significant shift in the Chinese state's macroeconomic and social policies, so much so that Derek Scissors (2009:24), an alarmist *Foreign Affairs* writer, proclaims that the year of 2008 "marked the 30th anniversary of the beginning of market reforms in China – and perhaps the third anniversary of their ending."

Conclusion

Anticipating a "new global financial system" in the aftermath of the collapse of the post-Bretton Woods system and noting how China, which has "capital controls and a managed currency," had become the largest creditor of the United States, the *Economist* ("Birth Pains," 2009: 80) posited, "It has been assumed that China will have to move toward the Western model. But why not the other way round? Western countries adopted free capital markets, as the British adopted free trade in the 19th century, because it suited them." To be sure, financial systems and media systems operate on different logics. To many, the thought that Western media models may converge on the Chinese model sounds truly horrifying, and I for one certainly do not anticipate, let alone advocate this. Moreover, the media in most countries "do not constitute any single 'system' with a single purpose or philosophy, but are composed of many separate, overlapping, often inconsistent elements with appropriate differences of normative expectation and actual regulation" (McQuail, 1994:133, cited in Hallin and Mancini, 2004b: 12). In China, although the party media model remains "structured in dominance," it is perhaps useful to move beyond a single model to understand Chinese media institutions and practices in the dynamic and creative tensions among political instrumentalization, commercial instrumentalization, professionalization, and pressures for popular participation in the era of digitalized and socialized communication.

Nevertheless, the *Economist*'s provocation does offer food for thought about the world's media systems and their future. That the Western media systems, despite all their freedoms, independence, public service professionalism, and variegated degrees of external and internal diversities, failed to provide any effective check on the excesses of global financial capitalism must be seen as an astonishing case of commercial instrumentalism. Now, after all the mega-mergers and market consolidations of the neoliberal era and after having played a sort of a Leninist "vanguard" role for the ascendancy of global financial capitalism, Western media systems are entering a profound and multifaceted crisis of their own. As the *Economist* ("Rebirth of News," 2009: 16) reported, in the aftermath of the burst of the global financial bubble and the ensuing advertising slump, along with the impact of the Internet, few other businesses are "doing as badly as the news business," with "[t]he crisis...most advanced in the Anglo-Saxon countries" and the newspaper industry the hardest hit sector. Beyond the parameters of the current economic crisis, consumer capitalism, in which advertising as a form of commercial propaganda has been the lifeblood for the news business, is no longer sustainable ecologically. Thus, there is indeed an urgent question regarding the long-term sustainability of advertising-dependent media systems, Western or non-Western alike. Certainly one does not have to invoke the Leninist notion of press freedom or endorse the CCP's self-serving media control regime to begin to challenge what McChesney et al. (2009: 19) have characterized as the "virtual civic religion" of the U.S. media system as the most powerful of all Western media systems – "that freedom of the press equals capitalistic, advertising-supported media."

Meanwhile, in China, state-controlled media continue to commercialize, capitalize, and expand domestically and, increasingly, globally in an attempt to project China's "soft power" outward. Although Chinese liberal intellectuals continue to view the Western media as embodying "universalist" values, there is also profound disillusionment among the Western-media–influenced and Internet-savvy youth generation with Western media's self-proclaimed ideals of freedom, autonomy, and impartiality. If CCTV's establishment of a CNN-inspired twenty-four-hour news channel, among other developments, can be seen as a response to the "forces of homogenization," Chinese Internet activists' creation of an "anti-CNN" website to expose the Western media for their coverage of the riots in Tibet in 2008 is a powerful reminder of the forces of nationalism and the different histories of nation-state formation that have underpinned both Western and non-Western media systems. At the same time, just as it is no longer, if it ever was, constructive to discuss whether the Chinese economy is moving toward the American model at a time when the two economies are so closely intertwined and when the "actually existing American model" has encountered such a profound crisis, it will be illuminating not only to compare national media systems within the relative confines of national political economies and cultures but also to study the dynamics of hybridization and contestation between different media systems and political cultures.

PART II

METHODS AND APPROACHES

9

The Rise of Transnational Media Systems

Implications of Pan-Arab Media for Comparative Research

Marwan M. Kraidy

The nation-state as unit of analysis underpins the three models of media and politics Hallin and Mancini develop in *Comparing Media Systems* (2004b). Although they "take the nation-state as [our] primary unit of analysis ... and media systems have to a large extent been organized at this level over the past couple of centuries," the authors recognize that "it is important to keep in mind that this in some ways misleading" (Hallin and Mancini, 2004b: 71). Livingstone similarly argued that "the nation is itself not a proper unit of comparison" and that "any project seeking to conduct cross-national comparisons must surely argue the case for treating the nation as a unit, rather than simply presuming the legitimacy of such a research strategy" (Livingstone, 2003: 479–80). This chapter explores one world region in which the primacy of the nation-state as an analytical category may indeed be misleading; through analyzing the rise of pan-Arab media as a transnational system, I raise questions about the universal applicability of the nation-state and provide significant fodder to Hallin's statement that "media systems do not necessarily coincide neatly with nation-state boundaries" (Hallin, 2009: 101).

Since 1990, Arab national broadcasting systems focused on development, propaganda, and national unity have been overshadowed by a pan-Arab satellite television industry whose ownership and agendas converge and compete with nation-state policies. This development encompasses twenty-two nation-states located in one of the world's intractable geopolitical flashpoints. Contemporary Arab media consist of an unevenly integrated regional (pan-Arab) market, superimposed onto national systems and increasingly integrated into the global media market, although in many respects distinct from both: It is a transnational media system.

The system is internally differentiated. Oil monarchies of the Gulf Cooperation Council (Bahrain, Kuwait, Oman, Qatar, Saudi Arabia, and the United Arab Emirates) are wealthier and socially more conservative than other countries in the Levant (Jordan, Lebanon, Palestinian Authority, and Syria) and the Maghreb (Algeria, Morocco, and Tunisia). Within each of these areas, political and media systems vary widely: Saudi Arabia's clerico-political authoritarianism and quiescent media contrast with Kuwait's feisty press and robust legislature, and Lebanon's fragmented polity and pluralist media differ greatly from Syria's one-party state and mostly monolithic press and broadcasting. The region's high-density urban centers have radically different social dynamics than do its rural areas. Another important cleavage exists between demographic heavyweights like Egypt and Saudi Arabia and small countries like Lebanon and Qatar. A sharp generational contrast, with youth accounting for more than 70 percent of the population (*World Population Prospects*, 2003), shapes media markets. Finally, the simultaneous rise of religiosity and consumerism undergirds a variety of sociocultural tensions and transformations.

These differences notwithstanding, a distinct transnational system has emerged. This chapter explores tensions between national and regional forces that shape the pan-Arab media system by focusing on Saudi Arabia and Lebanon, both instrumental in shaping the regional media order but occupying opposite poles of the sociopolitical spectrum: Saudi Arabia is the Arab world's most socially conservative nation, whereas Lebanon is its most socially liberal society. The two are joined by what I elsewhere called the "Saudi–Lebanese connection" (Kraidy, 2009): Saudi moguls with royal connections finance Arab media, while Lebanese journalists, producers, and managers populate the system. A direct comparative study of the two nation-states would gloss over the complexity and implications of this convergence. Saudi Arabia and Lebanon are better understood as a dynamic pair whose multifaceted interactions have shaped, along with those of other players, the rise of a transnational media system.

A Short History of Comparative Arab Media Research

In *The Arab Press*, first published in 1979, William Rugh classified the Arab press into three models: "mobilization," which includes Algeria, Egypt, Syria, Libya, Sudan, Iraq, and Yemen (People's Democratic Republic); "loyalist," encompassing Jordan, Saudi Arabia, Bahrain, Qatar, Oman, Tunisia, the United Arab Emirates, and Palestine; and "diverse," existing in Lebanon, Kuwait and Morocco. Reflecting a version of media-political parallelism, Rugh used "press characteristics" and "political conditions" as the two central dimensions of his typology. His analysis rested on four characteristics of the press – ownership, variety, view of (attitude toward the) regime, and style and tone – and three political conditions: the nature of the ruling group, the presence of public debate, and the existence of political opposition. Rugh mentioned *Four Theories of the Press* in his introduction and first chapter to endorse the view in Siebert et al. (1956) that media take on the "form and coloration of the social and political structure" where they operate and to note that none of the Arab systems falls within the book's categories. He concluded that because "none of the existing analytical categories helps us much in going beneath the surface of the Arab media systems, in order to explain their real functioning we must devise new theories designed to fit the cases at hand" (Rugh, 1979: 28). In the expanded version published a quarter-century later, *Arab Mass Media: Newspapers, Radio, and Television in Arab Politics* (2004), Rugh added a new category to his "Typology of Arab Print Media Systems" that he called "Transitional" and to which he moved Egypt, Jordan, Tunisia, and Algeria. Other changes include moving now unified Yemen from "mobilization" to "diverse" (Rugh, 2004).

Criticism of Rugh's taxonomy emerged in the 1980s, with one Arabic-language article attributing its lack of depth and sophistication to its weak contextualization of Western theories and its neglect of content in favor of a focus on ownership and state–press relations (Azzi, 1989). Yet it has been in the 2000s, when academic study of the Arab media achieved critical momentum at Western universities, that more scholars have attempted to typologize Arab media. Ayish (2002), for example, distinguished three models: "traditional government-controlled," like the Syrian Satellite Channel; "reformist government-controlled," like Abu Dhabi TV and Dubai TV; and "liberal commercial," like al-Jazeera. Mellor went further, arguing that Rugh's "typology has its shortcomings... based on *unclearly defined categories*... does not account for the *recent situation* in the Arab news media... its negligence of several factors, such as *the role of émigré media*" (2005: 51, emphasis added). She concluded that "the classification of the Arab press into four categories depending on the censorship exercised by the government does not account for the symbiotic relationship that takes place between the three actors involved in news production: government, journalists/editors, and the audience" (Mellor, 2005: 64). Rugh responded that "the most powerful factor influencing the structure and functioning of the media in the political process is the actual political reality that prevails in each country at a given time" (Rugh, 2007).

Most approaches to Arab media have emphasized the nation-state as a container and shaper of media, which may explain some of these disagreements. The nation is a problematic category for comparative analysis, and according to Livingstone (2003: 485), it can be approached in four different ways: as an object of study, as a context of study, as a unit of analysis, and as a "component of a larger international or transnational system." Rugh's and to a lesser extent Mellor's approach looked at nation-states as units of analysis. In contrast, this chapter proposes to move comparative research to the transnational realm. It develops an argument in favor of understanding contemporary Arab media, especially television, as a transnational system. Although Mellor gestured toward a transnational element when she emphasized the role of the Arab émigré press in the development of Arab media, she stopped short of making the transnational a central systemic feature. Rugh was correct in arguing that national political conditions are the primary shapers of Arab media, but he does not consider how transnational forces can shape national politics and in turn national media institutions. In turn, as numerous writings about al-Jazeera have demonstrated, transnational media institutions can shape national politics in specific countries, in addition to pan-Arab politics. Building on my previous research on Arab media controversies (Kraidy, 2009) and industries (Kraidy and Khalil, 2009), this chapter explores how interactions between national and supranational forces shape the transnational media system.

How does research on Arab media mesh with the four central dimensions of Hallin and Mancini's typology: the development of media markets, journalistic professionalization, media-political parallelism, and the role of the state? Economic forces are a powerful catalyst of transnationalization: Most Arab countries do not have the combination of purchasing power and population size to make them viable markets individually. The development of a transnational media market intersects powerfully with cross-national media professionalization. Saudi Arabia has had to rely on Egyptians and, most visibly, Lebanese to operate its media institutions, from early newspapers in the first decade of the twentieth century, to the revamping and expansion of the state television apparatus in the second decade of the twenty-first century. The Saudi and Lebanese cases also reflect two radically different roles for the state in the media system, which result in two different kinds of parallelism. These two countries offer an opportunity to explore parallelism from a transnational vantage point and to expand the notion of professionalization in comparative media research.

Arab Media and the Hallin and Mancini Model

The Development of Media Markets

The first Lebanese newspaper, *Hadiqat al-Akhbar* (News Garden), appeared in 1858, and the first Saudi newspaper, *Umm al-Qura* (Mother of Villages), was first published in 1924 and remains the state's official newspaper. (There have been several newspapers in the Hijaz since 1908, but the province was not integrated into Saudi Arabia until 1925.) Rugh argues that "real" newspapers did not develop in Saudi Arabia until the 1940s (Rugh, 1979). In 1975, Lebanon had 99 licensed political publications and 300 nonpolitical publications; of these, one newspaper had a circulation above 60,000 and two magazines above 100,000 (Dajani, 1975). The contemporary Lebanese press consists of a dozen national daily newspapers (most in Arabic, but a few in English, French, and Armenian), each distributing less than 50,000 copies. Both Lebanon and Saudi Arabia developed press laws in the 1960s that, among other features, enshrined private ownership and press autonomy.

Television in Lebanon was from the beginning a private–public venture. The national channel Télé-Liban was created by private businessmen who approached the government for a broadcasting license in the 1950s, and it remained a hybrid, half-private, half-state–owned institution until the early 2000s. By weakening the state's jurisdiction, the 1975–90 civil war created a media scene as fractured as Lebanon's political landscape, spawning dozens of unlicensed television and radio channels. A postwar 1994 Audio-Visual Media Law, implemented in 1996, reduced the number of private television stations to four and a few licenses have been awarded in the ensuing years (Kraidy, 1998, 1999).

The biggest challenge for Lebanese media is the small size of the national market, a challenge that has bedeviled media institutions from the early days of the press and continues to do so in the television era. In the 1950s, Beirut had more than fifty dailies, and even the Press Syndicate was concerned by this fragmentation. To remedy this issue, a 1953 legislative decree (see Rugh, 1979) stipulated a ceiling for the number of political dailies. In the 1970s, when Lebanon had the highest literacy rate in the Arab world, estimates had it that three of four Lebanese read a newspaper on a daily basis (Rugh, 1979). Since then, chronically shaky economic underpinnings have led the Lebanese press toward consolidation: Today most of the two dozen publishing houses publish several titles. Dar Assayad, for instance, publishes the daily newspaper *Addyar* and nine other titles. Market fragmentation has also made the Lebanese media vulnerable to instrumentalization by local and foreign forces.

In Saudi Arabia, the period 1962–75, known as the Faysal era (Kraidy, 2009), saw crucial developments in the national media market. When Prince Faysal Bin 'Abdul'aziz became prime minister for the second time in October 1962, there were no magazines, only one radio station, and three daily newspapers in Saudi Arabia. Although the U.S Air Force had been operating a station, AJL-TV, since 1955 (Boyd, 1999), and the Arabian American Oil Company (ARAMCO) ran another since 1957 (Rugh, 1980), Saudi Arabia did not have a national television service. Radio Mecca, the only radio station in existence, which had since 1948 broadcast religious programs, was audible only in the province of Hijaz, where 200,000 radio receivers existed at the time. The three newspapers together distributed 25,000 copies (Rugh, 1980). Between the time when Faysal became king in 1964 and his assassination in 1975, he expanded Saudi media to the point where there were seven dailies with a combined distribution of 100,000, Saudi radio could be heard across the kingdom, and Saudi television reached 1.5 million viewers (out of a population of around 7 million; *Saudi Arabia Country Profile*, 2008). As the Saudi economy grew and literacy rates rose, the number of newspapers increased. By 1976, there were seven Arabic and two English dailies (Rugh, 1979). Today the Saudi press consists of thirteen dailies (most in Arabic, but a few in English), approximately one per region, and a dozen companies control the market. For example, Saudi Research and Publishing issues seventeen publications, including five of the thirteen dailies.

With its wealth and large population, Saudi Arabia is the most important target of pan-Arab advertising and the largest market in the Gulf. Of its estimated 20 million viewers, 95 percent watch television at least six times a week, and 23 percent watch more than four hours of television per day (*Trends in Middle Eastern Arabic Television Series Production*, 2007). It is no surprise then that the marketing research company MindShare found that 80 percent of Saudi consumers believed that television was the most influential medium on their purchasing decisions. As a result, catering to the tastes of Saudi viewers is a priority for the Arab television industries throughout the year, but especially during the month of Ramadan when viewership reaches its peak and many channels spend a significant part of their yearly advertising budget (Kraidy and Khalil, 2009).

Media-Political Parallelism

Lebanon – and Saudi Arabia to a lesser extent – bears out Hallin and Mancini's claim that "where organized pluralism was strongly developed, the media were always integrated to a significant extent into the institutions of group representation" (2004b: 54). In both countries, media content reflects distinct political orientations, media are enmeshed in broader political structures, media workers tend to be active in political life, readers and viewers tend to be partisan, and journalists who work in that environment see themselves as analysts and commentators more than as "neutral" reporters of information. In Lebanon, parallelism clearly aligns with the country's consociationalism and political sectarianism (*al-ta'ifiyya al-siyasiyya*), according to which spoils are divided among the country's eighteen officially recognized groups, the largest three being Shi'i Muslims, Sunni Muslims, and Maronite Christians. Vertical networks of patronage and clientelism have historically permeated the system. In Saudi Arabia, although national broadcasting remains the property of the state, press parallelism reflects various clans within the royal family, which numbers thousands of princes and their business associates. The Saudi press, privately owned, has strong regional (subnational) characteristics. The first licenses for privately owned television, under discussion as of this writing, will most likely be given for regional, not national outlets.

National media in Lebanon and Saudi Arabia display a high level of external pluralism – that is, "pluralism achieved at the level of the media system as a whole" (Hallin and Mancini, 2004b: 29) – as opposed to internal pluralism, within each media entity. In terms of broadcast governance and regulation, whereas Saudi Arabia falls within the government model, with broadcasting directly controlled by the government through the Ministry of Culture and Information, Lebanon bears a striking resemblance to the "proportional representation model," although of mostly private, not public, broadcasters.

The 1975–90 Lebanese civil war spawned a national media explosion akin to situations in Southern Europe that led to the development of "savage deregulation" (Traquina, 1995). Unlike its neighbors, the Lebanese state had until recently never fully owned a television station. During the war political parties and warring factions launched several dozen unlicensed radio and television stations as mouthpieces: conservative and radical, Christian and Muslim, secular and religious, capitalist and communist (Kraidy, 1998, 2000). Just as the private–public broadcaster Télé-Liban was symptomatic of a weak state, so its unlicensed competitors symbolized the strength of civil society and sectarian politics. The new channels outperformed Télé-Liban in the ratings and became the most visible indication of the collapse of the Lebanese state.

A pressing postwar regulatory challenge was to restore state authority while preserving a politically representative media system. The "Document of National Understanding" – underwritten by Saudi Arabia, brokered by then Saudi special envoy to Lebanon, Rafiq Al-Hariri, and signed in the Saudi resort city of Ta'ef on October 22, 1989 – put an end to military conflict in Lebanon and called for the reorganization of the Lebanese media within a "modern" regulatory framework. The resulting 1994 Audio-Visual Media Law (AVML) was hailed as the first broadcasting law in the Arab world, but the licensing process was nakedly political. The AVML implementation in 1996 favored media institutions owned by leading politicians and cut down the number of privately owned television stations from sixty to four (Kraidy, 1998). Licensing followed the customary Lebanese sectarian formula. The four licensed TV stations were a Maronite station (LBC), a Sunni station (Future TV), a Shi'i station (National Broadcasting Network [NBN]), and a Greek Orthodox station with Druze influence (Murr Television [MTV]). Later, additional licenses were given to Al-Manar, Hizbollah's outlet; Télé-Lumière, a Christian station operated by the Maronite clergy; and New TV, formerly owned by the Lebanese Communist Party. Télé-Liban, whose monopoly ended with the AVML, fell into a protracted decline (Kraidy, 1998). The equilibrium achieved by licensing stations on sectarian bases, although periodically shaken by inflammatory broadcasts or state harassment (Kraidy, 1999), was punctured only by the shutdown of MTV by the Lebanese–Syrian security apparatus in September 2003.

As new political forces emerged, the government awarded new licenses, like the one won for OTV by the Free Patriotic Movement, a predominantly Christian political movement currently allied with Hizbollah. The momentous political upheaval and massive street demonstrations in 2005 reflected a flagrant polarization between two multisectarian blocks and strong parallelism between these forces and the country's print and electronic media.

Parallelism between the political structure and the media apparatus is less clearly defined in Saudi Arabia, where the media are aligned with government policy, but where, nonetheless, individuals and clans within the royal family have sway over different newspapers and satellite television channels. One way in which princes, their business associates, and state institutions subsidize Saudi newspapers is by purchasing advertising space, where the messages range from congratulations to official announcements similar to the ones found in the Israeli press (see Chapter 2). Parallelism emerges more clearly in Saudi-owned or controlled pan-Arab satellite channels; the control structure of these channels parallels the ongoing battle between liberals and conservatives in the kingdom, a battle in which the royal family plays the role of arbiter (Kraidy, 2009).

Professionalization

The freedom historically enjoyed by Lebanese journalists makes journalistic professionalization vulnerable because it opens the door for the instrumentalization of Lebanese journalism by local, but most importantly regional players. The late 1940s and early 1950s saw an intensification of foreign interest and influence. With Beirut benefiting from the fall of the port of Haifa, hitherto a major trading center in the Arab world, into the hands of the Israelis, and with Lebanon as a whole benefiting from the political and economic instability brought to Egypt by the 1952 coup, Lebanon solidified its role as a trading and publication center, and the press thrived as a result. Foreign money pouring in enabled the technological modernization of the printing process and the physical expansion of newspaper offices. Dajani (1975: 168) reported that a major Lebanese publisher then said that "the present situation of the Lebanese press is such that the publisher who does not take bribes is an ass." The Lebanese government, local business interests, foreign embassies, and international corporations "rented" editorial influence in the Lebanese press through subsidies, concentrated advertising, or direct payments to journalists.

Lebanese authorities were aware of these activities but unable to stop them because they often involved actors more powerful than the Lebanese government. The state of journalistic professionalization in Lebanon in the 1970s is reflected in the following story:

Toward the end of his term of office, the former President of Lebanon, Charles Helu, received the then newly-elected members of the Lebanese Press Union. After formal introduction, Helu jokingly, but with a mild tone of seriousness, addressed the Council members, saying: "Now that I have met you in your official capacities, may I learn what foreign countries your papers unofficially represent? . . . Welcome to your second country, Lebanon." (Dajani, 1975: 167)

In this environment, in which cynics argued that there was "no Lebanese press," only "a press in Lebanon," the Saudis found a space to influence Lebanese and pan-Arab politics, which is discussed in detail later in this chapter. For now, it suffices to keep in mind that the "rented" Lebanese press was regionally influential – Egyptian leader Gamal Abdel Nasser was known to read the Lebanese press before reading Egyptian newspapers in the morning (Kraidy, 1999) – and the Cold War and Arab tensions played out on its pages.

In what is now Saudi Arabia, newspapers were more critical of political leaders in the first three decades of the twentieth century, but when modern Saudi Arabia emerged in 1925, the press came under the sway of the al-Saud ruling family and turned its focus away from politics and toward poetry and literature. Since then, newspapers have reflected the importance of public consensus. When Saudi Arabia experienced the first oil boom and ensuing modernization of the state in the 1950s, newspapers prospered and grew more outspoken, especially in Jidda, the commercial center and most socially liberal city in the kingdom. The government cracked down in the late 1950s, shutting down the most critical dailies and merging others. In the 1960s, after several journalists were banned from writing in the country, the press grew even more quiescent. In the 1970s, according to the Ministry of Information the "common goal" of the government and the press was to develop the country, so Saudi journalists were "called upon" to write in support of that objective (Rugh, 1979: 85). In response to the siege of the Grand Mosque by radical militants in 1979, the royal family consolidated its grip on the media and instituted restrictive policies in the 1980s (Kraidy, 2009).

In the 1990s the rise of satellite television posed a challenge, not only by weakening the ability of government to control information but also by redefining the role of journalists from *sahafi* to *e'lami*. The first word, which means "journalist," customarily refers to print journalists, whereas the latter, which means "media personality," emerged with the advent of satellite broadcasting (Mellor, 2008), thus blurring the traditional boundary between information and entertainment. These developments, as I argue later in this chapter, call for a reconsideration of what "professionalization" means in comparative media research.

Role of the State
The Lebanese and Saudi states play different roles in media affairs. The press in both countries is privately owned, but whereas in Lebanon private ownership extends to television, in Saudi Arabia the state controls all

broadcasting activities in the country. The Lebanese state's role is a classic example of a laissez-faire approach to the media; the Saudi state's running of the media can be described as *dirigiste*.

Saudi Arabia has a unique philosophy of the role of television in society based on a combination of religion, nationalism, and developmentalism; this philosophy shapes the attendant media structure, policies, and regulations. Like many other rulers in the developing world in the middle of the twentieth century, the royal family of Saudi Arabia launched a television service in the 1960s to promote national unity and modernization; it continues to this day. In contrast to other countries, Saudi media policy is strongly influenced by religion, more specifically the puritanical version of Sunni Islam known as Wahhabiyya. (The Saudi system's peculiar combination could be compared to China's mix of communism, nationalism, and developmentalism, especially because both systems consider moral instruction to be important; see Chapter 8.) Saudi Arabia's large area (2.2 million square kilometers/830,000 square miles) is partly responsible for the country's low population density (11 inhabitants per square kilometer/29 per square mile). The population retains strong local and tribal identities, so television plays a crucial role in sustaining feelings of national belonging.

The Faysal era was critical for the development of a state media apparatus and for the creation of regulatory and supervisory institutions: the Ministry of Information and Culture in 1962, a new Press Code in 1964, and the Saudi News Agency in 1971. However, the Ministry of Information and Culture is not the only institution that addresses television policy. When they feel sidestepped by the royal family on matters of media policy, Saudi clerics feel empowered to make consequential public statements about the television industry (Kraidy, 2009). Every year during Ramadan, the holy month and most important season for the media market, several Saudi clerics are vocally critical of television programs that do not adhere to their strict standards (Kraidy and Khalil, 2009, especially chapter 5).

The Saudi government owns and operates all terrestrial and satellite television channels based on Saudi territory. The state-run Broadcasting Service of the Kingdom of Saudi Arabia (BSKSA) is in charge of all television activities, and private television channels are prohibited from satcasting from Saudi soil.[1] Saudi TV now has four channels, in addition to al-Ekhbariya, which was launched in 2004 in the wake of terrorist

---

[1] This may change, as discussions are underway for private licenses.

attacks in the kingdom as an all-news channel run by the Ministry of Culture and Communication from the capital Riyadh. As in the 1980s, changes in television policy reflect the government's desire to be able to provide news coverage at a time of crisis. Al-Ekhbariya was launched as part of wide-ranging television reforms that included revamping Channels 1 and 2 and launching a sports channel, all designed to attract Saudi viewers back to state television in the wake of their migration to al-Jazeera and al-Arabiya (Kraidy and Khalil, 2009).

If in Saudi Arabia, television reflects the mood of the society because of deliberate media policy, in Lebanon the same thing occurs in spite of media policies. Browne (1975) pointed out that during civil strife Lebanese television officials were instructed *not* to reflect what was occurring on the ground. Yet that occurred at a time when the government still held monopoly power over news on Lebanese television, a situation that changed radically during the 1975–90 civil war. The civil war unleashed chaos on the airwaves when the Lebanese Forces, a Christian-nationalist militia, launched LBC in 1985, followed by myriad other unlicensed stations (Kraidy, 1998).

Lebanon's 1994 AVML was the first Arab legislation that integrated privately owned radio and television. The 1989 Ta'ef Agreement – the official accord that ended the war, signed in the eponymous Saudi resort city – called for regulating the country's unlicensed media. These radio and television stations were a symbol of wartime anarchy and tarnished the prestige of a reemerging state. The AVML, which was passed in October 1994, revoked Télé-Liban's exclusive broadcasting rights, therefore legalizing private broadcasting. It reaffirmed that media freedoms were guaranteed by the constitution and gave the Council of Ministers the authority to issue licenses. The law also created the National Council of Audio-Visual Media (NCAVM) and charged it with setting technical standards, monitoring media performance, and recommending sanctions. It enhanced the powers of the Minister of Information to include the right to audit all financial records, because the law prohibited stations from operating in deficit for a protracted period. The NCAVM reported to the Minister of Information in a purely advisory role. The law affirmed core prohibitions against stirring up sectarian conflict, insulting the head of state and those of friendly countries, and endangering public order and national security (Kraidy, 1998). Today, the Lebanese state remains weak and generally unable to interfere strongly in media affairs. Télé-Liban, now fully owned by the state, is mired in a state of protracted decline.

In Saudi Arabia, the state has launched a vast modernization effort of its media sector, is even considering for the first time privatizing parts of the system, and in May 2010 announced that all state-owned satellite television channels will be webcast (Baqazi, 2010). 'Abdulaziz Khoja, the Minister of Culture and Information who is overseeing the modernization of Saudi state media, previously served as Saudi ambassador to Lebanon.

From a National to a Transnational System

Although both Lebanese and Saudi media play important roles in the contemporary pan-Arab media system, the two entered the transnational realms at different historical periods and with different motivations. Lebanese journalists fleeing Ottoman persecution in the late nineteenth century founded newspapers in Egypt and were active in newspapers in the Hijaz before the region became part of modern Saudi Arabia in 1925. Later, in search of economies of scale, Lebanese publications sought pan-Arab circulation. In the 1970s, according to Rugh, more than twenty Lebanese dailies were read regularly outside of Lebanon, and seven or eight titles were distributed more widely outside than inside the country (Rugh, 1979). This wide distribution, combined with the relative autonomy that Lebanese journalists have historically enjoyed, has made the Lebanese press a regional battleground for countries like Egypt, Saudi Arabia, Iraq, Syria, and others who at different stages financed Lebanese newspapers and journalists, a phenomenon discussed further in the section on professionalization.

Saudi Arabia stepped into the transnational realm as a reaction to external threats and developed a formidable transnational media capacity through various companies that it controls or influences. In the early 1960s, revolutionary Egypt subjected the House of Sa'ud to a relentless onslaught of propaganda that abated only after Nasser's defeat in the 1967 war. Egyptian accusations of Saudi treason and reaction reverberated in Saudi households tuned to Egyptian leader Gamal Abdel Nasser's Voice of the Arabs and Radio Cairo (Boyd, 2001). It was therefore imperative to develop a Saudi media capacity to retaliate. Faysal's strategy was to establish international media focused on a global Islamic audience, in line with the king's Islamic Solidarity Policy initiated in 1966 (Rugh, 1980). An effective media system was also needed internally because inhabitants of the Eastern Province were watching television from Kuwait, Iran, Qatar, and the UAE (Rugh, 1980). These two factors – economics and security, the latter including rhetorical and military conflicts – continue to this day to shape Lebanese and Saudi involvement in the pan-Arab media system.

The Arab television market today is one of the largest in the world: A 2003 United Nations report estimated the total Arab population at 330 million with an average 80 percent television penetration (*World Population Projections*, 2003). Before 1990, the regional advertising market was limited mostly to local consumer items within national television markets. Since the 1990s, the pan-Arab advertising market has expanded with the growth of the media. In Gulf Cooperation Council countries (Bahrain, Kuwait, Oman, Qatar, Saudi Arabia, and the UAE) alone, advertising expenditures rose from US $700 million in 1994 to US $4 billion in 2004 ("GCC Advertising Expenses," 2006). Satellite television is perhaps the most important advertising vehicle; in 2006 it captured US $2 billion out of a total regional annual advertising expenditure of US $5 billion (the total Arab advertising market grew from US $7.7 billion in 2007 to US 9.9 billion in 2008; Kraidy and Khalil, 2009). In its rapid commercialization, the Arab media system is similar to others in the Middle East like that of Israel (see Chapter 2) and Turkey.

The Saudi–Lebanese Connection in the Making of the Pan-Arab Media Order

After tightening their grip on the media internally in the 1980s, Saudi princes and their business partners expanded their stakes in transnational media, launching channels in London and Dubai and investing and developing transnational ventures with Lebanese media institutions and professionals. This was part of a radical transformation of the Arab media landscape and the rise of multiplatform conglomerates (LBC Group, MBC Group, al-Jazeera Network, Rotana; see Kraidy and Khalil, 2009, for details) operating transnationally with individual channels and publications targeting niche audiences. Of these, only al-Jazeera is not controlled by Saudi interests.

The gradual enmeshment of the Lebanese Broadcasting Corporation into the Saudi media apparatus reflects the synergies and tensions between the national and transnational realms. The Christian-nationalist Lebanese Forces militia launched LBC in 1985, making it the longest running privately owned Arab television channel. With its three-letter acronym, its emphasis on entertainment programs, and its advertising base, LBC reflects the rise of American-style commercial broadcasting over the older European system. Even as a partisan voice in Lebanon's war, LBC from its early days was run like a business, broadcasting Ramadan programs for Muslim viewers. After LBC went on satellite in 1996 and proved immensely popular in Saudi Arabia, Saudi investments poured in: First, Saudi mogul Saleh Kamel bought 49 percent of the total shares, which he later sold to Prince al-Waleed bin Talal for US $100 million (Kraidy, 2009). In 2007, al-Waleed's Rotana merged with LBC's satellite channel, with LBC General Manager Pierre el-Daher stating, "In today's media landscape only groups able to offer a comprehensive package of targeted channels to advertising markets are expected to grow two to three fold over the next five years and we intend to be part of that growth" ("LBCSAT and Rotana Television Channels Merge," 2007). These developments reflected commercial calculations in a market in which "everyone knows that the Saudi viewer is the target of satellite channels ... because he is the advertisers' target" (Badi, 2006). According to the manager of Future TV, another Lebanese channel, the Saudi market consisted of 60 percent of the Gulf market, "thus 60% of the satellite television market" (Haddad, 2006). Thus Future TV's strategy was to "become an Arab channel satcasting from Lebanon and not a Lebanese channel satcasting to Arabs" (Haddad, 2006).

In the pan-Arab market, channels are compelled to shed their national image to broaden their appeal. Although commercially successful, this model heightens tensions between countries as socially different as Lebanon and Saudi Arabia, even though both countries are increasingly integrated in the pan-Arab market. From 2004 to 2008, a wave of satellite television entertainment programs promoted under the rubric of "reality television," ostensibly unscripted and featuring audience voting for favorite contestants via the Internet and mobile telephones, generated wide-ranging controversies throughout the Arab world. The phenomenon compelled several national parliaments (notably Bahrain's and Kuwait's) to debate the social and economic impact of reality television shows, pushed Saudi Arabia's Higher Council of Ulemas to issue a *fatwa* against one of the programs, and caused the forced resignation of Kuwait's minister of information. Activists also used the verbal and visual languages of reality television in street demonstrations, most notably in Beirut during the spring of 2005 (see Kraidy, 2009, for details).

As the 2004–8 reality television controversies demonstrate, programs produced in Lebanon and financed by Saudi moguls regularly raise the ire of Saudi conservatives and radicals, some of whom have gone as far as to issue religious rulings fomenting violence against relatively liberal Saudi moguls (Kraidy, 2009). The reality television polemics also show that entertainment can have significant political repercussions in

non-Western contexts, in which "entertainment" has been integrated
into models of media and politics that have hitherto been concerned
exclusively with "information": These repercussions are exacerbated by
regular and heated polemics in Saudi Arabia over Lebanese-produced
popular culture. This expansion of the media–politics nexus has several important consequences, one of which is the need to redefine the
notion of professionalization to include media workers who are not
journalists.

Redefining Professionalization

Hallin and Mancini rely on Wilensky's definition of professionalization
as the practice of a profession "based on systematic knowledge or doctrine acquired only through long prescribed training" (Wilensky, 1964,
p. 138, quoted in Hallin and Mancini, 2004b: 33). In light of the rise
of Arab entertainment television as a politicized sphere, the definition
of professionalization needs to be expanded to include nonjournalistic
media labor.

The role of Lebanese media workers in Saudi-controlled institutions
is edifying in that regard, and it ranges from the staffing the press during Faisal's reign in Saudi Arabia to working in contemporary television.
Egyptian–Saudi rivalry set the ground for the Saudi–Lebanese connection. As prime minister, Faysal was concerned about the high number
of Egyptian journalists and technicians working in the Saudi press, at
a time of heightened tension between Saudi Arabia and Egypt. Faysal's
brother King Fahd's lavish lifestyle and conspicuous spending attracted
the lion's share of Egypt's anti-Saudi propaganda, but in 1962 Faysal
found himself featured with his brother on "Enemies of God," a program
on Nasser's Voice of the Arabs (James, 2006). Faysal's negative predispo-
sition toward Nasserist sentiments in Saudi newsrooms was exacerbated
when some Egyptian journalists working for Saudi newspapers went on
strike in solidarity with Egypt, after armed hostilities in Yemen began in
1962 between Egypt-backed republicans and Saudi-supported royalists
(Rugh, 1980). Another group of journalists who had mastered similar
technical skills but had different political orientations was required, a
development that aligned politics with media professionalization.

By the time Faysal died in 1975, the convergence of Saudi media institutions and Lebanese human resources had begun. In that year, the Saudi
brothers Hisham and Muhammad 'Ali Hafez launched the Arab world's
first English-language daily, *Arab News*. The sons of a Jeddah publisher,

they later founded Saudi Research and Marketing, a leading Arab media conglomerate (Loqman, 1997). The Hafez brothers' challenge was to find a qualified team of journalists and editors fluent in English and with knowledge of the Arab world, a challenge resolved by the Lebanese civil war. The war forced the Lebanese publisher Kamel Muruwwah to shut down the respected Beirut-based English-language newspaper *Daily Star* in 1975, leaving in its wake a group of unemployed journalists and editors experienced in publishing an English-language daily in the Middle East. *Arab News* recruited the group led by Jihad al-Khazen (Lebling, 2005). A former reporter at Reuters, al-Khazen was editor-in-chief of the *Daily Star* from 1968 to 1976[2] and went on to become one of the most prominent players in the Saudi–Lebanese connection, editing *Arab News* (1976–7) before going on to lead the two major Saudi-owned, London-based pan-Arab papers: first *Asharq Al-Awsat* (1978–86) and then *Al-Hayat* (1988–98). Al-Khazen also supervised the joint news venture Al-Hayat-LBC when it was set up in 2002 (Kraidy interview with al-Khazen, June 7, 2005).

A similar pattern occurred in television. The first Lebanese were recruited to MBC in the early to mid-1990s, followed by dozens who moved to Orbit, the Saudi-owned pay channel at first headquartered in Rome, when the drastic enforcement of Lebanon's 1994 Audio-Visual Media Law reduced professional media opportunities in Lebanon. As successive episodes of violence shook Lebanon, waves of journalists, news anchors, directors, producers, and managers found their way to higher wages in safer outposts (Dubai, London, Rome) of the sprawling Saudi media empire. At MBC in the late 1990s, for example, the majority of programs were presented in Lebanese Arabic rather than Egyptian Arabic (the two being dominant in Arab media), because "numerous non-Lebanese individuals in London [had] a tendency to adopt the Lebanese accent when they [went] on the air" (Le Pottier, 2003: 47). By the early 2000s, an MBC official estimated that half of the channel's staff was Lebanese (Le Pottier, 2003: 47). Around the same time, MBC established production studios in Beirut to produce its entertainment programs, and the channel's game, variety, and reality shows featured Lebanese hosts speaking in a Lebanese accent to their guests who were, in disproportionate number, Lebanese.

---

[2] Although the paper closed in late 1975, al-Khazen's biography lists 1976 as the last year of his editorship, probably reflecting contractual arrangements.

The Lebanese influence was also palpable in "branding" transnational channels in the highly competitive satellite era. A Saudi journalist summarized an Arabic *Forbes* report about the industry as follows:

The look that has come to dominate the new wave [of Arab satellite television channels] is derived primarily from Lebanese TV channels; they attracted a vast number of viewers as soon as they entered the arena . . . having a Lebanese element in a program's production and presentation can be a major contributor to the program's success. (Mishkhas, 2005)

The significant involvement of Lebanese human resources in the Saudi media apparatus set the ground for what could be described as transnational parallelism and mutual instrumentalization.

Transnational Parallelism and Mutual Instrumentalization?

In the relationship between Saudi Arabia and Lebanon, the former is clearly more powerful politically and economically. Thus the media-political parallelism between the two countries reflects a lopsided instrumentalization of Lebanese media workers and politicians by Saudi Arabia's rulers. Lebanon's influence is restricted to "cultural" matters, which connect to the ongoing battle between liberals and conservatives for the soul of Saudi Arabia.

Strong political ties between Saudi Arabia and Lebanon go back to the 1950s, when Hussein 'Uwayni, a Lebanese national, was Saudi Arabia's representative in Lebanon before he became prime minister in 1951 (Traboulsi, 2008). Similarly Rafiq al-Hariri, a Lebanese contractor, won Saudi citizenship and was the Saudi royal family's point man in the Ta'ef agreement ending the Lebanese war. He leveraged that experience to return to Lebanon as prime minister in 1992. Al-Hariri, unlike 'Uwayni, also controlled a media empire including Future TV, Radio-Orient, and the *al-Mustaqbal* newspaper. Al-Hariri, who was Lebanon's prime minister for most of the time between 1992 and 2005, when he was assassinated in Beirut, enjoyed unwavering Saudi support and aligned his policies with Riyadh.

The son of a Lebanese woman and a Saudi prince, Prince al-Waleed Bin Talal is also a dual citizen who has parlayed his media interests into political clout. His investments in LBC afforded the Lebanese channel a measure of political protection because he was close to Lebanese President Emile Lahoud, a major ally of the Syrians in Lebanon. This relationship was crucial because LBC had a history of opposition to Syrian interference in Lebanon and was vulnerable in 2000 when the Syrian-dominated

Lebanese state was clamping down on media dissenting from the Pax Syriana. He was a potent if unlikely critic of Rafiq al-Hariri's economic policies in postwar Lebanon. His close ties with al-Hariri's archrival Emile Lahoud, president of the Lebanese republic, fueled persistent rumors of his prime ministerial ambitions, a post for which he is eligible as a Sunni Muslim, according to Lebanese political tradition (Kraidy, 2009).[3] These relationships reflect transnational parallelism, with rival Saudi princes supporting rival Lebanese politicians, in political conflicts reflected in media outlets owned or influenced by the two camps.

This parallelism does not stem only from Saudi Arabia's desire to influence Lebanese politics and, through the Lebanese media, Arab politics; it also originates from a desire to influence internal Saudi politics through the Lebanese media-political system. For example, in the aftermath of the U.S.–UK invasion of Iraq, Saudi authorities asked LBC to host Muhammad Hussain Fadlallah, the towering Lebanese Shi'a *marja' al-taqlid* (source of emulation) who enjoys a large following among Saudi and other Gulf Shi'a. Through his appearance on an LBC talk show, Fadlallah was asked to soothe the anxieties of Saudi Shi'a, who were growing restive in their second-class status as they watched their Iraqi brethren rising to power.[4]

Such roundabout actions – Sunni Saudi authorities pushing a Shi'i Lebanese cleric to send a message of peace to Saudi Shi'a on a Christian Lebanese channel – help the Saudi royal family arbitrate the fierce battle between liberals and conservatives in the kingdom. Religious conservatives control religious satellite channels such as Iqra' and al-Majd, whereas MBC and LBC are considered liberal: The royal family uses this range of channels to send messages to the Saudi public. In the case mentioned earlier, the appearance of a preeminent Shi'i cleric like Fadlallah on a Saudi channel would be intolerable to the Sunni Wahhabi Saudi establishment, so LBC provided the needed platform. One Arab journalist captured the convoluted process thusly:

To break the chains imposed by religious institutions, the Saudi approach relies on channels of foreign origin but of Saudi affiliation, the most prominent of which is a Lebanese channel that manages the scheduling and content of its programs

---

[3] In addition to LBC, his Lebanese media assets have over the years included stakes in the now-defunct Murr Television (MTV), shut down by Lebanese authorities by Syrian orders in September 2003, and *Annahar* newspaper, which covers the activities of the prince and his Lebanese wing of the family.

[4] Author interview with a prominent LBC talk-show host, 2004, Lebanon [details omitted to protect anonymity].

according to Saudi timing [an unsubtle hint to LBC]. Here Saudis, hosts and participants, say what is prohibited in their country's channels because of the power of religious groups, or maybe because the ruling institution hides behind the putative power of these groups. (Rabahi, 2007)

Saudi "reformers" use Lebanese channels as platforms, like many Arab politicians used the Lebanese press in earlier decades. "The difference now," the journalist continued, "is that both the Saudi government and the opposition practice reform from the outside" (Rabahi, 2007), using LBC and others.

These media actions parallel political and economic processes. In Lebanon's consociational system dominated by institutionalized political sectarianism, Saudi Arabia historically supported the Sunnis and the office of prime minister, a post reserved for a Sunni according to tradition. Saudi interest and involvement in Lebanese affairs have increased recently, as the Saudi–Lebanese media connection has solidified.[5] Saudi princes use Lebanese politicians and media as proxies because, as a historian of Saudi Arabia explained, "[Lebanon] is an intermediary on which Saudi Arabia relies in various fields, a role that no other Arab country, large or small, is able to play. Lebanon, state and people, plays this role in different realms including culture, media, politics, economics, and even religion" (al-Rasheed, 2008).

Historically, Lebanese politicians, journalists, and media institutions have served Saudi agendas in several languages, regionally and internationally. "As a touristic destination," al-Rasheed continues, "Lebanon provides Saudi Arabia a social and entertainment space, a mediator between internal Saudi isolation and external Western openness" (2008). Controversial Saudi issues such as the rights of women, religion, and politics, banished from Saudi media space, find their way to the Saudi public through Lebanese-created and operated, but increasingly Saudi-owned, media:

(Television) programs that focus on the internal Saudi situation have become a Lebanese specialty, while (many) Saudis are kept away from these dialogues by the state. The Saudi person comes to this open, Saudi-owned, media space, carrying his concerns, sharing his private life and the secrets of his society with a Lebanese dialogue partner, on screens that appear to be Lebanese though in fact they are Saudi in both inclination and ownership (al-Rasheed, 2008).

---

[5] Al-Waleed Bin Talal increased his stake in LBC-Sat to "more than 85 per cent and less than 90" on July 5, 2008 (Abuzeid, 2008), effectively merging the two companies.

In the context of the Bush administration's "Greater Middle East" agenda and the stand-off between the United States and Iran, Saudi influence has grown in Lebanon. As a battleground of global and pan-Arab politics, Lebanon's media and political structures today parallel the regional struggle between Saudi Arabia and Iran. The Saudis support the "March 14" coalition headed by Rafiq al-Hariri's son in a protracted battle with Iran-supported Hizbollah and its allies (Abukhalil, 2008). Furthermore, some Lebanese journalists working for Saudi-aligned newspapers in Lebanon or Saudi-owned media in London and Dubai have been at the forefront of the recent Saudi rhetorical war against Iran and its ambition for regional hegemony.

If Lebanese media workers and institutions have served Saudi domestic and foreign policies, they have in turn influenced the ongoing debate between liberals and conservatives in Saudi Arabia, in addition to influencing musical, fashion, and culinary styles and tastes in the Gulf at large. Various controversies over popular culture, including the reality television wars (Kraidy, 2009), polemics over music videos and talk-shows, illustrate how Lebanese programs foment polemics in Saudi Arabia. Most recently LBC triggered a major upheaval in Saudi Arabia when it aired a Jerry Springer-like show that hosted a young divorced Saudi man, on camera in his bedroom, boasting of his sexual exploits and showing off his sex toys. The "LBC sex braggart" affair led to a highly publicized court case that convicted and jailed the man; in addition, several LBC offices in Saudi Arabia were closed, and LBC took the show off its satellite line-up, while keeping it on its terrestrial channel. Alhough this case has not led to a break between Saudi financing and LBC, it reflects the fragility of a relationship between the Arab world's most conservative society and its most socially liberal media institution.

There are other limits to transnational parallelism. When hostilities broke out between Israel and Hizbollah in 2006, Saudi leaders first condemned Hizbollah's "adventurism," but backpedaled in light of its resilience and the mounting civilian casualties caused by Israel's onslaught. Hizbollah's television station al-Manar climbed to the top ten in pan-Arab ratings, and talk-show hosts struggled to prevent callers from heaping verbal abuse on pro-U.S. Arab regimes. Under heavy Saudi (and Egyptian) lobbying, Arab information ministers met on February 12, 2008, and discussed a broad-ranging document, the Arab Satellite Television Charter (ASTC). The charter extended to the pan-Arab sphere provisions already in effect within nation-states. It penalized sexual content and that relating to alcohol consumption and purported to protect

"Arab identity from the harmful effects of globalization." It also banned content that would "damage social harmony, national unity, public order, or traditional values," thus affirming the current authoritarian catch-all provision against harming "national reputation," which enables a wide range of repressive measures (see chapter 6 in Kraidy and Khalil, 2009, for details). Although Saudi Arabia was one of the main sponsors of the ASTC, the Lebanese Information Minister stated that the charter was a "guiding, not binding" document. This reflects the limits of transnational parallelism and the major influence of national and regional politics. When many journalists objected that the Charter could be used to silence Lebanese and Palestinian media criticizing Israel, the director of the Saudi Information Ministry, 'Abdullah al-Jasir, hastened to explain that the charter "distinguishes between incitement to violence and resistance to occupation" (al-Barraq, 2008).

Conclusion

This chapter explored the implications of the rise of transnational media systems for comparative media research. My focus has been on investigating the role of two influential national media systems, the interaction of which is decisive in shaping the regional media order. Clearly, contemporary pan-Arab media draw on characteristics from various Arab countries. However, as this chapter has demonstrated, elements from the Lebanese and Saudi systems have been particularly influential. Perhaps more importantly, this chapter suggests that a transnational perspective may in some cases be more heuristic than a traditional comparative approach using the nation-state as a unit of analysis. Whereas the latter may have yielded insights about the peculiarities and diversity of Arab national systems, the former opens up an exciting avenue of research that emphasizes the complexities of media operations across borders and offers conceptual innovations, including notions of a transnational system, transnational parallelism, and an expanded understanding of media professionalization.

The Saudi–Lebanese connection served as the lynchpin of the analysis. It allows Saudi media companies access to qualified personnel in media writing, production, and management, while some Lebanese editors and journalists continue to be reliable spokespersons for Saudi agendas and policies. Concurrently, Lebanese media provide a platform for "reformist" princes and "liberal" activists to reach Saudi audiences.

Conversely, the Saudi media empire injects capital into cash-starved Lebanese institutions operating in a small domestic market and provides professional opportunities to numerous Lebanese journalists, editors, directors, producers, and managers, driven out of their native country by episodic violent conflicts or lured away from Lebanese companies by higher salaries. Finally, the influence of Lebanese style and culture on Saudi Arabia and other Gulf countries opens transnational markets for Lebanese product and enhances the status of Lebanese media corporations. The Saudi–Lebanese connection raises questions about the applicability of the center/periphery dichotomy (see de Albuquerque, Chapter 5) to characterize national media in a transnational system.

From the perspective of Hallin and Mancini's models, the transnational Arab media system is a hybrid of the Polarized Pluralist and the Liberal model, one in which the role of the state, parallelism, commercialism, and professionalization appear in different guises and give rise to different definitions. The system is liberal in the sense that it is increasingly commercialized, to a point where business calculations occasionally trounce political or religious considerations (Kraidy, 2009). At the same time, it is only quasi-liberal because it exhibits strong parallelism and a strong, even dominant role for the Saudi state. According to Hallin and Mancini (2004),

Polarized pluralist systems are typically complex political systems, with many contending parties, often themselves made up of contending factions. This results in a public sphere that is structured differently from the liberal public sphere in which the central element of political communication is assumed to be the appeal of political actors to a mass public of individual citizens. In a multiparty system of this sort, the most important element of political communication is the process of bargaining that takes place among parties, factions, and other social actors allied with them. Much of this process of communication takes place outside of the open public sphere, or enters it only tangentially or in coded, cryptic form. The negotiating process is delicate and messy and generally succeeds better if carried out informally, outside of the public arena. The media in such a system – especially newspapers – have historically served and participated in the process of bargaining. They are an important means by which elites follow and comment on the progress of negotiations, establish and agenda, signal positions and commitments, pressure one another, and arrive at an agreement. (p. 132)

In some way, this describes the pan-Arab media systems, its stars, and its rivalries. However, including "entertainment" alongside "information" in the analysis reveals a major difference: As the reality television polemics have shown (Kraidy, 2009), in an environment where nation-states and their political and media systems are increasingly enmeshed in a regional political and media order, elites have to bargain for power and resources publicly, contentiously, and across national boundaries.

Partisan Polyvalence

Characterizing the Political Role of Asian Media

Duncan McCargo

Generalizing about the media is fraught with risks, especially if we move beyond the West to make statements about the world as a whole. For example, newspaper sales are generally said to be falling, as traditional print media struggle to compete with broadcasting and online media; local newspapers are considered to be struggling everywhere. Actually, it turns out that everywhere does not really mean everywhere. Newspaper circulations are healthy in many low- and middle-income countries across Asia and Latin America: According to the World Association of Newspapers, in 2007 sales increased by 12 percent in Brazil, 11 percent in India, and 7 percent in Argentina. A thriving local newspaper sector in such countries might seem to reflect strong communities and emerging democracy – but not necessarily. I met a friend in Bangkok who had just come back from Nan, a sleepy province in northern Thailand. He reported that Nan has four local newspapers, a surprisingly large number. Yet when he made inquiries, he discovered that they were all in the extortion business, digging the dirt on local politicians and businesspeople, and asking to be paid not to publish it. The Committee for the Protection of Journalists reports numerous killings of local journalists in developing countries – the Philippines currently ranks number 5.[1] These murders of journalists are terrible abuses of human rights and democracy, but some of the victims were also small-town gangsters. And so it goes: Lurking behind every nice, simple, and attractive generalization are some messy

---

[1] For a summary of the data from 1992 to the present, see http://www.cpj.org/deadly/. Iraq tops the lists of journalists killed during this period; Algeria, Russia, and Colombia follow.

and uncomfortable realities that do not get in the way unless we talk about them. I talk about some of them in this chapter.

Like Hallin and Mancini (2004b: 10), I have always considered *Four Theories of the Press* (Siebert, Peterson, and Schramm, 1956) to be something of a "horror movie zombie" stalking the world of media studies. Like them, I would concur with Nerone (1995) that the four theories are ultimately predicated on one starting point, classical liberalism, and are deeply rooted in a North American understanding of how the world works. I am convinced that any conceptualization of media too firmly rooted, like *Four Theories*, in crude ideas of regime types will lack sufficient nuance to capture the ambiguous and even contradictory roles performed by different media actors.[2] *Comparing Media Systems* moves beyond such simplistic understandings, embracing Europe – including "Mediterranean" Europe – as well as North America. It is a great improvement on previous attempts to model the ways media work and offers a broadly convincing analysis of Western media paradigms. But where does it leave those of us who work on media in the rest of the world? Picking over the models themselves – Liberal, Democratic Corporatist, and Mediterranean – from a non-Western perspective is relatively straightforward. Details can be tweaked here and there, or a fourth model proposed, which might be essentially a variant on one of the others.

In my own work on the political role of media in the Asia-Pacific region, however, I have always resisted this form of modeling, partly because there are so many exceptions to every rule that rules tend to obscure rather than explain the nature of the game itself and partly because I discovered that media actors in the region persistently resist ready classification. Newspapers or broadcasters in countries such as Thailand and Indonesia have a chameleon-like capacity to refresh their colors at critical junctures. Yet the chameleon metaphor itself is both beguiling and misleading, because it implies that a particular publication or organization assumes only one coat of colors at a time. If we see media outfits as polyvalent, speaking with forked or multiple tongues, and given to acting in apparently contradictory ways, it becomes increasingly difficult to sustain attempts to model their behavior. For this reason, my own emphasis has always been on agency, rather than structure. My assumption is that media in Asia – always adept at creative borrowings and imitation – would at different junctures assume certain features of almost

---

[2] Huang (2009: 198–203), in a generous but confusing discussion of my work, incorrectly classifies my argument as supportive of a "regime type-based interpretation."

any given model, yet their attachment to such characteristics would be fickle, transitory, and ambiguous.

In other words, my primary interest is in trying to offer conceptualizations of media that embrace complexity and confusion and are firmly grounded in messy empirical realities. I am concerned with unpacking and problematizing received understandings of notions such as ownership, partisanship, and censorship – notions that parallel Hallin and Mancini's use of ideas about media markets, parallelism, professionalism, and state intervention. Underlying these critiques is a questioning of one major core assumption of media studies: that most media can be understood as business enterprises. My own conclusion, based on research in several Asian countries, is that many prominent media "businesses" are not profitable in a conventional sense. This finding carries important implications when we seek to describe, classify, or "model" the nature of media systems in the region.

For someone who is not especially enthusiastic about models in the first place, the idea of generalizing models developed in a Western context and applying them to "developing" countries with very different cultural and political contexts would seem quite a risky enterprise. I begin by sketching a description of the media in the Asian countries on which I work, using a set of headings based around Hallin and Mancini's four main criteria, but modified in accordance with my own language and preferences. Although I have conducted research in several Asian countries (including Cambodia, Hong Kong, Indonesia, and Japan), my core fieldwork site is Thailand; I therefore play to my strengths by using some detailed Thai examples to illustrate my approach, while always remaining alive to the possibility that they may not be broadly representative.

A passage from *The Golden Notebook*, a novel by Nobel-Prize–winner Doris Lessing (1999: 59), summarizes the view of the world I am articulating here:

Human beings are so divided, are becoming more and more divided, and more subdivided in themselves, reflecting the world, that they reach out desperately, not knowing they do it, for information about other groups inside their own country, let alone groups about other countries.... Inside this country, Britain, the middle-class has no knowledge of the lives of the working-people, and vice-versa; and reports and articles and novels are being sold across the frontiers, are read as if savage tribes were being investigated.

Although her novel is set in the 1950s, Lessing's organizing notion of subdivisions and gaps in social knowledge remains highly resonant. Less than a mile from my house near the University of Leeds campus, radical Muslims assembled the bombs that killed fifty-two people on the London transport system on July 7, 2005. I have literally no idea what people I pass on the street each day may be thinking. When I recently spent a month living on the forty-third floor of a Bangkok condominium building, I was utterly detached from the construction workers and street vendors living in the narrow alleys below me – many of them illegal Burmese immigrants with whom I had no common language. Despite the growth of mass media, life in the twenty-first century features far more division and divergence than it does convergence around agreed norms, ideas, and values.

Let me clear about my argument. I am suggesting that, to be able to study the media in a broader geographical context than is covered by *Comparing Media Systems*, we need to recognize the importance of diversity. Above all, the informal (in terms of markets, parallelism, partisanship, and censorship) will often loom larger in non-Western contexts than it does in Western ones. The proliferation of the informal makes the business of analysis and classification much more slippery. This is not to suggest that I am portraying "Western" media as an ideal type, devoid of informal pressures, hidden rules, and clandestine practices. Indeed, I strongly suspect that such informal dimensions are much more widespread in the West than is generally assumed, especially in Southern European (Mediterranean) cases. Nor does it mean that I am averse to all efforts at classification; it is simply that I approach them with some trepidation.

Media Markets and the Nature of Business

Hallin and Mancini argue that the development of a mass press is a crucial feature of certain media systems (those in North America and Europe), and is lacking in others (Southern Europe). In other words, their Mediterranean model relies on a "horizontal" print media, speaking largely to a small, urban political elite, whereas other models involve a "vertical" media addressing large numbers of ordinary citizens. It is tempting immediately to suggest that Thailand and Indonesia, for example, follow the Mediterranean model. *Thai Rath*, the top-selling newspaper in Thailand, has sales of only around a million copies in a country with a population of 64 million – and that only on the two days per month when the lottery results are announced in the press. On normal days, sales are much lower. Total average newspaper sales in Thailand are probably only around two million per day (McCargo, 2000: 1–2, 29). On one level, this looks like a horizontal model.

Yet the apparent identification of Thailand with a horizontal print media is not easily sustained. First of all, *Thai Rath* – which features blood-spattered corpses on every front page – is a mass-market newspaper, albeit one without conventional mass sales. Its influence greatly exceeds its sales, partly because in provincial Thailand few people buy their own copies of a newspaper. Newspapers are often read in cafes, markets, offices, or even in special village shelters (*sala*). The same copy of *Thai Rath*; downmarket rivals *Daily News*, *Khao Sot*, or *Khom Chat Luk*; or the more upmarket *Matichon*, may be read by twenty different readers during the course of a day. *Thai Rath* makes most of its profits from advertising and other activities; sales of individual copies are not the main focus.

And that is not all. The rise of talk radio and television talk shows in recent years has led to another trend: Broadcast media construct popular "news" programs that feature presenters reading aloud and discussing stories from the newspapers. Every morning, popular presenter Sorayuth Suthassanajinda appears on TV Channel 3 to give an extensive run-down of the stories and columns from the daily press.[3] This is the way Thais love to get their news: It provides them with edited highlights of the interesting bits in the newspapers, without the effort of actually reading (as a general rule, Thais are literate but prefer not to read much). Television provides a huge audience with a wide-ranging if highly selective briefing of newspaper coverage, saving them the trouble of buying a copy themselves. Because of Sorayuth's program – and a number of imitators, on radio as well as television – a story in *Thai Rath* readily reaches tens of millions of people who never pick up a newspaper at all. In such contexts, the distinction between horizontal and vertical print media turns out to be entirely empty. When exposed to empirical Asian scrutiny, models derived from Western experiences may slip through analytical fingers.

The underlying problem here is that we need to distinguish between formal and informal realities.[4] Taking external constructs too literally can be highly misleading. Simply because a newspaper or television station appears to be outwardly configured as a business enterprise

---

[3] Sorayuth's program, which previously appeared on Channel 9, has been running for several years with a series of different, usually female, co-hosts. The program retains its immense popularity despite (or perhaps because of) Sorayuth's persistent rudeness to his on-screen colleagues and his apparently inability to remember to look at the camera.

[4] The arguments in this section revisit many points made in the introduction to McCargo (2003: 1–18). This book focuses on agency rather than structure, distinguishing between three major modes of political agency exercised by media: the agency of change, agency of restraint, and agency of stability.

tells us very little about what is really going on. During the 1990s, for example, the Indonesian information minister was given shares in more than thirty media enterprises, by owners eager to ensure that their publications were not closed down. Most of these shares were "informal," held in the names of nominees. "Dividends" were handed over in cash, and no share certificates were issued. In other words, there was a discrepancy between the formal and informal ownership of these publications. Questioned by a researcher, Sok Eysan, the director of Cambodia's private Apasara TV station, refused to reveal the names of Apasara's shareholders – widely rumored to be senior figures in the ruling Cambodian People's Party (CPP; LICADHO, 2008: 29). Similar patterns of clandestine or informal ownership have long been widespread in countries such as Thailand and the Philippines. Some newspapers are simply vanity publications, underwritten or protected by influential politicians, businesspeople, or military officers.

Because of the rapid economic growth in the Asia-Pacific region over the past three decades, local stock markets have experienced regular, spectacular booms. One reason for the proliferation of newspapers in countries such as Thailand has been a desire to talk up particular stocks and shares. Owning newspapers allows proprietors to promote shares in companies in which they have an interest. The profits accruing from a single dramatic share-price rise, perhaps lasting only a few days, can often more than cover the annual running costs of a low-circulation newspaper. In this sense, media operate as businesses of an entirely different kind from their formal orientation; income derives not from advertising or sales, but from profits based on stock manipulation. Media specialists rarely discuss such matters, but they are actually crucial to understanding the role of the press in many rapidly growing economies (Coronel, 1999).

Nor is it necessary to own the entire newspaper. Individual columnists often have considerable license to pursue private political and commercial agendas through their writing. These columnists may or may not be in the regular or irregular pay of key power holders and may or may not receive protection or other incentives from them. In this sense, "owner-ship" needs to be completely problematized. It is very hard to know who owns and controls a particular column in a Thai newspaper. Is a given column owned by the formal owner of the newspaper (a family company or listed shareholders), the shadow owner of the newspaper (unlisted shareholders or power holders who enjoy close relationships with for-mal owners), the editor, the shadow editors (power holders who enjoy close relationships with the editor), the columnist, or the shadow colum-nist (power holders who enjoy close relationships with the columnist)?

A single publication may have an extremely wide range of lucrative visible and invisible business interests and yet make no profits of a conventional kind through sales and advertising.

My own research has been confined to Asia, but I strongly suspect that ambiguous ownership and murky relations with power holders characterize the media in most of the world's nations. In other words, far from being "peripheral" media, these forms of media are numerically and politically dominant globally. Labeling such realities "clientelism" and "instrumentalism," although perfectly reasonable, may be unhelpful unless we recognize these "isms" as the prevailing norms, rather than as peripheral deviations. In fact, North America and Western Europe are the marginal cases globally, the leading exceptions to how the media work in much of the world.[5] Rather than expecting the rest of the world to emulate some version of these marginal models, we should be more focused on the issue of divergence, the dominant theme of today's global media landscape.

Parallels and Connections: Politics and Media

Of Hallin and Mancini's four themes, political parallelism is the most complicated. Parallelism turns out to mean various different things at the same time; at its most simple, the way different newspapers in some countries are aligned with particular political parties and, more ambiguously, the way media content reflects the diversity of political perspectives in the wider society. It may also refer to the existence of formal connections between media and various politically oriented organizations. Hallin and Mancini distinguish between external pluralism (the big picture of how media outlets parallel political diversity) and internal pluralism, the pluralism that exists within individual media outlets.

In Asian contexts, some societies are characterized by a high degree of political parallelism: for example, Malaysia, in which major newspapers have close ties to individual political parties that are in turn tied to specific ethnic and linguistic groups, and the one-party states of China and Vietnam, where newspapers are directly or indirectly controlled by the Communist Party.[6] As I have argued elsewhere, "Thai language newspapers exist in a parallel world to that of Thai politicians and

---

[5] For a similar view, arguing that Brazilian media needs to be understood in its own cultural terms rather than as an inferior version of an American model, see Albuquerque (2005).

[6] For a discussion of media–politics interactions in various countries in the region, see Sen and Lee (2008).

political parties,"[7] Yet in most Asian contexts, newspapers do not endorse particular parties at election times. Influential publications prefer to go with the flow, maintaining strong connections with a wide range of formal and informal power holders and actors. Thailand's *Thai Rath* newspaper offers an extreme form of internal pluralism that might serve as a counter-model to received Western ideas of party-political parallelism (McCargo, 2000: 31–50). The newspaper has a political team of more than twenty columnists, editors, and reporters, each of whom is informally instructed to build close personal relations with one or more prominent politicians, faction bosses, ministers, military officers, social activists, and other influential figures. The journalist assigned to a key figure regularly provides that figure with broadly sympathetic coverage, keeping open strong channels of communication. This system is designed to ensure that if and when a particular figure ascends to a leadership position, the newspaper will already have an inside track to the top. Such a system is singularly appropriate to the rapidly changing Thai political order (Thailand has seen thirteen prime ministers, eight general elections, two military coups, and four constitutions since 1991), which is a highly unstable "new democracy"; yet no other media outlet has been able to match *Thai Rath's* successes in building such a formidable network of informal connections. *Thai Rath* combines very centralized family ownership with a remarkable degree of internal pluralism. Anyone seeking to track the tide of opinion in Thailand can gain a quick impression from comparing the various views to be found in the newspaper's various columns, notably those on pages three and four. At the same time, the front-page headlines strongly indicate the newspaper's collective view, as does an extended full-page Sunday political commentary. Editorials, crafted by superannuated senior editors who rarely set foot in the newsroom, are of no political importance.

For the most part, political parallelism in the Asian media context is not about formal organizational ties, but has everything to do with personal connections. Good journalists cultivate sources for years, even decades. Japanese reporters wander around the private residences of senior politicians, even helping themselves to drinks from the kitchen refrigerator (Freeman, 2000). Wherever possible, media organizations will assign reporters to key sources who are from the same region of the country, or the same ethnic or language group, or who graduated from the same university and faculty. Journalists who share common characteristics with their major sources are exponentially more effective in obtaining inside

---

[7] McCargo (2000: 2).

information than those who do not. Yet referring to these connections as "parallelism" may blur the fact that they are largely horizontal connections, sometimes overlaid by vertical ones (most commonly, senior political figures who exercise patronage power over more junior journalists, and sometimes up-and-coming political figures who cultivate powerful editors and proprietors). A more helpful way of understanding these connections may be through a critical review of ideas of partisanship, which themselves are inseparable from questions of professionalism.

Partisanship and Professionalism

Whereas Hallin and Mancini take questions of professionalism as a starting point, I tend to work backward from ideas of partisanship, because I assume that partisanship is the Asian (or global) norm and that professionalism is an ideal type that is quite difficult to locate in practice. In other words, I assume that journalists inhabit a realm of partisan pressures, both formal and informal, in which ideals of professionalism frequently have little space.

Whereas in Western countries positions such as the White House or Westminster correspondent are highly coveted assignments awarded to those who have proven their mettle in local and provincial journalism or have worked their way up after years on less important national beats, in many Asian countries kids fresh out of college (or even student trainees who have yet to graduate) are often sent to cover parliaments or seats of government in their first week on the job. Some of these reporters do have degrees from journalism or communication faculties, but the best and brightest of those graduates walk into better paid positions in advertising or public relations. This is because sharp-end political reporting is highly routinized.[8] Reporters hunt in packs, literally pursuing ministers or outspoken politicians around government buildings (or even ambushing them in parking lots) and soliciting quotes from them. In many countries, politicians freely comment on matters not under their jurisdiction and about which they know nothing. Typically, only a couple of senior reporters ask questions: The others simply get their tape recorders rolling or take copious notes. Afterward they huddle together in the press room, swapping recordings and trading quotes. This is a quasi-industrial and informally collectivized news-gathering process that

---

[8] The Thai version of this news-gathering process is described in McCargo (2000: 51–81); the Japanese version is a major theme of Feldman (1993).

requires little initiative. Those reporters who buck the trend and try to find their own exclusive stories are often ostracized by their colleagues. Such forms of news gathering are not part of a professional working culture, but a semi-tribal form of activity with its own rituals and unwritten rules. Again, I would venture to suggest that this sort of political news gathering may be the true global norm, far more widespread than the supposedly relentless, individualistic, and investigative endeavors of the Western journalist.[9]

In the Thai context, notions of journalistic professionalism have largely been reduced to a single axiom: "News" and "comment" must never be mixed. This principle – if it merits the term – actually derives from localized readings (misreading, on one level) of a 1960s American journalism text that warns against "editorializing" in the news.[10] News is largely defined as a set of stories that appear primarily on the front page of the newspaper (and are continued inside), in contrast with comment, which appears on inside pages. Political news comprises a few main facts, accompanied by quotations and summaries of opinions expressed by a range of political actors. Comment consists of opinions expressed by those working inside the newspaper – senior journalists who no longer have to work the beats, but simply pen responses to events and to the statements of external actors, often in very emotional and overblown terms. In short, there is a strong parallelism between news (comments by political actors) and comment (comments by journalists). Neither format offers much by way of analysis or explanation, and complex political stories are almost impossible to cover in a coherent fashion by either format. Both political actors and political columnists address one another in insider codes, codes

---

[9] To be clear, I am not suggesting that Hallin and Mancini subscribe to such a simplistic view of the Western journalist as entirely individualistic, and I am well aware of the literature criticizing similar forms of "pack journalism" in Western contexts. This is all a matter of degree, but in many Asian countries "pack journalism" has become the unapologetic default mode of operation, whereas reference to professional journalistic norms is often more rhetorical than real.

[10] "The principle of separating the news from editorial opinion is fully supported in every responsible area of American journalism": John Hohenberg (1969: 91). I found this book, *The Professional Journalist: A Guide to the Practices and Principles of the News*, in a cheap Indian reprint, gathering dust at the Faculty of Communication Arts, Chulalongkorn University, Bangkok. A professor at the Faculty once told me that Hohenberg's classic text had been enormously influential in providing an early American model for Thai journalism students to emulate. In fact, pp. 21–2 offer a much more nuanced discussion of the news versus comment distinction, but successive generations of Thai faculty and students took away the simple refrain that news and editorial opinion do not mix.

that go over the heads of all but the most politically aware, attentive, and diligent readers, who need to read a range of newspapers and columns to gain sufficient clues to understand what is going on. This model is not one of journalist as professional, but of journalist as privileged and partisan insider, whose aim is to show the reader how much he (almost invariably, it is he) knows, rather than what it is that he knows.

In other words, partisanship is the dominant mode of operation for Thai journalists of any seniority and supplants the role played by professionalism in other journalistic cultures. Partisanship is not defined in narrow terms such as party loyalty – because these loyalties are constantly shifting. Rather, it means that journalists of any importance are both entitled and expected to vent their opinions freely and in line with their own preferences; these preferences are in turn affected strongly by the personal – and sometimes financial – connections they enjoy with a range of power holders.[11]

Such phenomena have strong parallels in Hallin and Mancini's discussions of the Polarized Pluralist model in Southern Europe. Journalist Enzo Forcella's characterization of the Italian press fifty years ago would apply with equal force to today's Thailand: Newspapers are written for a readership of 1,500 members of the elite, in an "atmosphere of family discussion, with protagonists who have known each other since childhood, exchanging jokes, speaking a language of allusions."[12]

In other words, the primacy of partisanship over professionalism is by no means unique to Thai or Asian contexts. Indeed, it is becoming the dominant mode of the burgeoning blogosphere. This trend is epitomized by popular U.S. blogs such as the *Huffington Post* Web site, where opinions have completely displaced facts as the primary currency of journalistic exchange; these blogs play an increasingly central role in U.S. electoral politics. As Andrew Keen (2008: 52) writes,

At the moment, HuffPost works because the luminaries on Huffington's network have access to the reliable information derived from professional news journalists and commentators. But as the traditional newspaper business withers, media is liable to degenerate into a surreal Ponzi scheme of digital illusions and delusions where empirical facts will be replaced by opinion and professional news gatherers

---

[11] Detailed discussions of corrupt practices among journalists in Asia are relatively rare; for one example, see Romano (2003), chapter 11, "The Envelope Please," pp. 150–63.

[12] Faris (2009) notes that these newspapers provide little by way of context or background and quotes Paolo Mancini as saying: "The reader of the printed press already knows what's going on. They have the news. What they want is gossip." Again, this could be Thailand, Indonesia, or the Philippines.

by commentators-with-attitude. This represents a real threat to representative democracy.

In fact, the comment-rich, fact-poor, and analysis-thin form of blog journalism now emerging in developed democracies somewhat resembles the dominant mode of journalism that has long characterized many developing democracies, where representative politics remains weakly institutionalized. The Thai "model" is going global. Partisanship is both cheap and cheerful,[13] and professionalism is a luxury that few around the world can afford and that even the wealthy would prefer not to pay for. The evidence that new modes of media are undermining traditional outlets is widespread and growing. British politician Vince Cable recently suggested that he would now prefer to post his views on *The Guardian*'s blog than to give an interview on the same topic to a mass-circulation newspaper.[14] The blogosphere is a realm in which partisan polyvalence rules, the place where classical media systems are unraveling and where West meets East.

State Intervention and Censorship

Another set of factors characterizing the political role of the media concerns the form of state interventions. Put another way, how much freedom do the media have, and how far are they subject to formal and informal modes of censorship? Hallin and Mancini place their primary emphasis here on public service broadcasting, but this perspective may not translate into Asian perspectives. Japan has a major public service broadcaster (NHK), as does Hong Kong (RTHK), but the public service model is not widespread in less open Asian regimes. The very principle of public service implies a hands-off state, one that delegates powers to oversee the broadcaster to a relatively neutral regulator or to parliament itself. In most developing countries, such structures and models are gravely at odds with political realities. For a variety of reasons, the majority of states

---

[13] The British newspaper *The Guardian* runs an affiliated Web site titled "Comment is Free"; the irony of the name is that most contributors are unpaid. The same applies to the highly lucrative HuffPost.

[14] Vincent Cable, speaking at the University of Leeds on October 24, 2008. Now a cabinet member serving as Business Secretary and a former acting leader of the Liberal Democrat Party, Cable is widely regarded as the most intellectually impressive senior British politician today and one of the few capable of either understanding or explaining the post-2008 credit crunch and global recession.

are simply unable to resist meddling in the work of broadcasters. Public service broadcasting, like fully functioning parliamentary democracy, turns out to be a kind of media chimera, a rare beast often spotted in the nether distance but rarely living long once reared in captivity. The dominant order of state–media relations, especially as regards electronic media, is that states interfere wherever they can. This is particularly true in middle-income developing countries, where newspaper readership is typically low, yet most people have ready access to television and radio.

Yet the idea of state intervention is also complicated by questions concerning the nature of the state itself. In many developing countries, the state has a patrimonial character and is used as a vehicle for rent-seeking. In other words, the state – or certain elements thereof – has been captured by private, elite interests. In great swathes of the developing world, the much-vaunted distinction between public and private, on which so many heuristic categories and so much of the basic toolkit of social science relies, turns out to be something of an urban myth. Under such circumstances, state intervention in media is the norm rather than the exception. The same applies to censorship: Rather than imagining that media are free to report whatever they wish, unless subject to specific external interference, in much of the world it is safe to assume that such freedom is always highly contingent. In many Asian societies, it is not necessary for the authorities to intervene frequently to suppress media debate. In Singapore, for example, public discourse is delineated by what are termed "OB markers" (out-of-bounds markers) that preclude discussion of potentially sensitive questions such as interethnic relations. What is unusual about Singapore is that the term "OB markers" is bandied about openly; such markers are normally implicit, unspoken, but widely understood – such as the taboo on discussing the political role of the monarchy in Thailand.

Thus the state may be "intervening" in the media without doing anything at all. These interventions are programmed into citizens from a young age, as part of the schooling and socialization processes. Censorship is largely self-censorship and is mostly carried out by people who are not even critically aware of their own use of self-censorship – because most Asian educational systems do not teach or encourage critical self-awareness. In such contexts, blogs, e-mail lists, and Internet sites become the safest and most popular venues for more open discussion. Mainstream media that studiously ignore the topics of greatest popular interest may become increasingly irrelevant. New technology allows politically engaged netizens to create an alternative public sphere that appears open, safe, and anonymous (Klangnarong, 2009).

A second, related problem concerns the tendency of Western social science to view the state as a unitary actor or at least as an actor with certain broadly consistent core interests and positions. Again, this is simply not the case across much of Asia. Many states are not states as conventionally understood, but aggregations of competing bureaucratic, political, and private interests. For example, the military has long held an important political position in countries such as Thailand and Indonesia. In Thailand, the military owns and controls all radio frequencies, although most radio stations are privately operated. When radio broadcasters stray into sensitive political territory, they can find themselves abruptly cut off; more commonly, the military puts pressure on franchise holders to drop outspoken presenters. Locating the many hands of the state in Thai television broadcasting is even more difficult. Channel 11, now known as NBT, is operated by the government's Public Relations Department; Channel 9 is run by a state enterprise, the Mass Communications Organization of Thailand (sometimes confusingly compared with the BBC); a new channel, Thai TBS, claims to be a BBC-style public service broadcaster, but has been captured by "progressive" groups associated with the monarchy; and Channel 5 is directly controlled by the Thai Army. During clashes between pro- and anti-government forces in 2008, NBT adopted a hard-line pro-government stance, Thai PBS broadly supported anti-government demonstrators, and Channel 9 was more neutral.

Ironically, the root of the conflict between the two sides was an episode in 2005 when media magnate Sondhi Limthongkul's Channel 9 news commentary program was removed from the air; Sondhi proceeded to launch his own anti-government television station, ASTV, which remains illegal but now has hundreds of thousands of subscribers. The founders of ASTV have hailed the station as a new social mode for media in Thailand, a television channel based entirely around campaigning against the existing political order (Phiyarasot 2008). Sondhi went on to found an anti-government protest movement, the People's Alliance for Democracy; one of its most dramatic and controversial actions was to seize control of NBT by force on the morning of August 26, 2005. The protestors apparently wanted to broadcast the ASTV signal via the NBT government network, thereby effectively achieving a "revolution by television" (McCargo, 2009). In the event, they proved unable to achieve this goal and left the station at the end of the day.

The Thai protestors' seizure of a television station was an unusual event. However, such episodes illustrate that we need to think not simply in terms of state intervention in media but also in terms of media intervention in the state. In many countries that have experienced mass political movements or "democratic transitions" since the 1980s, the media have played a crucial role in undermining, perhaps even in toppling, a given political regime. For the most part, such movements have been lauded as progressive, popular, and participatory actions, even though their real internal politics may not bear particularly close scrutiny. The traffic between state and media is a two-way congress, not a zero-sum game of censorship and control. In any case, media in most Asian countries experience just as much intervention from private actors, individual power holders, and their freelance allies as from the state itself. Nor is the state a unitary actor: The seizure of television and radio stations is a standard feature of military coups the world over, in which one part of the state (typically, the armed forces) takes power from another (typically, the legislative and executive branch of government).[15]

Where the state is weak, and especially where it is divided against itself – such as during times of political transition or regime change – the mobilization of media is one crucial means by which competing political forces and rival power groups seek to act out their differences and to advance their causes. This has been clearly seen in numerous political crises in Asia and beyond, including the overthrow of Philippine president Ferdinand Marcos in 1986, the ouster of military-backed Thai premier Suchinda Kraprayoon in May 1992, and the downfall of Indonesian strongman General Suharto in 1998 (McCargo, 2003: 19–49). Recent incomplete upheavals – such as further rounds of "People Power" against more recent Philippine presidents – have assumed a similar character, illustrating a divided state and a factionalized political elite.

Sketching the Regional and Global Picture

Based on this discussion under four headings reworked from Hallin and Mancini, I am arguing that much of the media in Asia (and, by extension) the rest of the developing and non-Western world) is characterized by considerable diversity and subdivision. First, many media outlets do not operate as conventional businesses. Some are vanity projects operated on behalf of powerful or influential individuals or interests, for instrumental or prestige purposes. Some are involved in illegal or semi-legal

[15] Coups are far from going out of style: there have been at least twenty-nine successful and attempted coups since 2000, resulting in the ouster of more than ten serving governments, in countries ranging from Ecuador, Fiji, and Mauritania to Thailand and Togo.

activities ranging from share manipulation to extortion and are able to make profits with very little by way of conventional sales or advertising revenue. Despite these apparent shortcomings, such media organizations may also be doing positive and constructive work, supporting valuable social causes or progressive political goals. This is not a black-and-white picture. Shades of gray are needed in abundance to describe, measure, and evaluate the activities and performance of such media outlets. Second, Asian media organizations are often deeply implicated in politics, in ways that parallel, emulate, and even parody the politics of the societies in which they operate. Some of these political roles may be constructive, others less so. To survive in countries where politics is often relatively unstable and plural political actors abound, the media need to practice a form of internal pluralism, a polyvalence that somewhat resembles the sometimes chaotic conditions surrounding them. By contrast, where pluralism in the wider society is much less pronounced, media outlets will be far more monological and monotone. Third, ideas of professionalism derived from the West are not always viable in Asian contexts. Media partisanship of various kinds is highly normalized in many Asian countries, and journalists are often engaged in relatively mechanical news-gathering activities that serve the interests of the adjacent power holders.[16] Fourth, the boundaries between state intervention and media activity are often blurred. Censorship and state interference are virtually the norm for most Asian media. During times of crisis, Asian media often meddle in the workings of the state, contributing to processes of regime change; however, the state itself is generally plural rather than singular, characterized by intense internal contestation that makes state–media relations frequently messy and ambiguous.

This is my quick-and-dirty overview of the state of media and politics in Asia. I claim no academic expertise on my own country, Britain, let alone the rest of the world, but my cursory readings of literature about media and politics in Africa, the Middle East, and Latin America suggests to me that the global picture is generally closer to this kind of Lessing-style picture of a social politics of subdivision than to the Anglo-American and Continental European models that constitute the starting point for most literature in social science, political science, and media studies.

---

[16] Parvin (2006: 218–22, 197–9) argues that partisanship is a defining characteristic of the public sphere in Bangladesh, where many intellectuals practice what she terms "undercover partisanship" and both neutrality and moderation are in short supply. Partisanship is a basic operating procedure for the press there; indeed, the owners or co-owners of nine different newspapers stood as candidates in the 1996 elections.

In other words, I would like to suggest that, to conceptualize or to model the world's media, we might do best to start out from these uncomfortable realities. That is, North America and Western Europe constitute exceptions to the ways media and politics work (or do not work) in most of the world. Accordingly, it seems rather unlikely that global patterns of political communication would begin to converge around these exceptional paradigms. Indeed, it might equally be the case that Western patterns of media–politics relations could soon begin to unravel along "Asian" or non-Western lines – if, indeed, this is not already happening.

Back to the Models

If we return now to the three Hallin and Mancini models, where does Asia fit? Hallin and Mancini envisage "most of Asia" as somewhat resembling the Polarized Pluralist model, which they first developed to explain media systems in Southern Europe and France (2004: 306). This is slightly ironic, because Hallin and Mancini also suggest that the very same Polarized Pluralist model is rapidly going out of style in the Mediterranean, where the Liberal Model looks triumphant in the face of increasing homogenization and convergence. Reviewing most of Asia is rather a large task. Bearing in mind that Hallin and Mancini's three models are based on a close study of only eighteen countries, let me briefly outline here the region sometimes termed Pacific Asia, or East and Southeast Asia. This region comprises the following five East Asian countries – China, Japan, the Koreas (North and South), and Taiwan (a de facto country for these purposes) – plus the ten nations of ASEAN (Brunei, Indonesia, Malaysia, Philippines, Singapore, Thailand, Vietnam, Laos, Burma and Cambodia), and the tiny new nation of Timor Leste (East Timor). We might also add the two "special administrative regions" of Hong Kong and Macau, now part of China, but with distinctive political and media systems. In other words, the Pacific Asia region encompasses eighteen countries and territories, including much of the world's economic and industrial base, most of the non-Western countries of developed status, and several others that are rapidly approaching such status.

The difficulties inherent in applying the Polarized Pluralist model to Pacific Asia are readily apparent from a quick look at the regime types that characterize these eighteen territories. Brunei is an absolute monarchy, Burma a military dictatorship, and China, Laos, Vietnam, and North Korea are one-party states. Japan resembles a liberal democracy in many respects, but until the 2009 general elections, which saw a decisive

handover of power, had been controlled by the same party since 1955
(with a brief blip in the early 1990s). Malaysia and Singapore have been
controlled by the same party since independence. Hun Sen has served as
prime minister of Cambodia since 1985 (although from 1993 to 1998
he was technically "second prime minister"), irrespective of electoral
outcomes. In Hong Kong and Macau, chief executives are ultimately
appointed by Beijing, and elected representatives organized into political parties perform only legislative and veto functions. In other words,
twelve of Pacific Asia's eighteen territories have not experienced competitive political pluralism as understood in the West: Elections, where held,
do not normally change national governments. Elections have changed
governments successfully in Taiwan, South Korea (though only in the past
twenty years), Indonesia (but only in the last ten years), and the Philippines (although coup attempts and huge street protests also characterize
the political system). Thailand has also experienced numerous changes
of government after elections, as well as by successful military coups,
most recently in 1991 and 2006. East Timor, which has only officially
existed since 2002, has already seen a new party take power, but has also
experienced extensive civil disorder and an attempted coup.

   To summarize, politics in many Pacific Asian territories is rather plural
and highly polarized, but this pluralism often does not work along party-
political lines. Actors such as the military, the monarchy (in Brunei and
Thailand), and Diaspora communities (in Laos and Vietnam, for example) play roles with no direct equivalent in Western democracies. There
is no country in the region with a history of stable, competitive democracy going back more than a couple of decades, unless we count Japan.
Although it is certainly true that the media in several Pacific Asian territories are characterized by what Hallin and Mancini term: the "role of
clientelism, the strong role of the state, the role of media as an instrument
of political struggle, the limited development of the mass circulation press,
and the relative weakness of common professional norms," the meanings
of each of these terms in Asia is often very different from those that obtain
in a European context.

Media Systems and Political Systems
A core theme of Hallin and Mancini is the idea of parallelism – that
political systems (which means, at root, party systems) are paralleled by
media systems. The difficulty here is one that the authors acknowledge
quite frankly. Party systems are going out of style. As Angelo Panebianco
(1988) recognized with remarkable prescience in the 1980s, the lumbering

European-style "mass bureaucratic party," based on mass membership, party platforms, ideological orientations, resolutions at annual conferences, and dull leaders who were the captives of particular fractions, is virtually extinct in much of the Western world. With these lost parties has gone most of the academic literature on what constitutes a political party and, with that, much of our standard notions of what constitutes politics, political representation, and political participation. In place of the mass bureaucratic party we have the electoral professional party, epitomized for many by Tony Blair's New Labor – leader centered, media focused, sound-bite driven, policy light, ideologically barren, and voter focused rather than member oriented. In the Western world, the transition from mass parties to electoral professional parties has been a little-remarked transition from one form of liberal democracy to another.

Across much of the rest of the world, however, mass bureaucratic parties never took root in the European sense. In Pacific Asia, perhaps only the Japanese Socialist Party really merits the description. Other political parties are (or were) either communist behemoths (like the Chinese Communist Party), military front organizations (like Suharto's Golkar), ethnically oriented interest groups (like Malaysia's UMNO), or factionalized, personalized vote-gathering machines with little real collective identity (like most Thai and Philippine parties). Electoral professional parties and politics are now emerging across several Pacific Asian nations (including South Korea, Taiwan, Thailand, and the Philippines), but in Asian contexts their emergence does not represent the collapse of the traditional political party because traditional mass parties never existed. In other words, "new democracies" in Asia's economically rising countries have skipped the party system phase of political development (McCargo, 1997). They have gone straight from authoritarian or personalized forms of governance to hybridized forms of rule, based on an electoral politics that combines elements of political marketing and electoral professionalism with the persistence of some patrimonial and instrumental political practices (widespread vote buying and electoral manipulation, for example) (Shafferer, 2006). Because European and North American media systems are essentially the outcome of settled party systems and particular trajectories of political history, I would argue that these Asian territories do not really have media systems in the sense so ably captured by Hallin and Mancini. Where parties are less stable and where media often operate according to informal rather than formal norms, systems are harder to discern. As such, we cannot really expect to understand and analyze media in Pacific Asia successfully by applying the Polarized Plural model, even though we can certainly learn something about them from using some of the concepts and comparisons that Hallin and Mancini outline.

The Demise of Convergence?

The idea of convergence – that media systems around the world are growing more similar – is a major theme of Hallin and Mancini (2004b). In chapter 8, they elaborate on the "forces and limits of homogenization," hailing the "triumph of the Liberal Model" (2004b: 251–4). Despite some caveats about limits to the process of convergence, they conclude, "The differences among national media systems described in the preceding chapters of this book are clearly diminishing. A global media culture is emerging, one that closely resembles the Liberal Model" (2004b: 294). This argument, which forms a kind of codicil to the book, appears to me rather unconvincing and echoes some of the excessively teleological assumptions of Fukuyama's (1992) *The End of History and the Last Man*, and Huntington's (1991) *The Third Wave*.[17] In a later article entitled "Not the End of Journalism History," Hallin (2009: 334) distances himself from the convergence argument as follows:

Twenty years ago it was not uncommon to imagine that the end of journalism history was upon us, that for better or for worse all the world's media were going to wind up looking something like post-Second World War American media. Today it is very clear that diversity and often wrenching change are more likely to prevail over the coming decades.

In light of Hallin's recent clarification of his position, *Comparing Media Systems* might be read differently; in effect, the concluding discussion concerning homogenization and convergence may now be largely disregarded.[18] Diversity and change are the key to understanding today's media. However, the less things remain the same, the more difficult they are to generalize about, let alone to model. Media are becoming increasingly diverse, models and systems are breaking down, and Western

---

[17] Hallin insists that "No else but yourself" has read *Comparing Media Systems* as echoing Fukuyama's views. He and Mancini are adamant that I have misinterpreted their "convergence chapter," "ignoring repeated statements about limits and countertendencies, our critical view of straight-line modernization theories of media evolution, as well as our focus specifically on 'changes in European media systems.'" Dan Hallin, e-mail communication, July 6, 2009. I continue to see convergence as a core argument of the book. I invite readers to make their own judgments.

[18] Again, Hallin insists that "My own recent article certainly represents no change of heart." E-mail communication, July 6, 2009.

countries such as those forming the focus of *Comparing Media Systems* now look more marginal in global terms.

Toward a Conclusion

Hallin and Mancini have developed three eminently persuasive and valuable models to account for the development of media systems (paralleling political systems) in Western Europe and North America. Their models are based on a comparative study of eighteen countries. Because of their level of economic development and their stable political systems – all are essentially mature liberal democracies – these 18 countries are deeply unrepresentative of the wider world, which contains at least 192 nations.[19] Although these eighteen countries have certainly played leadership roles in shaping both media and politics far beyond their boundaries, it would be premature to assume that the models underpinning their media systems can be readily exported.

Many of the remaining 175-plus countries in the world share some features in common with the Polarized Pluralist model developed by Hallin and Mancini to summarize media-politics parallelism in Southern Europe. Yet the nature of non-European polarization and the forms of non-European pluralism are often very different from their Mediterranean varieties. If we take as our starting point the eighteen territories of Pacific Asia – which include China, Japan, South Korea, Vietnam, and Indonesia, all major nations of considerable importance – modeling the diversity of political and media systems in this region proves extremely hard. What we find instead is a picture of contradictions and subdivisions that defies considered classification. I would venture to suggest that if we were to throw in South Asia, Africa, the Middle East, and Latin America, the task of classification and modeling would prove completely overwhelming. It would certainly be possible to spend some time applying various of the three models to individual Asian countries, but it is unclear what would be learned by doing so.

Generalizing the Hallin and Mancini models is made more difficult by the rise of Pacific Asia, especially the recent emergence of China as a major global power. Such changes seriously challenge the dominance of Liberal models, whether in politics, the economy, or the media. Even the Polarized Pluralist model, for all its shortcomings, is far a more liberal way of doing politics and media than China would wish to encourage in

---

[19] Actually, more than 200 by most counts.

its backyard.[20] Without seeking to echo crude representations of China as a threat to the West,[21] it is clear that the rise of China does offer an alternative way of understanding future political directions for both the Asia Pacific region and the rest of the world.

Beyond the scope of this chapter is this question: How sustainable are the four defining factors (media markets, parallelism, professionalism, and state intervention) that Hallin and Mancini use to create the groundwork for their models? As the 2008 American presidential election campaign abundantly illustrated, new online media outlets now enjoy huge audiences and engage directly with voters and citizens on public issues. Yet these outlets do not work on conventional business models, are inherently unprofessional (some have no paid staff at all), and are largely beyond the reach of conventional state intervention.

The highly participatory parallelisms inherent in political blogs such as HuffPost – where postings on topical issues may attract several thousand comments within a few hours – and their counterparts across the world may soon demand a complete rethinking of what we mean by media systems. This in turn will entail radically remodeling or demodeling the media, both in Asia and elsewhere. The rise of new media and the growing ascendancy of the blogger over the journalist may mean the unraveling of "media systems" as conventionally understood in developed democracies. In those developing countries that currently lack institutionalized political and media systems, the rise of new media may allow societies to skip the "system" stage or at least to generate very different forms of structure. In fact, mass political parties and conventional mass media may never emerge in such countries – instead, these nations may proceed directly to a twenty-first-century mode of political and informational participation, in which the election of representative elites operates through hybridized, marketized campaigning, and the medium persistently trumps the ideological and policy message. Insofar as this new mode of media and politics can be modeled, we would need to develop appropriate "anti-models" that can embrace an emerging global picture of fragmentation, subdivision, and a lack of overarching systems. Such anti-models would begin by problematizing and questioning notions such as the marketization of media, political parallelism, professionalism, and state intervention.

---

[20] For the idea of China as offering a nondemocratic alternative to the West, see Daniel C. Lynch (2007).

[21] For a critical discussion of this debate, drawing on numerous Chinese sources, see Callahan (2005).

Orderly media systems are the exception rather than the rule, and their successful export to Asia or the rest of the developing world looks rather unlikely.

To adopt a skeptical stance toward the idea of modeling media systems is not to question the value of comparing media in different countries or in different parts of the world. Media in the new democracies, illiberal democracies, and semi-authoritarian nations of Pacific Asia are commonly characterized by intense partisanship, persistent state interference, ambiguous modes of ownership, and questionable profitability. Although these features are too miscellaneous to amount to a model, there is ample scope for comparative research concerning the ways in which similar media characteristics recur around the region. In short, rapid economic growth and rapid social change give media a heightened political salience, empowering media to be much more potent political actors in their own right than has generally been the case in the West. At times of transition from authoritarian to more open regimes – such as the fall of Marcos in 1986, the 1992 Black May events in Bangkok, or the 1998 ouster of General Suharto – media have repeatedly played a pivotal role. Where such changes have been averted, media have been crucial in promoting state stability or in moderating the actions of the state in line with popular sentiment. As potential agents of change, media in Cambodia, Hong Kong, Indonesia, Malaysia, the Philippines, South Korea, Taiwan, and Thailand, for example, have much in common.

In short, a polyvalent clamor, sometimes latent or incipient, sometimes vocal and outspoken, challenges a more settled, state-sanctioned information order. This polyvalence often takes place at the margins, on dissident Web sites, in small-circulation print media, and through community radio stations. In the one-party states of China and Vietnam, polyvalence is more aspiration than reality, operating only tentatively and primarily online. The media in much of the Asia-Pacific might be given the working designation "Partisan Polyvalence." Such a designation does not constitute a new model, but attempts to capture the persistent tensions between authorized and unauthorized voices that characterize the media in this region and beyond.

11

How Far Can Media Systems Travel?

Applying Hallin and Mancini's Comparative Framework outside the Western World

Katrin Voltmer

Introduction

Only a few books in communication studies have triggered as lively a debate in the academic community as Hallin and Mancini's (2004b) *Comparing Media Systems*. For decades communication scholars have pushed for more comparative research to advance the theoretical foundations of the field and to generate more systematic knowledge of the differences and similarities of systems of communications across time and space (Blumler, McLeod, and Rosengren, 1992; Esser and Pfetsch, 2004). Even though there have been a number of important collections of country studies (see, for example, Gunther and Mughan, 2000; Kaid and Holtz-Bacha, 1995; Kelly, Mazzoleni, and McQuail, 2004), most of these volumes lack a unifying conceptual framework that would allow us to draw generalizable conclusions beyond the individual cases at hand. Hallin and Mancini's "three models of media and politics" therefore provide a much needed intellectual toolkit for understanding the immense variations between systems of public communication in different cultural and political contexts.

Since its publication several scholars have tried to apply the framework to countries other than the group of advanced democracies that are covered in *Comparing Media Systems* (for Eastern Europe, see Jakubowicz and Sükösd, 2008; for Brazil, Albuquerque, 2005; for South Africa, Hadland, 2007). These studies attempt to classify a particular country into one of the three models – Polarized Pluralist, Democratic Corporatist, or Liberal – usually with the conclusion that it is the Polarized Pluralist model that captures best the features of the country under study. With its defining characteristics of journalistic partisanship, political instrumentalization of the media, and uncontrolled commercialization of the media industry, all of which are regarded as problematic and potentially obstructive to a healthy democratic public sphere, the Polarized Pluralist model seems to have become something like a catch-all category for media systems outside the Western world of established democracies. However, it is rather implausible to assume that, whereas eighteen countries in Western Europe and North America are diversified into three distinct constellations of media–politics relationships, all the remaining media systems around the world can be sufficiently understood by only one model. Classifying non-Western media systems as Polarized Pluralist not only implies that these systems are deficient in one way or the other[1] but also that there is no significant variation in institutions and practices except for those that can be observed in the established democracies of the West.

Hence, if we are to understand the nature and variety of media systems outside the group of advanced Western democracies, we have to expand and refine the analytical categories suggested by Hallin and Mancini. Doing so will contribute not only to broadening the theoretical framework but also to the "de-Westernization" (Curran and Park, 2000) of media studies. Like Hallin and Mancini's study, this chapter focuses on democratic media systems (i.e., countries that meet the minimum requirements of democratic governance).[2] For this reason, countries like Burma, Zimbabwe, but also China and most countries of the Middle East, interesting as they might be, are not considered here.

---

[1] It has to be emphasized that Hallin and Mancini reject any value judgments as to which of the three models might be preferable. Instead they point out the strengths and weaknesses of each model. Nevertheless, although the Liberal and the Democratic Corporatist models each have their advantages – most notably a high level of political independence and public service broadcasting, respectively – the Pluralist Polarized model appears to be less advanced.

[2] The question as to what can be regarded a democracy and what not is highly disputed. The positions range from minimalist views that regard regular contested elections as sufficient (for example Przeworski, 1991) to maximalist approaches that include a large range of additional conditions, such as a democratic political culture, state capacity, and socioeconomic equality, to name but a few (for example Dahl, 1989; Merkel, 2004; see for a general discussion Grugel, 2002). I am following here the pragmatic approach suggested by Bernhagen (2009: 31) that stipulates a core definition of democracy as "a political system in which the government is held accountable to citizens by means of free and fair elections," complemented by a number of "necessary preconditions," such as basic liberties, including freedom of association, expression, and the press.

Most non-Western democracies are new, or emerging, democracies that abandoned autocratic rule during the so-called third wave of democratization (Huntington, 1991), which started in the 1970s, culminated in the dramatic events surrounding the fall of the Berlin Wall, and then spread to many countries in Asia and Africa. Much of the discussion of this chapter is therefore informed by the rich body of literature on democratization that has accompanied the events of the "third wave" over the past couple of decades. Students of new democracies are confronted with similar questions to those faced by communication scholars seeking to expand comparative research outside the Western world. What kind of systems – political, media – are emerging in these newly established democracies? Are the existing analytical concepts sufficient to understand these cases, or do we need additional categories? What are the prospects for these emerging systems? Can we expect them to develop into one of the Western models, or are they now and will remain genuinely different from what we know from Western democracies, with different institutional structures and different internal rules and norms?

The chapter starts with a brief reconstruction of Hallin and Mancini's analytical framework and some suggestions as to possible refinements. This is followed by a discussion of possible future pathways of political and media systems in non-Western new democracies. I argue that the coincidence of convergence and divergence of political and media systems is likely to result in new and hybrid patterns of politics–media relationships. Taking recent political science debates on the emergence of hybrid regimes as a starting point, the chapter then identifies specific constellations of politics and the media in emerging democracies that can serve as starting points for future research.

Three Models and Four Pillars

The three models suggested by Hallin and Mancini to describe media–politics relationships are understood as "ideal types" as defined by Max Weber. That is, rather than denoting an ideal, or normatively desirable, state of affairs they systematically describe the empirical reality by summarizing and compressing the richness of social structures and behavior into summative categories. Hallin and Mancini's typology comprises three models, each of which is predominant in particular geographical areas: the Polarized Pluralist model that can be found in Mediterranean countries, the Democratic Corporatist model of North and Central Europe, and the Liberal model that dominates the Anglo-Saxon countries of the North Atlantic. These models are based on four dimensions of media systems that serve as pillars, or supporting elements, which are again composed of various sub-aspects: (1) media markets, (2) political parallelism, (3) journalistic professionalism, and (4) the degree and nature of state intervention.

The particular constellation of these four dimensions then constitutes the three models and is the basis for the classification of individual countries. It can be argued that dimensions 1, 2, and 4 refer to the media's relationship with their economic, social, and political environments, whereas the third dimension describes the internal rules and norms of media institutions. Because all media systems have to address these external and internal relationships, the four dimensions can be regarded as universally applicable tools for describing the dynamics of media and politics in different contexts: All media organizations have to generate revenues to produce their outputs; decide on whether or not to engage in alliances with social groups and, if so, which ones; internally agree on the rules of operation and the norms that set the standards for evaluating their outputs; and finally position themselves vis-à-vis the actors and institutions of political power. For the most part, these relationships are not entirely determined by the media themselves. Instead, their discretionary power varies considerably, depending on the ability of their counterparts to impose their own rules and interests on the media. In particular the media's relationship with their political environment is highly determined by the state's capacity to issue policies and regulations, even though in turn the media affect the way in which political institutions operate. Overall, although the applicability of the dimensions is universal, the specific pattern of the relationships they describe can take on very different forms, and it remains an open question whether these variations constitute new models other than the three suggested by Hallin and Mancini.

Several problems arise when applying the four dimensions and the resulting models to non-Western contexts. One relates to the *scope* of the dimensions. For the purpose of classification Hallin and Mancini break them up into "high" and "low" or "strong" and "weak." Whereas in established democracies with highly developed market economies, the scope of these dimensions is confined to a relatively limited range of possible values, in non-Western countries the scope of these dimensions might go far beyond what is included in the categories '"high" or "low."[3]

---

3 I owe thanks to Hartmut Wessler, University of Mannheim (Germany), who has pointed me to this problem.

For example, newspaper circulation in the Polarized Pluralist model is classified as low compared to the strong print markets of the countries belonging to the Democratic Corporatist model. However, some media markets of the developing world fall far below this range. High levels of illiteracy, underdeveloped consumer markets, and inadequate technological infrastructure might even constitute a totally different quality of the economic foundations of the media than would be captured by simply expanding the dimension to, for example, "very weak media market." In addition, developing countries are usually characterized by extreme inequality, which is also reflected in their media markets. Whereas some parts of the population are virtually excluded from public communication, others, usually the urban, economically thriving middle classes, are hardly different from their counterparts in the industrialized West. Thus, when classifying media markets we have to consider not only the average degree of development but also the variance within the system as a defining element of possible resulting models.

Similar arguments can be made with regard to state intervention. Democratic Corporatist countries score high on this dimension in particular because of the central role of public service broadcasting, which is usually subjected to a higher degree of regulation than the commercial media systems of the Liberal model. However, even though the relationship between the state and public service broadcasting is often problematic and prone to conflicts, there is a substantial difference between even extensive regulation of public service broadcasting and excessive state interference into the running of media organizations and their editorial decision making, which characterizes many post-authoritarian democracies. Again, even though the dimension of state intervention is conceptualized as a continuum, there might be a certain threshold that marks a new quality in the relationship between the media and the state.

Another aspect that can potentially affect the boundary and meaning of the models is the *kind*, or specific nature, of the dimensions that should be taken into account alongside measurements of degree. In the present conceptualization only the dimension "state intervention" includes both its nature and degree. The reason for considering both aspects is that it does make a great difference whether there is a high degree of intervention with the objective to ensure the quality of programming, or whether the intervention aims to increase the government's control over the media. The means of intervention are equally important; for example, whether regulation uses direct intervention into the production process and its outcomes or primarily indirect incentives such as taxation, prices, and certain privileges. Thus, it is not only the degree of state intervention but also its objectives and instruments that determine the eventual classification of a country into a particular model.

Similar considerations apply to the other dimensions as well; for example, political parallelism between partisan media and the political groupings they support. European politics has traditionally been shaped by the ideological difference between left and right or, in the U.S. context, liberal and conservative. The terms denote antagonistic economic interests and, related to them, conflicting values of equality that evolved from the historical struggle between labor and capital (Bobbio, 1996; Lipset and Rokkan, 1967). Because of its roots in the economic and political traditions of European history, the ideological distinction of left and right often does not make much sense in countries outside the Western world. Instead, religious, ethnic, and regional identities, but also clientelistic loyalties play a much more important role.[4] The nature of these conflicts has a significant impact on the way they are dealt with in the political arena. The antagonism between left and right has almost entirely been reduced to issues of redistribution (i.e., the question of how much of the national wealth is allocated to whom). Depending on the bargaining power of the antagonists, the gains and losses of either side are a matter of more or less and are therefore negotiable. In contrast, when it comes to identities or (divine) truth, political controversies can quickly turn into unsolvable conflicts. It is difficult to bargain about giving away or gaining some identity or some truth. Hence, polarization along religious or ethnic lines bears the risk of spinning out of control and turning into hatred or even civil war.[5] In other words, the nature and the degree of political conflict and its reflection in the media system do make a difference.

Furthermore, the dynamics of the political conflict and the resulting media parallelism are determined by the social structure of the conflict (i.e., the strength of the opposing camps). Polarization usually denotes the antagonism between two opposing camps. However, a different pattern arises when the political contest is fragmented into multiple small groups, none of which is able to control the scene over a substantial period of time. Where these groups are unable to reach compromises and form

---

[4] It has to be emphasized that these conflicts are also present in Western European politics, but they have largely lost their divisive force. Remaining examples are Northern Ireland and the Basque country.

[5] An extreme example of the media's potentially disastrous role in ethnic conflicts is the genocide in Rwanda, which was fueled by inflammatory media campaigns (Thompson, 2006).

coalitions, this type of fragmented pluralism can result in a permanent stalemate and the inability of governments to make binding decisions. Yet another configuration of conflict emerges from the continuous dominance of one camp or party at the expense of all the other groups, so that elections rarely result in an alternation of power. As a consequence, the ruling party is able to concentrate the resources of power, including the ability to control the public agenda, in its hands.

Whatever the specific constellation of the conflict, the pattern of media allegiances is of crucial importance for the dynamics of the political process. The media can reflect the strength of the conflicting parties in a fairly one-to-one fashion, thereby paralleling the conflict. Or they can disproportionally ally with a particular group, resulting in a distorted pluralism in the system (for a discussion of different constellations of press-party parallelism, see Seymour-Ure, 1974: 156–76). This constellation of political parallelism often generates a structural "spiral of silence" (Noelle-Neumann, 1993) in which the continuous underrepresentation of large parts of existing interests and identities on the media agenda leads to their marginalization in political life.

Political parallelism of the media can be an important contribution to a lively public sphere. It can strengthen citizens' party attachment and encourage political participation. However, media parallelism with political parties – or any other politicized grouping – can be detrimental if no effective mechanisms of moderation are in place. One such mechanism is a forum medium that serves as a platform where all voices can be heard and – even more important – listen to each other. In Western Europe and in Canada, public service broadcasting has fulfilled the role of a forum medium, and even though it has been threatened by the rise of commercial broadcasting it is still able to attract large parts, if not the majority, of the national audience. However, in recently emerging democracies the attempt to establish public service broadcasting has been largely unsuccessful. Unlike in Western democracies, the frequent political parallelism of the media – be it polarized, fragmented, or hegemonic – is not complemented by a public forum, making these countries' attempt to develop a new political identity with shared values and norms an extremely difficult endeavor.

This brief discussion of the dimensional elements of Hallin and Mancini's theoretical framework shows that variations both in terms of scope and kind may indicate specific constellations that fall outside the present three models. These differences are likely to arise when looking at cases outside advanced Western democracies and may or may not constitute new and distinct models of media systems.

It could be argued that any new models would only be of transitory relevance because the forces of convergence will eventually lead to the homogenization of media systems around the world. In fact, Hallin and Mancini wonder about a possible convergence toward the Liberal model even within the range of their sample of advanced Western democracies. However, the reemergence of partisan media in the United States can be taken as an indication that the dynamic of media systems is more complex and by no means unidirectional (Hallin, 2009).

Convergence, Divergence, and Hybridity

One of the main forces that drives media systems toward convergence is the globalization of media markets. Media organizations around the world are owned by a decreasing number of transnational media conglomerates that are trying to expand their audiences both within and across national boundaries. The initial response of the media industry to globalization was to produce media products of high uniformity to make them saleable everywhere in the world. However, international media corporations quickly realized that the successful export of media products requires cultural sensitivity and the willingness to adapt to the preferences of local audiences. For example, Rupert Murdoch's Star TV, arguably the most successful international media enterprise, not only transmits in dozens of different languages, including local dialects, but has also modified its products to adjust to the viewing habits and cultural values of its diverse audiences. There is also resistance to globalization from below. The global flow of information from the West has often led to a growing awareness of existing traditions and values and, as a consequence, has strengthened the demand for local media products. Here lies the reason for the enormous success of Bollywood, the Indian film industry located in Bombay (now named Mumbai), across Asia, or its equivalent Nollywood, Nigeria's film industry, in African countries. Hence, today's media markets are international and local at the same time. Yet rather than resulting in a simple mix of ingredients or a range of different shades of gray, this has brought about new, unique forms of media products and practices (Rantanen, 2004; Thussu, 2009).

Similar trends can be observed with regard to democracy. Over the last two decades or so, democracy has become a globalized idea that continues to inspire people from all over the world. Alternative discourses have largely lost their legitimacy, forcing even die-hard autocrats to adopt democratic rhetoric or to introduce some sort of elections (Grugel, 2002; Levitsky and Way, 2010). Indeed, at the peak of the democratization wave in the mid-1990s political observers and scholars alike were convinced that the global victory of democracy was unstoppable and that the newcomers would soon adopt the institutions and practices of liberal democracy as known from the West. The idea of global democracy is reflected in the theoretical concepts that were developed to understand the spread of democracy around the globe. The terms "democratization" and "transition" implicitly carry the assumption of a unidirectional process toward liberal democracy. Thus developments diverging from this path were regarded as failed or incomplete transitions. A similar line of thought believed that the media in emerging democracies would adopt Western models of operation, preferably the Liberal one with its emphasis on minimal state regulation and neutral reporting.

Policy makers of international nongovernmental organizations (NGOs) and Western governments are working toward similar objectives. Countless democracy support programs have been set up to encourage and strengthen democratization around the world (Carothers, 1999). Initially, these programs were focused on the core political institutions, such as the implementation of electoral systems, the reconstruction of parliaments and the judiciary, and the strengthening of political parties. However, international donors and policy makers have become increasingly aware of the crucial role played by the media in the transition process. They believe that many of the flaws in the functioning of the newly established institutions can be put down to inefficient and unfree media. The link between effective democracy and the media becomes most obvious during elections, which can only be fair and free when oppositional voices have access to the media and when all citizens have the opportunity to learn about the alternatives at hand. Many organizations that are working toward democratization have therefore initiated media development schemes (among others, see Global Forum for Media Development [n.d.] ; for an academic discussion see Price, Rozumilowicz, and Verhulst [2002]) with the aims of strengthening civil society, fighting corruption, and fostering development – to name but a few of the goals that are hoped to be achieved. A prominent example is the World Bank's CommGAP program (Communication for Governance and Accountability Program) that was launched in 2006 to promote good governance and democratic public spheres, in particular in the developing world (World Bank, 2009).

The policy documents of this scheme, even though aware of the importance of local contexts, clearly reflect a preference for private media, factual reporting, and adversarial journalism – in other words, the key elements of the Liberal model in Hallin and Mancini's framework. Another organization in the international arena whose work promotes the homogenization of political and media systems is the European Union. In the negotiations for accession the EU has made it a condition for prospective new member states to adhere to its media policy.

However, evidence from the new democracies of the third wave indicates that neither the export of political institutions nor of journalism and media has resulted in uniformity, let alone convergence toward the Liberal model of media systems. To the contrary, what we can observe now – a quarter-century after the onset of the "third wave" – is a puzzling diversity of institutions and practices of public communication. Few hail this diversity, and there is growing skepticism as to the fate of these new democracies and the quality of their media (Carothers, 2002; Diamond, 1996). Whereas some countries have been remarkably successful in transforming their institutions, others appear to be stuck in transition and even to be developing in a reverse direction. It seems that on their way from their Western origin to their destination in a new political and cultural environment institutions change their structure and functioning, often in a subtle, but almost always in a fundamental way. What are the reasons for the limited capability of institutions – and particularly media institutions – to travel? Why is it so difficult, often impossible, to implement institutions in a one-to-one fashion in a different context?

Media Systems as a Social Construction

One of the reasons is that concepts such as representative government, elections, and media pluralism are not as unanimous as they appear to the Western eye. Neither democracy nor the notion of a democratic media – nor that of related ideas such as press freedom, objectivity, and the watchdog role – has a fixed meaning that could claim validity outside time and space. In fact, the meaning of these notions is far more elastic than textbook knowledge usually implies and therefore has to be renegotiated in the context in which they are implemented. Regime changes raise the question of the meaning of democracy in a very dramatic way. With the breakdown of the old autocratic regime, some agreement has to be reached as to how the new regime differs from the previous one, how institutions should be designed, and what is accepted as proper democratic practice and what not (Dryzek and Holmes, 2002). Political scientist Laurence

Whitehead (2002: 187) therefore proposes an "interpretavist" perspective on democratization, in which the meaning and practices of democratic politics are achieved in a process of social construction. Instead of having a fixed meaning that can be applied universally, the meaning of democracy is anchored in broader cultural, historical, and political discourses that eventually shape the outcome of the transition process. Even established democracies periodically go through times of interpretative uncertainty and self-reflection, especially in situations of high-profile political scandals or national disasters. However, they can rely on an accumulated set of previous agreements, often laid down in official documents (court decisions, committee reports, etc.) that serve as a point of reference in the actual debate. Policy makers in new democracies operate on far less solid grounds.

The reconstruction of the media is an area of change in which an "interpretavist" view proves particularly fruitful. Even though press freedom is regarded as a litmus test of democracy, most people, practitioners and scholars alike, would agree that it is not an absolute value. Rather, press freedom has to be balanced with other, sometimes competing values; for example, the public interest, national security, privacy and minority rights, and even taste and decency. The exact balance of these values is a matter of collective debate and therefore varies not only across cultures but also over time. Similar ambiguities exist with regard to journalistic role expectations. Empirical research shows that journalistic cultures differ significantly around the world (Hanitzsch, 2007; Weaver, 1998). Chalaby (1998) even goes so far as to argue that the notion of neutral and detached journalism is essentially American and far from a universal norm.

However, an "interpretativist" approach to democratization and the media bears the risk of losing sight of core standards and eventually ending up in an "anything goes" position that might even justify the persistence of autocratic practices. The rediscovery of Asian, especially Confucian, values by the Chinese and other authoritarian East Asian governments is an example of the attempt to use cultural traditions as a line of defense against further liberalization (Chan, 1997; Massey and Chang, 2002). Hence, without identifying the defining threshold, the concepts of democracy and democratic media would evaporate into empty words. Whitehead (2002: 19) suggests the notion of a "floating but anchored" conception of democracy and its key values where the core meaning is anchored, but the margins are open to debate and interpretation. Similarly, it can be argued that, although it is essential to ensure the media's ability to fulfill their key functions of informing the citizens and controlling political power holders, the understanding of the relative importance of each of these roles and the criteria as to how they are performed are shaped by a complex set of cultural and situational factors.

These are not just esoteric questions that are best dealt with in an academic seminar. Rather, the meaning of democracy and the role of the media therein are closely linked to the power relations in a society. Access to the media is one of the main resources in winning and maintaining power positions. In many new democracies where political parties and candidates often lack alternative channels of mobilization, such as strong grassroots organizations or stable loyalties of voters, control of the media becomes a matter of political survival. Therefore, the definition of press freedom and press responsibility and the resulting course of media policy frequently turn into a fierce battlefield between political groups who are trying to secure their position in the political contest (Wasserman, 2010; Wasserman and De Beer, 2006). Hence, which and whose definition prevails greatly affects the relationship between politics and the media and the resulting media system.

Transforming Media Institutions from the Rubble of the Past

Another reason for the assumption that emerging democracies develop new types of media systems rather than copying Western models lies in the trajectories of the transition itself. Unlike other democratic institutions, such as electoral systems or parliaments, the media are not newly created after the regime change. Rather, they are transformations of existing institutions that carry with them the norms and power relations of the old regime. The result is a unique mix of persisting structures inherited from the past alongside newly adopted elements from existing – usually Western – role models and, in addition, specific features born out of the desire to implement something different and better than the institutional predecessor (Milton, 2000). Continuity applies not only to institutional structures and norms but also to the individuals who are part of these institutions (Sparks, 2008). Numerous journalists who worked under the old regime remain in their position after the regime change, and the rules and practices they have been brought up with continue to guide their work. Even more continuity can be observed among the political elites, however. Being used to subservient media, they often react with anger and aggression to media that see themselves as an adversary rather than as a mouthpiece of the government. Rather than accepting the media as an independent player and learning the more subtle strategies of news management, these political elites stick to the old tricks of direct pressure, threats, and editorial interference (Adam and Pfetsch, 2009; Dobreva, Pfetsch, and Voltmer, 2011). Surprisingly enough, even former opposition activists who fought for freedom of expression and the press under the old regime frequently have difficulties dealing with the new media environment. In addition to the earlier mentioned necessity to secure access to the media as a political resource, they seem to assume that under democratic circumstances the media are their "natural" allies that should support their cause.

Given the continuity of organizational structures, personnel, and practices, we have to factor in the particular features of the preceding authoritarian regime as a determinant of the emerging media systems in new democracies. Elsewhere I have argued that different types of authoritarian regimes have generated specific patterns of politics–media relations that affect the outcome of the transformation process of political and media institutions after the demise of the old regime (Voltmer, 2008; for a discussion of nondemocratic regimes in general, see Brooker, 2009). It should be noted that the discussion that follows presents ideal typical constellations, and individual countries and particular historical periods might differ significantly from these summary accounts.

More than any other nondemocratic regime type, communist regimes, especially the former Soviet Union and its satellites, are based on a comprehensive ideology that positions itself in opposition to capitalism and liberal democracy. Consequently, market structures and free enterprise were destroyed and replaced by nationalized (i.e., state) ownership. Thus, virtually all media were owned by the government or state organizations. Moreover, the attempt to educate the masses according to communist ideals put the media into the role of the main instrument of mass mobilization. Media content was therefore highly politicized, leaving little space, if any, for nonpolitical issues or entertainment.

These characteristics still shape political communication in postcommunist countries. The need to privatize the entire media industry has caused enormous turbulence, especially where the newly created markets remained weak. Newspapers were particularly easy prey for international media conglomerates, leading to a high proportion of foreign ownership. Most postcommunist countries in Eastern Europe tried to transform the former state television channel into public service broadcasting, but largely failed to create a politically independent and, at the same time, a socially responsible institution (Open Society Institute/EU Monitoring and Advocacy Program, 2005; Paletz and Jakubowicz, 2003). Instead,

public service broadcasting remains extremely vulnerable to state interference. Meanwhile, newspapers are highly politicized and opinionated,
which still resonates with the socialist model of journalism that sees itself
in the role of intellectual leader and interpreter of political issues rather
than reporter of mere facts (Hall and O'Neil, 1998; Voltmer, 2000).

Military dictatorships, which dominated Latin America before democratization began in the late 1970s, are in many respects the flipside of communist regimes. This regime type never touched the capitalist structure
of the economy, so except for a few selected state outlets the media were
highly commercialized and even benefited in some cases from the industrial policy of the government (Tironi and Sunkel, 2000). Even though the
political leaders of military dictatorships used nationalistic and anticommunist rhetoric, ideology did not play a significant role in ensuring the
legitimacy of the regime. Hence, there were no attempts to mobilize the
masses. In the contrary, the stability of the regime was built on acquiescence and depoliticization (Linz and Stepan, 1996). The best way for the
media to survive was therefore to stay away from politics as much as possible and resort to entertainment programs. After the withdrawal of the
generals from the political scene, the media did not seem to require particular attention to be transformed into democratic institutions, because
marketization and commercialization correspond neatly with the Anglo-
Saxon notion of independent media. However, below the surface of a
strong media industry, the political independence of the media remains
precarious. Political ownership is widespread, with influential politicians
or their family members controlling key media outlets and leaving the
media squeezed "[b]etween the rock of the state and the hard place of the
market" (Waisbord, 2000a: 50).

Authoritarian developmental states under one-party rule were a typical pattern in East Asia, most notably the so-called tiger states. These
regimes used a strong state bureaucracy and close ties with the industry to
push for development (Clark, 2000). The media were part of this industrial project; they were used to propagate the government's development
policies and in turn benefited from state subsidies and protectionism.
Hence, like the media under military dictatorship, the media in authoritarian developmental states were part of a thriving capitalist market,
but like their counterparts in communist regimes they were subjected to
serving political goals and objectives. Political change did not occur with
a "big bang," but came gradually and without dramatic disruptions. In
fact, a high degree of continuity is a striking feature of this transition
pathway. Even though basic liberties including freedom of the press are

now guaranteed, the media remain under tight state control, with most national television stations and high-circulation newspapers still being owned by the state.

One-party rule also dominated the developing countries in Africa. However, state institutions were – and still are – weak and often unable to perform their basic functions. Like other resources, the media were seized by a small clique of political elites who used them for their own purposes. Democratization has been greeted with great enthusiasm in this part of the world, but has suffered many setbacks and breakdowns (Nyamnjoh, 2005). The problems of the past – state incapacity and underdevelopment – still persist. Weak consumer markets, insufficient infrastructure, and low educational levels leave the media extremely vulnerable to political interference. Many outlets would not be able to survive on their own terms and remain dependent on state subsidies, whether directly transferred or in the form of state advertising. Given the dependence of the media on the state, investigative journalism becomes a risky enterprise, and individual journalists who dare to dig into cases of corruption and mismanagement have been harassed, physically attacked, and even imprisoned. Liberalization of public communication has also brought about negative consequences. Ethnic, regional, and/or religious differences now can openly be expressed in public and as a consequence have become more salient as political forces. Because most media are affiliated with particular group interests, this open expression of differences has frequently led to hostilities and even the outbreak of violence.

To sum up, the trajectories of the past alongside the (re-)interpretations of institutions make it unlikely that media systems outside the Western world fit into the models that have been developed to describe media and politics in Europe and North America. Especially in new democracies, which make up most non-Western countries, media systems are built on their institutional predecessors and have inherited some of their features. They are also the cognitive constructions of the policy makers of the transition process, who shape them according to their own values, worldviews, and interests. The outcome are hybrid media systems that correspond, and are closely interrelated, with the political systems in which they operate.

Toward Models of Hybrid Media Systems

The notion of hybridity is a useful analytical tool in understanding the unique nature of media systems that have emerged in the context of the "third wave" of democratization, but it can easily become a catch-all category that disguises different patterns of politics–media relations within this group of media systems. The following discussion therefore suggests strategies to break down the broad category of hybrid media systems with the aim of identifying specific constellations that might constitute distinct models of media systems other than the three suggested by Hallin and Mancini.

The discussion in the previous section drew on types of autocratic regimes to understand the historical origin of emerging hybrid media systems. What is striking is that these types of autocracy are clustered in particular geographical regions – very much like with Hallin and Mancini's models. Apparently, cultural norms and social practices are not randomly distributed in space. The high density of exchange of goods and ideas alongside shared political destinies often leads to similar institutional preferences. However, taking regional proximity – Asian, African, Latin American – as a defining element for models of media systems makes it difficult both to account for the heterogeneity that can be found within regions and to identify possible similarities across regions. Furthermore, even though the preceding autocratic regime constrains in specific ways the range of choices available to political and media elites after regime change, the influence of the past is far from deterministic. Other influences, such as international politics, traditions reaching back before authoritarian rule, or socioeconomic factors, also influence the direction a country and its media system take after transition. The huge differences between the countries that emerged from Soviet-style communism illustrate this point. Russia, Ukraine, Romania, and Hungary, for example, all experienced communist rule, but differ significantly with regard to the political institutions, including media, that have been implemented after the breakdown of communism.

Thus, although geographical location and the preceding autocratic regime are useful foci of classification, they can also be misleading because of the heterogeneous distribution of regime types across space and time. Instead, we have to turn to key characteristics of the existing political system and its dominant structures as the defining point of departure. Hallin and Mancini take a similar approach (2004b: 69). In fact, the labels they use to identify the three models – Democratic Corporatist, Polarized Pluralist, and Liberal – are well-established categories in comparative politics. The underlying argument for looking at the political system to understand the media system is that, even though a close interrelationship and mutual dependence exist between the political and the media system, it is the political system that ultimately has the power to make binding decisions and thus shapes the basic structure and functioning of the media system. This does not mean that the media system mirrors the political system in a one-to-one fashion. In fact, there can be significant incongruities and tensions between the structures of the two systems caused, for example, by ambiguities in the surrounding culture or the internal logic of operation of the media system itself. Nevertheless, it is plausible to assume that by and large the media system reflects the norms and structures of the political system.

Like media systems, the political systems of new democracies often seem to defy the institutional norms known from established Western democracies. Starting with Karl's (1995) seminal article on the "hybrid regimes of Central America," the notion of hybridity has become a buzzword among political scientists who are trying to come to grips with the messy reality of the large range of new democracies that in some way or the other do not live up to the ideal of Western liberal democracy. If the hybridity of both political and media systems were just a transitory phase in a country's journey from autocratic to democratic rule, it would hardly be worthwhile to identify specific types or models. We would just have to wait until these systems reached democratic maturity and could then be classified into one of the existing models. However, this is not the case. Instead, hybrid systems show a surprising level of persistence, and in many cases the peculiar mix of democratic and autocratic practices has to be regarded as an equilibrium rather than a transitory state of affairs (Carothers, 2002; Morlino, 2009). What then are the particular characteristics of hybrid regimes, and what kind of media systems have emerged in these contexts?

By combining elements of the preceding regime with elements of democratic rule, hybrid regimes inhabit a gray zone between authoritarianism and democracy (Alexander, 2008). They seem to be somewhere halfway: no longer autocratic, but not yet fully democratic. Generally speaking, hybrid regimes have introduced some kind of competitive elections, but fail to deepen democratic governance beyond basic formal requirements. However, the degree to which hybrid systems have adopted democratic practices varies.[6] In some cases they fall below even a minimalist

---

[6] Diamond (2002) locates hybrid regimes on a continuum between liberal democracy at one end and closed authoritarianism on the other. The suggested hybrid categories are electoral democracy (but not liberal), ambiguous regimes, competitive authoritarianism, and hegemonic electoral authoritarianism (p. 26).

conception of democracy – for example, the hybrid regime type of "competitive authoritarianism" (Levitsky and Way, 2010); in other cases they can be regarded as diminished forms of democracy (Bernhagen, 2009). It is the lighter shades of gray, (i.e., democratic hybrid regimes) that are the focus of the present discussion.

A common feature of these democratic hybrid regimes is the existence of competitive and reasonably free elections, but a weak institutionalization of the rule of law and civil liberties (Rose, 2009). One recurring element of what Zakaria (1997) calls "illiberal democracy" is the restriction of the independence of the media and resulting limitations of media pluralism, which go far beyond the degree of state interference that can be observed in the Polarized Pluralist model of Hallin and Mancini's framework.

In the following I draw on two particular hybrid regime types that have been widely researched and that appear to be of particular interest for understanding the specific constellation of politics and the media in hybrid regimes: delegative democracy and one-party predominance. It should be emphasized that there are many more types of hybrid regimes than just these two. However, delegative democracy and one-party predominance make up a significant number of new democracies and are therefore a fruitful starting point for expanding the range of models of media systems.

The notion of *delegative democracy* has been introduced by O'Donnell (1994) as a "new species" of democracy that differs in important ways from representative democracy. Delegative democracy flourishes in countries with presidential systems of government. They are based on the premise that "whoever wins election to the presidency is thereby entitled to govern as he or she sees fit" (O'Donnell, 1994: 59). This type of democracy has been extensively described with regard to new democracies in Latin America, but it has also become the dominant political form in the successor states of the Soviet Union, most notably Russia (Kubicek, 1994). In delegative democracies presidents represent themselves as standing above the divisions of party politics, claiming to represent the nation as a whole rather than particular interests or groups. Delegative democracies employ presidential rule in a way that weakens democratic institutions, such as parliament and the judiciary. Presidents frequently rule by decree to avoid negotiations and compromises that are time consuming and uncertain in outcome. Further, by dismissing party politics and the articulation of group interests, delegative presidents undermine intermediary structures that would counterweigh or even question their almost absolute power. Instead of relying on party organizations for winning elections, presidential candidates seek to establish direct links with the people, which once in office they continuously try to mobilize as a resource of power. Delegative democracies therefore show strong plebiscitary tendencies. It is this aspect that creates a symbiotic relationship between delegative democracy and the media. One could even argue that it would have been impossible for delegative democracy to develop without a media-rich environment. As Waisbord (1995: 216) argues in relation to Latin American countries, the fusion of personalism and a highly commercialized television industry has brought about a "new brand of caudillos" who build their power on a successful adaptation of media logic as a political strategy. Populist appeals to the masses and attractive images have recently paved the way for outsiders like Alberto Fujimori in Peru or Evo Morales in Bolivia to move onto the television screen and then into political office (Boas, 2005; Waisbord, 2003). This mutual dependence of delegative presidentialism and the media further undermines the already weak institutions in a vicious circle that may obstruct the consolidation of stable democracy.

Another hybrid type of (new) democracy is *one-party predominance.* Unlike delegative democracy it is less confined to particular geographical regions, but can be found in contexts as different as Africa, Asia, and Latin America. Even though one-party rule is a defining element of authoritarian regimes, many new democracies are dominated by one particular party even after the introduction of free and fair elections. It was Sartori (1976: 35–49) who developed different categories for one-party rule to distinguish between autocratic forms where oppositional parties are restricted to an extent that they do not pose any threat to the ruling party, and power relations in "predominant party systems" that are based on a genuine majority of the population.[7]

In many new democracies, one-party dominance continued after the end of authoritarian one-party rule and the implementation of democratic institutions, at least for several elections after the regime change. Taiwan and South Korea are examples for this pathway of transition that protected these countries not only from dramatic ruptures but also from the experience of renewal that has inspired many other transition processes (Chu, 2001; Rawnsley and Rawnsley, 1998; Solinger, 2001). In other cases, especially in some of the emerging democracies in Africa,

---

[7] Note that Sartori (1976) uses the adjective "hegemonic" to describe a nondemocratic one-party system, and the term "predominant" for a democratic type of one-party dominance. In this chapter the two terms – hegemonic and (pre)dominant – are used interchangeably.

the persistence of one-party dominance is more dubious and involves irregularities in the voting process. Another interesting case is South Africa where the ANC won for the fourth time by large margins in elections that were internationally recognized as free and fair. Because the power of the ANC rests on the support of the black majority of the country, there is little chance for one-party dominance to be challenged in the foreseeable future, unless internal divisions lead to breakaways that are able to bring large parts of the electorate behind them (Giliomee and Simkins, 1999).

The consequence of one-party predominance is usually a hegemonic public sphere in which the ruling party's interpretation of the political situation prevails while oppositional views are marginalized and even delegitimized. Usually the ruling party has almost unlimited access to the media agenda, frequently enabled by the fact that the government owns the main national television channels. In addition, deep-rooted networks of clientelism and patronage do not stop at the doorsteps of the media. Many journalists are beneficiaries of the hegemonic system and have bought into the worldview of the dominant party (Sen and Lee, 2007; Willnat and Aw, 2004). In developed economies the Internet has evolved as an alternative public forum that has the potential to counterbalance and challenge the hegemonic discourse of mainstream media. Yet this is hardly an option in poorer countries with weak infrastructure and low literacy rates.

One could argue that, because of the deep gulf between the dominant party and the opposition parties, these systems could best be described within the framework of the Polarized Pluralist model. However, the nature of pluralism – hegemonic versus fragmented – results in a very different dynamic of public discourse and popular opinion building. In a hegemonic pluralist system the competition of different viewpoints does not occur on a level playing field. Not only does the ruling party dominate the public agenda, but it also has the power to control access to the decision-making positions within the relevant media organizations. This combination of formal and informal power over public communication generates the earlier mentioned structural spiral of silence that systematically disadvantages oppositional voices.

The brief discussion of two types of hybrid forms of democracy – delegative democracy and one-party predominance – shows that these regimes have developed a distinct pattern of politics–media relations that differs from Western representative democracies in significant ways. However, whereas delegative democracy is deeply rooted in cultural and historical traditions and therefore a rather permanent constellation of institutions and practices, one-party dominance seems to be a more transient category. Some of these systems that emerged from one-party authoritarianism have been successfully defeated (for example, South Korea, Taiwan, and Mexico), whereas in other cases a formerly pluralist system has been taken over by one particular party.

Conclusion

The dramatic spread of democratic rule across the globe over the past quarter-century has put an end to democracy and pluralist media being mainly an achievement of the West. However, the de-Westernization of democracy has brought about new forms of democratic practice that differ from, often even contradict, the expectations of Western observers. In spite of the forces of globalization, the transitions from authoritarian rule have not resulted in a homogenization of democratic practice. Rather, the trajectories of the past and the cultural frames within which the new political institutions are interpreted by those who are putting them into practice have given way to a puzzling diversity of what is broadly labeled "democracy" and "democratic media." Thus, neither the political systems nor the media systems that emerged during the recent wave of democratization fit easily into the concepts and models that have been developed for Western contexts.

With regard to media systems, this raises the question whether, and if so in what way, the three models of politics–media relationships developed by Hallin and Mancini (2004) have to be amended when studying countries other than the eighteen European and North American cases included in their analysis. In this chapter I argued that classifying the media systems of non-Western and, specifically, new democracies into one of the existing three models leads to conceptual overstretching and disguises the broad variation of constellations that can be found empirically outside the Western world. To apply Hallin and Mancini's framework to new contexts, it is therefore necessary to revisit the intellectual toolkit that underlies the three models. In particular, I suggested that we need to think more systematically about the content and boundaries of the four dimensions – media markets, political parallelism, journalistic professionalism, and state intervention – that are the foundation of the models. Media systems in many new democracies are characterized by a degree of state intervention that goes far beyond what is known from established democracies; media markets are often considerably weaker and more divided between developed and underdeveloped segments; journalists combine universally acknowledged professional standards with the specific values and norms of their own culture and traditions; and parallelism follows different lines of conflict that in some instances are less open to consensus or compromise. These differences in both scope and kind might indicate a new quality that constitutes distinct models in their own right.

To illustrate media–politics relationships that can be considered as potentially additional models of media systems, this chapter drew on the concept of hybrid regimes, which has been used in transition research to understand the way in which new democracies differ from their established Western counterparts. Delegative democracy was presented as an example of the symbiotic relationship between the media and a charismatic leader that characterizes many new democracies not only in Latin America but also in some of the successor states of the Soviet Union. In this type of democracy close ties between extensive presidential powers and mediated populism undermine the further consolidation of institutionalized politics. One-party predominance entails a type of pluralism – and resulting media parallelism – in which one particular party controls the public discourse to an extent that prevents the competition of ideas on a level playing field. Even though this constellation of media–politics relationship seems to be more transient than delegative democracy, because oppositional parties have successfully challenged the predominance of the ruling party, one-party predominance is a frequent constellation of limited pluralism that can be found both on national and subnational levels. More conceptual and empirical research is needed to identify possible additional media system models.

I2

Comparing Processes

Media, "Transitions," and Historical Change

Natalia Roudakova

Introducing their seminal volume, Hallin and Mancini (2004b) pay tribute to Siebert, Peterson, and Schramm's (1956) *Four Theories of the Press*, acknowledging the validity of the general question the authors of the *Four Theories* were interested in – namely, how and why is it that "the press always takes on the form and coloration of the social and political structures within which it operates" (Siebert et al., 1956: 2). However, the authors of *Comparing Media Systems* part company with the authors of the *Four Theories* as they shift their focus from the political philosophies that Siebert et al. presumed undergird the flavor, "form and coloration" of mass media around the world. Instead, Hallin and Mancini (2004b) focus on empirical analyses of relations between media and politics in particular locales in Western Europe and North America and on the rootedness of those relations in specific histories of social and political change.

Yet, despite Hallin and Mancini's admirable wish to give the *Four Theories* "a decent burial and move on," two aspects of their seminal work continue to bear resemblance to some of the original tenets of the *Four Theories*. The first aspect is Hallin and Mancini's commitment to the continual search for *models* of media and politics (as per the book's subtitle), albeit with the crucial stipulation that the models proposed in the 2004 volume are empirical, not normative. Second is their commitment to analyze relations between media and politics worldwide on a *systems* level (as per the book's title), but again, with the crucial specification that media systems are often dynamic, not always stable, and undergo constant historical change.

While acknowledging the importance of structural or systems-level analysis, I argue here for an approach that foregrounds *processes* rather than systems or structures in studying the interplay of media and politics. The difficulty with a processual approach is that it forces the researcher to accept the untidiness and dynamism of media–political relations while still trying to discern some logic behind those relations, such as how they are maintained, how and when they begin to change, and how we know the change is of historical significance rather than a unique adjustment to a particular situation. In a way, the difficulty with the processual approach lies in its ambition to document history in the making, to discern "the emergent" and "the residual" (Williams, 1977) in cultural and political formations out of the endless fluctuations of everyday life.

My attention to studying processes grew out of my effort to understand the political transformation of "what was socialism and what came next" (Verdery, 1996). Throughout the late 1980s and 1990s, political change in the former Soviet bloc was studied most authoritatively (with little attention paid to the role of the media) under the "transitions" paradigm, where the change worth waiting for and paying attention to was the long-awaited transition away from authoritarianism and toward liberal democracy. During those fifteen years or so, the field of "transitology" was seen as bringing what used to be ghettoized as Soviet studies into the mainstream of comparative politics (e.g., Linz and Stepan, 1996; Markwick, 1996). With the excitement around the "third wave" of democratization eventually waning by the end of the 1990s (with many presumed democratic "candidates" getting stuck, derailed, or lost in the transition), political observers began to talk about "hybrid" regimes as a new and durable form of political rule that combines democratic and authoritarian elements (Alexander, 2008; Carothers, 2002; Diamond, 2002; Karl, 1995; Levitsky and Way, 2010). Moreover, there seems to be a consensus now in comparative politics that hybrid regimes have become the most common form of political organization around the world.

As is often the case with knowledge generated in the tradition with strong roots in structural-functionalism, "transitologists" turned "hybridologists" have set out a new task for their field: to formulate a *typology* of hybrid regimes. Thus appeared "illiberal democracy" (Zakaria, 1997), "delegative democracy" (O'Donnell, 1994), "imitation democracy" (Shevtsova, 2007), "electoral democracy" and "electoral authoritarianism" (Schedler, 2002), "competitive authoritarianism" (Levitsky and Way, 2002), "multi-party authoritarianism" (Linz, 2000), "non-cooperative transitions" (McFaul, 2002), "limited multi-party regimes"

(Hadenius and Teorell, 2007), and many other subtypes in the political "gray zone" (Carothers, 2002) between classic liberal democracy and classic dictatorships.

While acknowledging that building typologies can be a useful analytical tool, I believe that the "foggy" (Schedler, 2002) or gray zone between democracy and dictatorship is not the best place to attempt such an exercise.[1] I *am* sympathetic to the desire to classify and systematize because I am also dissatisfied with the use of "hybrid" when it denotes a lump of features that the researcher does not know how to untangle. However, the very grayness or fogginess of the intermediary zone in question is a signal that we must shift gears and drop down into the level of analysis where things are clearer. I suggest that the ethnographic method, among other things, allows us to clear up some of the analytical fog that is inevitable in structural-typological analysis, because it connects changes that are happening "on the ground" (micro level) to changes that are potentially historical (macro level). I hope to demonstrate in this chapter that such an approach gets at the hybridity in question by untangling the complexities of media–political relations without sacrificing their dynamism or their frequent contradictions and tensions.

The plan for this chapter is then as follows. First, I further identify what I mean by "process" and how it is implicated in the maintenance of both order and change. I pay special attention to the interplay between micro and macro levels of analysis that gives the processual approach its particular advantage. In an ironic twist, I am attempting what could be interpreted as a typology of processes to help us identify what kinds of processes can and cannot be potentially compared to one another. I then move on to regard media organizations as *sites* where different kinds of processes intersect with and feed off of one another. Throughout, I draw on my work and the work of colleagues to point to some examples of what different processes and their interrelations might look like. In some respects, my analysis runs counter to Hallin and Mancini's goal of sharpening the dimensions along which media and politics can be compared around the world (media markets, "political parallelism," professionalization of journalists, and state–media relations), because the

---

[1] I agree with Colin Sparks here when he notes that such "seemingly endless proliferation of different intermediate stages between democracy and dictatorship not only reduces the elegance of the paradigm but also calls into question its explanatory power" (Sparks, 2008: 46).

processual approach I am advocating cuts across many of those dimensions. In other respects, however, the focus on process opens up those dimensions, revealing links among them, which *is* one of Hallin and Mancini's goals. The hope is that the focus on process will offer a useful tool for studying patterns and especially shifts in relations between media and politics in societies that are changing in uncertain directions or seem to be permanently "stuck in transition" – shifts that are sometimes subtle, sometimes contradictory, and often historically significant.

Order and Change

In many works drawing inspiration from poststructural theory, the idea of process is often contrasted with the idea of structure or with a stable social and political order (e.g., Buyandelgeriyn, 2008; see also Vincent, 1986). Process is seen as fluid, dynamic, and full of human agency, whereas structure is seen as stable, static, and full of rules. This is a mistaken dichotomy, however: Process can be both about the maintenance of order and about the transformation of that order; not infrequently, it is about both of those things at once. Anthropologist Sally Falk Moore (1978) calls the first type of processes "regularizing"; I call them "order-maintaining." These processes are geared toward producing continuity, consistency, and regularity in social relations, and they do so through a continual renewal and reenactment of existing norms and rules. The countervailing variety of processes – through which social orders are dismantled or transformed rather than maintained – are rooted in what Moore (1978: 50) calls "situational adjustment." This refers to people's attempts to use "whatever areas there are of inconsistency, contradiction, conflict, and ambiguity . . . to achieve immediate situational ends." What results from situational adjustment may or may not help generate new norms and rules and may or may not be historically significant, but it does help erode regularities if those regularities were there to begin with. I call these processes "order eroding."

How can both order-maintaining and order-eroding processes coexist or even be in competition with one another? This is possible, Moore (1978) explains, because at bottom, social life does not exhibit a proclivity toward either regularity or change; rather, it rests on the basic premise of *indeterminacy* of most social situations, which turn out one way or another depending on the articulation of social forces and the circumstances at play. This is the idea that I aimed for in Roudakova (2009) by describing the tension between centripetal and centrifugal forces in post-Soviet Russian journalism. Had the centripetal forces been stronger, I argued, they would have helped carry Russian journalism more or less intact through the tribulations of the early post-Soviet period, helping maintain some regularity in professional norms and rules. However, it was the centrifugal forces that ended up being stronger in that particular period in Russia; those forces splintered journalism along the lines of situational adjustment, when every practitioner ended up, as they put it, "on their own" and "working primarily for themselves."

The dynamic tension between order maintenance and order erosion is particularly useful in theorizing about hybrid regimes and their prospects. Several theorists of hybrid regimes (e.g., Diamond, 2002; Levitsky and Way, 2002; McFaul, 2002) explicitly recognize this dynamic as they point to tensions and ambiguities that underlie hybrid regimes. McFaul, for instance, invokes the image of "a stalemate between competing forces" [of autocracy and democratization] as a characteristic feature of hybrid regimes (McFaul, 2002: 224). Levitsky and Way, in their turn, speak of "the contradictions inherent in competitive authoritarianism" as political incumbents have to continuously "choose between egregiously violating democratic rules, at the cost of international isolation and domestic conflict, and allowing the [democratic] challenge to proceed, at the cost of possible defeat" (Levitsky and Way, 2002: 59). Significantly for us here, Levitsky and Way identify what they call "independent media" as one of their four "inherent sources of instability" in hybrid regimes, in addition to the electoral, legislative, and judicial arenas. Independent media in hybrid regimes "are not only legal but often quite influential," Levitsky and Way note, and journalists working for those outlets, "though frequently threatened and periodically attacked, often emerge as important opposition figures" (Levitsky and Way, 2002: 59).

There is an important point to be made here about the meaning of political change. Conventionally, much of transitology was pegged to the notion of political change away from authoritarianism and toward liberal democracy (and hybrid regimes have often been seen as states where such movement has been stalled). Many of us continue to assume, along with transitologists, that change means a shift from one state of affairs to another. However, if we look at it more processually, keeping in mind the interplay between order maintenance and order erosion in the basic field of indeterminacy, the notion of change has to be rethought in important ways. Change could indeed mean a shift from one set of regularities to another; however, it could also mean, more subtly, a shift from regularity to indeterminacy, or from indeterminacy to regularity, or from one version of indeterminacy to another (Greenhouse et al., 2002; Moore, 1978, 1987; Ortner, 1984, 2006).

In each of these scenarios, change can be conceptualized as the result of a competition between order-maintaining and order-eroding processes. In the first and third scenario, order maintenance would be seen as temporarily prevailing over order erosion; in the other two scenarios, it would be the other way around. In the transitions literature, some of these more subtle shifts are referred to as "limited political openings" or "liberalization without democratization." While acknowledging that, of course, "every step toward political liberalization matters" (Diamond, 2002: 33) where repression is rampant, I want to point out that conceiving of political shifts two-dimensionally (toward liberalization – away from liberalization) might be robbing us of the fuller understanding of history as it unfolds. As I argue later in this chapter, what often come to matter historically with hybrid regimes are the specific *sequences* of the shifts to and from indeterminacy. These historical shifts might be easily overlooked if we understand political change in binary terms.

Micro and Macro

In addition to thinking about processes in terms of order and change, another way to approach them is in terms of their scale. For simplicity's sake, we can divide them into micro and macro, and the articulations between the two are a favorite topic of ethnographers. Micro processes are the "stuff" of everyday life; they are about the daily movement of people through their social roles, situations, institutions, and positions of power. In contrast, macro processes are the material of history. They are about shifts, continuities, contradictions, and tensions in the social, political, and economic organization of societies.

Both micro and macro processes can be order maintaining and order eroding. A micro process is order maintaining when people's daily interactions help reproduce people's existing positions in power hierarchies. It can be order eroding if people begin to respond to those situations in novel, unanticipated ways as they detect shifts in circumstances; if enough people do so and do so often enough, these actions may become socially and historically meaningful. It is at this point that the micro and the macro level articulate with one another: after all, the making of history happens in many different places and with the help of many actors at once (Moore, 1987: 730). The making of history can indeed be order transforming; this is our conventional understanding of history as a series of revolutions, uprisings, coups, elections, accessions to the throne, and the like. Yet history making can also be much more mundane. Historical continuity – as a process – is also a variety of history making. In that process, events may unfold in a regular, predictable manner or sequence, or as I suggested earlier, historical continuity may manifest itself through a sequence of subtle shifts from one state of indeterminacy to another. We need analytical tools that would account for both.

Structure and Agency

The last component in the analysis of processes I am suggesting is closely connected to the points made earlier. In the same way in which process links order and change, and micro and macro levels, it usefully brings together structure and agency (another pair of concepts that are some-times seen in opposition to one another in social analysis). The mutual constitution of structure and agency through process is by no means a novel idea – it is at least as old as Marx's adage about people making history but not in circumstances of their choosing. Yet it has taken on a new significance in the human sciences and in anthropology in particu-lar with the revival of what has come to be known as "practice theory" (Bourdieu, 1977; Ortner, 1984, 2006; Vincent, 1986). Practice theory restored the agent to the social process without losing sight of the larger structures that both constrain that agency, but are ultimately susceptible to being transformed by it (Ortner, 2006). It reminded researchers that social and political structures are rarely seamless or harmonious wholes; rather, they are made up of inconsistencies, tensions, and struggles for power both on the micro and macro levels. When participants in a social situation are successful in (temporarily) quelling those inconsistencies – whether through discursive enactment, performance, or representation of "the structure" – then structures emerge as durable social facts (cf. Geertz, 1980; Turner, 1974). Performing and representing "the struc-ture" are none other than order-maintaining processes discussed earlier. When, however, actors cannot contain tensions within the structure for one reason or another, order erosion takes center stage. What becomes equally important, then, are the *conditions* and *circumstances* in which social structure emerges as a coherent entity and the conditions and cir-cumstances when it does not.

   To see what all of this means for analyses of media and politics, and in hybrid regimes in particular, let us turn to Hallin and Mancini's four dimensions as jumping-off points. Hallin and Mancini mention in the introduction to this volume that one can ask these questions of media and politics in *any* country: What is the role of the state? What is the level of professionalism of journalists? What is the extent of the links between the media and organized social and political groups? And how are media markets developed? Asking these questions, however, presupposes an analytical separation between the domains of the state, the market, and civil/political society (where social and political groups "reside" and can organize). Such analytical separation carries with it a set of core assumptions about what the nature and function of the state might be, what the nature and function of the market might be, and what civil/political society "is" and "is for."

What the processual approach purports to do is to help us *not* make those assumptions at the outset. Once we start thinking of relations between media and politics as a set of overlapping and interlocking processes, it quickly becomes clear that Hallin and Mancini's dimensions cannot be studied in isolation from one another. They have to be opened up, linked together, and put into motion. Let us attempt to do that, turning first to the state, then to political parallelism, and then to journalistic professionalism. (I do not devote a separate section to media markets, but simply assume that they, too, are not only a "dimension" but also a process connected to other processes, and highlight those connections as necessary throughout my analysis.)

The State as a Process

One useful place to start seeing the state as a process is the fast-growing literature on the anthropology of the state, which builds on poststructural developments in social theory (Comaroff, 1998; Gupta, 1995, forthcoming; Hansen and Stepputat, 2001; Mitchell, 1991; Navaro-Yashin, 2002; Sharma and Gupta, 2006). This literature makes the unity of the state a phenomenon to be explained, instead of taking that unity as a point of analytical departure. States come to us culturally embedded, these anthropologists argue, and a significant amount of cultural labor goes into the everyday production of what "the state" is and does. In other words, assuming that "the state has to be imagined no less than the nation" (Gupta and Sharma, 2006: 278), anthropologists ask, How is what we recognize as "the state" culturally produced, perceived, and experienced as such?

Put differently, a cultural approach to the state attempts to simultaneously *disaggregate* and *decenter* the state as an object of analysis.

Disaggregating the state means giving up the notion of the state as an a priori entity and seeing in its place assemblages of interlinked governmental and interpretive practices that sometimes do and sometimes do not add up to an overarching governing structure. Inter-bureaucratic tensions and alliance building, as well as intra-institutional contestation and conflict (considered dysfunctional in an ideal-typical Weberian bureaucracy), come to the fore here as social situations through which "the state" is actually produced (of course, in a very extended and complex way). Interestingly, this "messiness" and unevenness of state practices are something that every ethnographer of the state is immediately confronted with, yet have rarely been built into social scientists' analytical frameworks. Instead, like governmental officials themselves, social scientists have tended to reify the state through their discourses and representations of it (Mitchell, 1991). Borrowing a provocative phrase from Philip Abrams, an early proponent of studying the state processually, "since the task of the social scientist is to demystify," in studying the state it should mean "attending to the senses in which the state does *not* exist [as much as] to those in which it does" (Abrams, 1988: 82, emphasis added).

In addition to disaggregating the state, the second emphasis is on *decentering* it. This means putting the state in a relational frame – that is, focusing on the processes through which the state's institutional frames articulate with discourses about the state, representations and performances of the state, and perceptions of what the state is and does. It means seeing the state as a set of social relations enacted every day through the daily encounters and meaning-making practices between and among state officials and other people who come into contact with the state, including, in our case, various media actors. As people come in contact with and represent the state to one another, these performances and representations, in turn, feed into people's subsequent perceptions of and actions on "the state."

When we think of the state in this way, we are able to put a finger on that "mushy concept that political analysts do well to avoid" (Huntington, 1991: 46), namely the question of state legitimacy and its maintenance through the media, especially through state-owned, state-funded, and government-aligned media outlets. In many respects, this is the old question of hegemony as a lived, active, shifting, "formative but also transformative" process and practice (Williams, 1977: 113), where the dominant, the residual, and the emergent elements of ideology are in a dynamic interplay and often tension. Hallin and Mancini (2004b) curiously do not focus on the ideological maintenance of state authority as an avenue along which the state "intervenes" into the media (they focus, instead, on questions of state ownership, regulation, and funding). This is perhaps in part because in the Western European democracies they study, the legitimacy of government stems from the very procedure through which those governments come to power. Yet in hybrid regimes where governmental legitimacy is often maintained through mechanisms other than elections, how media organizations "perform" the state to citizens is one of the most important processes to pay attention to.

Let me start with the case I am most familiar with, the story of state–media relations in the Soviet Union and their transformation in post-Soviet Russia. The image of the Soviet press that many Westerners continue to have is of stolid, turgid, unbroken columns of gray text glorifying the Soviet Union's superiority and achievements. The press as a "transmission belt" between the communist party-state and the Soviet masses, and journalists as the compliant "lapdogs" or "cogs" in the Soviet propaganda machine, are the key images Western imagination conjures up of the social institution that produced those texts. Much interesting work has come out in the last decade and a half that challenges this widespread perception. This line of work (Boyer, 2003, 2005; Boyer and Yurchak, 2010; Wolfe, 2005; Yurchak, 1997, 2003, 2006) approaches Soviet-style media precisely along the lines discussed earlier, drawing out the interconnections among media representations of the state, performances of it, citizens' perceptions of it, and what "it" ended up being as a result of all those manipulations.

Drawing on what Zizek (1991) has called "totalitarian laughter," and what Sloterdijk (1987) has called "humor that has ceased to struggle," this new line of work elucidates the connections among representation, performance, and perception of states and their media in the former Soviet bloc in the following way. In encountering (and producing) turgid ideological columns of newspaper text, the reader (and the writer) were acutely aware of both the *inevitability* and the *vacuity* of those official representations. Instead of openly recognizing that, however, citizens preferred to *mis*recognize it, because such acts of misrecognition opened doors for them to develop relations with the state they did find meaningful and fulfilling (more on this later). As people misrecognized the inevitability of the official Soviet rhetoric while enjoying what such misrecognition enabled, most could not help but notice a dissonance at the heart of such practice. Most people found that dissonance ironic, which found expression in an exquisite collection of political jokes (*anekdoty*) known to and performed across the former Soviet bloc and across all social strata (Lampland, 1991; Verdery, 1996; Yurchak, 1997). Yurchak (2003) in particular argues that such subtle shifts in the representation, performance, and perception of the Soviet state, occurring as they did during the last few decades of Soviet rule, likely played an important role in bringing about the restructuring and eventual collapse of Soviet governmental institutions in the late 1980s and early 1990s.

Another commonly elided aspect of discussions about the Soviet party-press is that the latter pages of quality Soviet newspapers usually carried much livelier content than the requisite official rhetoric of the first pages. It is in those latter pages that one can get a glimpse of the *social relations* that readers were developing with newspaper journalists and, through them, with the Soviet state. In the city of Gorky (Nizhny Novgorod) in Russia where I have been conducting research, journalists who worked for the newspaper for young adults (called *Leninskaya Smena* [*LS*]) in the mid-1980s spent less time actually writing for the newspaper and more time working closely and carefully with readers' letters, phone calls, and visits to editorial offices. Journalists held weekly writing workshops for high school and college students and coordinated the activities of the cartoonists' club and the film lovers' club linked to the newspaper and open to the public. They opened their offices for regular informal discussions between newspaper readers and local dignitaries. They also routinely organized professional and neighborhood competitions, festivals, restoration drives for historical monuments, environmental clean-up campaigns, rock concerts, film screenings, and many other public events in the city. Lively reports about these events would then end up on the latter pages of the newspaper. It is fair to say that the majority of socially active Gorky residents who are middle-aged today subscribed to *LS* in the 1970s and 1980s, enjoyed reading it, and took advantage of the opportunities for socialization it offered at some point or another during their teens and twenties.[2]

One of the main reasons for the popularity of *LS* with young adults was that its texts and the opportunities for engagement with the Soviet state it offered lacked what I call "ideological closure." That is, in their work, *LS* journalists, instead of papering over the discursive and governmental tensions inherent in the Soviet project, often managed to capture those

---

[2] The circulation of the newspaper during the mid-1980s was around 170,000 copies a day, with most of the subscribers living in the city of Gorky, which had a little more than a million inhabitants.

tensions and sometimes even brought them to the fore. They did so both unwittingly (because those tensions were objectively present in the Soviet project) and purposefully (when they acted on their understanding of their civic and professional roles or when they tried to stay creative in the face of "boring" orthodox practices like the requisite production of ideologically correct passages for the front pages of the newspaper).

A good example of how ideological closure was avoided was *LS* journalists' interest in working with so-called difficult letters that arrived by the hundreds to its offices every week. *LS* published some of those letters as invitations to a conversation under the "Discussion Club" rubric that ran regularly in the newspaper. Readers wrote back, *LS* published some of the responses, and *LS* journalists chimed in on the discussions as well. In 1983–5, conversation threads around uncomfortable but enormously popular topics included debates about the value of money and consumption in opposition to socialist ideals of modesty and intellectual pursuits; the tension between a formal approach to Komsomol (Communist Youth League) activities and a substantive one; conversations about boredom and depression and why they persist in a socialist society; discussions about the tension between individuality and collectivity and whether one should try to change oneself to "fit in"; arguments over what it meant to be a "modern" young person in the 1980s; and debates on whether listening to Western rock bands (an under-the-radar activity in the USSR) without understanding the lyrics still counted as supporting those bands' "glorification" of self-indulgence, naval gazing, egotism, and other capitalist vices. The tensions that these discussions would highlight would be the very same tensions woven into the Soviet governmental project itself, most notably the tension between liberal humanism (with its key ideas of inquisitiveness, creativity, self-realization, and self-fulfillment) and socialism's more community-oriented values of selflessness, altruism, modesty, and discipline.

LS journalists' being attuned to their readers' experiences of socialism as paradoxical and contradictory was none other than the act of journalists and readers representing and performing the Soviet state to one another, and this activity – this process – helped nurture a particular kind of cultural contract between Soviet journalists and their audiences that became especially important during the transformative late 1980s. Specifically, this process helped build trust between journalists and readers, without which Soviet journalists would not have emerged in the late 1980s as an independent cultural and moral force that propelled perestroika forward. We could say that this process drew both on order erosion and order maintenance: order erosion when journalists would capture and highlight for readers the contradictions of the Soviet governmental project, and order maintenance when journalists would appear before their readers as representatives of "the most humane (*chelovekoo-braznym*) department of Soviet power" (Gutiontov, 2005) when they served as intermediaries between readers and various party-state bureaucracies.

The formation of this important cultural contract (the contract that would be broken in the late 1990s) was a process that involved not only representations and performances of the state but also acting on the institutional inconsistencies in the mechanisms of ideological control of the Soviet press. *LS* was a newspaper for the young, and in the official hierarchy of Soviet media outlets, newspapers for the young were afforded more room for experimentation and criticism than their "adult" counterparts. This, I was told, was because the press's Communist Party overseers understood that people in their teens and twenties are in a period in their lives when they intensely search for answers, ask more questions, are less compromising, more easily feel betrayed by insincerity, and are less tolerant of hypocrisy. Journalists knew that, and many of them preferred to work in outlets for young adults until retirement, despite the official expectation that they would move on to work in an "adult" newspaper once they reached their late thirties. Readers also knew that, and quality newspapers for the young like *LS* maintained large audiences in part because they included many older readers (noticeable through readers' letters).

Of course, all of this meant that *LS* journalists had a little more leeway compared to their colleagues in other newspapers when it came to relations with their party overseers. The *LS* chief editor, who happened to have good leadership skills and was a journalist at heart, knew how to walk a very fine line: On the one hand, he knew to keep the newspaper in line with the general mission of the state-party press, and on the other hand, he worked hard not to stifle the creativity of *LS*'s more adventurous journalists (a number of whom were not party members). That meant the editor knew whom to assign the more ideologically stodgy tasks, and whom to spare, and how to edit the texts of his more spirited colleagues so that they would retain their critical edge yet would be amenable to at least some party officials. Himself a seasoned party worker, the chief editor knew how to work the corridors of the party organization overseeing the newspaper. That meant enlisting tacit support of more open-minded party officials there or knowing which battles to fight and which to drop.[3]

Finally, the officials themselves at the oblast (regional) committee of Komsomol (Obkom), the organization that oversaw *LS*, varied greatly. There were some, as journalists put it, who tried to "order them around" (*pytalis' stroit' zhurnalistov*) and from whom journalists sought protection through their chief editor. Yet there were also many horizontal links between the newspaper and the Obkom because of the mirror-like doubling of many departments in the two organizations: Many journalists and rank-and-file Obkom "instructors" often worked jointly on projects, which allowed both groups to develop social and human relations with one another. In the language of the 2000s, many Obkom workers were "adequate" (*adekvatyne*) people – that is, people you could reason with, who were not mortally scared of their own superiors or seeking promotion at all costs; in other words, they were people with a sense of integrity and often humor. Perhaps, more significantly, Obkom activists were often the very same people who had gone through the discussion clubs at *LS* and who, therefore, had grown up ideologically in the fairly relaxed and intellectually uninhibited atmosphere of those gatherings (not to mention that, initially, they had come to know many *LS* journalists as their writing mentors and were often hesitant to talk "down" to them from their new positions as Obkom overseers).[4]

All of these practices helped sustain a generally positive, relaxed, and creative atmosphere in *LS* offices in the 1970s and 1980s; this atmosphere was felt on newspaper pages, in the editorial offices that readers frequented, and at public events *LS* journalists organized. In conjunction with *LS* representational practices that highlighted the unique paradoxes of the Soviet governmental project, this atmosphere helped people experience the Soviet state as something meaningful, and not only as something inevitable and ridiculous, as when it was the butt of (anti)Soviet jokes. Significantly, as I already mentioned, this complex process, through which the Soviet state was co-produced by *LS* journalists and audiences, helped

---

[3] Sometimes it meant smoothing out explosive situations with humor or doing contradictory things like apologizing to the officials while simultaneously rewarding journalists. It also meant knowing how to keep cool under pressure when, for instance, a party superior would find out about *LS* plans for a "sensitive" publication and would "highly recommend" against publishing it, but would refuse to take responsibility for a flat-out prohibition of the publication.

[4] During perestroika in the late 1980s, Obkom leaders in the Gorky region began to emerge as the region's first successful entrepreneurs.

foster a cultural contract between these two groups that became central to Soviet journalists' emergence as an independent cultural and moral force during perestroika (1985–91). During that period, journalists, building on the trust they had developed with citizens, crucially contributed to the transformation of the Soviet party-state and its eventual dissolution in 1991.[5] Since the fall of the Soviet Union, however, the relation in Russia between the media, the state, and the public has undergone a series of important shifts. Some of those shifts have been subtle, some less so, but each new articulation of relations in the media–state–public triangle has owed significantly to what had come before it. This is important, because without studying the sequence of those shifts, one cannot get an adequate picture of state–media transformation and its dynamics in Russia, which many Western liberal accounts of post-Soviet media and politics lack.[6]

One critical juncture in those relations crystallized around the mid-1990s, when Russian journalists put their renewed moral authority to the cause of state-building, as they began to involve themselves in electoral campaigns, supporting some candidates and denouncing others. This was simultaneously a cultural, political, and economic move on the part of journalists: Their compulsion to act as moral guardians of the nation articulated with the privatization of media outlets, the near absence of consumer advertising, and the willingness of electoral contenders to generously fund electoral battles. This period culminated in 1996 with journalists reluctantly throwing their moral weight behind Boris Yeltsin's reelection campaign, funded by the newly emerged "oligarchs," against Yeltsin's communist contender. This was a decision most Russian journalists today bitterly regret, because it opened the floodgates for the so-called media wars of the late 1990s, when political and economic elites began buying up media outlets for the sole purpose of using them as weapons in political battles.

The media wars of the late 1990s therefore mark another key node in Russia's state–media transformation, one that came as a response to the developments of the early 1990s and one that simultaneously laid the groundwork for a dismal future for Russia's journalists in the 2000s. Intense media wars splintered the remaining professional solidarity among journalists, undercut their moral authority, and irreparably

---

[5] See also Hosking (2007).
[6] It hardly needs mentioning that according to those accounts, the 1990s in Russia were a period of attempted liberal democracy and press freedom, whereas the 2000s have witnessed a reimposition of censorship and authoritarian control under President Putin.

alienated their labor as it came to be "freely" bought and sold on the market of electoral promotion and political persuasion. A new and wide-spread discourse of journalism as "prostitution" that had been absent in the Soviet Union emerged as one of the unintended consequences of that period.

The media wars, funded by Russia's new oligarchs, were both a symptom of and (at least partially) a cause of their spectacular rise to power. It thus makes sense that President Putin, elected in 2000 and determined to "rein in" the oligarchs, identified reimposition of state control over the oligarchs' media resources as his key policy objective. The reintroduction of partial censorship in both state and privately owned outlets was therefore a decision *made possible* by the very political developments that brought Putin's team to power in the first place.

Ironically, once political control over most of the journalistic field was reestablished in Russia in the early 2000s, the country's leaders and their ideologists found themselves in a new and awkward predicament. The control they had secured was control over those media producers who continue to be distrusted and disrespected by their audiences. With time, this distrust has become circular: Citizens are disdainful of both journal-ists and the government (e.g., Bogdanov, 2007; Levada, 2006; Oushakine, 2009a; Vedomosti, 2005); government officials distrust both journalists and citizens (e.g., Dubin, 2005; Gaaze, 2009; Larina et al., 2009); and many journalists are contemptuous both of their government overseers and of their audiences, privately referring to the latter as "the rabble" (*bydlo*) and *pipl khavaet* ("the people [who] are eating it up;" Nenashev, 2004; Petrovskaya and Larina, 2010; Shestopal and Kachkaeva, 2006; "Svoboda Mnenii v Internete," 2010).

Needless to say, this circular disrespect in the state–media–society tri-angle complicates and possibly undermines the very task of ideological closure the Kremlin had set out to achieve. The ideological situation in Russia today is therefore precarious, and to be able to govern through consent and not only coercion, Russia's leaders once again need the sup-port of journalists and intellectuals whose moral authority had *not* been compromised by the "chaos" of the transition or has somehow been "repaired." Russia's current leaders are reluctant to go that route, yet there are many indicators that some feel compelled to do *something*, because most of their own attempts to offer citizens a new set of cultural-ideological coordinates *without* the help of uncompromised intellectuals have thus far succeeded only marginally at best (Borodina, 2008; Dubin et al., 2009; Gaaze, 2009; Kolesnikov, 2009; Zygar et al., 2009). What that "something" will be, when it will be done, and how it will articulate with other loci of power in Russia are still difficult to predict, but it will be a shift of possible historical significance, another nod in Russia's continuing media–political transformation, coming out of what has come before.

Cultural Production of States: Comparisons

Using the processual framework outlined earlier, how do we begin to compare the processes through which state legitimacy is maintained across countries and historical periods? This is not an easy task, but one that we can attempt nonetheless. The key to this task is the unity of ethnographic or other qualitative research methods that allows one to simultaneously tease out and link order and change, macro and micro, and structure and agency, through process. Despite the recent proliferation of scholarship aimed at de-Westernizing media studies, unfortunately there is still a real dearth of historically sensitive field research on the state–media–society dynamic, especially in countries that do not neatly fit the liberal "media and democratization" narrative. In what follows, I draw on existing qualitative research on state–media and state–community relations in China and Venezuela, in part because there is good qualitative work there and in part because those countries share with Russia an ongoing history of profound yet uncertain political change, in which the media have been a key player. Not having done any work in those countries myself, I am inevitably presenting my reading of existing research, with all the potential pitfalls of that enterprise.

It is probably important to remind readers here what kind of comparison between Russia, China, and Venezuela this will *not* be. By examining media–political relations in these three countries side by side, I am not implying that Russian, Chinese, and Venezuelan governments are "illiberal" in the same way in the political projects they are pursuing (they are not); or that they practice press censorship and political violence against media actors in a similar way (they do not). These kinds of comparisons have been made many times by Freedom House and other organizations and are not particularly insightful, in my view. The kind of comparison I am offering below, and for which I have been developing tools in this chapter, aims to find comparable and overlapping elements in the media-political *processes* happening in the three countries. These processes may be similar in some respects and different in others; what unites them is that these processes are open-ended, are happening relatively fast, and are therefore of profound historical significance. Let us then first turn to historical shifts in China's relations between the state, the media, and the public, as they have more obvious similarities to the (post)Soviet story presented earlier. China's history over the last several decades has been punctuated just as much as Russia's (and probably more so) by ongoing experiments with new forms of social, political, and economic organization. Following Rofel (1999, 2007) and Zhao (1998, 2008), both of whom draw on Wang (2004, 2006), I understand China's socialist[7] decades (1949–79) as a period of real, if wrought, intense, and deeply conflicting public mobilization around communist ideals and goals. More historical research needs to be done to understand the role the Chinese press played in the cultural production and reproduction of the revolutionary state during that period. The available research is on the postsocialist period, so that is where we must inevitably start. In the same way in which I identified critical junctures, or forks in the road, for Russia's media–political transformation, similar junctures can be identified for China. The socialist Democracy Movement of 1979; Deng Xiaoping's neoliberal reforms in the 1980s; the June 4th Movement of 1989; the near-collapse of state legitimacy that followed; the explosive market growth in the 1990s and the seeming restoration of the state's authority; the mounting challenge to the party-state in the 2000s, as the gap between wealth and poverty widened; and the party-state's response to that challenge – all of these can be read as key junctures in the recent history of China's media–political relations.

The critical political economy perspective from which Yuezhi Zhao (2008) and her colleagues work helps identify many of those forks in the road; however, this approach is less helpful in fleshing out the actual process through which state legitimacy has been maintained (or eroded) "on the ground" over time. For instance, Zhao (2008; see Chapter 8) reminds us that the Chinese Communist Party (CCP) has always been built on intra-elite tensions and struggles, including disagreements between "liberal," "neoliberal," and Maoist factions; tensions between central, municipal, and local governments; disagreements between those in the CCP favoring a more popular participatory press and those favoring a more bureaucratic elitist one; and recent tensions between those who

---

[7] The question of whether China is socialist or postsocialist continues to be a matter of debate for some; following many China scholars, I take the introduction of neoliberal reforms by Deng Xiaoping in 1978 and their acceleration throughout the 1980s and 1990s as the key development that marks the end of China's socialism.

control the flows of information and those who control financial flows within media outlets and conglomerates. These intra-elite struggles have inevitably pulled media actors into their orbit over the years, sometimes creating spaces for the media to step into the political fray and "speak up for the people," or spaces for the everyday people to "speak bitterness" – a discursive practice that both addresses the state and critiques it, with the potential both to reinforce and fragment state power. ("Speaking bitterness" has interesting parallels to readers' "difficult" letters in the Soviet Union and to *denuncias*, or people's complaints about the state in contemporary Venezuela; more on that later.)

Following media scholars such as Zhao (1998, 2008), Pan and Lu (Pan, 2000; Pan and Lu, 2003), He (2000, 2003), and Tong and Sparks (Tong, 2007a, 2007b; Tong and Sparks, 2009), we can begin to glimpse how the maintenance of state legitimacy has been carried out in China through the everyday practices of representing and performing the state through the media; what institutional tensions have fueled those practices; and how the articulation of institutions, performances, and perceptions of the state has been contributing to shifts in what the Chinese state means to its citizens. Zhao (1998, 2008) shows particularly well how Deng's "no debate" policy after the Tiananmen Square crackdown led to mounting social tensions that the media tried to contain and how the explosive growth of media markets happening at the same time was creating new, competing loci of social and economic power. Together, these developments both reinforced and weakened state authority by the end of the 1990s. Zhao (2008) also shows how the party-state has attempted to respond to mounting crises of authority throughout the 1990s and 2000s: The introduction of an investigative series, *Focus Interviews*, on CCTV and the greater critical "bite" of the *People's Daily* are two such examples. Pan and Lu's ethnographic research (Pan, 2000; Pan and Lu, 2003) portrays how journalists were reinventing themselves and their organizations in the midst of China's economic boom in the late 1990s – practices that ended up contributing both to new forms of corruption in journalism and to the rise of respectable investigative reporting. However, Pan and Lu stop short of linking how these practices contributed (or not) to the relegitimization of the Chinese party-state throughout the 1990s. Tong and Sparks' research (Tong, 2007a, 2007b; Tong and Sparks, 2009) several years later illuminates how investigative journalists in China "perform" the state and their new professional identities to their sources, their audiences, and their party overseers, in the face of what seems not only like stricter rules of engagement between journalists and propaganda officials but also like a greater level of trust between journalists and audiences, compared to the late 1990s. Zhou He (2000, 2003) is less optimistic: He does not see China's journalists developing any new, culturally meaningful links to their audiences or to the Chinese state throughout the 1990s. The postsocialist period, he argues, "alienated [journalists] from Communist ideology," but did not bring about any new "solid bonds with alternative ideologies" (He, 2003: 208). As a result, the majority of China's journalists in the 2000s are guided by "a mesh of vague, embryonic, and transient ideas" in their relations with the state and the public (ibid.).

Perhaps not surprisingly, it is from the work of anthropologists and cultural theorists (Anagnost, 1997; Rofel, 1999, 2007; J. Wang, 2001) who do not work specifically on media organizations, but who are particularly attentive to the interplay of order and change, micro and macro, and structure and agency within a cultural process, that I was best able to grasp the changing dynamics of state–media–society relations in China over the last three decades. According to Jing Wang (2001), it was the transnational capital that came to China in the 1990s that saved the Chinese state from a crisis of confidence that almost collapsed after the Tiananmen Square crackdown in June 1989. The fact that the Chinese state managed throughout the 1990s to regulate, contain, and more or less "socialize" that windfall capital – through its preoccupation with legality, regulation, and "democratic consumerism" – greatly helped the Chinese state reestablish its legitimacy. Interestingly, according to Wang (2001), the state was able to step in and take control over public representations and perceptions of itself in the mid-1990s, in part because by then, China's intellectuals (which include journalists) had become splintered by a decade and a half of Deng's pro-market restructuring. When the intellectuals could no longer speak cohesively of "what was best for the people," state actors stepped in and did so for them. This is an important point, because if it is true, there are interesting parallels here with the cultural contract between journalists and audiences in the Soviet Union I described and with the rupture of that contract as Russia's market reforms picked up in the mid- and late 1990s. Much literature (e.g., Faraday, 2000; Oushakine, 2009b) exists on the crisis of post-Soviet intelligentsia, showing that intellectuals' unique claim to moral authority is recognized under socialism by audiences as long as those intellectuals act as mediators between those audiences and the ethical ideals of the socialist state. Once that state is transformed by the market, the discursive unity – and moral power – of the intelligentsia is eroded.

Lisa Rofel (2007) draws out another interesting set of conclusions about the state–media–public dynamic in China, based on her long-term fieldwork. She is struck by the fact that almost every conversation she initiated in the late 1990s and early 2000s with young and middle-aged urban Chinese women, including a number of journalists, began with their declaration – "I am completely uninterested in politics" – even as most of them "volubly, vociferously, and satirically condemned the government's treatment of Falun Gong, for example" (Rofel, 2007: 124). Rofel eventually realizes that these women's declarations of "disinterest" in politics were meant to underscore their desire to unlink their identities from the idea of government. Assertions that one is uninterested in politics stressed that one's passions "were not in the least bit directed toward the state" (ibid.). The history behind those desires, Rofel argues, is rooted in the decades of intense political mobilization under Mao, when people were invited to direct "the passions of the self" to the revolutionary state and its projects. Claims of "disinterest" in politics also come out of the decade and a half under Deng of recasting socialism as full of sacrifice, deprivation, and unneeded hardship. The post-Deng discourse of politics of *any* stripe as "uninteresting" or "boring" is thus meant to rectify what Boyer (2005) has called "the surfeit of history" with reference to contemporary West German discourses about East Germany. Boyer argues that many East Germans today have withdrawn into private lives, in part because their socialist past is authoritatively recast for them as having "too much politics of the wrong kind." A parallel can also be drawn to postsocialist, postwar Serbia, where young people are similarly politically apathetic, this time as a result of international democracy promoters urging them to abandon an emotional investment into the "wrong" kind of political passions, presumably located in Serbian nationalism of the 1990s (Greenberg, 2010).

Venezuela's trajectory of recent political change is in many respects the reverse of that of Russia and China; after all, Hugo Chavez has been pursuing an anti-neoliberal revolution there with the goal of building socialism, rather than moving away from it. Yet precisely because this transformation involves profound changes to Venezuela's social and political fabric, the question of maintaining state legitimacy *through* the transformation has been of critical importance there as well. Significantly for our analysis, supporters often colloquially refer to Venezuela's ongoing political restructuring as *el proceso* (Schiller, 2009).

In the same way we identified key historical junctures in state–media–society relations for China and Russia, we can do so for Venezuela as well.

Most observers consider the *Caracazo* – the popular riots of 1989 against the government's neoliberal structural adjustment programs that were violently put down by the military – as "year zero" of Venezuela's contemporary political change (Leary, 2009; Samet, 2009; Schiller, 2009; Smilde, 2009). Of key importance for us here, the *Caracazo* signaled a real crisis of legitimacy for the presidency of Carlos Andres Perez, elected just weeks before the riots began. Through televised appearances on private channels, government officials resorted to misrepresenting the rioting poor as "savages" and attempted to cover up state violence against the rioters, all in an effort to paint a coherent picture of the state being "in control." This effort failed: The riots continued, and when the minister of the interior went live on television to announce a curfew, he was "so overcome by nerves that he could not deliver his speech. Disney cartoons abruptly interrupted the broadcast of the suddenly helpless minister" (Leary, 2009: 31).

After the *Caracazo*, Venezuela experienced an almost decade-long crisis of state authority: During the 1990s, two failed coups shook the country, two main parties that had dominated politics for decades collapsed, and the president (Andres Perez) was jailed for misuse of public funds. The failed coup of 1992, led by General Hugo Chavez, is now remembered for Chavez's ninety-second televised address to the nation, because that address captured many Venezuelans' disaffection with the state and paved the way for Chavez's return as a legitimate president in 1998. Importantly, in the political uncertainty of the 1990s, Venezuelans placed a great deal of faith in the press (Samet, 2009). Newspapers like *El Nacional* wielded a significant amount of power, "playing an active role in setting the country's political agenda" (Samet, 2009: 5). For instance, *El Nacional*, along with other major news outlets, actively supported Hugo Chavez's campaign for presidency in 1998.

Once Chavez came to power, his intense anti-neoliberal rhetoric and sweeping political reforms turned most private media outlets and most middle- and upper-class Venezuelans away from him. At the next historical juncture, in 2002–4, it was time for Chavez's authority to be seriously tested – through an attempted commercial "media" coup against him, a nationwide strike by oil producers, and a recall referendum aimed to remove him from power. It is no doubt that it is *in response to* those events that Chavez and his allies have been trying to centralize power and bolster their authority since then – efforts that have included a dramatic increase in the number of state media outlets, a de facto expansion of the Popular Power branch of government (aimed at bypassing governing

structures of the pre-Chavez era), new legislation allowing Chavez's political appointees to bypass some of the authority of governors and mayors,
and new defamation and libel statutes that make it harder for the press to
gain access to official information and criticize officials (Human Rights
Watch, 2008; Smilde, 2009).

Naomi Schiller's (2009) careful ethnography of relations between the
Venezuelan state and government-aligned community media in Caracas is particularly illuminating of the fluctuations and shifts in how the
Venezuelan state has been culturally produced and maintained over the
last several years. Since coming to power, the Chavez government has
centrally relied on community organizers and media producers from
Venezuela's *barrios* to maintain its claim to being "of the people" and "for
the people." State television workers have been recruited from the ranks
of community media producers, and state TV programming has been
borrowing the aesthetic of grassroots media to perform its allegiance to
"the people" (Schiller, 2009). In turn, community media have been urged
to take part (and often take center stage) in numerous governmental
press conferences, official election coverage, state-sponsored marches,
festivals, international conferences, and other events through which
the Venezuelan state has been simultaneously performed and culturally
(re)produced.

Yet participating in *el proceso* has been neither smooth nor complete
for community media producers in Caracas, as Schiller (2009) demonstrates beyond doubt. The Venezuelan state has been more successful in
pulling community media into its orbit during crucial moments of its
recent history when the very existence of the Chavez government was
in question – the presidential recall referendum of 2004 and the presidential election of 2006. Yet relying on community media to provide
everyday cultural support to the legitimacy of Chavez's "Bolivarian revolution" has been a much more contested, open-ended, and uncertain
process. The practice of televising *denuncias* – simultaneous complaints
to and criticisms of the government – has been one troubled area for
community media producers. On the one hand, many people from the
barrios perceive community media as "the last resort" for them to be
heard by the government, when all other avenues have been exhausted.
In this respect, *denuncias* are similar to Soviet citizens' "difficult letters"
to newspapers and Chinese citizens' "speaking bitterness" through the
press – phenomena that both invoke the state into being and criticize
it and that interpolate government-aligned media workers as "the most
humane branch" of state power.

On the other hand, broadcasting *denuncias* has been a fraught practice for government-aligned community media outlets. In the context of intense political polarization in contemporary Venezuela, any *denuncia* aired on community television can be construed as an indictment of the Chavez government and its social programs. In fact, as Samet (2009) shows, crime reporters in Caracas working for private newspapers often press crime victims from poor neighborhoods to *produce* a *denuncia* into a camera or a tape recorder, aware of its power to help mount a political challenge against political incumbents.

Providing ongoing cultural legitimization to Chavez's "Bolivarian revolution" was particularly difficult in 2007, Schiller (2009) explains, when the government decided to effectively revoke the broadcast license of one of the oldest commercial stations in Caracas, RCTV, which had been an active participant in the coup against him in 2002. In contrast to generating political and cultural support for Chavez during the 2004 and 2006 campaigns, community and government media in 2007 "faced an uphill battle in building support among poor neighborhoods" for the government's decision to exile RCTV from public airwaves (Schiller, 2009: 336). Many community media producers explicitly perceived the public cultural battle around RCTV's license revocation as "a test to prove the legitimacy of their revolutionary project . . . negotiating the terms through which the revolution's 'respectability' or legitimacy would be judged" (p. 332). There was an ongoing tension, Schiller reports, between "whether state institutions were merely consulting with community organizations" or truly collaborating with them about what kind of television should replace RCTV (p. 330). Community media suggested the creation of a national community media channel, but were themselves ambivalent about such an idea, because they were unsure what such a channel would mean for their base of power (p. 348). Eventually, and without much discussion, the Ministry of Communication went for officially certified "Independent National Producers" – people who are largely educated, middle class, and produce "professional quality" programming for whoever is footing the bill. Understandably, this introduced tensions in the relations between community producers and Independent National Producers, as well as tensions *among* community media producers, because some of them had registered with the state as Independent National Producers while others saw this route as a petit bourgeois betrayal of "the people" (p. 356). How these tensions will play out in the future and what role (if any) they will have in the future of "the Bolivarian revolution" are hard to predict; however, what this development highlights and brings us back to is the difficult, ambivalent, and multifaceted role of intellectuals in the continuous legitimization (and sometimes delegitimization) of state power.

What Schiller's (2009) and Samet's (2009) ethnographies get at is the actual process through which state legitimacy has been maintained (or, possibly, has begun to be eroded) via media institutions in Venezuela over the last few years. Their analysis helps capture the dynamic between centripetal and centrifugal forces of the kind I identified for post-Soviet Russia and that can probably be identified for postsocialist China as well. On the one hand, there is a continuing process of centralization of state power (manifested in the many legal and political moves described earlier) that continues to draw legitimacy from the work of state and community media producers. On the other hand, there is a centrifugal pull for decentralization, destabilization, and delegitimization of state power – the effect of "media wars"[8] and other battles the government and the opposition continue to fight. Neither government-aligned nor opposition-aligned media producers would likely want either of those pulls to reach its logical conclusion (authoritarianism or civil unrest), yet they are caught in the middle of a process that, to a certain extent, contains both of those pulls at once.

Political Parallelism as a Process

Hallin and Mancini (2004b) define "political parallelism" as the extent and the character of the links between media outlets and organized social and political groups. Partisanship of media content and of media audiences and personnel connections between media organizations and social and political groups they represent are all key features of political parallelism for Hallin and Mancini. Overall, political parallelism is a useful term for the analysis of media and politics beyond Western Europe, but just like with the analysis of "the state," it needs to be opened up and put into motion to capture the dynamics of political change in much of the non-Western world.

First, it is important that we include into the definition of an "organized social group" not only parties, churches, trade unions, and other organizations claiming political participation but also individual capitalists with connections in government and factions within state bureaucracies.

---

[8] A note here on possible comparisons between Chavez opposition media wars in Venezuela and Russia's media wars of the late 1990s and early 2000s and their outcome.

Second, I welcome de Albuquerque's move (see Chapter 5) to distinguish analytically between political partisanship of media outlets, on the one hand, and an active role of media actors and organizations in the political and state-making process, on the other. Some examples of media organizations actively intervening into the political process include commercial media staging a coup against Chavez in 2002; the same outlets urging people in 2003 to join the nationwide oil strike and not to pay taxes to paralyze the working of the Venezuelan state; Brazilian journalists' throwing unqualified support behind Color's bid for the presidency, announcing later they made a mistake, and contributing to his removal from power a few years later (Albuquerque, 2005); Russian journalists' crucial intervention into the electoral process in 1996 and 1999; and "Radio Maria" contributing decisively to the election of Lech Kaczyński in Poland in 2006.[9] Perhaps even China's *People's Daily*'s notorious "Nine Commentaries" (see Chapter 8), published as "Open Letters to the Communist Party of the Soviet Union" and credited with bringing about the Sino-Soviet split, could be considered as an example of active "interventionism" of media organizations into the political process that goes beyond mere "parallelism." What is important here is that media outlets in these cases intervene not only in politics but also in state formation – if we think of states, as argued in the previous section, as "works in progress" (Schiller, 2009).

Next, Hallin and Mancini make an important point that organized social groups are historical formations and change over time. This historical dimension is particularly important in non-First World contexts, especially in recently postcolonial, postsocialist, postdictatorship, and postwar contexts in which intense, turbulent political change is a matter of recent history or of the present, compared to the 300-year span of Western European history with which Hallin and Mancini deal. Just as journalists' intervention into politics is often inseparable from state formation, so is the formation of social groups. State formation and social groups' formation do not run "in parallel," but are part of the same historical process. Stuart Hall (2006) makes these links clear[10] with respect to the English state and class structure, highlighting the historical junctures at which the relationship between the English state and the

---

[9] See http://www.catholicnewsagency.com/news/radio_maria_played_decisive_role_in_latest_elections_in_poland/, accessed May 31, 2010.
[10] Similar arguments are advanced in Corrigan and Sayer (1985) and Joseph and Nugent (1994).

English class structure would reach a relative "settlement" and identifying periods of "transition," when both the *form* of the English state and England's class structure would be fundamentally and thoroughly reshaped and transformed.

For postcolonial, postconflict, postdictatorship, and postsocialist societies in which state formation and the formation of classes, parties, and other social groups are a matter of ongoing historical process, media outlets have been particularly important sites for social and political mobilization, division, containment, and conflict. They have also been sites in which power relations between intellectual elites, the imagined "people," and the transforming state have been playing out. In studying these processes, it might be helpful to think of "organized social groups" as fluid and changing rather than durable entities, as they tend to appear in Hallin and Mancini's analysis. A good example here are my illustrations from early 2000s Russia, where the partisan links between media outlets and powerful (or not so powerful) political players would sometimes last no longer than a month, after which relations of partisanship would have to be renegotiated (Roudakova, 2008). Duncan McCargo's (see Chapter 10) description of "partisan polyvalence" in Thailand, where journalists are valued for playing many different political "cards" at once, is another example in which "organized social groups" are fluid rather than durable.

Yet we might be better off by not drawing too hard a distinction between durable and fluid political groupings in the first place. For instance, Zhao (see Chapter 8) argues that the Chinese Communist Party, which some might consider one of the most "durable" political organizations out there, has been constantly transforming and has had many of its own "forks in the road." Zhao reminds readers that Deng Xiaoping's rise to power, for example, was made possible only after Deng had traveled to southern China and was able to mobilize the more liberal media in Shanghai and Guangdong provinces to help him "win over" more conservative Beijing party circles. In her turn, Schiller (2009) studies what might appear, to outsiders, as a well-organized political grassroots movement that forms the base of Chavez's "Bolivarian revolution." However, on ethnographic examination, the movement turns out to be a shifting and contested terrain, a political project open to multiple and strategic deployments, contingent on various occlusions, and advanced by the erasure of some experiences while privileging others. Precisely because this political project is fluid, community organizers in Caracas are able to articulate and at times disarticulate their positions and actions with the contemporary Venezuelan state, and they do it sometimes willingly, sometimes reluctantly, and often strategically.

In evaluating the usefulness of the term "political parallelism" proposed by Hallin and Mancini, Colin Sparks (2008) suggests that we switch to political "alignment" instead of "parallelism," to avoid the unwanted connotations of straight, parallel lines present in the latter term. It seems to me that "alignment" still keeps us within the geometry of lines; to steer clear of that, I suggest "political articulation and disarticulation" as a pair of concepts that might help us better account for the interplay of the continuities and the breaks in the processes described.

Journalistic Professionalism as a Process

In *Comparing Media Systems*, Hallin and Mancini (2004b) admirably break the analytical link between commercialism (of news media) and professionalism (of journalists), which was presumed universal by liberal and "Whig" theories of press freedom and which still underpins many democracy-promotion activities worldwide. Instead, the authors argue, the link between commercialism and professionalism in news media is specific to countries with an early history of liberal economic and political institutions. What is *not* historically specific about professionalism, say Hallin and Mancini, is the presence of group autonomy for journalists, shared ethical norms, and a commitment to public service (rather than to particularistic interests).

This new three-pronged approach to journalistic professionalism is useful in many ways, not in the least because it allows the acknowledgment of professional practices in media systems with no commercial presence at all (Curry, 1990; Roudakova, 2007). However, the new three-pronged definition, like the earlier one, can quickly become ahistorical and acultural, unless the processual character of journalistic professionalism is brought center stage. (This is similar to the concern Hallin and Mancini express in the introduction to this volume that many scholars around the world are starting to treat *Comparing Media Systems* as the new *Four Theories*.)

To approach professionalism as a process, we need, again, to open it up, "lay it on thick" (Geertz, 1973; Scott, 1990), and put it into everyday and historical motion. In addition, like we did with the concept of "the state," we need to attend to the articulations between the institutional settings that enable the practice of professionalism, on the one hand, and the performances and perceptions of the *idea* of professionalism, on the other. To save space, I focus on the commitment to public service – the third element in Hallin and Mancini's definition of professionalism – and demonstrate what attending to the interplay of institutions, performances, and perceptions of "the public" over time might look like. However, similar explications could be done for the group autonomy[11] and shared ethical norms components of professionalism as well.

The public has been understood as a protean concept for quite some time now (e.g., Gal, 2002; Peters, 1995; Warner, 2002). Following this line of thought, rather than asking whether or not a group of journalists is committed to public service, it might be more interesting to ask these questions: How is the notion of the public understood, performed, and deployed? Under what conditions and to what end are those performances and deployments carried out? What institutional incongruencies make possible subtle shifts in those deployments, and to what results? Or we could ask a related set of questions, especially important in societies undergoing a thorough social transformation: What is the difference, if any, between the public and the social? Which public is being hailed by journalists? Do journalists know their public "when they see it"? Even more interestingly, how does the hailed public recognize itself as such?

The significance of these questions is underscored by research documenting the so-called soul searching among journalists in contemporary Russia, China, and Venezuela (Dinges, 2005; He, 2003; Pan and Lu, 2003; Roudakova, 2007; Yu, 2006). Journalists' soul searching signals a genuine sentiment that they might have lost a connection to their "public" somewhere along the way in their country's recent history. This soul searching might be better understood as a social anxiety, the result of a social mismatch between journalists and their "publics," when the two groups are unable to recognize one another or speak past one another. One of the more striking examples comes from Russia in the early 2000s, when a group of well-known journalists from what was considered the most professional private television station, NTV, made repeated calls to "the public" to support their protests against the effective renationalization of their station by the Russian government. Those journalists were the same ones who had given their cultural support to liberal democracy *and* oligarchic capitalism in Russia throughout the 1990s. It is perhaps

---

[11] A good place to start would be Schudson (2005).

of little surprise that those journalists' efforts to shore up "public support" for their protests were met with a wall of silence by the majority of Russian viewers (Levada, 2001).

Dinges (2005) reports on the "crisis of conscience" in Venezuela's professional media circles. This crisis has to do with professional journalists identifying with what passes as "civil society" in Venezuela, a concept that has explicitly bourgeois connotations in that country because it is used to mark itself off from "the mob" – the frame frequently reserved for Chavez supporters (Gottberg, 2004; Leary, 2009; Schiller, 2009). In a similar vein, Yu (2006) and Zhao (2008) draw attention to the coverage of the story of Sun Zhigang in China a few years ago, coverage that would count as "professional" by many journalists' standards. This was an investigation into the death of a young university graduate after being detained by Guangzhou police for failing to produce his temporary resident card. Yu (2006) and Zhao (2008) both underscore that what made the reporters pick up and pursue the story out of countless other cases was the fact that it was "a university graduate beaten to death" rather than simply "a citizen beaten to death" (Yu, 2006: 321).

As journalists search for and experiment with meanings of "the public" in the shifting social terrain of their respective countries, some of their actions add up to subtle shifts in the processes of "everyday state formation," including state legitimization, whereas others do not. For instance, the unexpectedly wide coverage of the Sun Zhigang case helped bring about the abolition of "anti-vagrancy" laws in China, so the police can no longer imprison people unable to produce their ID cards on the spot. In Venezuela, professional journalists' soul searching has helped tame down the explicitly racist language of commercial print and airwaves over the last few years, and some professional journalists have joined the ranks of Chavez-supported Independent National Producers (Schiller, 2009). In Brazil, as Albuquerque and his colleague show (see Chapter 5; Albuquerque and Silva, 2009), communist journalists, acting on *their* understanding of their "public mission," played an important role both in the emergence of professional journalism in Brazil *and* in the erosion of state legitimacy during the military reign of 1964–85. In fact, Albuquerque and Roxo da Silva's story – of communist journalists' strategic collaboration with Brazil's commercial media owners, the military regime's move to "tame down" communist journalists, the inadvertent pushing of more radical varieties of communism into universities after that move, universities beginning to train a new generation of journalists, and the new generation contributing to the cultural de-legitimation of the military regime – is a chain of developments that is a particularly good example of journalistic professionalism being not merely a separate "dimension" of analysis, but a historical and cultural process intertwined with other processes, including the formation and transformation of the Brazilian state and its "organized social groups."

Conclusion

This chapter outlined an approach to studying relations between media and politics that foregrounds processes rather than systems or structures. I identified some of the elements that a processual analysis of media and politics can build on: the interplay of continuity and change, the articulation between situational (micro) and historical (micro) developments, and the mutual constitution of human agency and social structure. I suggested that a processual analysis of this sort is particularly helpful in studying media–political relations in the so-called hybrid regimes, said to occupy the "political gray zone" between classic liberal democracy and classic dictatorship. Importantly, analysis in this chapter proceeded on the assumptions that hybrid regimes are constantly changing political formations and that this change is historical even if does not have a clear trajectory toward or away from textbook liberal democracy.

With the focus on processes, I attempted to unpack and dynamically link together three of the four dimensions proposed by Hallin and Mancini (2004b) for studying media and politics worldwide. Doing so, I assumed that media organizations are sites in which many overlapping, interconnected processes feed off of one another; among such processes are the exercise of political power, the staging of ideological performances, the accumulation of economic capital, the carrying out of social struggles, the production of cultural representations, and the creation of professional identities. Carefully tracking the articulations of these different processes is a difficult task. Comparing these articulations across countries is even more difficult, because any approach that treats ethnography as history refuses to "check" historical and cultural context at the door of comparison. With context being indispensable to treating the present as historically significant, there is therefore a *tentativeness* to processual comparisons that is absent in structural comparisons. That is "not because of some paradigmatic failure," to go back to Sally Falk Moore (1987: 730), but because the researcher embarking on processual comparisons is willing to admit "two significant zones of ignorance."

The first is detailed knowledge of every context being compared; the second is knowledge of the future. As contemporary ethnographies become "more candid about what cannot be ascertained . . . analyses of 'current history' must be made *more candid* about what *cannot* be predicted" (Moore, 1987: 731; emphasis added). This does not mean processual comparisons cannot be attempted at all, but it does mean that they must be undertaken carefully, cautiously, and with an explicit understanding of the purpose – the politics – of such comparisons.

13

Conclusion

Daniel C. Hallin and Paolo Mancini

In this concluding chapter we focus on a number of central issues that emerge from the contributions presented here. As with the volume as a whole, we take the conceptual framework of *Comparing Media Systems* as a point of departure, and to some extent we use this chapter to respond to issues the various contributors have raised about our concepts and argument.[1] Beyond this, we try to summarize some of the central arguments put forward in this volume about how the field of comparative media studies can move forward with the study of media and politics across a wide range of media and political systems. Of course, the contributions included here are far too rich for us to summarize in more than a very selective way. This chapter deals with these four broad issues: (1) the nature of the Polarized Pluralist model put forward in *Comparing Media Systems* and the question of its relevance to understanding non-European systems; (2) the issue of whether world media systems are converging toward the Liberal model; (3) the conceptualization of the four dimensions proposed in *Comparing Media Systems* as a framework for comparison; and (4) a set of methodological issues, raised principally in Part II of this volume, which have to do with the use of "models" in *Comparing Media Systems*, the concept of "system," the units of analysis for comparative analysis, and related issues of structure and agency.

---

[1] Additional reflections on the critical reception of *Comparing Media Systems* can be found in Hallin and Mancini (forthcoming a).

The Polarized Pluralist Model as a Worldwide Model?

In the conclusion to *Comparing Media Systems*, we make the observation (p. 306) that our Mediterranean or Polarized Pluralist model, more than the other two we discuss, would be "most widely applicable to other systems as an empirical model of the relation between media and political systems." We drew this parallel not because the concept of polarized pluralism in the narrow sense is likely to apply to a wide range of cases: As de Albuquerque points out in Chapter 5, Giovanni Sartori (1976), who coined the term "polarized pluralism," had in mind a very specific type of political party system that does not even clearly fit all the cases in Southern Europe that we discuss under our Polarized Pluralist model. We borrowed Sartori's term because the broader pattern of political development associated with the party systems that Sartori calls polarized pluralist – including, among other characteristics, a later and more contested transition to liberal institutions; polarization, or broad differences among political parties about the basic shape and norms of the political order; clientelism; a stronger role of the state; and historically lower literacy rates – did indeed seem broadly relevant across Southern Europe, as it does also to many other systems worldwide. The analyses presented in this collection essentially confirm our observation about the broad prevalence of this pattern. Many of the authors note important parallels between the cases they study and the characteristics of our Polarized Pluralist model: a strong prevalence of partisan media, a tendency to instrumentalization of media by political and economic elites and their use as tools of bargaining and maneuvering among those elites, frequent state intervention and involvement in the media system, lesser development of journalistic professionalism, lower newspaper circulation, and so on. At the same time, many of our participants raised questions about the use of our Polarized Pluralist model in wider comparative analysis. These questions were essentially of two kinds. The first had to do with the concern that the Polarized Pluralist model would wind up being a catch-all residual model, lumping together diverse media systems under a category that comprised everything other than North America and Northern Europe; the second, with the question of whether the conceptualization of our Polarized Pluralist model involved negative normative implications that were problematic for comparative analysis.

Certainly we concur with the view that our Polarized Pluralist model cannot be treated as a catch-all model to be applied to media systems around the world. This would contradict the most basic methodological premise of our research, which is the idea that the conceptualization of media systems needs to be rooted in detailed empirical analysis of particular systems in their own historical and structural context. Our point in making our concluding observation about the relevance of the Polarized Pluralist model was to stress that *if* other media systems were going to be compared with North American or European ones, the most relevant comparison would probably *not* be to the systems most often used as normative reference points, particularly those we classify under our Liberal model, but to the type of system that prevails in Southern Europe. We stressed this in part to underscore our argument that comparative analysis should be based on empirical investigation of media systems and not on normative models, as well as our view that it was important to try to conceptualize what we called the Polarized Pluralist model as a distinct system, and not simply to ignore it in the belief that it was nothing more than a less fully developed version of a general Western model.

The countries covered in *Comparing Media Systems* are very unusual cases by global standards – unusual in the way liberal institutions of capitalism and democracy were consolidated so early and so strongly. However, this is a bit less true of the countries of Southern Europe. In their recent transitions to democracy, their greater ideological heterogeneity, the larger role the state has played in their social and economic development relative to the market and the lesser differentiation of political and economic institutions, in the prevalence of clientelism, in the fusion of journalism with both literature and politics – in all these things their experience is closer to that of most of the rest of the world than is the experience of the United States or Sweden. Of course, their experience is also distinct from that of other regions in many ways, and in empirical analysis of media systems there is no reason we should privilege any set of cases as standard points of reference – they way media studies has, historically, privileged the systems of Northern Europe and North America as normative ideals. Southern European systems may be an interesting point of comparison in many cases, but if we are dealing, say, with an African or Southeast Asian media system, it is hardly likely that they will be the closest comparisons or the best frame of reference for conceptualizing a model of a distinct pattern of media system development.

Many commentators have raised the issue of whether our analysis of Southern European media systems portrays them as "backward" in relation to our other two models, despite our rejection of modernization theory and our stated intention to construct empirical, rather than normative, models of media systems; this issue was also part of the discussion among our participants. It is related to an analytical issue raised by de Albuquerque in Chapter 5, about whether our Polarized Pluralist model, in contrast to the other two, is defined negatively by what it *lacks* in comparison to them. We are not surprised that these issues have come up; it seemed to us almost inevitable that they would, given the fact that Southern European media systems deviate from the dominant normative models, and even the research and media discourse within these countries is heavily influenced by a consciousness of that fact. Our intent, however, was certainly to understand Southern European media systems on their own terms, as systems with highly specific forms of interaction between media and politics that are deeply rooted in the specific historical evolution of these countries. One reason we organized *Comparing Media Systems* with the discussion of the Polarized Pluralist model first, before the discussion of the other two, was to avoid the tendency to judge that model by reference to the others; we tried to be very explicit in arguing that we could find no body of evidence in our research to justify a conclusion that Southern European media systems are in general deficient from the point of view of democratic performance. In fact, the countries we discuss under the Polarized Pluralist model are typically characterized by a very active democratic life in many respects, with high levels of participation in community and particularly in political life, high voting turnout, and a very lively public sphere in which different views meet and contend through the mass media as well as in other ways. The politicization of media in Southern Europe, although it may be seen as normatively problematic in some ways, is intimately related to this active democratic life.

Any system, of course, can be defined in part by its difference with others, which means that it can be understood in part by what it is not. This is what comparison is about, to see one pattern in terms of its difference from another. So, yes, when we compare our Polarized Pluralist model with our other two, we can say that it lacks a strongly developed culture of journalistic professionalism, lacks a mass-circulation press, lacks a strong tradition of rational-legal authority, lacks autonomous public service broadcasting, lacks effective public interest regulation of media industries in important ways, and lacks differentiation between media and political institutions. (Of course, if we compared these Southern European countries with other parts of the world, rather than with Northern Europe or with North America, these contrasts would in many cases be reversed.) Similarly we can say that the Liberal model is

characterized by a lack of pluralism and political diversity in media, by
the absence of what could be called "representative media" (media that
serve to represent parties and other kinds of organized social groups in the
public sphere), by the lack of the positive role of the state more commonly
found in Continental Europe, and by a lack of differentiation between
the media and the market (the high circulation of tabloid press in some
of these countries is a good indicator of the lack of civil and political
involvement of many of its readers). Both systems can be also be seen
in terms of their positive characteristics – "positive" here understood in
analytical rather than normative terms. What are the "positive" characteristics of the Polarized Pluralist model? Pluralism, partisanship – which
as McCargo points out in Chapter 10, is certainly as significant a form of
media agency as is professionalism – a strong political role of the media,
and a close relation between the political and media fields, to use the
terms of Bourdieu's field theory.

Since *Comparing Media Systems* was finished, Mancini (2009) has
published a new book assessing the significance of the Italian *lottizzazione* – the division of power, of jobs, of airtime, and so on, among
political parties in the Italian state broadcaster. As Mancini points out,
the *lottizzazione* can be understood as a form of clientelism or of "par-
tiocracy," which we may judge as negative from a normative point of
view (although they are certainly coherent forms of social organization
with their own social functions). Yet this is too simplistic a way to understand the politics of Italian broadcasting. The *lottizzazione* was three
things simultaneously: a manifestation of clientelism, an expression of
the strong value Italian society placed on political pluralism, and a manifestation of consociationalism, of power sharing, which was fundamental to the consolidation of Italian democracy. In Chapter 5 Albuquerque
writes, "According to [Hallin and Mancini] one of the chief traits of
the Polarized Pluralist model is the absence of consensual values among
the media and political actors. Thus, how could the absence of unifying
values exert some kind of normative role?"[2] Yet an absence of consensus does not imply an absence of ideas, and in fact Southern European
countries have generated plenty of ideas about media and politics and
plenty of institutional achievements, which, though they might not have

[2] To clarify, Polarized Pluralist systems are characterized by relatively low political consensus, as well as relatively low consensus on journalistic norms. In another way, however,
it is important to keep in mind that journalists and politicians do share values with
one another: values of party loyalty, for example, and a belief that parties are the most
authentic representatives of society.

become dominant globally, either institutionally or as normative models, are worthy of study. Often these are ideas precisely about how a democratic media system can deal with the absence of consensus, and they may be of special relevance to media systems in periods of transition. These achievements include the *lottizzazione*; the ideal of the journalist as an activist in the world of politics and ideas; the vision, strongly expressed in France after World War II, of a journalist-run press autonomous of political and economic control (Frieburg, 1981); and the French success in shifting from a highly "instrumentalized" public broadcasting and regulatory system to a more autonomous one.

Of course, there are also normative issues that come up in relation to clientelism, instrumentalization, lack of consensus on journalistic norms, and other problems endemic to what we call the Polarized Pluralist system. These may well be problematic for the improvement of democratic life and for a more equal access to public resources. They are certainly seen so by many members of those societies, and we do not believe it makes sense to avoid making reference to these concepts because they are seen as normatively tinged or could be interpreted as "smuggling in" modernization theory, a phrase we have heard in discussions on a number of occasions. We have emphasized that we believe the comparative analysis of media systems should avoid normative ideals as a conceptual starting point, but we certainly do not believe we should avoid mention of phenomena that raise normative issues. As political scientists have observed (e.g., Diamond and Morlino, 2005), however, the quality of democracy cannot be understood as varying only along a single dimension, and democracy has many forms. Who has a better democratic life – the citizen who needs to call in a friend with political connections to improve his or her career or the one whose daily paper is focused on sexual affairs of a star football player? Any normative judgment we may make about democracies and about the role of media in them is likely to be complex.

One final thought here about comparing the "West" and "the rest." The concept of "the West" and its division from the rest of the world is obviously problematic in many ways, which we need not enumerate here. We believe it is important to follow a middle course in thinking about this contrast; that is, we need to be conscious of the sharp differences that separate the historical experience of Western Europe and North America from other world regions, but we should not treat the differences between "Western" and "non-Western" media systems as more radical than they actually are. Many phenomena found in non-Western media systems that are commonly seen as divergences from Western models – the use of media as tools for private intervention in politics, reliance of media on state financial support, "formal and informal links between political or integrated political/economic elites and journalists" (Vartanova, Chapter 7), the selective application of media regulations, journalistic forms that merge opinion and reporting –are not unknown in the West. They are easiest to see when we look at Southern Europe, and in that sense the comparison with Southern Europe helps relativize a bit the dichotomy of "the West" and "the rest of the world."

Convergence and Hybridity

Another important theme addressed by most of the chapters in this volume has to do with the question of convergence or homogenization. In the final chapter of *Comparing Media Systems*, we address the commonly held argument that the differences among media systems, which are the central focus of the early chapters of the book, are diminishing as the growth of global media markets, European integration, and a number of other forces drown national differences in a homogenized global media culture. We conclude that this argument is correct to a significant extent. In the European countries we studied, the most important forces of change include commercialization of the media, which began with the decline of the party press in competition with the commercial press and accelerated with the introduction of commercial television; European integration, which has been preoccupied with the formation of a Europe-wide commercial media market; and the decline of traditional mass parties in favor of more individualized, media-centered forms of political mobilization. These changes can be seen as pushing European media systems closer to the Liberal model, centered around commercial media in which market forces are dominant, as well as around more individualized forms of political communication rooted in the culture of marketing. We speculate that these forces are probably significant in most of the rest of the world as well. We also argue that there are important forces that limit these tendencies to homogenization or convergence, including structural differences between political systems, and we caution that we do not think one can simply project the tendency toward convergence into the future and assume that differences among national media systems will disappear.

The participants in this project were very consistent in rejecting the idea that global media systems are converging toward the Liberal model.

Of course, many did see significant manifestations of forces that under-mine national differences. For example, Vartanova concludes, "The profit-based logic of media organizations using the matrix of the 'West-ern' (Liberal) model has put Russian media far beyond the traditional practices." Even in China, certainly one of the strongest cases that can be cited for the consolidation of a media system model distinct from the Lib-eral one, Zhao notes the influence of Anglo-American ideas of independent, "impartial" journalism. Many other authors note the influence of both Anglo-American professional norms and the globalization of media markets. None, however, concludes that convergence toward the Liberal model is a dominant tendency. Dobek-Ostrowska and Balčytienė find substantial convergence of East European media systems toward Euro-pean models – but toward hybrid systems more similar in many ways to the Polarized Pluralist than the Liberal model. Obviously, a strong assertion of the thesis of convergence toward the Liberal model would contradict our point about the greater relevance of the Polarized Pluralist model for understanding media systems outside of Western Europe.

Peri argues that the Israeli media system might have converged toward the Liberal model, had war and the culture of national security not pushed it in a different direction. Peri's analysis takes on the differen-tiation theory of Jeffrey Alexander, according to which media systems tend to develop from particularistic to universalistic forms of informa-tion, thereby shifting away from political parallelism, to use the term we employ in *Comparing Media Systems*, and toward autonomous profes-sionalism. Peri argues that the fact of protracted conflict in the Israeli case has intensified the "particularistic-nationalistic foundations of culture," undermining this shift to universalism. His analysis is a reminder that history does not move in straight lines and that political conditions can shift the direction of media development. A parallel might be drawn to the intensification of conflicts over immigration and multiculturalism in Europe, which have produced a shift away from moderate pluralism – with the rise of new anti-system parties – and similar tendencies toward "particularistic-nationalistic" forms of communication.

De Albuquerque finds a strong influence of American norms on Brazil-ian journalism, but also argues that Brazilian journalists and media own-ers actively appropriated and reinterpreted these norms in ways that fun-damentally transformed their meaning. In fact, it is probably the rule more than the exception that imported global media norms are reinter-preted to fit local political structures and cultures and combined with "indigenous" practices. Papathanassopoulos (2001) has made a similar point about Greek journalists' appropriation of global norms. De Albuquerque goes on to argue that it would make sense to introduce the distinction between central and peripheral systems as a variable in comparative analysis to reflect the openness or vulnerability of systems to influence from other systems. This would be an example of what Tilly (1984: 125) called an "encompassing" comparison, one that "select[s] locations within the structure or process and explain[s] similarities or differences among those locations as consequences of their relation to the whole"; Zhao also endorses this approach, advocating that we "analyze world media systems in their structural relationships, not simply in comparative terms, which tends to flatten asymmetric power relations."

Other contributors argue for the consolidation of models quite different from the Liberal model, models deeply rooted in the realities of political life in the cases they study. Many of these authors stress, with McCargo, the continued centrality of media partisanship, and many also stress the strong role of the state, both characteristics that separate other systems from the Liberal model. Voltmer's argument in Chapter 11, that globalization is an important force but that it typically produces a variety of forms of hybridization, rather than homogenization – seems to summarize well the findings of our contributors.

One of the greatest surprises in the reception of *Comparing Media Systems* was that many readers attributed the convergence hypothesis, sometimes in fairly extreme versions, to us, as "Hallin and Mancini's convergence hypothesis." The convergence chapter was actually not part of the original plan of our book. However, when we made initial presentations of our work, many scholars voiced the criticism that we were ignoring forces that were diminishing the differences among media systems and between nation-states in general. This argument has been around for a long time. It has its roots in the modernization theory of the 1960s, then in a different form in the cultural imperialism theory of the 1970s, and more recently has been put forward by many scholars writing about globalization, neoliberalism, and the "Americanization" of politics, among other themes. The criticism of our focus on the sharp differences between national media systems seemed valid. It was clear that the differences among the media systems we were analyzing had been much greater a generation earlier, when, for example, the party press predominated in most of Europe and commercial broadcasting did not exist there legally – outside of Luxembourg, than they were at the turn of the twenty-first century. We tried in our concluding chapter to use our analysis of the historical development of European media systems to clarify how the forces of convergence had transformed the media systems we studied. It seems clear that the diffusion of Western press models, the growth of global media markets, democratization, neoliberalism, and the like have transformed media systems in other parts of the world in important ways. If we had believed that the differences among media systems were actually on the verge of disappearing, however, it would not have made much sense to write the book we did. This was exactly what some critics had argued – that we were producing something of merely historical interest and should foreground convergence, not difference. We were not persuaded to go that far, however, and persisted in our original plan to focus primarily on contrasting models of media system development in the West.

Comparative analysis is valuable only to the extent that context matters, and we certainly think it still does. Media partisanship, as we see in more detail later, is not the same where there is only one party or where parties are transitory and tied to individual actors. Journalism is not the same thing in Italy as in the United States, and it is different still in Russia or South Africa. Even if journalists perceive that there exists a "dominant" model of journalism whose practices and principles are spreading around the world, even if they may claim to follow that normative model, nevertheless in their everyday activity they perform in substantially different ways. This observation underscores the importance of abandoning the traditional Western-centrism of media studies, the assumption, for example, that Western journalism, what Jean Chalaby (1998) defines as the Anglo-American model, *is* "journalism." If we gave the impression in our book that these kinds of differences are becoming irrelevant, the contributions presented here are a good corrective.

Reconceptualizing Media System Variables

As noted in the introduction to this volume, the four dimensions we use for comparing media systems probably "travel" better than do our three ideal types, at least in the sense that one can ask these questions about any media system: What is the structure of the media market? What is the degree and what are the forms of journalistic professionalism? and so on. Clearly, however, the particular variables on which we focus in our comparison of Western media systems, and the particular values of these variables we consider, are, like our three models, rooted in the context of Western Europe and North America, and we need to begin rethinking them as soon as we consider other systems. As we noted in the introduction, one of the main reasons for the "most similar systems design" of *Comparing Media Systems* was that it served to reduce the number and complexity of variables with which we would have to deal – which implies that expanding the number of cases would of course require a new conceptual apparatus. In this section we consider some of the issues with the conceptualization of media system variables that arose in our discussions.

Structure of Media Markets

In *Comparing Media Systems* we focused on a particular difference among media markets in Western systems, which seemed to us fundamental to understanding their development. This difference is reflected in widely varying statistics on newspaper readership (from more than 700 copies circulated per thousand population in Norway to about one-tenth that rate in Greece). However, we believe that the numbers also reflect profound differences in the fundamental historical development of media systems, between those (in North America and Northern Europe) in which the press developed as a part of mass culture and those (in the South) in which it developed primarily as part of the world of elite culture and of elite political discussion and where electronic media strongly dominate the field of mass diffusion. These patterns are rooted in differences of culture (e.g., between Protestant and Catholic or Orthodox culture) and of economic and social development (urbanization, mass literacy, consumer markets), and they deeply affect many aspects of the role of media in society and the relation between media and politics.

With the exception of a small number of countries in East Asia, along with Israel, Australia, and New Zealand, almost all the rest of the world would fall in the category of low newspaper circulation, usually lower still than the Southern European countries of our study. In the end, though, as Voltmer points out in Chapter 11, it will not be very enlightening simply to extend the newspaper circulation variable to include a "very low" category into which we would lump most world media systems. We will need to conceptualize a much wider range of patterns in the way media and information are produced and circulated, including paying more attention to inequality of media access (between classes, genders, urban and rural areas, and linguistic groups)[3] and to variations in the development of electronic media (those variations are not particularly

---

[3] Here again there is a parallel with our Polarized Pluralist model, which is characterized by much greater divergences between demographic groups in newspaper readership – divergences between regions, between urban and rural areas, and between genders.

significant within Western Europe). McCargo mentions the significance of sensationalist tabloids in Asian countries with low aggregate newspaper circulation, a phenomenon not found not in Western Europe, but found in other regions, including Latin America. In the Middle East, as Kraidy stresses in Chapter 9, the role of transnational media is clearly of great importance. Kraidy also argues that, although our analysis focuses on news media, entertainment media are also implicated in the world of politics, and it will often be important, across all the variables of the analysis, to conceptualize their relation to political processes as well as to news media. In China, as Zhao notes, for many years newspapers were not consumed individually but distributed through work units and village committees, and they were often read collectively. As this last point suggests, the term "media markets" itself is too narrow, because it implies that media are distributed as commodities to individual consumers; a broader concept would have to encompass patterns of media distribution and of circulation of information and might, for example, take into account such things as the role of oral communication and its relation with mass media.

Another obvious limitation of *Comparing Media Systems* is the fact that it says little about the Internet and new media. Comparative research on these topics is just beginning to emerge, and the discussion in this volume remains limited. However, some important points emerge in the analyses presented here that are worth underscoring. First, new media markets will not necessarily reflect the same patterns of development as other media markets. (We consider it an important point in general that media systems, although they may be interdependent, are not homogeneous and that different sectors may operate according to different logics.) For example, Balčytienė points out that, although print media circulation is lower in Central and Eastern Europe than Western Europe, CEE countries are above the European norm in Internet use. Second, many of the contributors to this volume confirm what is certainly a widespread assumption in popular discussion of new media: In at least some important ways new media are less subject to political control than more traditional media and frequently serve as a site for "new exciting links between journalism, civil society and democracy" (Balčytienė), activism (Vartanova), "broaden[ing] the terms of political discourse" and "mobilizing social protests" (Zhao), or as the "safest and most popular venues for more open discussion" (McCargo). The political rebellions in Tunisia, Egypt and other parts of the Arab world in 2011 are certainly a dramatic example of this pattern, which may reflect the globalized character of the Internet, its less resource-intensive character, demographic patterns in its diffusion – its use by younger generations and more educated sectors, for example – or the fact that power holders exercise the tightest control over the most widely diffused media and the Internet does not yet fall into this category. Clearly this is a phenomenon worthy of systematic comparative study. The actual pattern may be complex. Peri stresses continuity of the Internet with traditional media forms more than difference, at least in a common focus on "hard news." Zhao notes that, although the Internet may be more open in important ways, the state also has an important presence and quotes Zheng (2008) as saying that "the Internet has concurrently empowered the state and the society." She also notes that its predominant use by educated urban youth has "intensified the urban bias of the Chinese communication system." Finally, Voltmer questions whether the vision of the Internet as a broad public forum is really "an option in poorer countries with weak infrastructure and low literacy rates."

Professionalism

Reading the contributions to this volume, we were struck by the fact that most devote less attention to the discussion of journalistic professionalism than to political parallelism and the role of the state. This no doubt reflects the fact that, as McCargo says, partisanship dominates over professionalism in most of the world. Consolidation of professionalism is difficult where both political and commercial pressures are too strong: When the main goal of the news organization is to support particular politicians, factions, parties, or business organizations, news organizations may need skilled public relations people or media producers, but the development of a profession with strong "field autonomy," in Bourdieu's terms,[4] is unlikely. One of the arguments we tried to make in *Comparing Media Systems*, however, was that the concept of journalistic professionalism needs to be unpacked and relativized – it has different dimensions that may not all develop in the same way. Professionalism also has taken different forms in different contexts; for example, it has not always been associated with the "objectivity norm" that is central to its American variant. We suspect that a variety of hybrid and partial forms of professionalization will exist in different systems, and they are worthy of further study. Kraidy adds the point that we can study professionalism not only in journalism but also in entertainment media, and this also may be relevant to the relationship of media and politics.

---

[4] See Benson and Neveu (2005).

As noted earlier, in one common pattern globalized forms of pro-fessionalism – professional education and ideologies often modeled on those of the United States or Europe – are adopted, but their influence remains superficial or, perhaps more correctly, becomes transformed and hybridized. Afonso de Albuquerque, for example, argues that Brazilian journalists adopted the rhetoric of an independent Fourth Estate, but attached it to a much more interventionist conception of the role of the media, rooted in Brazilian history, than in the United States. Albu-querque's account of the role of communist journalists in conservative Brazilian newspapers also underscores the fact that professionalism is not purely about autonomy, but is in its own way a form of social control. There are interesting parallels between his account and British accounts of communist journalists working in the conservative press in post–World War II Britain, something that was possible because journalists were pro-tected but also disciplined by the codes of professionalism (Smith et al., 1975).

Meanwhile in Chapter 6, Adrian Hadland draws attention to the per-sistence of the ideology of "development journalism" in Africa. Devel-opment journalism is seen by its critics as "government say-so journal-ism" and defined in terms of lack of autonomy from the state. Yet it does include a conception of public service, and it has some parallels to the deferential, consensual forms of professionalism often found in the West in the 1950s, when the journalist was often what Olsson (2002: 62) describes (in the Swedish case) as "the enthusiastic, not to say offi-ciously supportive proponent of modernization and progress." Obviously the contexts of racial segmentation in South Africa and democratic cor-poratism in Sweden, among other things, make the two cases different (although both also had dominant majority parties), but perhaps not so different as to say they have nothing to do with one another.

Yuezhi Zhao's contribution on Chinese journalism suggests that by the criteria of professionalism we put forward in *Comparing Media Sys-tems* – relative autonomy, consensus on standards of practice distinct to the journalistic field, and an ideology of public service – it does make sense to talk about a form of professionalism existing in communist systems, even in the absence of the structural conditions of autonomy from the state that are assumed under Western accounts of journalistic profession-alism. Other authors have made similar points, including Curry (1990), writing about communist Poland. Zhao points both to a strong ideology stressing the role of the press as a servant of "the people" as a whole and to a degree of success in the efforts of the Communist Party to stamp out the forms of journalistic corruption and clientelism that had emerged with the introduction of market relationships, resulting in reestablishing some degree of consensus on professional ethics. In this respect there is an interesting contrast between contemporary Russia, where the sale of journalists' services to private parties is more widespread, and China, where it seems to have been controlled more strongly. One important argument of *Comparing Media Systems* has to do with the relation between rational-legal authority and journalistic professionalism. Perhaps there is an interesting story to be told about the development of a form of rational-legal authority in communist systems and, again, a set of links to a form of journalistic professionalism. Both Hadland's discussion of the competition between development journalism and liberal conceptions of journalistic professionalism, and Zhao's discussion of Chinese journalism, resonate with Roudakova's argument in Chapter 12, that it would be valuable to focus on journalistic professionalism as a process interlinked, among other things, with the constitution of a particular conception of what "the public" actually is.

Political Parallelism

Among the most important contributions of the chapters in this collection are a set of observations about the concept of political parallelism, the ways in which our conceptualization of that concept is tied to the particular political history of Western Europe, and the ways we might have to reconceptualize the concept to apply to other kinds of systems. All the cases covered in this book have relatively highly politicized media systems, and all the authors find plenty to say about the ways in which the structure of the media and the practice of journalism reflect and participate in the ideological and factional divisions of the political system. This is even true of systems that do not have the formal structures of pluralistic democratic politics: Thus Zhao observes that the Chinese media not only had organizational ties to the Communist Party and a political role in disseminating its views but also that "different sectors of the print and broadcast media took different positions and articulated different social interests in a multifaceted Chinese 'public sphere.'" This is political parallelism, even if it exists in the absence of multiparty politics and a liberal "civil society."

If the fundamental concept of political parallelism is widely applicable, however, it is also clear that the conceptualization we present in *Comparing Media Systems* is closely tied to particular Western patterns of political development. Those patterns center around multiparty democracy, built around the competition of mass parties and other independently organized groups (e.g., unions) rooted in broad socioeconomic interests. In Europe mass parties historically have represented the most important means to participate in the life of the community and to address problems of general interest; they had a strong influence on many processes of socialization, including the mass media, which in the strongest forms of party-press parallelism played the roles of diffusing political "faith" and information to members and of reinforcing and linking together the organization of the party. The mass party systems of Western Europe provided a clear structure to political conflict mostly centered around the left–right spectrum, and media tended to have stable relationships with these groups and/or stable ideological identities rooted in their conflicts. The print media in most of the West, and broadcast media in many countries, were born within this framework of ideological links and affiliations.

Yet this is a very particular political history, and in most of the countries addressed in this volume political divisions and political competition are organized in other ways. In many countries, for example, political parties tend to be relatively shallow and transient: They do not have deep social roots or clear ideological identities, they tend to appear and disappear quickly, and neither voters nor political leaders have strong, stable attachments to them. This is true, for example, of the Polish, Lithuanian, Russian, and Brazilian cases. Balčytienė argues that in Lithuania the political role of the media centered historically around the defense of national culture rather than around the left–right ideological divisions that organized the West European party system and that, with the transition to democracy, parties have become fragmented, media highly commercialized, and the political relations between them, although important, are fluid and often obscure. In many of these cases political competition is organized more around individual politicians and their followers and allies than around parties and interest groups. McCargo, discussing media and politics in Asia, makes a particularly strong case for the importance of understanding the relationship of media and politics in this context and connects it with a pattern of "partisan polyvalence" that, he argues, prevails in much of Asia: In this pattern individual journalists have ties to particular politicians, and media organizations employ journalists with a wide range of such ties, making it possible for them to adapt easily to shifting political alliances. A related issue is raised by de Albuquerque, who notes that only one of the eighteen countries covered in *Comparing Media Systems* (the United States) has a presidential political system and that our work does not include the distinction between presidential and parliamentary systems as a variable. Among the cases covered here, Brazil and Russia have varieties of presidential systems; it does seem likely that presidentialism is associated with more personalized rather than party-centered forms of politics, which would make West European understandings of political parallelism less relevant to these systems.

Political diversity and competition may also be organized in other ways than through competing political parties, which will clearly require different ways of thinking about forms of parallelism between media and politics. In some cases political diversity is organized around factions of the state, more than around separate political parties: Vartanova quotes S. Oates as noting that "the presidential administration and other powerful bureaucracies" tend to organize the process of "marketing" political candidates in Russia; Zhao's analysis indicates that, in China as well, political parallelism has to do largely – although not exclusively – with competition and debate among factions of the ruling party and of official institutions. In other cases ethnicity, language, religion, or clan may be central. These kinds of divisions are not unknown in the European context, of course. In the origins of the European media system, many media were vehicles of religious conflict, and linguistic or religious divisions have been central to both the media and political systems in countries like Belgium or the Netherlands. However, in these countries in the twentieth century, religious and linguistic divisions were expressed largely through the system of mass parties and interest groups, which is likely to be very different from their organization in other systems. Finally, Kraidy argues that understanding media and politics in Lebanon requires us to think in terms of "transnational parallelism," in which Lebanese media are structured in part by their functions within *Saudi Arabian* politics.

Of course, there are some cases considered here in which political parties are indeed well developed and play central roles in shaping political communication, including China and South Africa. Here, however, it is important to note, as de Albuquerque points out, that *Comparing Media Systems* deals with only a limited number of types of party systems, excluding, among others, all forms of noncompetitive systems. As Hadland shows, South Africa would be an example of a one-party-dominant system or, as Sartori called it, a "hegemonic party system," as the ANC competes with other parties but clearly dominates political power. Such a case clearly requires a different conceptualization of the relation of media and politics than anything we develop in *Comparing Media Systems*.

In his contribution to this volume, de Albuquerque goes on to develop an argument that the notion of "political parallelism" should be abandoned as a general concept and seen instead as a special condition associated with the Polarized Pluralist model. We are not so sure we agree with this argument, both because the specific phenomenon of partisan identifications and alliances of media is actually found in many different systems (increasingly so, for example, in the United States) and because we believe the broader concept seems to be reasonably robust; that is, we can ask about most systems to what extent and in what forms the media systems reflect the divisions of the political system. A news report (Mitton, 2008) about the trial of two Vietnamese journalists involved in reporting on official corruption begins, "The conviction of two senior journalists in Hanoi last week had more to do with tussles within the leadership of the ruling Vietnam Communist Party than anything else. The much-derided show trial of the journalists and two anti-corruption investigators indicates the intensity of the conflict between the party's conservatives and reformists." Obviously this example does not fit European patterns of party-press parallelism, but to us, it clearly makes sense to talk about it as a form of political parallelism.

Albuquerque's proposal that we disaggregate the concept of political parallelism and, in particular, that we separate *external pluralism* – that is, the tendency for different media to express different partisan tendencies – from the *political activity* of media – the tendency of media to intervene in political debate, to engage in advocacy, or to try to influence political events – seems like a potentially valuable idea, and it fits the findings of other contributors, including Balčytienė and McCargo. As with the case of journalistic professionalism, the phenomenon of political parallelism may in fact be multidimensional, and it is an open question to what extent its different forms or elements will vary together. It is quite possible that we will find cases in which political parallelism seems high on some subdimensions and low on others, just as it is the case that it may be high in some segments of a media system and low in others (high in the British print press, but low in broadcasting; high in the French national press, but low in the local press). We will then have to conceptualize the conditions under which these various mixed forms develop.

The Role of the State

Zhao points out in Chapter 8 that we discuss the role of the state last, among our four dimensions, and that we tend to use the term "intervention" to discuss that role, which implies that the state and the media are separate to begin with. The order in which we discuss the four dimensions in *Comparing Media Systems* is not intended to reflect a hierarchy of their importance. However, it is true that we tend to begin the story of the development of these media systems by talking about the emergence of media markets and that we assume the media and the state to be essentially differentiated social institutions, even if they clearly interpenetrate in important ways. There is no doubt that we had in mind a "Western" idea of the state and its relation to the media. We were assuming a welfare state that intervenes in the market to support political pluralism and to facilitate the participation of all citizens in decision-making processes, as was characteristic especially of the Nordic democracies; or a regulatory state that modifies the market in keeping with some conception of the "public interest"; or, at times, a state intervening in the public arena to influence citizens in the course of a struggle over competing ideas, interests, and visions. In this last case the state may try to limit the power of the media or to manipulate or instrumentalize them, but even here the state is one among a number of competing actors and its power and functions are limited or have to be negotiated with other actors and their interests. All of the countries covered in *Comparing Media Systems* are essentially liberal systems with limited state power, relatively high degrees of rational-legal authority, and a relatively high degree of differentiation between the state and other social institutions, including the mass media. In most of the cases covered in this volume, by contrast, the role of the state is clearly much stronger (the main exception is Lebanon, where the state is weak and highly subject to penetration by outside actors). There is considerable variation among these cases in the degree of the state's strength – it plays a more central role in China, Russia, or Saudi Arabia than in Israel, Poland, Lithuania, or Brazil. Clearly, in the former countries we have to see the media as to some degree an integral part of the state itself. As this last point suggests, we can also look at these differences in terms not only of the degree of power of the state relative to the media but also of the degree of differentiation between the two. In the Russian case, for example, Vartanova stresses the formation of an "integrated political and business elite backed by the state" that exercises control over much of the media. Several of the contributors to this volume (Vartanova, Voltmer, Zhao) mention a related pattern, which has been observed by various scholars, of "market authoritarianism" – the synergy that often develops between authoritarian regimes and commercialized media for which depoliticized, entertainment-oriented media are mutually beneficial; in this respect there is a close parallel between 1970s Brazil or Mexico and China or Russia in the period after commercialization.

In many cases, the role of the state in the systems covered here appears more negative and more problematic than in the Western cases discussed in *Comparing Media Systems*, with their public service broadcasting systems and strong legal protections for press freedom. In many other systems around the world, the idea of an autonomous state serving the "public interest" is weaker, and the state, as McCargo argues, is often "captured by private, elite interests." State intervention may also be more coercive in character; as Hadland points out, "governments in Denmark or Great Britain are unlikely to send paramilitary police into newsrooms. Sadly, this is a more common phenomenon in newer democracies." Norris (2009) has criticized our analysis in *Comparing Media Systems* for the fact that it does not include press freedom as a major variable. This reflects the fact that press freedom does not differ greatly among the systems we analyze there. Obviously, however, in a wider analysis it will indeed be an important variable, although undoubtedly one that involves as many conceptual issues as others we have covered here.[5]

One of the ways in which the cases covered in *Comparing Media Systems* – and especially those of the Liberal and Democratic Corporatist models – are distinctive is in the high development of rational-legal authority in the Weberian sense. We believe this is an important variable, one that has to do not only with the relative size and power of the state but also with its character. It seems to us that many of the observations the authors of this volume make about the ways in which relations between media and politics in other cases differ from those we describe – the absence of clear differentiation between state and society, public and private; the tendency for the state to intervene in media and media to intervene in the state; and the particularism of the links between media

---

[5] Norris and Ingelhart (2009) propose a classification of world media systems based on an index of "cosmopolitanism" in which press freedom is a central component. Their quantitative, large-*N* comparative study represents a very different tradition of comparative analysis from the one represented by our book and by the contributions presented here. We certainly believe it makes an important contribution in understanding cross-system variation in the impact of mass media. We also believe, however, that in essentially conceptualizing media systems in terms of a unidimensional hierarchy defined by distance from the most "developed" Western systems, it reproduces many of the same problems of conceptual flattening that characterized early comparative work rooted in modernization theory. Russia and India, for example, had nearly identical scores on their Cosmopolitanism Index (for 2005), both a bit toward the lower ("provincial") end of their spectrum. However, clearly those media systems are sharply different in many important ways. Our methodological approach, as mentioned at the beginning of this chapter, is based on detailed analysis of media systems in their own historical and structural context, an approach that draws more on the tradition of small-*N* comparative analysis.

and political actors – are related to the relative development of rational-legal authority, in contrast to clientelist relationships and other forms of social organization. These differences, moreover, have to do not only with the structures of the state but also with political culture more generally. Rational-legal authority is a general variable that is manifested in society at large from the simplest and most common behaviors in everyday life up to the most important decisions regarding the life of the community; this aspect of the relation of state and society is part of what Blumler and Gurevitch (1995: 20) have defined as the "overall cultural mix" and what Michael Schudson (1995), borrowing a phrase from Hoggart's introduction to the old classic *Bad News* (1976), refers to as "the cultural air we breathe." (Vartanova, for example, refers to a "set of informal rules and enforcement practices" that persisted in the Russian case even as formal structures changed and that, she argues, make the role of the state in Russia distinct from anything found in Western Europe.) Rational-legal authority is, among other things, central to the cultural environment in which journalistic professionalism, in the sense that we discuss it – with its emphasis on the media as a social institution serving society as a whole – is able to develop.

These kinds of contrasts – between a coercive and a limited state, or between more autonomous states and those more easily instrumentalized by private interests – are important. However, it is also important not to force our analysis of media and state into the dichotomies of traditional liberal media theory, not to reduce the role of the state to control or censorship, or to assume a dichotomy between commercialism and state control or a clear separation between a coercive realm of political power and a private realm of free speech. We have to understand the functions of the state in their full complexity. As Zhao says of the Chinese case, "the state, despite all its authoritarian and patrimonial dimensions, is invested with the normative expectations of promoting positive freedoms, defending territorial sovereignty, promoting national integration, as well as engendering social and economic development." In many other cases and in a variety of different ways, the state has had among its primary functions that of "nation building" and may have strongly developed conceptions of the public interest that exist outside the context of the liberal concept of a limited state or the West European concept of rational-legal authority.

We have also to remember, as many of the authors here point out, that the state is not a unified actor, but is often complex, internally pluralistic, and in some cases unable to exercise power effectively, for good or ill. We have to remember that interventions, including coercive interventions, originate not only in the state but also, as McCargo puts it, "from private actors, individual power holders and their allies," who may in fact instrumentalize parts of the state as well as parts of the media. We have to remember that media may intervene in the state as well as the other way around. We have to remember, as both Peri and McCargo argue, that self-censorship, rooted in the media's relationship with culture and public opinion, is often as important as state censorship. Roudakova in Chapter 12 argues that we should see the media as playing a role in the process of state formation – or, as the case may be, fragmentation – "representing and performing" the state and hence constituting its meaning; this argument resonates with many of these points. Her emphasis on understanding "the state as culturally produced, perceived and experienced" would seem to be useful for conceptualizing such phenomena as the integration of media into the nationalist state, described by Peri, even where direct control or pressure by the state apparatus is not particularly strong. All of these points, emphasizing, as they do, the importance of seeing relations between state and media as interdependent and mutually constituting, rather than as separate and opposed, may apply more to non-Western than to Western states, but they do apply to the West as well. In our discussion of differentiation theory in *Comparing Media Systems* (pp. 290–1), we make the point that, although Western media systems generally became "differentiated" from political parties and social groups over the course of the twentieth century in the context of the welfare state, the consolidation of rational-legal authority, and the world wars and Cold War, in some ways they actually became *more* integrated with the state.

Methodological Issues: Models, Systems, Structure, and Agency

Comparing Media Systems was organized around a particular unit of analysis – the media system, understood as corresponding with a nation-state – even if these systems were not understood as internally homogeneous or as entirely independent of one another. The contributions to this volume, particularly in Part II, raise a number of issues about this approach to comparative analysis.

First, Marwan Kraidy, focusing on the Arab world where transnational media in various forms play an important role, raises the issue of whether we need to move away from the nation-state as a unit of analysis. He deals with two national cases – Lebanon and Saudi Arabia – that certainly differ from one another and can be compared in the traditional way.

Yet he makes a convincing case that neither can be understood without reference to the relations between them and to the wider transnational context of media and politics in the Arab world, which shifts the frame of analysis to a transnational level.

Another set of issues centers around the use of models, the concept of "system," and the relation of structure and agency. Duncan McCargo writes that "media actors in [Asia] persistently resist ready classification.... If we see media outfits as polyvalent, speaking with forked or multiple tongues, and given to acting in apparently contradictory ways, it becomes increasingly difficult to sustain attempts to model their behavior. For this reason, my own stress has been on agency rather than structure." The utility of "models" came up often in our discussions; it has been raised in other discussions of *Comparing Media Systems* as well and provides a good place to begin an analysis of this set of interrelated methodological issues. In an insightful commentary on our book, Humphreys (2009: 11) argues that "rather than expend time and energy on producing neat typologies, it is more important to explore in depth a more comprehensive range of variables that bear on the complex media-politics relationship and also to explore more levels of analysis of this relationship." We are not at all unsympathetic to these concerns. When we were writing the book, we had some discussion about the advantages and disadvantages of introducing a typology of distinct models as part of the conceptual apparatus. It seemed obvious that it would have great conceptual power, derived from its ability to summarize a complex pattern of similarities, differences, and relationships, but that it would be potentially problematic precisely because of its power to simplify and the consequent danger that the typology would become reified and obscure the more complex analysis it was supposed to summarize. Certainly we did not want to encourage the reduction of comparative analysis to a categorization of cases, in which a label becomes a substitute for more concrete explanation.

We decided in the end to put forward the set of three ideal types for several reasons. We wanted to be able to talk about individual cases in relation to *patterns* of media system development and structure; the models were meant to draw attention to these patterns and to pose the question of why they took the forms they did. Often scholars working on individual cases would have idiosyncratic explanations for the patterns found in that system. Yet once we can identify similar patterns across a number of cases, we can begin to conceptualize and explain them more systematically. It seemed to us that there were strong resemblances among media systems that followed a geographical pattern; we believed these similarities were rooted in both structural and cultural patterns shared within particular geographical regions and patterns of cultural and political influence, like the British colonization of Ireland and North America or French influence on the Iberian peninsula. The use of models allowed us to address these patterns. This point is echoed by some of the scholars contributing to this volume, including Hadland, who argues that there are commonalities among African media systems, and Vartanova, who argues for a "Eurasian" model. Of course, it is important to note that comparisons by no means need to be intra-regional, as ours was. Roudakova's comparisons of Russia, China, and Venezuela underscore this point.

Second, we wanted to be able to deal with media systems holistically, giving a sense of their historical development, the relationships among their parts, and the logics and tensions that structured them. Many of the contributions to this collection again echo this point, stressing the "path dependence" of media systems and the importance of history in understanding why they take the forms they do. We felt that what might be called a more mechanistic approach, which would focus solely on the relationships among variables, would make this holistic and historical approach difficult.

We introduced our three models with a lot of qualifications – that individual cases did not necessarily correspond to the ideal types, that they were not conceived as internally homogeneous, and so on. Yet it is probably not surprising that they are appropriated – and criticized – as a "broad-brush" approach, as Humphreys writes. The framework seems to have been productive of much new theorizing about comparative analysis, and we think it is probably a useful enterprise to think about what other patterns might be conceptualized in this way, as Hadland does, for example, in discussing whether there is a distinct African model of media system or, more likely, a number of them. To some degree, however, we would agree with Humphreys that an overemphasis on typologies is a danger in comparative analysis and that a stronger emphasis on variables and their relationships is in order.

This issue is closely related to the question of structure and agency, or system and process, and it comes up particularly in the chapters by McCargo and by Roudakova. McCargo argues that because the role of the media is so polyvalent and situational, with media actors and organizations shifting roles from situation to situation, borrowing from different models, and adapting to changing conditions, agency rather than structure is the proper focus for analysis. Roudakova, whose work is based on ethnography, analyzes in detail the way particular actors shape their roles and the ways in which they constitute, through their agency, institutions like the state. These are important points. The relation between media and politics is situational, and any comparative analysis that ignores this fact, that assumes that journalists or media owners, for example, will act the same way toward political parties, the state, or social movements in every instance, is going to be a poor analysis. For example, American media are much more aggressive toward state actors in some situations than others. British newspapers, meanwhile, manifest a form of partisanship that fits the third of Blumler and Gurevitch's (1995: 65) four levels of political parallelism, in which media organizations tend to support particular parties but do so conditionally – which implies situational variation: For example, Rupert Murdoch's *Sun* shifted from its normal conservative orientation during the Blair years and then shifted back. Dobek-Ostrowska argues that the same is true of many Polish media. Political and media institutions, moreover, are indeed constituted and changed by particular actors and cannot be taken as preexisting or fixed. Certainly a focus on this process of constitution is crucial to a sophisticated analysis of media and politics.

However, does this mean that it is not valid to speak at all about structure or system? We would say that this does not follow. As Roudakova observes, many social theorists have addressed the issue of how to avoid the kinds of oversimplifications that arise from reductive approaches to the aporia of structure and agency – Giddens, for example, or Bourdieu. We think it is evident that the comparative analysis of media and politics needs to keep the two perspectives in balance. Agents shift and innovate in ways that cannot be reduced to any fixed, all-determining structure. Yet their agency is also shaped by conditions that are outside of their control, by realities of where their news organizations get the resources to function, for example, or the power relationships that prevail in the political system in which they live. In reading McCargo's work, in particular (in this volume and McCargo, 2000, 2003), we wonder if the baby of comparative analysis is not being thrown out with the bath water of "structure" and "modeling." McCargo argues that "the role of the press in Thailand is highly situational: sometimes progressive, sometimes just the opposite." He also describes sharp shifts in Asia between periods when media owners defer to the state or begin to become power brokers in their own right. He makes these points very convincingly, but he does not make much attempt to explain under what circumstances they might play one role or another. Is not this kind of explanation, this search for patterns, essential to what social science is about? We suspect that the polyvalence and fluidity McCargo describes so eloquently do have patterns, and our own preference would be for a stronger focus on trying to identify what these patterns are. That could mean developing ideal types similar to our models. In many ways, McCargo seems to have described a kind of media system – characterized by "partisan polyvalence," personalized relationships between media actors and political actors, and a number of other characteristics that he summarizes very effectively – which suggests a "model" just as coherent as any of those we put forward. If this pattern characterizes a number of Asian countries – McCargo identifies it with Cambodia, Hong Kong, Indonesia, Malaysia, the Philippines, South Korea, Taiwan, and Thailand in whole or in part – and if there are underlying historical and structural explanations for it, it may indeed make sense to characterize the pattern as a "model." Or maybe it makes more sense, shifting the emphasis in the direction Humphreys has urged, to try to specify variables that account at least in part for the kinds of shifts in media roles McCargo describes. Either way, we suspect it is possible to find structure in the agency.

One final issue that arises here has to do with the unit of analysis for comparative research and with the question of whether we are comparing "media systems" or something else. McCargo's work suggests a need for comparative analysis of particular cases of political intervention in media and the reverse, of media intervention in politics; this might take the form of a comparative analysis of political crises or other kinds of political conjunctures, the different roles media can play in them in relation to political actors, and the factors that account for these differences. Voltmer's work suggests the need for comparative analysis of political transitions, which again can be conceived as a process or a kind of conjuncture, rather than as a system. Finally, Roudakova develops an argument for comparison of processes. Processes are certainly among the standard units of analysis in the tradition of comparative social history (Tilly 1984). We suspect that all of these kinds of analysis would probably benefit from comparative analysis at the level of systems, although there may be some conditions under which media and political institutions are so unstable that the notion of a coherent "system" does not really make sense. The reverse would also be true; that is, the analysis of media systems could benefit considerably from these other modes of comparative analysis.

Our work fits a particular style of comparative analysis. For one thing it is an attempt to synthesize across many cases, and we think the concept of "system" has many advantages for this purpose, including, importantly, the comprehensive aggregation under one unit of different features, performances, and structures that – we believe – cannot be understood in isolation from one another. In some ways, the concept of process proposed by Roudakova is similar; both approaches involve "dynamically linking together" the different dimensions of the phenomenon under study, but with a focus more on time than on space, more on transformation than on difference. Comparative analysis can take a number of different forms, and we would not argue for privileging the particular approach or "moment" in the wider enterprise of comparative analysis that we took in *Comparing Media Systems*. It is fitting to emphasize this point in ending this volume, which is intended to provide a kind of bridge between our work and new research, which we hope will enter into dialogue with ours – and not, as we have stressed many times, to "apply" it in any mechanical way. We hope that the contributions presented here will help the field move in the direction not of a single conceptual framework, which is probably unrealistic and counterproductive, but of a broad and deep tradition of comparative analysis of media and politics that will involve an increasingly global and diverse frame of reference.

References

Abramo, Cláudio (1988). *A regra do jogo*. São Paulo: Companhia das Letras.

Abramo, Perseu (1997). *Um trabalhador da notícia: textos de Perseu Abramo*. São Paulo: Fundação Perseu de Abramo.

Abrams, Philip (1988). "Notes on the Difficulty of Studying the State." *Journal of Historical Sociology*, 1(1), 58–89.

Abreu, Alzira Alves de (2003). "Jornalistas e jornalismo econômico na transição democrática." In Alzira Alves de Abreu et al. (eds.), *Mídia e Política no Brasil: Jornalismo e Ficção* (pp. 13–74). Rio de Janeiro: FGV Editora.

Abukhalil, As'ad (2008). "Determinants and Characteristics of Saudi Role in Lebanon: The Post-Civil War Years." In M. Al-Rasheed (ed.), *Kingdom without Borders: Saudi Arabia's Political, Religious and Media Frontiers* (pp. 79–88). New York: Columbia University Press.

Abuzeid, Rania (2008, July 6). "Alwaleed Expands Media Empire." *The National*.

Adam, Jens and Barbara Pfetsch (2009). "Remodeling Dependency – Commercialization and Politicization as Constraints of Political Communication in Poland." Paper presented at the conference "Beyond East and West – Two Decades of Media Transformation after the Fall of Communism," June 25–27, Budapest.

Adghirni, Zélia Leal (2004). Hibridação e gêneros midiáticos. A informação jornalística mediada pelas instituições de comunicação. *Ícone*, 7, 140–52.

Agh, Attila (2001). "Early Consolidation and Performance Crisis: The Majoritarian-Consensus Democracy Debate in Hungary." *West European Politics*, 24(3), 89–112.

AKAR (2009). *Assotsiatsija kommunikatsionnyh agentsv Rossiji (Association of Russian Communication Agencies)*. Available at http://www.akarussia.ru/.

Akhmadullin, Yevgenij (2000). *Pravitelsvennaya pechat' Rossii, konetz 19–fevral' 1917* (The Government Press in Russia, from the End of the 19th Century–February 1917). Rostov-na-Donu: Izd-vo Kniga.

al-Barraq, Nabil (2008, February 20). "Abdallah al-Jaser: Satellite Charter distinguishes between incitement to violence and resistance to occupation." *Al-Hayat* [accessed October 15, 2008, at http://www.alhayat.com]

Albuquerque, Afonso de (1999). *Aqui você vê a verdade na tevê. A propaganda política na televisão.* Niterói: Edições do MCII.

Albuquerque, Afonso de (2005). "Another 'Fourth Branch': Press and Political Culture in Brazil." *Journalism*, 6(4), 486–504.

Albuquerque, Afonso de and Ariane Diniz Holzbach (2008). "Metamorfoses do contrato representativo: jornalismo, democracia e os manuais da redação da Folha de S. Paulo." *Comunicação, Mídia e Consumo*, 5(14), 149–70.

Albuquerque, Afonso de and Marco Antonio Roxo da Silva (2009). "Skilled, Loyal, and Disciplined: Communist Journalists and the Adaptation of the American Model of 'Independent Model' in Brazil." *International Journal of Press/Politics*, 14(3), 376–95.

Alexander, Jeffrey C. (1981). "The Mass News Media in Systemic, Historical, and Comparative Perspective." In E. Katz and T. Szecsko (eds.), *Mass Media and Social Change* (pp. 17–51). Beverly Hills: Sage.

Alexander, Marcus (2008). "Democratization and Hybrid Regimes: Comparative Evidence from Southeast Europe." *Eastern European Politics and Societies*, 22(4), 928–54.

Ali, Tariq (2002). *The Clash of Fundamentalisms: Crusades, Jihads and Modernity.* London: Verso.

Almeida, André Mendes de (1993). *Mídia eletrônica: seu controle nos EUA e no Brasil.* Rio de Janeiro: Forense.

Almeida, Maria Hermínia Tavares de and Luiz Weis (1998). "Carro-zero e pau-de-arara: o cotidiano da oposição de classe média ao regime militar." In Fernando A. Novais and Lilia Moritz (eds.), *História da Vida Privada no Brasil 4. Contrastes da Intimidade Contemporânea* (pp. 319–410). São Paulo: Companhia das Letras.

al-Rasheed, Madawi (2008, April 12). "The Saudi Sect Joins Lebanon's Seventeen Sects." *Al-Quds Al-'Arabi* [Arabic].

Anagnost, Ann (1997). *National Past-Times: Narrative, Representation, and Power in Modern China.* Durham, NC: Duke University Press.

Anderson, Benedict (1983). *Imagined Communities: Reflections on the Origin and Spread of Nationalism.* London: Verso.

Antanaitis, Kastytis (1998). "Lietuviškoji sovietinė nomenklatūra." *Darbai ir dienos*, 7(16), 161–257.

Arab Human Development Report 2003: Building a Knowledge Society (2003). New York: United Nations Development Program.

Arian, Asher (1985). *Politics in Israel.* Chatham, NJ: Chatham House.

Axworthy, Thomas S. and Mathew Johnson (2008, May). *New State to Sustained Democracy: The Case of Israel.* Center for the Study of Democracy. Kingston, Ontario: Queens University.

Ayish, Muhammed (2002). "Political Communication on Arab World Television: Evolving Patterns." *Political Communication*, 19(2), 137–54.

Azevedo, Fernando (2006). "Mídia e democracia no Brasil: relações entre o sistema de mídia e o sistema político." *Opinião Pública*, 12(1), 88–113.

Azzi, Abdel-Rahman A. (1989). "The Arab Press: An Evaluation of William Rugh's Typology." *al-Fikr al-'Arabi*, 58, 169–83 [Arabic].

Badi, Ibrahim (2006, December 16). "'Gulf Pages' Follows 'Live with Us' in Beirut . . . Saudis behind the Cameras . . . Anchors or Emigrants?" *Al-Hayat* [Arabic].

Bajka, Zbigniew (2000). "Dziennikarze lat dziewięćdziesiątych." *Zeszyty Prasoznawcze*, 3–4, s. 42–63.

Balčytienė, Auksė and Halliki Harro-Loit (2007). "Preserving Journalism." Paper presented at the conference "Comparing Media Systems: West Meets East," April 23–25, Wroclaw.

Balčytienė, Auksė and Epp Lauk (2005). "Media Transformations: The Post-Transition Lessons in Lithuania and Estonia." *Informacijos mokslai*, 33, 96–109.

Balčytienė, Auksė, Aaudronė Nugaraitė, and Kristina Juraitė (2009). "Journalism Training and Education in Lithuania." In G. Terzis (ed.), *European Journalism Education* (pp. 447–63). Bristol: Intellect.

Baqazi, A. (2010, May 20). "Saudi Satellite Channels Poised for Live Web-Casting." *Asharq al-Awsat* [Arabic].

Barratt, Elizabeth (2006). *Part of the Story: 10 Years of the South African National Editors' Forum*. Johannesburg: Sanef.

Batalov, Eduard (2002). "Politicheskaya Kultura Rossii Skvpz Prizmu (Political Culture in Russia through Civic Culture)." *Pro et Contra*, 3.

Becker, Jonathan (2004). "Lessons from Russia: A Neo-Authoritarian Media System." *European Journal of Communication*, 19(2), 139–63.

Bell, Daniel C. (2008). *China's New Confucianism: Politics and Everyday Life in a Changing Society*. Princeton, NJ: Princeton University Press.

Bellah, Robert N. (1967). "Civil Religion in America." *Daedalus*, 96(3), 1–21.

Benavides, J. L. (2000). "'Gacetilla': A Keyword for a Revisionist Approach to the Political Economy of Mexico's Print News Media." *Media, Culture & Society*, 22(1), 85–104.

Benson, Rodney and Erik Neveu (eds.) (2005). *Bourdieu and the Journalistic Field*. Cambridge: Polity.

Berger, Guy (2002). "Theorising the Media-Democracy Relationship in Southern Africa." *International Journal for Communication Studies*, 64(1), 21–45.

Berger, Guy (2004). "More Media for Southern Africa? The Place of Politics, Economics and Convergence in Developing Media Density." *CriticalArts*, 18(1), 42–75.

Bernhagen, Patrick (2009). "Measuring Democracy and Democratization." In Christian W. Haerpfer, Patrick Bernhagen, Ronald F. Inglehart, and Christian Welzel (eds.), *Democratization* (pp. 24–40). Oxford: Oxford University Press.

"Birth Pains" (2009, May 16). *The Economist*, 80.

Blumler, Jay G. and Michael Gurevitch (1995). *The Crisis of Public Communication*. London: Routledge.

Blumler, Jay G., Jack M. McLeod, and Karl Erik Rosengren (eds.) (1992). *Comparatively Speaking: Communication and Culture across Space and Time*. Newbury Park: Sage.

Boas, Taylor C. (2005). "Television and Neopopulism in Latin America. Media Effects in Brazil and Peru." *Latin American Research Review*, 40(2), 27–49.

Bobbio, Noberto (1996). *Left and Right: The Significance of a Political Distinction*. Cambridge: Polity.

Bogdanov, Vsevolod (2007, May 3). "V obshchestve net doveria slovu." *Novaya Gazeta*, 32. Retrieved May 25, 2010, from http://novayagazeta.ru/data/2007/32/24.html.

Borodina, Arina (2008). "Ludi zhdut novyh slov. Rukovoditeli telekanalov podvodiat itogi telesezona 2007–2008." *Kommersant*. Retrieved June 5, 2010, from http://www.kommersant.ru/doc.aspx?DocsID=908232.

Bortnowski, Stanisław (1999). *Warsztaty telewizyjne*. Warsaw: Stentor.

Bourdieu, Pierre (1977). *Outline of a Theory of Practice*. Cambridge: Cambridge University Press.

Boyd, Douglas A. (1999). *Broadcasting in the Arab World, 2nd ed*. Ames: Iowa State University Press.

Boyd, Douglas A. (2001). "Saudi Arabia's International Media Strategy: Influence through Multinational Ownership." In K. Hafez (ed.), *Mass Media, Politics and Society in the Middle East* (pp. 43–60). Cresskill, NJ: Hampton Press.

Boyer, Dominic (2003). "Censorship as a Vocation: The Institutions, Practices, and Cultural Logic of Media Control in the German Democratic Republic." *Comparative Studies in Society and History*, 45, 511–45.

Boyer, Dominic (2005). *Spirit and System: Media, Intellectuals, and the Dialectic in Modern German Culture*. Chicago: University of Chicago Press.

Boyer, Dominic and Alexei Yurchak (2010). "American *Stiob*: Or, What Late Socialist Aesthetics of Parody Reveal about Contemporary Political Culture in the West." *Cultural Anthropology*, 25(2), 179–221.

Brady, Anne-Marie (2008). *Marketing Dictatorship: Propaganda and Thought Work in Contemporary China*. Lanham, MD: Rowman & Littlefield.

Bratton, Mike and Nicolas Van Der Walle (1997). *Democratic Experiments in Africa: Transitions in Comparative Perspective*. Cambridge: Cambridge University Press.

Brooker, Paul (2009). *Non-Democratic Regimes* (2nd ed.). Basingstoke: Palgrave Macmillan.

Browne, Donald (1975). "Television and National Stabilization: The Lebanese Experience." *Journal of Broadcasting*, 52(4), 692–8.

Buyandelgeriyn, Manduhai (2008). "Post-Post-Transition Theories: Walking on Multiple Paths." *Annual Review of Anthropology*, 37, 235–50.

Callahan, William A. (2005). "How to Understand China: The Dangers and Opportunities of Being a Rising Power." *Review of International Studies*, 31, 701–14.

Calland, Richard (2006). *Anatomy of South Africa: Who Holds the Power?* Cape Town: Zebra Press.

Carothers, Thomas (1999). *Aiding Democracy Abroad: The Learning Curve*. Washington, DC: Carnegie Endowment.

Carothers, Thomas (2002). "The End of the Transition Paradigm." *Journal of Democracy*, 13(1), 5–21.

Caspi, Dan (1996). "American Style Electioneering in Israel: Americanization versus Modernization." In D. Swanson and P. Mancini (eds.), *Politics, Media, and Modern Democracy* (pp. 175–92). Westport, CT: Praeger.

Castells, Manuel, Mireia Fermandez-Ardevol, and Jack Linchuan Qiu (2006). *Mobile Communication and Society: A Global Perspective.* Cambridge, MA: MIT Press.

Cater, Douglass (1965). *The Fourth Branch of Government.* New York: Vintage Books.

Chakrabarty, Dipesh (2000). *Provincializing Europe: Postcolonial Thought and Historical Difference.* Princeton, NJ: Princeton University Press.

Chalaby, Jean (1996). "Journalism as an Anglo-American Invention: A Comparison of the Development of French and Anglo-American Journalism, 1830s-1920s." *European Journal of Communication,* 11(3), 303–26.

Chalaby, Jean (1998). *The Invention of Journalism.* London: Macmillan.

Chalaby, Jean (ed.) (2005). *Transnational Television Worldwide.* London: I. B. Tauris.

Chalaby, Jean (2009). *Transnational Television in Europe.* London: I. B. Tauris.

Chalhoub, Sidney (1986). *Trabalho, lar e botequim: o cotidiano dos trabalhadores no Rio de Janeiro da Belle Époque.* São Paulo: Brasiliense.

Chan, Joseph M. (1993). "Commercialization without Independence: Trends and Tensions of Media Development in China." In J. Cheng and M. Brosseau (eds.), *China Review 1993* (pp. 25.1–25.21). Hong Kong: Chinese University of Hong Kong Press.

Chan, Joseph (1997). "Hong Kong, Singapore and Asian Values: An Alternative View." *Journal of Democracy,* 8(2), 35–48.

Cheibub, José Antonio (2007). *Presidentialism, Parliamentarism, and Democracy.* Cambridge: Cambridge University Press.

Chen, Lidan (2002). *Makesizhuyi winwenxue cidian.* Beijing: Zhongguo guangbo dianshi chubanshe.

Chu, Yun-han (2001). "The Legacy of One-Party Hegemony in Taiwan." In Larry Diamond and Richard Gunther (eds.), *Political Parties and Democracy* (pp. 266–98). Baltimore: Johns Hopkins University Press.

Clark, Cal (2000). "Modernization, Democracy, and the Developmental State in Asia: A Virtuous Cycle or Unravelling Strands?" In James F. Hollifield and Calvin Jillson (eds.), *Pathways to Democracy: The Political Economy of Democratic Transition* (pp. 160–77). New York: Routledge.

Comaroff, John. (1998). "Reflections on the Colonial State, in South Africa and Elsewhere: Factions, Fragments, Facts, and Fictions." *Social Identities,* 4, 321–61.

Cook, Timothy (1998). *Governing with the News: The News Media as a Political Institution.* Chicago: University of Chicago Press.

Coronel, Sheila (1999, April–June). "Lords of the Press." *Public Eye.* Philippine Center for Investigative Journalism. Available at http://www.pcij.org/imag/PublicEye/lords.html.

Corrigan, Philip and Derek Sayer (1985). *The Great Arc: English State Formation as Cultural Revolution.* Oxford: Blackwell.

Couldry, Nick (2005). "Book Review." *Political Studies Review*, 3(2), 308.

Croteau, David and William Hoynes (2006). *The Business of Media: Corporate Media and Public Sphere*. London: Pine Forge Press.

Cruise O'Brien, Donal B. (1999). "Does Democracy Require an Opposition Party? Implications of Some Recent African Experience." In Herman Giliomee and Charles Simkins (eds.), *The Awkward Embrace: One-Party Domination and Democracy* (pp. 319–36). Cape Town: Tafelberg.

Curran, James (1978). "The Press as an Agency of Social Control: An Historical Perspective." In Gorge Boyce, James Curran, and Pauline Wingate (eds.), *Newspaper History: From the Seventeenth Century to the Present Day* (pp. 51–75). London: Constable.

Curran, James and Park Myung-Jin (eds.) (2000). *Dewesternizing Media Studies*. London: Routledge.

Curran, James and Jean Seaton (1997). *Power without Responsibility: The Press and Broadcasting in Britain* (5th ed.). London: Routledge.

Curry, Jane Leftwich (1982a). "Conclusion: Media Management and Political Systems." In Jane Leftwich Curry and Joan R. Dassin (eds.), *Press Control around the World* (pp. 255–70). New York: Praeger.

Curry, Jane Leftwich (1982b). "Media Control in Eastern Europe: Holding the Tide on Opposition." In Jane Leftwich Curry and Joan R. Dassin (eds.), *Press Control around the World* (pp. 104–27). New York: Praeger.

Curry, Jane Leftwich (1990). *Poland's Journalists: Professionalization and Politics*. Cambridge: Cambridge University Press.

Dahl, Robert (1989). *Democracy and Its Critics*. New Haven, CT: Yale University Press.

Dajani, Nabil H. (1975). "Press for Rent." *Journal of Communication*, 25(2), 165–70.

Daniels, Christine and Michael V. Kennedy (2002). *Negotiated Empires. Centers and Peripheries in the Americas, 1500–1820*. New York: Routledge.

De Smaele, Hedwig (1999). "The Applicability of Western Media Models on the Russian Media System." *European Journal of Communication*, 14(2), 173–89.

De Smaele, Hedwig and Elena Vartanova (2007). "Russia." In L. d'Haenens and F. Saeys (eds.), *Western Broadcast Models: Structure, Conduct and Performance* (pp. 341–60). Berlin: de Gruyter.

Dekmejian, Richard (2003). "The Liberal Impulse in Saudi Arabia." *Middle East Journal*, 57(3), 381–99.

Desai, Radika (2008). "Introduction: Nationalisms and Their Understandings in Historical Perspective." *Third World Quarterly*, 29(3), 397–428.

Diamond, Larry (1996). "Is the Third Wave Over?" *Journal of Democracy*, 7(3), 20–37.

Diamond, Larry (2002). "Thinking about Hybrid Regimes." *Journal of Democracy*, 13(2), 21–35.

Diamond, Larry and Leonardo Morlino (2005). *Assessing the Quality of Democracy*. Baltimore: John Hopkins University Press.

Dinges, John (2005). "Soul Search: Letter from Caracas." *Columbia Journalism Review*, 44(2), 52–8.

Dobek-Ostrowska, Bogusława (2001). "Process of Transition to Democracy and Mass Media in Central and Eastern Europe." In Janusz Adamowski and Marek Jabłonowski (eds.), *The Role of Local and Regional Media in the Democratization of the Eastern and Central European Societies* (pp. 55–64). Warszawa: Oficyna Wydawnicza ASPRA–JR.

Dobek-Ostrowska, Bogusława (2006). "Miejsce i rola mediów masowych w procesach demokratyzacyjnych." In Bogusława Dobek-Ostrowska (ed.), *Media masowe w demokratyzujących się systemach politycznych* (pp. 11–36). Wrocław: Wydawnictwo Uniwersytetu Wrocławskiego.

Dobek-Ostrowska, Bogusława and Michal Głowacki (2008). "Introduction: Central European Media between Politicization and Commercialization." In Bogusława Dobek-Ostrowska and Michal Głowacki (eds.), *Comparing Media Systems in Central Europe: Between Commercialization and Politicization* (pp. 9–26). Wrocław: University of Wroclaw Press.

Dobek-Ostrowska, Bogusława and Bartolomiej Łódzki (2008). "Election News Coverage in Poland." In Jesper Strömbäck and Lynda L. Kaid (eds.), *Election News Coverage around the World* (pp. 226–45). New York: Routledge.

Dobreva, Alina, Barbara Pfetsch, and Katrin Voltmer (2011). "Trust and Mistrust on Yellow Brick Road. Political Communication Culture in Postcommunist Bulgaria." In Bogusława Dobek-Ostrowska and Michal Głowacki (eds.), *Making Democracy in Twenty Years*. Wroclaw: University of Wroclaw Press.

Downing, John D. H. (1996). *Internationalizing Media Theory: Transition, Power, Culture: Reflections on Media in Russia, Poland and Hungary, 1980–95*. Thousand Oaks, CA: Sage.

Dryzek, John S. and Leslie Holmes (2002). *Post-Communist Democratization. Political Discourses across Thirteen Countries*. Cambridge: Cambridge University Press.

Duarte, Celina (1980). "A Lei Falcão: antecedentes e impacto." In *Voto de desconfiança, eleições e mudança política no Brasil: 1970–79* (pp. 173–216). Petrópolis: Vozes.

Dubin, Boris, Daniil Dondurei, and Irina Poluektova (2005). "Vlast, Massa I Mass Media v Segjodnyashney Rossii (The Strangers: Power, Mass and Media in Contemporary Russia)." *Otechestvenniye Zapiski*, 6(26).

Dubin, Boris, Daniil Dondurei, Irina Poluektova et al. (2009). "Sotsiologi v programme Anny Kachkaevoi: nuzhna li televideniyu perezagruzka i chto mozhet ob'edinit' sovremennogo telezritelia u ekrana." *Radio Free Europe/Radio Liberty*. Retrieved June 05, 2010, from http://www.svobodanews.ru/content/transcript/1802025.html.

Duncan, Jane and Ian Glenn (2009). "Turning Points in South African Television Policy and Practice since 1990." Unpublished manuscript.

Elias, Hanna (1993). *La presse arabe*. Paris: Maisonneuve et Larose.

El-Oifi, Mohamed (2006, December). "Voyage au coeur des quotidiens panarabes." *Le Monde Diplomatique*.

Esser, Frank and Barbara Pfetsch (eds.) (2004). *Comparing Political Communication: Theories, Cases, and Challenges*. Cambridge: Cambridge University Press.

Ezrahi, Yaron (1998). *Rubber Bullets*. Berkeley: University of California Press.

Faraday, George (2000). *Revolt of the Filmmakers: The Struggle for Artistic Autonomy and the Fall of the Soviet Film Industry*. University Park: Pennsylvania State University Press.

Faris, Stephan (2009, September 7). "Italy's Newspapers: Untrusted Sources." *Time*.

Feinstein, Andrew (2007). *After the Party: A Personal and Political Journey Inside the ANC*. Cape Town: Jonathan Ball.

Feldman, Ofer (1993). *Politics and the News Media in Japan*. Ann Arbor: University of Michigan Press.

Feres Junior, João (2004). "Spanish America como o outro da América." *Lua Nova*, 62, 69–91.

Folha de S. Paulo (1984). *Manual Geral da Redação*. São Paulo: Folha de S. Paulo.

Fomicheva, I. (2005). *Sociologia SMI* (Mass Media Sociology). Moscow: Aspect-Press.

Fossato, Florain (2003). Medialandshaft: 1991–2003 (In Russian: Media Landscape: 1991–2003), Otechestvennyje Zapiski. 4. Available at: http://magazines.russ.ru/oz/2003/4/2003_4_7.html.

Freeman, Laurie Ann (2000). *Closing the Shop: Information Cartels and Japan's Mass Media*. Princeton, NJ: Princeton University Press.

Freiberg, J. W. (1981). *The French Press: Class, State and Ideology*. New York: Praeger.

Frias Filho, Octavio (2003). "Interview." In Alzira Alves de Abreu et al. (eds.), *Eles mudaram a imprensa: depoimentos ao CPDOC* (pp. 344–84). Rio de Janeiro: FGV Editora.

Friedman, Stephen (1999). "No Easy Stroll to Dominance: Party Dominance, Opposition and Civil Society in South Africa." In Herman Giliomee and Charles Simkins (eds.), *The Awkward Embrace: One Party-Domination and Democracy* (pp. 97–126). Cape Town: Tafelberg.

Fukuyama, Francis (1992). *The End of History and the Last Man*. Harmondsworth: Penguin.

Futurefact (2004). *Report: Media Use Survey Data and Presentation*. Available from http://www.futurefact.co.za.

Gaaze, Konstantin (2009). "Desiat let Surkova: Kulturnoi revolutsii 'po Surkovu' ne poluchilos, hotia dlia nee byli vse predposylki." Retrieved May 30, 2010, from http://www.slon.ru/blogs/gaaze/post/106226/.

Gal, Susan (2002). "A Semiotics of the Public/Private Distinction." *Journal of Feminist Cultural Studies*, 13(1), 77–95.

"GCC Advertising Expenses Rise by 464 Percent in Ten Years" (2005). *Kuwait News Agency* [Arabic]. Retrieved November 30, 2005, from http://www.kuna.net.kw/newsagenciespublicsite/homepage.aspx?language=ar.

Geertz, Clifford (1973). *The Interpretation of Cultures: Selected Essays*. New York: Basic Books.

Geertz, Clifford (1980). *Negara: The Theatre State in Nineteenth-Century Bali*. Princeton, NJ: Princeton University Press.

Gilboa, Eytan (2008). "The Evolution of Israeli Media." *Middle East Review of International Affairs*, 12(3), 88–101.

Giliomee, Herman and Charles Simkins (eds.) (1999). *The Awkward Embrace: One Party-Domination and Democracy*. Cape Town: Tafelberg.

Glenn, Ian and Jane Duncan (2010). "Turning Points in South African Television Policy and Practice since 1990." In D. Moyo and W. Chuma (eds.), *Media Policy in a Changing South Africa* (pp. 39–72). Pretoria: Unisa Press.

Global Forum for Media Development (n.d.). *Media Matters: Perspectives on Advancing Governance and Development*. Retrieved August 28, 2009, from http://www.internews.org/pubs/gfmd/mediamatters.shtm.

Głowacki, Michal (2008). "Political Pressure on Public Television in Poland: The Case of the National Broadcasting Council." In Bogusława Dobek-Ostrowska and Michal Głowacki (eds.), *Comparing Media Systems in Central Europe: Between Politicization and Commercialization* (pp. 111–122). Wroclaw: University of Wroclaw Press.

Goban-Klas, Tomasz (1997). "Politics versus Media in Poland: A Game without the Rules." In Patrick O'Neil (ed.), *Post-Communism and the Media in Eastern Europe* (pp. 24–41). London: Frank Cass.

Goldenstein, Gisela Taschner (1987). *Do Jornalismo Político à Indústria Cultural*. São Paulo: Summus.

Goryainov, Vladimir (2009). *Tzennostnyie suzhdeniya v Rossii I Zapadnoi Yevrope: sravnitel'nyi analis* (Value Judgments in Russia and Western Europe: Comparative Analysis). Socis, N, pp. 114–20.

Gottberg, Luis Duno (2004). "Mob Outrages: Reflections on the Media Construction of the Masses in Venezuela (April 2000-January 2003)." *Journal of Latin American Cultural Studies*, 13(1), 115–35.

Greenberg, Jessica (2010). "'There's Nothing Anyone Can Do about It': Participation, Apathy, and 'Successful' Democratic Transition in Postsocialist Serbia." *Slavic Review*, 69(1), 41–64.

Greenhouse, Carol J., Elizabeth Mertz, and Kay B. Warren (2002). *Ethnography in Unstable Places: Everyday Lives in Contexts of Dramatic Political Change*. Durham, NC: Duke University Press.

Gross, Peter (2004). "Between Reality and Dream: Eastern European Media Transition, Transformation, Consolidation and Integration." *East European Politics and Societies*, 18(1), 110–31.

Gross, Peter (2008). "Dances with Wolves: A Meditation on the Media and Political System in the European Union's Romania." In Karol Jakubowicz and Miklós Sükösd (eds.), *Finding the Right Place on the Map: Central and Eastern European Media Change in a Global Perspective* (pp. 125–45). Bristol: Intellect.

Gross, Peter, Ray Hiebert, and Owen Johnson (eds.) (1999). *Eastern European Journalism. Before, During and After Communism*. Cresskill, NJ: Hampton Press.

Grugel, Jean (2002). *Democratization: A Critical Introduction*. Basingstoke: Palgrave.

Guimarães, César and Roberto Amaral (1988). "Brazilian Television: A Rapid Conversion to the New Order." In Elizabeth Fox (ed.), *Media and Politics in Latin America: The Struggle for Democracy* (pp. 125–37). Newbury Park, CA: Sage.

Gumede, William M. (2005). *Thabo Mbeki and the Battle for the Soul of the ANC*. Cape Town: Zebra Press.

Gunther, Richard and Anthony Mughan (eds.) (2000). *Democracy and the Media: A Comparative Perspective*. Cambridge: Cambridge University Press.

Gupta, Akhil (1995). "Blurred Boundaries: The Discourse of Corruption, the Culture of Politics, and the Imagined State." *American Ethnologist*, 22(2), 375–402.

Gupta, Akhil (forthcoming). *Red Tape: Corruption, Inscription and Governmentality in Rural India*. Durham, NC: Duke University Press.

Gupta, Akhil and Aradhna Sharma (2006). "Globalization and Postcolonial States." *Current Anthropology*, 47(2), 277–307.

Gutiontov, Pavel (2005). "Iz zapisok vodoprovodchika. Vremia gniet i lomayet tekh, kto gotov gnutsia i lomatsia." Retrieved May 26, 2010, from http://www.library.cjes.ru/online/?b_id=686.

Gwiazda, Andrej (2008). "Party Patronage in Poland: The Democratic Left Alliance and Law and Justice." *East European Politics and Societies*, 22 (Fall), 802–27.

Habielski, Rafał (1999). "Dwudziestolecie mię dzywojenne." In D. Grzelewska, R. Habilski, A. Kozieł, J. Osica, L. Piwońska-Pykało, and F. Skierawski (eds.) *Prasa, radio i telewizja w Polsce. Zarys dziejów* (pp. 61–93). Warsaw: Elipsa.

Hachten, William and Anthony Giffard (1984). *The Press and Apartheid*. London: Methuen.

Hackett, Robert A. and Yuezhi Zhao (1998). *Sustaining Democracy? Journalism and the Politics of Objectivity*. Toronto: Garamond Press.

Hadamik, Katharina (2005). "Between East and West or Simply 'Made in Poland:' The Many Different Styles of Today's Polish Journalism." In Svennik Høyer and Horst Pottker (eds.), *Diffusion of News Paradigm 1850–2000* (pp. 211–24). Goteborg: Nordicom.

Haddad, Viviane (2006, September 17). "Lebanese Satellite Channels Compete for Saudi media Personalities." *Asharq Al-Awsat* [Arabic].

Hadenius, Alex and Jan Teorell (2007). "Pathways from Authoritarianism." *Journal of Democracy*, 18(1), 143–56.

Hadland, Adrian (2007). "State-Media Relations in Post-Apartheid South Africa: An Application of Comparative Media Systems Theory." *Communicare*, 26(2), 1–17.

Hadland, Adrian, L. Cowling, and F.-T. Tabe (2007). *Advertising in the News: Paid-for Content and the South African Print Media*. Cape Town: HSRC Press.

Hadland, Adrian and K. Thorne (2004). *The People's Voice: The Development and Current State of the South African Small Media Sector*. Cape Town: HSRC Press.

Hall, Richard A. and Patrick H. O'Neil (1998). "Institutions, Transitions, and the Media: A Comparison of Hungary and Romania." In Patrick H. O'Neil (ed.), *Communicating Democracy: The Media and Political Transitions* (pp. 125–45). Boulder: Lynne Rienner.

Hall, Stuart (2006). "Popular Culture and the State." In A. Sharma and A. Gupta (eds.), *The Anthropology of the State: A Reader* (pp. 360–80). Oxford: Blackwell.

Hallin, Daniel C. (1986). *The "Uncensored War": The Media and Vietnam*. New York: Oxford University Press.

Hallin, Daniel C. (1992). "Sound Bite News: Television Coverage of Elections: 1968–1988." *Journal of Communication*, 42(2), 5–24.

Hallin, Daniel C. (2009, June). "Not the End of Journalism History." *Journalism*, 10(3), 332–4.

Hallin, Daniel C. and Paolo Mancini (1984). "Speaking of the President: Political Structure and Representational Form in U.S. and Italian TV News." *Theory and Society*, 13, 829–50.

Hallin, Daniel C. and Paolo Mancini (2004a). "Americanization, Globalization, and Secularization: Understanding the Convergence of Media Systems and Political Communication." In Frank Esser and Barbara Pfetsch (eds.), *Comparing Political Communication: Theories, Cases, and Challenges* (pp. 25–44). Cambridge: Cambridge University Press.

Hallin, Daniel C. and Paolo Mancini (2004b). *Comparing Media Systems: Three Models of Media and Politics*. Cambridge: Cambridge University Press.

Hallin, Daniel C. and Paolo Mancini (forthcoming a). "Commentary on the Use and Critical Reception of *Comparing Media Systems*." In F. Esser and T. Hanitzsch (eds.), *Comparing Media Systems: A Response to Critics*. London: Routledge.

Hallin, Daniel C. and Paolo Mancini (forthcoming b). "Comparing Media Systems between Eastern and Western Europe." In Peter Gross and Karol Jakubowicz (eds.), *Fighting Windmills: A Retrospective on 20 Years of Media Transformation in the Post-Communist World*. Frankfurt am Main: Peter Lang.

Hallin, Daniel C. and Stylianos Papathanassopoulos (2002). "Political Clientelism and the Media: Southern Europe and Latin America in Comparative Perspective." *Media, Culture & Society*, 24(2), 175–95.

Hampton, Mark (2005). "Media Studies and the Mainstreaming of Media History." *Media History*, 11(3), 239–46.

Hanitzsch, Thomas (2007). "Deconstructing Journalism Culture: Towards a Universal Theory." *Communication Theory*, 17(4), 367–85.

Hansen, Thomas Blom and Finn Stepputat (2001). *States of Imagination: Ethnographic Explorations of the Postcolonial State*. Durham, NC: Duke University Press.

He, Zhou (2000). "Working with a Dying Ideology: Dissonance and Its Reduction in Chinese Journalism." *Journalism Studies*, 1(4), 599–616.

He, Zhou (2003). "How Do the Chinese Media Reduce Organizational Incongruence? Bureaucratic Capitalism in the Name of Communism." In C.-C. Lee (ed.), *Chinese Media, Global Contexts* (pp. 196–214). London: Routledge.

Heilmann, Sebastian and Elizabeth J. Perry (2011). *Mao's Invisible Hand: The Political Foundations of Adaptive Governance in China*. Cambridge, MA: Harvard University Asia Center.

Herbut, Ryszard (2002). *Teoria i praktyka funkcjonowania partii politycznych*. Wrocław: University of Wroclaw Press.

Herscovitz, Heloíza Goldspan (2000). "Jornalistas de São Paulo: quem são e o que pensam em comparação com os jornalistas americanos e franceses." *Revista Brasileira de Ciências da Comunicação*, 23(2), 65–86.

Hoggart, Richard (1976). "Foreword." In Glasgow Media Group (ed.), *Bad News*. London: Routledge and Kegan Paul.

Hohenberg, John (1969). *The Professional Journalist: A Guide to the Practices and Principles of the News Media* (2nd ed.). New York: Columbia University Press.

Hong, Yu (2011). *Labor, Class Formation, and China's Informationized Policy of Economic Development*. Lanham, MD: Lexington Books.

Horwitz, Robert (2001). *Communication and Democratic Reform in South Africa*. Cambridge: Cambridge University Press.

Hosking, Jeffrey (2007). "Struktury doverija v poslednie desyatiletiya Sovetskogo Soyuza." *Neprikosnovennyi Zapas*, 4(54). Retrieved May 25, 2010, from http://magazines.russ.ru/nz/2007/54/ho5.html.

Høyer, Svennik, Epp Lauk, and Peeter Vihalemm (1993). *Towards a Civic Society: The Baltic Media's Long Road to Freedom*. Tartu: Nota Baltica.

Hu, Jintao (2004). "Zai silujie sizhong quanhui disanci quantihuiyi shang de jianghua" *(jiexuan)*. Presented at the 16th National Congress (excerpts). Retrieved July 5, 2008, from http://www.gzswdx.gov.cn/librarynewweb/showcontent.asp?TitleID=29874.

Huang, Xiaoming (2009). *Politics in Pacific Asia: An Introduction*. Basingtoke: Palgrave.

Human Rights Watch (2008). *A Decade under Chavez: Political Intolerance and Lost Opportunities for Advancing Human Rights in Venezuela*. New York: Human Rights Watch.

Humphreys, Peter (2009). "A Political Scientist's Contribution to the Comparative Study of Media Systems in Europe: A Response to Hallin and Mancini." Paper presented at the 2009 ECREA Communication Policy and Law Workshop, Zurich.

Huntington, Samuel P. (1991). *The Third Wave: Democratization in the Late Twentieth Century*. Norman: University of Oklahoma Press.

Ismail, Jamal abdi and James Deane (2008). "The 2007 General Election in Kenya and Its Aftermath: The Role of Local Language Media." *International Journal of Press/Politics*, 13(3), 319–27.

Ivanitsky, Valerij (2009). *Rynok SMI v postsovetskoi Rossii* (Mass Media Market in Post-Soviet Russia), 6, 114–31. Moscow: Vestnik Moskovskogo Universiteta.

Jacques, Martin (2009). *When China Rules the World: The Rise of the Middle Kingdom and the End of the Western World*. London: Allen Line.

Jakubowicz, Karol (1995). "Media within and without the State: Press Freedom in Eastern Europe." *Journal of Communication*, 45, 125–39.

Jakubowicz, Karol (2002). "Media in Transition: The Case of Poland." In Monroe Price, Beata Rozumilowicz, and Stefeen Verhulst (eds.), *Media Reform: Democratizing the Media, Democratizing the State* (pp. 203–31). London and New York: Routledge.

Jakubowicz, Karol (2007a). "The Eastern European/Postcommunist Media Model Countries." In George Terzis (ed.), *European Media Governance. National and Regional Dimensions* (pp. 303–13). Bristol: Intellect.

Jakubowicz, Karol (2007b). *Rude Awakening. Social and Media Change in Central and Eastern Europe.* Cresskill, NJ: Hampton Press.

Jakubowicz, Karol (2008a). "Finding the Right Place on the Map: Prospects for Public Service Broadcasting in Post-Communist Countries." In Karol Jakubowicz and Miklós Sükösd (eds.), *Finding the Right Place on the Map: Central and Eastern European Media Change in a Global Perspective* (pp. 101–24). Bristol: Intellect.

Jakubowicz, Karol (2008b). "Riviera on the Baltic? Public Service Broadcasting in Post-Communist Countries." In Bogusława Dobek-Ostrowska and Michal Głowacki (eds.), *Comparing Media Systems in Central Europe: Between Commercialization and Politicization* (pp. 41–54). Wrocław: University of Wroclaw Press.

Jakubowicz, Karol and Miklós Sükösd (eds.) (2008). *Finding the Right Place on the Map: Central and Eastern European Media Change in a Global Perspective.* Bristol: Intellect.

James, Laura (2006). "Whose Voice? Nasser, the Arabs, and 'Sawt al-Arab' Radio." *Transnational Broadcasting Studies,* 16, http://www.tbsjournal.com/James.html (accessed November 1, 1998).

Jobim, Danton (1954). "French and U.S. Influences upon the Latin American Press." *Journalism Quarterly,* 31(1), 61–6.

Johnston, Alexander (2005). "The African National Congress, the Print Media and the Development of Mediated Politics in South Africa." *CriticalArts,* 19(1&2), 12–35.

Joseph, G. M. and D. Nugent (1994). *Everyday Forms of State Formation: Revolution and the Negotiation of Rule in Modern Mexico.* Durham, NC: Duke University Press.

Kaid, Lynda L. and Christina Holtz-Bacha (eds.) (1995). *Political Advertising in Western Democracies. Parties and Candidates on Television.* Thousand Oaks, CA: Sage.

Kangaspuro, Markku (ed.) (1999). *Russia: More Different than Most.* Helsinki: Kikimora.

Karl, Terry L. (1995). "The Hybrid Regimes of Central America." *Journal of Democracy,* 6(3), 72–86.

Keane, John (1991). *The Media and Democracy.* London: Polity Press.

Keane, Michael (2006). "Once Were Peripheral: Creating Media Capacity in East Asia." *Media, Culture and Society,* 28(6), 835–55.

Keen, Andrew (2008, August). "Portrait: Arianna Huffington." *Prospect.*

Kelly, Mary, Gianpietro Mazzoleni, and Denis McQuail (eds.) (2004). *The Media in Europe: The Euromedia Research Group.* London: Sage.

Kempen, Hetty van (2007). "Media-Party Parallelism and Its Effects: A Cross-National Comparative Study." *Political Communication*, 24(3), 303–20.

Khan, Joseph (2006, March 12). "A Sharp Debate Erupts in China over Ideologies." *New York Times*.

Khlebnikov, Pavel (2001). *Boris Berezovsky, krestnyi otetz Kremlja*. Moscow: Detective Press.

Kimmerling, Baruch (2001). *The Invention and Decline of Israeliness: State, Society and the Military*. Los Angeles: University of California Press.

Kinzo, Maria D'Alva Gil (1988). *Oposição e autoritarismo. Gênese e trajetória do MDB (1966–1979)*. São Paulo: Vértice.

Kit-Wai Ma, Eric (2000). "Rethinking Media Studies: The Case of China." In James Curran and Myung-Jin Park (eds.), *De-Westernizing Media Studies* (pp. 21–34). London: Routledge.

Klangnarong, Supinya (2009). "'Netizens' and Political Agency in Thailand: Cyber Liberty vs. National Security." Paper presented at the Association for Asian Studies Annual Meeting, March 25–27, Chicago.

Klimkiewicz, Beata (2005). *Media Pluralism: European Regulatory Policies and the Case of Central Europe*. Florence: Badia Fiesolana European University Institute EUI Working Papers RSCAS No. 2005–19.

Kochanowicz, Jacek, Piotr Kozarzewski, and Robert Woodward (2005). *Understanding Reform: The Case of Poland*. CASE Reports 59/2005. Warsaw: Center for Social and Economic Research.

Koikkalainen, Katja (2007). "Business Media in Nordic Countries and Russia: Global Trends, Local Content." In Elena Vartanova (ed.), *Media and Change* (pp. 180–90). Moscow: MediaMir.

Kolesnikov, Andrei (2009). "Politekonomiya: Russkyi sopromat." *Vedomosti*, 228(2498). Retrieved December 2, 2009, from http://www.vedomosti.ru/newspaper/article/2009/12/02/220342.

Koltsova, Olesya (2005). "News Production in Contemporary Russia: Practices of Power." In D. McQuail, P. Golding, and E. De Bens (eds.), *Communication Theory & Research: An EJC Anthology* (pp. 220–234). Thousand Oaks, CA: Sage.

Kopecký, Peter and Peter Mair (2006). "Political Parties and Patronage in Contemporary Democracies: An Introduction." Paper presented at the ECPR Joint Session of Workshop, Nicosia, Cyprus.

Kosto, Pal (2000). *Political Construction Sites: Nation Building in Russia and Post-Soviet States*. Boulder, CO: Westview Press.

Kraidy, Marwan M. (1998). "Broadcasting Regulation and Civil Society in Postwar Lebanon." *Journal of Broadcasting and Electronic Media*, 42(3), 387–400.

Kraidy, Marwan M. (1999). "State Control of Television News in 1990s Lebanon." *Journalism and Mass Communication Quarterly*, 76(3), 485–8.

Kraidy, Marwan M. (2000). "Television Talk and Civic Discourse in Postwar Lebanon." In Leon A. Gher and Hussein Y. Amin (eds.), *Civic Discourses in the Middle East and Digital Age Communications* (pp. 1–17). Norwood, NJ: Ablex.

Kraidy, Marwan M. (2009). *Reality Television and Arab Politics: Contention in Public Life*. New York and Cambridge, UK: Cambridge University Press.

Kraidy, Marwan M. and Joe F. Khalil (2009). *Arab Television Industries*. London: British Film Institute/Palgrave Macmillan.

Kubicek, Paul (1994). "Delegative Democracy in Russia and Ukraine." *Communist and Post-Communist Studies*, 27(4), 423–41.

Kucinski, Bernardo (1991). *Jornalistas e revolucionários. Nos tempos da imprensa alternativa*. São Paulo: Editora Página Aberta.

Kucinski, Bernardo (1998). *A síndrome da antena parabólica: ética no jornalismo brasileiro*. São Paulo: Editora Fundação Perseu Abramo.

Lampland, Martha (1991). "Pigs, Party Secretaries, and Private Lives in Hungary." *American Ethnologist*, 18(3), 459–79.

Larina, Ksenia, Irina Petrovskaya, Stanislav Kucher, et al. (2009). "Chinovnik i SMI." On *Kulturnyi shok* [Radio broadcast] (Echo of Moscow). Retrieved May 26, 2010, from http://echo.msk.ru/programs/kulshok/588995-echo.

Lauk, Epp (2008). "How Will It All Unfold? Media Systems and Journalism Cultures in Post-Communist Countries. In Karol Jakubowicz and Miklós Sükösd (eds.), *Finding the Right Place on the Map: Central and Eastern European Media Change in a Global Perspective* (pp. 193–212). Bristol: Intellect.

Lawson, Chappell H. (2002). *Building the Fourth Estate: Democratization and the Rise of a Free Press*. Berkeley: University of California Press.

"LBCSAT and Rotana Channels Merge in One Entity" (2007, August 9). *Al-Riyadh* [Arabic].

"LBCSAT and Rotana Television Channels Merge to Form Media Powerhouse" (2007, August 9). Press Release.

Le Pottier, Gaelle (2003). "Le monde de la télévision satellitaire au Moyen-Orient et le rôle des libanais dans son développement." In F. Mermier (ed.), *Mondialisation et nouveaux médias dans l'espace arabe* (pp. 43–72). Paris: Maisonneuve et Larose.

Leary, John Patrick (2009). "TV Urgente: Urban Exclusion, Civil Society, and the Politics of Television in Venezuela." *Social Text*, 27(2), 25–53.

Lebling, Robert (2005, April 22). "From Beirut to Jeddah: A Desk Editor Reminisces." *Arab News*.

Lee, Chin-Chuan (2000). "State, Capital, and Media: The Case of Taiwan." In James Curran and Myung-Jin Park (eds.), *De-Westernizing Media Studies* (pp. 124–38). London: Routledge.

Lenin, Vladimir (1901). "Where to Begin," *Iskra*, no. 4, May. Available at http://www.marxists.org/archives/lenin/works/1901/may/04.htm.

Lessing, Doris (1999). *The Golden Notebook*. New York: Perennial Classics (original work published 1962).

Levada, Yury (2001). "Chelovek stal meniatsia, no drugim ne stal." *Index on Censorship*, 13(2001). Retrieved June 15, 2011, from http://index.org.ru/journal/13/levada1301.html.

Levada, Yury (2006). "Staryi novyi neporiadok: Rossiiskie grazhdane ne doveriayut vlastnym institutam vne zavisimosti ot svoikh politicheskikh ubezhdenii." *Kommersant*, 33(3364). Retrieved May 30, 2010, from http://www.kommersant.ru/doc.aspx?DocsID=652822.

Levitsky, Steven and Lucian Way (2002). "The Rise of Competitive Authoritarianism." *Journal of Democracy*, 13(2), 51–65.

Levitsky, Steven and Lucian Way (2010). *Competitive Authoritarianism: Hybrid Regimes after the Cold War.* Cambridge: Cambridge University Press.

Li, Cheng (2009). "China's Team of Rivals." *Foreign Policy*, March/April, 88–93.

Li, Yahong (2009). "Citizens' Political Participation Inspired by the Internet." *China Today*, 58(4), 12–17.

LICADHO (2008, May). *Reading between the Lines: How Politics, Money and Fear Control Cambodia's Media.* Phnom Penh: LICADHO.

Liebes, Tamar (2000). "A Socio-Schematic History of Broadcasting in Israel." In James Curran and Myung-Jin Park (eds.), *De-Westernizing Media Studies* (pp. 305–24). London: Routledge.

Lieven, Anatol (1994). *The Baltic Revolution: Estonia, Latvia, Lithuania and the Path to Independence.* New Haven, CT: Yale University Press.

Lijphart, Arend (1971). "Comparative Politics and the Comparative Method." *American Political Science Review*, 65(3), 682–93.

Lima, Venício A. de (2004). *Mídia: teoria e política.* São Paulo: Editora Fundação Perseu Abramo.

Lin, Chun (2006). *The Transformation of Chinese Socialism.* Durham, NC: Duke University Press.

Lindberg, Steffan I. (2006). *Democracy and Elections in Africa.* Baltimore: Johns Hopkins University Press.

Linz, Juan J. (1990). "The Perils of Presidentialism." *Journal of Democracy*, 1, 51–69.

Linz, Juan J. (1994). "Presidential or Parliamentary Democracy: Does it Make a Difference?" In Juan J. Linz and Arturo Valenzuela (eds.), *The Failure of Presidential Democracy: The Case of Latin America* (pp. 3–90). Baltimore: Johns Hopkins University Press.

Linz, Juan J. (2000). "Further Reflections on Authoritarian and Totalitarian Regimes." In J. Linz (ed.), *Totalitarian and Authoritarian Regimes.* Boulder, CO: Lynne Rienner.

Linz, Juan and Alfred Stepan (1996). *Problems of Democratic Transition and Consolidation: South Europe, South America, and Post-Communist Europe.* Baltimore: Johns Hopkins University Press.

Lipset, Seymour M. and Stein Rokkan (1967). "Cleavage Structure, Party Systems, and Voter Alignments." In Seymour M. Lipset and Stein Rokkan (eds.), *Party Systems and Voter Alignments: Cross-National Perspectives* (pp. 1–67). New York: Free Press.

Livingstone, Sonia (2003). "On the Challenges of Cross-National Comparative Media Research." *European Journal of Communication*, 18(4), 477–500.

Łódzki, Bartłomiej (2010). *informacyjnych ustanawianie agendy mediów podczas kampanii wyborczych w 2005 r.* Wrocław: Wydawnictwo Uniwersytetu Wrocławskiego.

Loqman, Faruq (1997). *Internationalizing the Arab Press: Hisham and Muhammad 'Ali Hafez.* Jeddah: Saudi Distribution Company [Arabic].

Lustosa, Isabel (2000). *Insultos impressos. A Guerra dos jornalistas na independência 1821–1823.* São Paulo: Companhia das Letras.

Lynch, Daniel C. (2007). "Envisioning China's Political Future: Elite Responses to Democracy as a Global Constitutive Norm." *International Studies Quarterly*, 51(3), 701–22.

Mabuza, Ernest (2009, August 1). "Court Strikes Blow for Free Media." *Business Day*, p. 4.

Mączak, Antoni (1994). *Klientela*. Warsaw: Semper.

Mainwaring, Scott (1995). "Brazil: Weak Parties, Feckless Democracy." In Scott Mainwaring and Timothy Scully (eds.), *Building Democratic Institutions: Party Systems in Latin America* (pp. 354–98). Stanford, CA: Stanford University Press.

Mamdani, Mahmood (1996). *Citizen and Subject: Contemporary Africa and the Legacy of Late Colonialism*. Princeton, NJ: Princeton University Press.

Mancini, Paolo (1991). "The Public Sphere and the Use of News in a 'Coalition' System of Government." In Peter Dahlgren and Colin Sparks (eds.), *Communication and Citizenship* (pp. 135–54). London: Routledge,

Mancini, Paolo (2009). *Elogio della lottizzazione*. Bari: Laterza.

Markwick, Roger D. (1996). "A Discipline in Transition? From Sovietology to Transitology." *Journal of Communist Studies and Transition Politics*, 12(3), 255–76.

Martinsen, Deborah (1998). *Literary Journals in Imperial Russia*. Cambridge: Cambridge University Press.

Massey, Brian L. and Li-jing A. Chang (2002). "Locating Asian Values in Asian Journalism: A Content Analysis of Web Newspapers." *Journal of Communication*, 52(4), 987–1003.

Mato, Daniel (2005). "The Transnationalization of the *Telenovela* Industry: Territorial References, and the Production of Markets and Representations of Transnational Identities." *Television and New Media*, 6(4), 423–44.

Matos, Carolina (2008). *Jornalismo e política democrática no Brasil*. São Paulo: Publifolha.

Mattelart, Michèle and Armand Mattelart (1989). *O carnaval das imagens: a ficção na TV*. São Paulo: Brasiliense.

McCargo, Duncan (1997). "Thailand's Political Parties: Real, Authentic, and Actual." In Kevin Hewison (ed.), *Political Change in Thailand: Democracy and Participation* (pp. 114–31). London: Routledge.

McCargo, Duncan (2000). *Politics and the Press in Thailand: Media Machinations*. London: Routledge.

McCargo, Duncan (2003). *Media and Politics in Pacific Asia*. London: Routledge.

McCargo, Duncan (2009). "Thai Politics as Reality TV." *Journal of Asian Studies*, 68(1), 7–19.

McChesney, Robert C., John Bellamy Foster, Inger L. Stole, and Hannah Holleman (2009). "The Sales Effort and Monopoly Capital." *Monthly Review*, 60(11), 1–35.

McCormack, Gilian (ed.) (1999). *Mass Media in CIS: Analysis of Political, Legislative and the Socio-Economic Framework*. Brussels: European Institute for the Media.

McFaul, Michael (2002). "The Fourth Wave of Democracy and Dictatorship: Noncooperative Transitions in the Postcommunist World." *World Politics*, 54, 212–44.

McNair, Brian (1991). *Glasnost, Perestroika and the Soviet Media*. London: Routledge.

McNair, Brian (2000). "Power, Profit, Corruption, and Lies: The Russian Media in the 1990s." In James Curran and Myung-Jin Park (eds.), *De-Westernizing Media Studies* (pp. 79–94). London: Routledge:

McQuail, Denis (1994). *Mass Communication Theory: An Introduction*. London: Sage.

McQuail, Denis (2005). *McQuail's Mass Communication Theory* (5th ed.). London: Sage.

MDDA (2009, June 15). *Trends of Ownership and Control of Media in South Africa*. Report by the Media Development and Diversity Agency. Retrieved August 31, 2009, from http://www.mdda.org.za.

Mellor, Noha (2005). *The Making of Arab News*. Lanham, MD: Rowman & Littlefield.

Mellor, Noha (2008). "Arab Journalists as Cultural Intermediaries." *Press/Politics*, 13(4), 465–83.

Merkel, Wolfgang (2004). "Embedded and Defective Democracies." *Democratization*, 11(5), 33–58.

Miceli, Sergio (2001). *Intelectuais à brasileira*. São Paulo: Companhia das Letras.

Miguel, Luis Felipe (2004). "Mídia e vínculo eleitoral: a literatura internacional e o caso brasileiro." *Opinião Pública*, 10(1), 91–111.

Milne, Claire and Anne Taylor (2006). *South Africa: Research Findings and Conclusions*. London: African Media Development Initiative, BBC World Service Trust.

Milton, Andrew K. (2000). *The Rational Politician: Exploiting the Media in New Democracies*. Aldershot: Ashgate.

Mirsky, Dmitry Petrovich (1999). *The History of Russian Literature from Its Beginnings to 1900*. Evanston, IL: Northwestern University Press.

Mishkhas, Abeer (2005, January 27). "Who's Who Out There?" *Arab News*.

Mitchell, Timothy (1991). "The Limits of the State: Beyond Statist Approaches and Their Critics." *American Political Science Review*, 85(1), 77–94.

Mitton, Roger (2008, October 24). "Vietnam: Behind the Journalists' Jailings." *Asia Sentinel*.

Moore, Sally Falk (1978). "Uncertainties in Situations, Indeterminacies in Culture." In S. F. Moore (ed.), *Law as Process: An Anthropological Approach* (pp. 32–53). London: Routledge.

Moore, Sally Falk (1987). "Explaining the Present: Theoretical Dilemmas in Processual Ethnography." *American Ethnologist*, 14(4), 727–36.

Morlino, Leonardo (2009). "Are There Hybrid Regimes? Or Are They Just an Optical Illusion?" *European Political Science Review*, 1(2), 273–96.

Mozaffar, Shaheen (2006). "Understanding Party Dominance in Africa." In *Challenges to Democracy by One-Party Dominance* (pp. 1–14). Johannesburg: Konrad-Adenauer-Stiftung.

Mtyala, Quinton (2009, July 23). "184 N2 Stonings, but Only One Arrest." *Cape Times*, p. 1.

Muratov, Sergei (2008). "Legendy I Mify vokrug TV (Legends and Myths about TV)." In A. Kachkayeva (ed.), *Teleradioefir: istorija I sovremennost* (pp. 21–40). Moscow: Aspekt Press.

Nathan, Andrew (2003). "Authoritarian Resilience." *Journal of Democracy*, 14(1), 6–17.

Navaro-Yashin, Yael (2002). *Faces of the State: Secularism and Public Life in Turkey*. Princeton, NJ: Princeton University Press.

Negrine, Ralph (1994). *Politics and the Mass Media in Britain*. London: Routledge.

Negrine, Ralph and Stylianos Papathanassopoulos (1996). "The 'Americanization' of Political Communication: A Critique." *Harvard International Journal of Press/Politics*, 1(2), 45–62.

Neiger, M., E. Zandberg, and M. Meyers (2008). *The Rhetoric of Criticism: Challenging Criticism, Reaffirming Criticism, and Israeli Journalism during the Second Lebanon War*. The Media in the Lebanon War series. Tel Aviv: Rothschild-Caesarea School of Communication, Tel Aviv University. [In Hebrew]

Nenashev, Mikhail (2004). "Nastala pora platit' po dolgam." *Zhurnalist*, 2. Retrieved April 19, 2006, from http://www.journalist-virt.ru/2004/2/10.php.

Nerone, John C. (ed.) (1995). *Last Rights: Revisiting Four Theories of the Press*. Urbana: University of Illinois Press.

Nieminen, Hannu (2009). "Russian Media 2008: The View from Outside." In E. Vartanova, H. Nieminen, and M.-N. Salminen (eds.), *Perspectives to the Media in Russia: "Western" Interests and Russian Developments* (pp. 107–13). Helsinki: Aleksanteri Institute.

Nieroda, Marcin (2008). *Program Trzeci Polskiego Radia S.A. w systemie medialnym Polski*. Unpublished masters thesis.

Nisbet, Eric and Devra Moehler (2005). "Emerging Political Communication Systems in Sub-Saharan Africa: Some Preliminary Models." Paper presented at the annual meeting of the American Political Science Association, September 1, Washington, DC.

Noelle-Neumann, Elisabeth (1993). *The Spiral of Silence. Public Opinion – Our Social Skin*. Chicago: University of Chicago Press.

Nord, Lars (2008). "Comparing Nordic Media Systems: North between West and East?" *Central European Journal of Communication*, 1(1), 95–110.

Nordenstreng, Kaarle and Reino Paasilinna (2002). "Epilogue." In Kaarle Nordenstreng, Elena Vartanova, and Yassen Zassoursky (eds.), *Russian Media Challenge* (2nd ed., pp. 189–198). Helsinki: Kikimora Publications.

Norris, Pippa (2009). "Comparative Political Communications: Common Frameworks or Babelian Confusion?" *Government and Opposition*, 321–35.

Norris, Pippa and Ronald L. Ingelhart (2009). *Cosmopolitan Communications: Cultural Diversity in a Globalized World*. Cambridge: Cambridge University Press.

North, Douglass C. (1990). *Institutions, Institutional Change and Economic Performance.* Cambridge: Cambridge University Press.

North, Douglass C. (1994). "Economic Performance Through Time." *The American Economic Review*, 84(3), 359–68.

Nyamnjoh, Francis B. (2005). *Africa's Media, Democracy, and the Politics of Belonging.* London: Zed Books.

O'Donnell, Guillermo A. (1994). "Delegative Democracy." *Journal of Democracy*, 5(1), 55–69.

Oates, Sarah (2006). *Television, Democracy and Elections in Russia.* London: Routledge.

Ogan, Christine L. (1980). "Development Journalism/Communication: The Status of the Concept." Paper presented at the 63rd Annual Meeting of the Association for Education in Journalism, August 9–13, Boston.

Olsson, Tom (2002). "The Right to Talk Politics in Swedish Journalism 1925–1995." In M. Hurd, T. Olsson, and P. Åker (eds.), *Storylines: Media, Power and Identity in Modern Europe. Festschrift for Jan Ekecrantz.* Stockholm: Hjalmarson & Högberg.

Olukoshi, Adebayo (2008). "Bringing the Public Sphere into African Democratic Theory." Paper delivered at the 12th General Assembly of the Council for the Development of Social Science Research in Africa (Codesria), December 7–11, Yaounde, Cameroon.

Opatrny, Lukas (2007). *The Post-1990 Demise of the Alternative Press.* Unpublished masters thesis, University of Cape Town.

Open Society Institute/EU Monitoring and Advocacy Program (2005). *Television across Europe: Regulation, Policy and Independence.* Budapest and New York: Open Society Institute.

Oppelt, Phylicia (2008, July 5). "Airwaves of Discontent." *Sunday Times Review*, p. 2.

Ortiz, Renato (1988). *A moderna tradição brasileira.* São Paulo: Brasiliense.

Ortner, Sherry (1984). "Theory in Anthropology since the Sixties." *Comparative Studies in Society and History*, 26, 126–66.

Ortner, Sherry (2006). *Anthropology and Social Theory: Culture, Power, and the Acting Subject.* Durham, NC: Duke University Press.

Oushakine, Serguei (2009a). *The Patriotism of Despair: Nation, War, and Loss in Russia.* Ithaca, NY: Cornell University Press.

Oushakine, Serguei (2009b). "Wither the Intelligentsia: The End of the Moral Elite in Eastern Europe." *Studies in East European Thought*, 61, 243–8.

Ovsepyan, Rafall (1979). *Sovetskaya zhurnalistika I kommunisticheskoye vospitanije trudyashikhsya* (Soviet Journalism and Communist Upbringing of Workers). Moscow: Izd-vo Mosk.

Ovsepyan, Rafall (1999). *The Contemporary History of Russian Journalism.* Moscow: Izd-vo MSU; TNS Gallup Media.

Paasilinna, Reino (1995). *Glasnost and Soviet Television: A Study of the Soviet Mass Media and Its Role in Society from 1985–1991.* Helsinki: Yleisradio Research Report, 05/1995.

Paletz, David L. and Karol Jakubowicz (eds.) (2003). *Business as Usual: Continuity and Change in Central and Eastern European Media*. Cresskill, NJ: Hampton Press.

Pan, Zhongdang (2000). "Improvising Reform Activities: The Changing Reality of Journalistic Practice in China." In Chin-Chuan Lee (ed.), *Power, Money and Media: Communication Patterns in Cultural China* (pp. 68–111). Evanston, IL: Northwestern University Press.

Pan, Zhongdang and Ye Lu (2003). "Localizing Professionalism: Discursive Practices in China's Media Reforms." In C.-C. Lee (ed.), *Chinese Media, Global Context* (pp. 215–336). New York: Routledge.

Panebianco, Angelo (1988). *Political Parties: Organization and Power*. Cambridge: Cambridge University Press.

Papathanassopoulos, Stylianos (2001). "Media Commercialization and Journalism in Greece." *European Journal of Communication*, 16(4), 505–21.

Papatheodorou, Fotini and David Machin (2003). "The Post-Dictatorial Intimacy between the Political Elite and the Mass Media in Greece and Spain." *European Journal of Communication*, 18(1), 31–54.

Park, Myung-Jin, Chang-Nam Kim, and Bying-Woo Sohn (2000). "Modernization, Globalization, and the Powerful State: The Korean Media." In James Curran and Myung-Jin (eds.), *De-Westernizing Media Studies* (pp. 111–23). London: Routledge.

Parvin, Nelofar (2006). *Public Intellectuals and Partisanship in Bangladesh*. Unpublished Ph.D. thesis, University of Leeds.

Pasti, Svetlana (2007). *The Changing Profession of a Journalist in Russia*. Linna: Tampere University Press.

Pempel, T. J. (1990). *Uncommon Democracies: The One-Party Dominant Regimes*. Ithaca, NY: Cornell University Press.

Peri, Yoram (1999). "Media, War and Citizenship." *Communication Review*, 3(4), 323–52.

Peri, Yoram (2004). *Telepopulism; Media and Politics in Israel*. Stanford, CA: Stanford University Press.

Peri, Yoram (2007). "Intractable Conflict and the Media." *Israel Studies*, 12(1), 79–102.

Perry, Elizabeth (2007). "Studying Chinese Politics: Farewell to Revolution?" *China Journal*, 57, 1–25.

Peters, John Durham (1995). "Historical Tensions in the Concept of Public Opinion." In T. L. Glasser and C. Salmon (eds.), *Public Opinion and the Communication of Consent* (pp. 3–32). New York: Guilford Press.

Petrovskaya, Irina and Ksenia Larina (2010). *Chelovek iz televizora* (Echo of Moscow). Retrieved May 29, 2010, from http://echo.msk.ru/programs/persontv/674223-echo/.

Phiyarasot, Suwicha (2008). *ASTV kabot sua thorathat thai: sua thi mai yom yuen mong khwam toktam khong sangkhom baep muenchaei* (ASTV Revolutionizes Thai Television: Media That Refuses to Stand Back and Watch Indifferently as Society Declines). Bangkok: Ban Phra Athit Publishing.

Pietilainen, Jukka (2002). *The Regional Newspaper in Post-Soviet Russia: Society, Press and Journalism in the Republic of Karelia 1985–2001*. Linna: Tampere University Press.

Piombo, Jessica (2005). "Party Politics, Social Demographics and the Decline of Ethnic Mobilization in South Africa, 1994–1999." *Party Politics*, 11 [Special issue on "Political Parties, Party Systems and Democracy in Africa"], 447–70.

Pisarek, Walery (1999). "Kontinität und Wandel auf dem Tageszeitungsmarkt." In Gerd Kopper, Ignacy Rutkiewicz, and Katherina Schliep (eds.), *Medientransformation und Journalismus in Polen 1989–1996* (pp. 129–45). Berlin: Vistas.

Pivovarov, Jurij (2002). "Russkaya Politicheskaya Kultura I (In English: Political Culture and 'Political Culture')." *Pro et Contra*, 3.

Porto, Mauro (2002). "Novos apresentadores ou novo jornalismo? O Jornal Nacional antes e depois da saída de Cid Moreira." *Comunicação e Espaço Público*, 1–2, 9–31.

Porto, Mauro (2006). "Political Advertising and Democracy in Brazil." In Lynda Kaid and Cristina Holtz-Bacha (eds.), *Handbook of Political Advertising* (pp. 129–43). Newbury Park, CA: Sage.

Potter, Elaine (1975). *The Press as Opposition: The Political Role of South African Newspapers*. Toronto: Chatto & Windus.

Price, Monroe E., Beata Rozumilowicz, and Stefaan G. Verhulst (eds.) (2002). *Media Reform: Democratizing the Media, Democratizing the State*. London: Routledge.

Przeworski, Adam (1991). *Democracy and the Market*. Cambridge: Cambridge University Press.

Puppae, Yakov (2000). ≪*Oligarkhi*≫. *Ekonomicheskaya khronika 1991–2000* (in English: ≪*Oligarchs*≫. The Economic Chronology 1991-2000). Moscow: State University/High School of Economics.

Qiu, Jack Linchuan (2009). *Working-Class Network Society: Communication Technology and the Information Have-Less in Urban China*. Cambridge, MA: MIT Press.

Rabahi, Tawfiq (2007, July 17). "Saudi Loyalty and Dissent... From Abroad, and War of Attrition in Qassem and Haddad's Topics." *Al-Quds Al-'Arabi* [Arabic].

Rafael, Vince (2003). "The Cell Phone and the Crowd: Messianic Politics in the Contemporary Philippines." *Popular Culture*, 15(3), 399–425.

Rantanen, Terhi (2004). *The Media and Globalization*. London: Sage.

Rawnsley, Gary D. and Ming-Yeh T. Rawnsley (1998). "Regime Transition and the Media in Taiwan." *Democratization*, 5(2), 106–24.

"The Rebirth of News" (2009, May 16). *The Economist*, pp. 15–16.

Reddy, Thiven (2006). "INC and ANC: A Comparative Analysis." In *Challenges to Democracy by One-Party Dominance* (pp. 55–63). Seminar Report. Johannesburg: Konrad-Adenauer-Stiftung.

Reich, Zvi (2009). *Sourcing the News*. Cresskill, NJ: Hampton Press.

Resnyanskaya, Ludmilla (ed.) (2007). *SMI I politika* (Mass Media and Politics). Moscow: Aspekt Press.

Ribeiro, Ana Paula Goulart (2001). "Clientelismo, corrupção e publicidade: como sobrevivem as empresas jornalísticas no Rio de Janeiro dos anos 50?"

In Marialva Barbosa (ed.), *Estudos de Jornalismo (I)* (pp. 42–55). Niterói: Intercom/Edições do PPGCOM/UFF.

Ribeiro, Ana Paula Goulart (2003). "Memória de jornalista: um estudo sobre o conceito de objetividade nos relatos dos homens de imprensa dos anos 50." In Vera França et al. (eds.), *Livro do XI Compós – Estudos de Comunicação* (pp. 285–99). Porto Alegre: Sulina.

Ribeiro, Ana Paula Goulart (2006). "Modernização e concentração. A imprensa carioca nos anos 1950–1970." In Lucia Maria Bastos, P. Neves, et al. (eds.), *História e imprensa: representações culturais e práticas de poder* (pp. 426–35). Rio de Janeiro: DP&A.

Rofel, Lisa (1999). *Other Modernities: Gendered Yearnings in China after Socialism.* Berkeley: University of California Press.

Rofel, Lisa (2007). *Desiring China: Experiments in Neoliberalism, Sexuality, and Public Culture.* Durham, NC: Duke University Press.

Röger, Maren (2010). "Political and Commercial Interests? The Polish Axel Springer-Tabloid 'Fakt' and Its Coverage about Germany." In Bogusława Dobek-Ostrowska, Michal Głowacki, Karol Jakubowicz, and Miklós Sükösd (eds.), *Media Systems East and West: How Different, How Similar?* Budapest: Central European University Press.

Romano, Angelo (2003). *Politics and the Press in Indonesia: Understanding an Evolving Political Culture.* London: Routledge.

Roppen, Johann (2008). "Public Service Market? Commercial Activities of the Norwegian Broadcasting Corporation (NRK)." *Central European Journal of Communication,* 1(1), 79–94.

Rose, Richard (2009). "Democratic and Undemocratic States." In Christian W. Haerpfer, Patrick Bernhagen, Ronald F. Inglehart, and Christian Welzel (eds.), *Democratization* (pp. 10–23). Oxford: Oxford University Press.

Rossiiskyi rynok periodicheskoi pechati. Sostoyanie, tendentsii I perspektivy razvitija in 2008. (2009). Moscow: FAPMK.

Roudakova, Natalia (2007). *From the Fourth Estate to the Second Oldest Profession: Russia's Journalists in Search of Their Public after Socialism.* Ph.D. dissertation, Department of Cultural and Social Anthropology, Stanford University.

Roudakova, Natalia (2008). "Media-Political Clientelism: Lessons from Anthropology." *Media, Culture & Society,* 30(1), 41–54.

Roudakova, Natalia (2009). "Journalism as 'Prostitution': Understanding Russia's Reactions to Anna Politkovskaya's Murder." *Political Communication,* 26(4), 412–29.

Rugh, William (1979). *The Arab Press.* Syracuse, NY: Syracuse University Press.

Rugh, William (1980). "Saudi Mass Media and Society in the Faysal Era." In W. A. Beling (ed.), *King Faysal and the Modernization of Saudi Arabia* (pp. 125–44). Boulder, CO: Westview Press.

Rugh, William (2004). *Arab Mass Media: Newspapers, Radio, and Television in Arab Politics.* Westport, CT: Praeger.

Rugh, William (2007). *Do National Political Systems Still Influence Arab Media? Arab Media and Society.* Available at http://www.arabmediasociety.com/?article=225.

Rutkowski, Piotr (2008). "Klientelizm a perspektywie wyborów samorządowych – stadium miasta średniej wielkości. Hipoteza klientelistyczna jako próba wyjaśnienia fenomenu reelekcji." In Jacek Raciborski (ed.), *Studia nad wyborami. Polska 2005–2006* (pp. 48–69). Warszawa: Wydawnictwo Naukowe Scholar.

Samaras, Athanassious N. (2000). "The Decline of Partytocracy and the Transformation of the Greek Political Communication Systems." Paper presented at the XVIII World Congress of IPSA, August 1–5, Quebec City.

Samet, Robert (2009). "Denouncing Violence: Crime Reporting and the Politics of Citizen Security in Caracas, Venezuela." Paper presented at the XXVIII International Congress of the Latin American Studies Association, "Rethinking Inequalities," June 11–14.

Samuels, David (2002). "Presidentialized Parties: The Separation of Powers and Party Organization and Behavior." *Comparative Political Studies*, 35(4), 461–83.

Santos, Boaventura de Sousa (2008). "Plurality of Public Spheres? From Participatory Budgeting to Plurinationality?" Paper presented at the 12th General Assembly of the Council for the Development of Social Science Research in Africa (Codesria), Dec. 7–11, Yaounde, Cameroon.

Sartori, Giovanni (1976). *Parties and Party Systems: A Framework for Analysis*. Cambridge: Cambridge University Press.

"Saudi Arabia Country Profile" (2008). Retrieved June 23, 2008, from http://earthtrends.wri.org.

Schedler, Andreas (2002). "Elections without Democracy: The Menu of Manipulation." *Journal of Democracy*, 13(2), 36–50.

Schiller, Naomi (2009). *"Don't Watch Television, Make It!" Community Media, the State, and Popular Politics in Caracas, Venezuela*. Ph.D. dissertation, Department of Anthropology, New York University.

Schlemmer, Lawrence (1999). "Democracy or Democratic Hegemony? The Future of Political Pluralism in South Africa." In Herman Giliomee and Claire Simkins (eds.), *The Awkward Embrace: One-party Domination and Democracy* (pp. 281–300). Amsterdam: Harwood Academic Publishers.

Schramm, Wilber (1964). *Mass Media and National Development: The Role of Information in the Developing Countries*. Stanford, CA: Stanford University Press.

Schreiner, Wadim (2004). "Media's Perception of Political Parties in South Africa in the Run-Up to the National Elections in April 2004." Presentation at Mediatenor, Pretoria.

Schudson, Michael (1978). *Discovering News: A Social History of American Newspapers*. New York: Basic Books.

Schudson, Michael (1982). "The Politics of the Narrative Form: The Emergence of News Conventions in Print and Television." *Daedalus*, 3(4), 97–112.

Schudson, Michael (1995). *The Power of News*. Cambridge, MA: Harvard University Press.

Schudson, Michael (2002). "The Objectivity Norm in American Journalism." *Journalism*, 2(2), 149–70.

Schudson, Michael (2005). "Autonomy from What?" In R. Benson and E. Neveu (eds.), *Bourdieu and the Journalistic Field* (pp. 214–23). Malden, MA: Polity Press.

Scissors, Derek (2009). "Deng Undone: The Costs of Halting Market Reform in China." *Foreign Affairs* (May/June), 24–39.

Scott, James C. (1990). *Domination and the Arts of Resistance: Hidden Transcripts*. New Haven, CT: Yale University Press.

Sen, Krishna and Terence Lee (eds.) (2007). *Political Regimes and the Media in Asia*. London: Routledge.

Senn, Alfred Erich (2004). "How Russia Has Acknowledged the Lithuanian Nation." Paper presented at the conference *Valstybė, kalba, spauda*, Department of Journalism at Vytautas Magnus University, May 5, Kaunas.

Sevcenko, Nicolau (1983). *Literatura como missão. Tensões sociais e criação cultural na Primeira República*. São Paulo: Brasiliense.

Seymour-Ure, Colin (1974). *The Political Impact of Mass Media*. London: Constable/Sage.

Shafferer, Christian (ed.) (2006). *Election Campaigning in East and Southeast Asia: Globalization of Political Marketing*. Aldershot: Ashgate.

Sharma, Aradhana and Akhil Gupta (2006). *The Anthropology of the State: A Reader*. Oxford: Blackwell.

Shestopal, Elena and Anna Kachkaeva (2006). "Televidenie glazami uchenykh." On *Chas Pressy* [Radio broadcast]: Radio Liberty/Radio Free Europe. Retrieved May 22, 2010, from http://www.svobodanews.ru/articleprintview/271909.html.

Shevtsova, Lilla (2007). *Russia Lost in Transition: The Yeltsin and Putin Legacies*. Washington, DC: Carnegie Endowment for International Peace.

Shkaratan, Ovsei and Vladimir Iljin (2006). *The Social Stratification of Russia and East Europe*. Moscow: High School of Economics

Shugart, Matthew Soberg and John M. Carey (1997). *Presidents and Assemblies: Constitutional Design and Electoral Dynamics*. Cambridge: Cambridge University Press.

Shugart, Matthew Soberg and Scott Mainwaring (1997). "Presidentialism and Democracy in Latin America: Rethinking the Terms of the Debate." In Matthew Soberg Shugart and Scott Mainwaring, *Presidentialism and Democracy in Latin America* (pp. 12–54). Cambridge: Cambridge University Press.

Siebert, Fred, Thodore S. Peterson, and Wilbur Schramm (1956). *Four Theories of the Press*. Urbana: University of Illinois Press.

Siebert, Fred, Thodore S. Peterson, and Wilbur Schramm (1963). *Four Theories of the Press* (rev. ed.). Urbana: University of Illinois Press.

Silva, Carlos Eduardo Lins da (1991). *O adiantado da hora: a influência americana sobre o jornalismo brasileiro*. São Paulo: Summus.

Skolkay, Andrej (2008). "Research on Mass Media in Central/Eastern Europe and Southern Europe in Comparative Analysis." In Bogusława Dobek-Ostrowska and Michal Głowacki (eds.), *Comparing Media systems in Central Europe: Between Politicization and Commercialization* (pp. 27–40). Wroclaw: University of Wroclaw Press.

Sloterdijk, Peter (1987). *Critique of Cynical Reason*. Minneapolis: University of Minnesota Press.

Smilde, David (2009). *Three Stages in the Chavez Government's Approach to Participation*. Retrieved May 29, 2010, from http://www.wilsoncenter.org/topics/pubs/Venezuela.pdf.

Smith, A. C. H. with Elizabeth Immirzi and Trevor Blackwell (1975). *Paper Voices: The Popular Press and Social Change 1935–1965*. Totowa, NJ: Rowman & Littlefield.

Smith, Anne-Marie (1997). *A Forced Agreement: Press Acquiescence to Censorship in Brazil*. Pittsburgh, PA: University of Pittsburgh Press.

Solinger, Dorothy J. (2001). "Ending One-Party Dominance: Korea, Taiwan, Mexico." *Journal of Democracy*, 12(1), 30–42.

Soloski, John (1989). "News Reporting and Professionalism: Some Constraints on the Reporting of News." *Media, Culture and Society*, 11(2).

Sosnovskaya, Anna (2000). "Social Portrait and Identity of Today's Journalist: St. Petersburg, a Case Study." In Jan Ekecrantz and Kerstin Olofsson (eds.), *Russian Reports: Studies in Post-Communist Transformation of Media and Journalism* (pp. 139–96). Stockholm: Södertörn Academic Studies.

Southall, Roger (2005). "The 'Dominant Party Debate' in South Africa." *Afrika Spectrum*, 39(1), 61–82.

Sparks, Colin (1995). "The Media as a Power for Democracy." *Javnost (The Public)*, 2(1), 45–59.

Sparks, Colin (1998). *Communism, Capitalism and the Mass Media*. Newbury Park, CA: Sage.

Sparks, Colin (2008). "After Transition: The Media in Poland, Russia and China." In K. Jakubowicz and M. Sükösd (eds.), *Finding the Right Place on the Map: Central and Eastern European Media Change in a Global Perspective* (pp. 43–72). Bristol: Intellect.

Splichal, Slavko (1994). *Media beyond Socialism: Theory and Practice in East-Central Europe*. Boulder, CO: Westview Press.

Splichal, Slavko (2001). "Imitative Revolutions. Changes in the Media and Journalism in East-Central Europe." Paper presented at the conference "Democratization and Media," Bellagio.

Steinberg, Jonny (2008). *Three-Letter Plague: A Young Man's Journey through a Great Epidemic*. Cape Town: Jonathan Ball.

Steyn, Elaine and Arrie S. De Beer (2002). "South African National Skills Audit." Unpublished report prepared for the South African National Editors Forum (Sanef) and the Sanef Education and Training Committee. Available at http://scribe.co.za, or http://www.mediatenor.co.za.

Stranahan, Patricia (1990). *Molding the Medium: The Chinese Communist Party and the Liberation Daily*. Armonk, NY: M. E. Sharpe.

Street, John (2001). *Mass Media, Politics and Democracy*. London: Palgrave Macmillan.

Štromas, Aleksandras (2001). *Laisvės horizontai* (Horizons of Freedom). Vilnius: Baltos lankos.

Sükösd, Miklós (2000). "Democratic Transformation and the Mass Media in Hungary: From Stalinism to Democratic Consolidation." In Richard Gunther and Anthony Mughan (eds.), *Democracy and the Media: A Comparative Perspective* (pp. 122–64). Cambridge: Cambridge University Press.

Sükösd, Miklós (2007). "Hungary's Media System on the Way from Polarized Pluralism to a Mixed Mode. Entering the Post-Objectivity Era?" Paper prepared for the workshop "Comparing Media Systems beyond the Western World," March 23–24, University of Perugia.

Sun, Wanning and Yuezhi Zhao (2009). "Television Culture with 'Chinese Characteristics': The Politics of Compassion and Education." In Graeme Turner and Jinna Tay (eds.), *Television Studies after TV: Understanding Television in the Post-Broadcast Era* (pp. 96–104). London: Routledge.

Suttner, Raymond (2004). "The Great 'One Party State' Debate." *This Day*, March 26.

"Svoboda Mnenii v Internete" (2010). On *Svoboda Mysli* [TV Broadcast]: 5 Kanal. Retrieved May 22, 2010, from http://www.5-tv.ru/programs/broadcast/504795/.

Swanson, David L. and Paolo Mancini (1996). *Politics, Media, and Modern Democracy*. Westport, CT: Praeger.

Switzer, Les and Donna Switzer (1979). *The Black Press in South Africa and Lesotho: A Descriptive Bibliographic Guide*. Boston: G. K. Hall.

Tan, Zixue (2006). *Internet and Civil Society in China*. New York: Routledge.

Teer-Tomaselli, Ruth (2004). "Transforming State-Owned Enterprises in the Global Age: Lessons from Broadcasting and Telecommunications in South Africa." *CriticalArts*, 18(1), 7–41.

Tettey, Wisdom J. (2001). "The Media and Democratisation in Africa: Contributions, Constraints and Concerns of the Private Press." *Media, Culture & Society*, 3(1), 5–31.

Thompson, Allan (ed.) (2006). *The Media and the Rwandan Genocide*. London: Pluto Press.

Thussu, Daya K. (2009). *International Communication: A Reader*. Abingdon: Routledge.

Tilly, Charles (1984). *Big Structures, Large Processes, Huge Comparisons*. New York: Russell Sage Foundation.

Tironi, Eugenio and Guillermo Sunkel (2000). "The Modernization of Communications: The Media in the Transition to Democracy in Chile." In Richard Gunther and Anthony Mughan (eds.), *Democracy and the Media: A Comparative Perspective* (pp. 165–94). Cambridge: Cambridge University Press.

Tocqueville, Alexis de (1969). *Democracy in America*. New York: Doubleday.

Tomaselli, Keyan (1997). "Ownership and Control in the South African Print Media: Black Economic Empowerment after Apartheid, 1990–97." *Ecquid Novi*, 18(1), 21–68.

Tomaselli, Keyan, Ruth Tomaselli, and Johan Muller (1987). *The Press in South Africa*. Johannesburg: Richard Lyon & Co.

Tong, Jingrong (2007a). "Decentralisation in the Chinese Government-Media Relation: How Powers Struggle in Journalistic Field in China." Paper presented at the International Communication Association Meeting, San Francisco.

Tong, Jingrong (2007b). "Guerilla Tactics of Investigative Journalists in China." *Journalism*, 8(5), 530–5.

Tong, Jingrong and C. Sparks (2009). "Investigative Journalism in China Today." *Journalism Studies*, 10(3), 337–52.

Traboulsi, Fawwaz (2008). "Saudi Expansion: The Lebanese Connection, 1924–1952." In M. Al-Rasheed (ed.), *Kingdom without Borders: Saudi Arabia's Political, Religious and Media Frontiers* (pp. 65–78). New York: Columbia University Press.

Trachtenberg, Anna (2007). "Transformation without Change: Russian Media as a Political Institution and Cultural Phenomenon." In Elena Vartanova (ed.), *Media and Change* (pp. 122–8). Moscow: MediaMir.

Traquina, Nelson (1995). "Portuguese Television: The Politics of Savage Deregulation." *Media, Culture & Society*, 17(2), 223–38.

Trends in Middle Eastern Arabic Television Series Production – Opportunities for Broadcasters and Producers (2007). Dubai: Booz Allen and Hamilton.

Turner, Victor W. (1974). *Dramas, Fields, and Metaphors: Symbolic Action in Human Society*. Ithaca, NY: Cornell University Press.

Tyla, Antanas (2004). "Tautos tvirtybė: kova dėl savosios spaudos (The Strength of the Nation: The Struggle for an Indigenous Press)." *Darbai ir dienos*, 38, 7–16.

Vartanova, Elena (2002). "Media Structures: Changed and Unchanged." In Kaarle Nordenstreng, Elena Vartanova, and Yassen Zassoursky (eds.). *Russian Media Challenge* (pp. 21–72; 2nd ed.). Helsinki: Kikimora Publications.

Vartanova, Elena and Yassen Zassoursky (2003). "Television in Russia: Is the Concept of PSB Relevant?" In G. Lowe and N. Hujanen (eds.), *Broadcasting and Convergence: New Articulations of Public Service Remit* (pp. 93–108). Moscow: Nordicom.

Vedomosti (2005). "Russkie otvety." *Vedomosti*, 122(1403). Retrieved May 25, 2010, from http://www.vedomosti.ru/newspaper/article/2005/07/06/94314.

Velloso, Mônica Pimenta (1982). "Cultura e poder político. Uma configuração do campo intelectual." In Lucia Lippi Oliveira, Mônica Pimenta Velloso, and Ângela Maria de Castro Gomes (eds.), *Estado Novo: ideologia e poder* (pp. 69–108). Rio de Janeiro: Zahar Editores.

Verdery, Katherine (1996). *What Was Socialism, and What Comes Next?* Princeton, NJ: Princeton University Press.

Vihalemm, Peeter, Epp Lauk, and Marju Lauristin (1997). "Estonian Media in the Process of Change." In Marju Lauristin and Peeter Vihalemm (eds.), *Return to the Western World: Cultural and Political Perspectives on the Estonian Post-Communist Transition* (pp. 227–41). Tartu: Tartu University Press.

Vincent, Joan (1986). "System and Process: 1974–1985." *Annual Review of Anthropology*, 15, 99–199.

Vishnevsky, Anatolij (2010). Serp I rubl. *Konservativnaja modernizatsija* v SSSR (In Russian: Sickle and Rubl: the Conservative Modernization in USSR). Moscow: High School of Economics.

Voltmer, Katrin (2000). "Constructing Political Reality in Russia. Izvestiya – Between Old and New Journalistic Practices." *European Journal of Communication*, 14(4), 469–500.

Voltmer, Katrin (2008). "Comparing Media Systems in New Democracies: East Meets South Meets West." *Central European Journal of Communication*, 1(1), 23–40.

Waisbord, Silvio R. (1995). "The Mass Media and Consolidation of Democracy in South America." *Research in Political Sociology*, 7, 207–27.

Waisbord, Silvio R. (2000a). "Media in South America: Between the Rock of the State and the Hard Place of the Market." In James Curran and M.-J. Park (eds.), *De-Westernizing Media Studies* (pp. 50–62). London: Routledge.

Waisbord, Silvio (2000b). *Watchdog Journalism in South America: News, Accountability and Democracy*. New York: Columbia University Press.

Waisbord, Silvio (2003). "Media Populism: Neo-Populism in Latin America." In Gianpietro Mazzoleni, Juliane Stewart, and Bruce Horsfield (eds.), *The Media and Neo-Populism: A Contemporary Comparative Analysis* (pp. 197–216). Westport, CT: Praeger.

WAN (World Association of Newspapers) (2006). *World Press Trends 2006*. Paris: Zenith Optimedia.

Wang, Guoqing (2005). "Zhongguo baoye de fazhan fangwei." *Xinhua Net*, September 19, 2005, http://news.xinhuanet.com/newmedia/2005-09/19/content_3513225.htm, accessed May 21, 2009.

Wang, Hui (2004). "The Year 1989 and the Historical Roots of Neoliberalism in China." *Positions: East Asia Cultures Critique*, 12(1), 7–69.

Wang, Hui (2006). "Depoliticized Politics: From East to West." *New Left Review*, 41 (Sept/Oct), 29–45.

Wang, Jing (2001). "Culture as Leisure and Culture as Capital." *Positions: East Asia Cultures Critique*, 9(1), 69–104.

Waniek, Danuta (2007). *Dylematy ładu medialnego RP. Standardy europejskie a praktyka polityczna*. Kraków: Oficyna Wydawnicza AFM.

Ware, Alan (1996). *Political Parties and Party Systems*. Oxford: Oxford University Press.

Warner, Michael (2002). *Publics and Counterpublics*. New York: Zone Books.

Wasserman, Herman (2010). "Freedom's Just Another Word? Perspectives on Media Freedom in South Africa and Namibia." *International Communication Gazette*, 72(7), 567–88.

Wasserman, Herman and Arrie S. De Beer (2005). "A Fragile Affair: The Relationship between the Mainstream Media and Government in Post-Apartheid South Africa." *Journal of Mass Media Ethics*, 20(2), 192–208.

Wasserman, Herman and Arrie S. De Beer (2006). "Conflicts of Interest? Debating the Media's Role in Post-Apartheid South Africa." In Katrin Voltmer (ed.), *Mass Media and Political Communication in New Democracies* (pp. 59–75). London: Routledge.

Weaver, David H. (ed.) (1998). *The Global Journalist: News People Around the World*. Cresskill, NJ: Hampton Press.

Weimann, Gabi (2007). *Public Criticism of the War in Lebanon 2006*. The Media in the Lebanon War series. Tel Aviv: Caesarea-Rothschild School of Communication, Tel Aviv University [Hebrew].

Whitehead, Laurence (2002). *Democratization: Theory and Experience*. Oxford: Oxford University Press.

Williams, Raymond (1977). "Dominant, Residual, and Emergent." In *Marxism and Literature* (pp. 121–7). Oxford: Oxford University Press.

Willnat, Lars and Annette J. Aw (2004). "Political Communication in Asia: Challenges and Opportunities." In Lynda L. Kaid and Christina Holtz-Bacha (eds.), *Handbook of Political Communication Research* (pp. 479–503). Mahwah, NJ: Erlbaum.

Witschge, Tamara and Gunnar Nygren (2009). "Journalism: A Profession under Pressure?" *Journal of Media Business Studies*, 6(1), 37–59.

Wolfe, Thomas C. (2005). *Governing Soviet Journalism: The Press and the Socialist Person after Stalin*. Bloomington: Indiana University Press.

Wolfsfeld, Gadi (2004). *Media and the Path to Peace*. Cambridge: Cambridge University Press.

Wolinetz, Steven B. (2002). "Beyond the Catch-All Party: Approaches to the Study of the Parties and Party Organization in Contemporary Democracies." In J. R. Montero, R. Gunther, and J. J. Linz (eds.), *Political Parties: Old Concepts and New Challenges* (pp. 136–65). Oxford: Oxford University Press.

World Bank (2009). Communication for Governance and Accountability Program. Retrieved August 28, 2009, from http://web.worldbank.org/commgap.

World Population Prospects, the 2002 Revision Highlights (2003). United Nations. Retrieved October 18, 2008, from http://www.unpopulation.org.

Woźna, Jusytna (2008). "The Impact of Foreign Ownership on the Regional Press." In Bogusława Dobek-Ostrowska and Michal Głowacki (eds.), *Comparing Media Systems in Central Europe: Between Commercialization and Politicization* (pp. 149–62). Wrocław: University of Wroclaw Press.

Wyka, Angelika (2008). "In Search of the East Central European Media Model – The Italianization Model? A Comparative Perspective on the East Central European and South European Media Systems." In Bogusława Dobek-Ostrowska and Michal Głowacki (eds.), *Comparing Media Systems in Central Europe: Between Commercialization and Politicization* (pp. 55–71). Wrocław: University of Wroclaw Press.

Yang, Guobin (2009). *The Power of the Internet in China: Citizen Activism Online*. New York: Columbia University Press.

Yu, Haiquing (2006). "From Active Audience to Media Citizenship: The Case of Post-Mao China." *Social Semiotics*, 16(2), 303–26.

Yu, Haiqing (2009). *Media and Cultural Transformation in China*. New York: Routledge.

Yu, Xu (1994). "Professionalization without Guarantees: Changes of the Chinese Press in Post-1989 Years." *Gazette*, 53(1–2), 23–41.

Yurchak, Alexei (1997). "The Cynical Reason of Late Socialism: Power, Pretense, and the *Anekdot*." *Public Culture*, 9(2), 161–88.

Yurchak, Alexei (2003). "Soviet Hegemony of Form." *Comparative Studies in Society and History*, 45(3), 480–510.

Yurchak, Alexei (2006). *Everything Was Forever, until It Was No More: The Last Soviet Generation*. Princeton, NJ: Princeton University Press.

Zakaria, Fareed (1997). "The Rise of Illiberal Democracy." *Foreign Affairs*, 76(6), 22–43.

Zassoursky, Yassen (ed.) (2008). *Mass Media in Russia* (In Russian: SMI Rossii). Moscow: Aspekt Press.

Zassoursky, Yassen and Boris Esin (eds.) (2003). *Russkaja zhurnalistika v dokumentakh. Istorija nadzora.* (In English: Russian journalism in documents. The history of control.) Moscow: Aspekt Press.

Zeng, Genan (2008). "2010: qianren ribao yongyouliang lizhen dadao 90 fen (2010: Strives to Achieve 90 Daily Newspapers per One Thousand People)." Retrieved May 21, 2009, from http://www.cnci.gov.cn/content%5C2009414/news_44230.shtml.

Zhao, Yuezhi (1998). *Media, Market, and Democracy in China: Between the Party Line and the Bottom Line.* Urbana: University of Illinois Press.

Zhao, Yuezhi (2000a). "From Commercialization to Conglomeration: The Transformation of the Chinese Press within the Orbit of the Party State." *Journal of Communication,* 50(2), 3–26.

Zhao, Yuezhi (2000b). "Watchdogs on Party Leashes? Contexts and Limitations of Investigative Reporting in Post-Deng China." *Journalism Studies,* 1(4), 577–97.

Zhao, Yuezhi (2003). "Falun Gong, Identity, and the Struggle for Meaning inside and outside China." In James Curran and Nick Couldry (eds.), *Contesting Media Power: Alternative Media in a Networked Society* (pp. 209–24). Lanham, MD: Rowman & Littlefield.

Zhao, Yuezhi (2004). "Underdogs, Lapdogs, and Watchdogs: Journalists and the Public Sphere Problematic in China." In Gu Xin and Merle Goldman (eds.), *Chinese Intellectuals between State and Market* (pp. 43–74). London: Routledge Curzon.

Zhao, Yuezhi (2008a). *Communication in China: Political Economy, Power, and Conflict.* Lanham, MD: Rowman & Littlefield.

Zhao, Yuezhi (2008b). "Neoliberal Strategies, Socialist Legacies: Communication and State Transformation in China." In Paula Chakravartty and Yuezhi Zhao (eds.), *Global Communications: Toward a Transcultural Political Economy* (pp. 23–50). Lanham, MD: Rowman & Littlefield.

Zhao, Yuezhi (2009). "Communication, the Nexus of Class and Nation, and Global Divides." *Nordicom Review,* 30(2), 91–104.

Zhao, Yuezhi (2011). "Sustaining and Contesting Revolutionary Legacies in Media and Ideology." In Sebastian Heilmann and Elizabeth J. Perry (eds.), *Mao's Invisible Hand: The Political Foundations of Adaptive Governance in China* (pp. 201–36). Cambridge, MA: Harvard University Asia Center.

Zhao, Yuezhi and Zhenzhi Guo (2005). "Television in China: History, Political Economy, and Culture." In Janet Wasko (ed.), *A Companion to Television* (pp. 521–39). Oxford: Blackwell.

Zhao, Yuezhi and Dan Schiller (2001). "Dances with Wolves? China's Integration into Digital Capitalism." *Info,* 3(2), 137–51.

Zhao, Yuezhi and Wusan Sun (2007). "'Public Opinion Supervision': The Role of the Media in Constraining Local Officials." In Elizabeth Perry and Merle Goldman (eds.), *Grassroots Political Reform in China* (pp. 300–24). Cambridge, MA: Harvard University Press.

Zheng, Yongnian (2008). *Technological Empowerment: The Internet, State, and Society in China*. Stanford, CA: Stanford University Press.

Zizek, Slavoj (1991). *For They Know Not What They Do: Enjoyment as a Political Factor*. London: Verso.

Zygar, Mikhail, Maria Zheleznova, and Yulia Taratuta (2009). "Televidenie novogo pokolenia." *Russian Newsweek*. Retrieved June 5, 2010, from http://www.runewsweek.ru/country/31472.

Index

Continue from page iii